Black Stereotypes
in Popular Series Fiction,
1851–1955

ALSO BY BERNARD A. DREW

Henry Knox and the Revolutionary War Trail in Western Massachusetts (McFarland, 2012)

Literary Afterlife: The Posthumous Continuations of 325 Authors' Fictional Characters (McFarland, 2010)

Black Stereotypes in Popular Series Fiction, 1851–1955

Jim Crow Era Authors and Their Characters

BERNARD A. DREW

McFarland & Company, Inc., Publishers
Jefferson, North Carolina

LIBRARY OF CONGRESS CATALOGUING-IN-PUBLICATION DATA

Drew, Bernard A. (Bernard Alger), 1950–
Black stereotypes in popular series fiction, 1851–1955 : Jim Crow era authors and their characters / Bernard A. Drew.
     p.   cm.
Includes bibliographical references and index.

ISBN 978-0-7864-7410-3 (softcover : acid free paper) ∞
ISBN 978-1-4766-1610-0 (ebook)

1. American fiction—19th century—History and criticism.
2. American fiction—20th century—History and criticism.
3. African Americans in literature.   4. Stereotypes (Social psychology) in literature.   I. Title.

PS374.N4D68 2015   813'.409352996073—dc23   2015009144

BRITISH LIBRARY CATALOGUING DATA ARE AVAILABLE

© 2015 Bernard A. Drew. All rights reserved

No part of this book may be reproduced or transmitted in any form or by any means, electronic or mechanical, including photocopying or recording, or by any information storage and retrieval system, without permission in writing from the publisher.

On the cover: Herman and Verman, characters in Booth Tarkington's Penrod stories, 1914

Printed in the United States of America

*McFarland & Company, Inc., Publishers
Box 611, Jefferson, North Carolina 28640
www.mcfarlandpub.com*

For Donna,
Jessie and Darcie

Table of Contents

Preface 1

Introduction: If That Is the Way They Are in Stories, That Must Be the Way They Are in Life 4

I. Writers of the Antebellum, Reconstruction and Early Jim Crow Era (1851–1899) 19

Harriet Beecher Stowe (1811–1896) 20
Mark Twain (1835–1910) 23
Joel Chandler Harris (1848–1908) 25
George Washington Cable (1844–1925) 29
Thomas Nelson Page (1853–1922) 30
Charles W. Chesnutt (1858–1932) 32
Paul Laurence Dunbar (1872–1906) 35

II. Writers of the Late Jim Crow Era (1900–1955) 37

Richard F. Outcault (1863–1928) 37
Henry Edwards Cowen ("Red Buck") Bryant (1873–1967) 45
Bridges Smith (1848–1930) 49
Harris Dickson (1868–1946) 71
Irvin S. Cobb (1876–1944) 77
E.K. (Eldred Kurtz) Means (1878–1957) 88
Booth Tarkington (1869–1946) 96
James P. Alley (1885–1934) and Calvin Alley (1915–1970) 106
Ambrose E. Gonzales (1857–1926) 113
Robert McBlair (1888–1976) 118
Octavus Roy Cohen (1891–1959) 122
Harry Stillwell Edwards (1855–1938) 159
Arthur LeRoy Kaser (1890–1956) 164
Hugh Wiley (1884–1968) 170
Arthur K. Akers (1886–1980) 179
Roark Bradford (1896–1948) 183
Charles Correll (1890–1972) and Freeman F. Gosden (1899–1982) 199
Paul F. Ernst (1899–1985) 215
Will Eisner (1917–2005) 218
Langston Hughes (1902–1967) 228

III. Additional Writers of Interest   244

Phillis Wheatley (1753–1784)   245
Robert Roberts (1780–1860)   245
Thomas D. Rice (1808–1860)   245
John Pendleton Kennedy (1795–1870)   246
George Washington Dixon (1801–1861)   246
Augustus Baldwin Longstreet (1790–1870)   247
Caroline Gilman (1794–1888)   247
Lydia Maria Child (1802–1880)   247
Frederick Douglass (1818–1895)   248
William Wells Brown (1814–1884)   248
E.D.E.N. Southworth (1819–1899)   249
Mary Henderson Eastman (1818–1887)   249
Maria J. McIntosh (1803–1878)   250
Caroline Lee Hentz (1800–1856)   250
Mary J. Holmes (1825–1907)   250
Thomas Chandler Haliburton (1796–1865)   251
Johnson Jones Hooper (1815–1862)   251
Martin Delany (1812–1885)   251
Harriet E. Wilson (1825–1900)   252
Harriet Ann Jacobs (1813–1897)   252
Petroleum V. Nasby (1833–1888)   253
Samuel W. Small (1851–1931)   253
Irwin Russell (1853–1879)   254
Thomas Worth (1834–1917)   254
Colonel Prentiss Ingraham (1843–1904)   255
Louise Clarke Pyrnelle (1850–1907)   255
Katherine Sherwood Bonner McDowell (1849–1883)   256
Ruth McEnery Stuart (1849–1917)   256
Frances Ellen Watkins Harper (1825–1911)   256
Polk Miller (1844–1913)   257
John Trotwood Moore (1858–1929)   257
Kate Chopin (1851–1904)   258
Opie Pope Read (1852–1939)   258
Bob Cole (1868–1911)   259
Miss Howard Weeden (1846–1905)   259
Martha Sawyer Gielow (1860–1933)   260
Helen Bannerman (1862–1946)   260
Alice Dunbar-Nelson (1875–1935)   261
Will N. Harben (1858–1919)   261
Booker T. Washington (1856–1915)   261
Martha Strudwick Young (1862–1941)   262
John Charles McNeill (1874–1907)   262
Frederick H. Seymour (1850–1913)   262
James D. Corrothers (1869–1917)   263
W.E.B. Du Bois (1868–1963)   263
Ella Middleton Tybout (1871–1952)   264
Silas Xavier Floyd (1869–1923)   264
William Marriner (1873–1914)   265

John F. Dixon Jr. (1864–1946)   265
Sara Cone Bryant (1873–?)   266
Frances Boyd Calhoun (1867–1909) and Emma Speed Sampson (1868–1947)   266
Joseph S. Cotter, Jr. (1861–1949)   267
James Weldon Johnson (1871–1938)   267
Marion F. Harmon (1861–1940)   268
B.B. Valentine (1862–1919)   269
Julia Mead Peterkin (1880–1961)   269
Robert Emmet Kennedy (1877–1941)   269
Jane Baldwin Cotton (d. 1932)   270
Nella Larsen (1891–1964)   270
Charles E. Mack (1887–1934)   271
Annie Vaughan Weaver (1905–1982)   271
Inez Hogan (1895–1973)   272
E.V. White (1879–1955)   272
Zora Neale Hurston (1891–1960)   272
Richard Wright (1908–1960)   273
Ellen Tarry (1906–2008)   273
Enid Blyton (1897–1968)   274
Jackie Ormes (1911–1985)   274
Ralph Ellison (1914–1994)   275
James Baldwin (1924–1987)   275
Lorraine Hansberry (1930–1965)   275

Index   277

Preface

This book is about white writers and their fiction series featuring black characters. Published in popular magazines, major newspapers and books, these series appeared during what I have called the late Jim Crow era, which fell mainly in the first half of the twentieth century.

Squarely in focus are Octavus Roy Cohen's Florian Slappey stories, E.K. Means's Skeeter Butts episodes, Roark Bradford's tales of Little Bee Bend Plantation and even James P. Alley's Hambone cartoons.

The author profiles in this book are presented approximately chronologically, based on their first or most significant work. Each profile is followed by selected bibliographic and source material. Some authors, like Mark Twain, have sections for particular series included as well. These items are presented as a numbered list and the numbers, in turn, are used in other entries to indicate if a portion of the entire work appeared elsewhere—in periodicals, for instance. For example, Twain has a section for "Selected Huck Finn and Tom Sawyer Books," which lists the following:

SELECTED HUCK FINN AND TOM SAWYER BOOKS
  (1) *Adventures of Tom Sawyer* (1876)
  (2) *Adventures of Huckleberry Finn* (1884)
  (3) *Tom Sawyer Abroad* (1894)
  (4) *Tom Sawyer Detective* (1896)
  (5) *Huck Finn and Tom Sawyer Among the Indians and Other Unfinished Stories* (1989)
  (6) *Adventures of Huckleberry Finn: The Only Comprehensive Edition* (1996) ed. Victor Doyno, restored passages
  (7) *Adventures of Huckleberry Finn: Mark Twain Library* (2001) ed. Victor Fischer, Lin Salamo, Harriet E. Smith and Walter Blair, restored passages
  (8) *The Annotated Huckleberry Finn* (2001) ed. Michael Patrick Hearn and E.W. Kemble, restored passages
  (9) *Adventures of Tom Sawyer and Huckleberry Finn: The New South Edition* (2011) ed. Alan Gribben, expurgated

A bibliographic section following this one is "Huck Finn and Tom Sawyer Stories in Periodicals," which lists the various places individual stories appeared in print outside of the entire book. An entry such as "Adventures of Huckleberry Finn" (*Century Magazine*, December 1884) chapters 17 and 18, and a portion of 19, edited (2) indicates that these stories (in edited form) were taken from number two of the preceding list. In this case, from *Adventures of Huckleberry Finn* (1884).

The first section of the book looks at seven writers active in earlier decades whose stories, novels and poems with black characters and themes laid the groundwork for the generation of popular literature writers that followed.

Among this early group are some familiar names, including Harriet Beecher Stowe, Mark Twain and Joel Chandler Harris—whose Br'er Rabbit stories now embarrass Disney, yet were universally known in the late 1800s. In addition to two other writers who were better known then than now, George Washington Cable and Thomas Nelson Page, there are also Paul Laurence and Charles W. Chesnutt, black writers who found a niche with a general audience.

The second section, which makes up the bulk of the book, examines 22 writers who were among the first to be able to take advantage of an emerging popular literature—particularly general-interest periodicals such as the *Saturday Evening Post* and *Collier's*. The introduction of ongoing series meant consistency for readers, who knew what to expect with continuing characters, and could seek them out.

And those characters were easily found. Bridges Smith, Ambrose E. Gonzales, Harry Stillwell Edwards and H.E.C. Bryant wrote primarily for newspapers; Harris Dickson, Irvin S. Cobb, Booth Tarkington, Octavus Roy Cohen, Hugh Wiley, Arthur K. Akers and Bradford Roark wrote for the slick magazines such as the *Saturday Evening Post*; R.F. Outcault, James P. and Calvin Alley and Will Eisner syndicated their cartoons and graphic art; and E.K. Means, Robert McBlair and Paul Ernst toiled for the pulps. Charles Correll and Freeman F. Gosden wrote radio shows, but their scripts were also syndicated in newspapers. Arthur LeRoy Kaser wrote blackface stage skits.

Langston Hughes is included as a counterpoint. He was of course a black writer. He had the editorial support to write a newspaper column the way he wanted to. His columns appeared in the most widely circulated black newspaper of his day, but the stories could be appreciated by attuned white readers.

The third section, which includes brief write-ups, creates something of a timeline, placing in a general context the writers just mentioned and several dozen more who were further shaping a black literature—albeit an at times quirky literature, distorted as white writers threatened to outnumber black writers.

Little has been written about most of these authors, and to my knowledge no one has examined them as a group. But it is as a group that the degree of their impact on the generally white reading public of the late Jim Crow era emerges. Whatever their intentions, they either (1) perpetuated black stereotypes at a time when the general population needed to be steered toward acceptance, (2) made black characters acceptable to white readers and thereby opened the doors to black writers writing fiction about black characters, or (3) maybe both.

Readers today will be aghast at the audacity of the white writers, who blithely assumed they could write about black characters. These writers are not overtly racist, but their generally stereotypical depictions would—or at least should, as we must admit racism hasn't by any means vanished from our society—draw disdain today. And few have fared well with history. Except for Booth Tarkington, today considered a leading regionalist writer, and Will Eisner, whose genius as a graphic artist is widely understood, and Langston Hughes, whose verses yet shine bright, there's no reason you should recognize them.

If their work is so dubious, why should we know more about Harris Dickson and

Robert McBlair and Roark Bradford and the others? The better we are able to recognize the peripheral elements of racism during the Jim Crow era, the better we can recognize its remnants in popular culture and literature today. Appearing under the radar, these popular writers did more to influence rural and suburban readers of little means in the 1910s to 1940s than did mainstream literature.

All these writers reflect a curious, now largely scorned, literature.

Introduction:
If That Is the Way
They Are in Stories,
That Must Be the Way
They Are in Life

In the United States we believe racism evolved as an attempt to justify slavery, segregation, discrimination and the economic exploitation of black people. These practices came to be based on ideas of racial inferiority which were elaborated into pseudo-scientific theories.

—John Silk and Catherine Silk,
Racism and Anti-Racism in American Popular Culture[1]

Sambo was an extraordinary type of social control, at once extremely subtle, devious, and encompassing. To exercise a high degree of control meant also to be able to manipulate the full range of humor; to create, ultimately, an insidious type of buffoon. To make the black male into an object of laughter, was to strip him of masculinity, dignity, and self-possession. Sambo was, then, an illustration of humor as a device of oppression, and one of the most potent in American popular culture.

—Joseph Boskin,
Sambo: The Rise and Demise of an American Jester (1986)[2]

Among its other purposes and effects, literature has a responsibility and an established function to draw attention to social problems and to provide the moral leadership to search for solutions.

—Terrence Craig,
Racial Attitudes in English-Canadian Fiction 1905–1980 (1987)[3]

Wildcat Marsden, Jeff Poindexter, Widow Duck or Mush and Poke—they aren't as recognizable as Jay Gatsby, Ma Joad, Todd Hackett or Sam Spade. But they were compatriots on the printed page, fictional characters who vied for readers' attention in North America's dynamic literature of the 1920s and '30s.

This book examines a narrow, overlooked subgenre of American popular literature: short-form humorous fiction featuring continuing black characters, written by white authors for general-interest periodicals and broad-circulation newspapers in the late Jim Crow era.

A good example is Octavus Roy Cohen's Florian Slappey stories. Set in Birmingham's Darktown, they appeared in the *Saturday Evening Post* (166 stories) and other publications (151 stories) for more than three decades beginning in 1918. The writer depicted a fantasy world that southern readers found safe and northern readers believed to be accurate.

Works by Cohen and other authors profiled in this book have largely disappeared from bookstore, library and private bookshelves, in part because they are decades old and very much of their time period but also because they are generally weak on character and plotting. Not incidentally, the stories are laden with vernacular conversations and stereotyped characters of the type greatly (and thankfully) now out of vogue.

They're racist.

The stories aren't incitefully racist, but in their time, they served as reinforcement of Jim Crow etiquette (a term that will be defined below). They spread concepts of Negro inferiority into the American North and West. Not that the North and West were exempt from racism or Jim Crow; the influx of newly freed blacks

Cohen's Florian Slappey appeared in four black-and-white films in 1929. Charles Olden played the lead.

after the Civil War heightened demand for jobs, and, coupled with a general unfamiliarity with people of a different race, inspired a less formal set of rules, but an etiquette nevertheless.

"There were those who railed against the image," noted historian-scholar Joseph Boskin, "and its acceptance by a majority of the populace. Yet their energies were not enough to prevent the figure [stereotype] from assuming iconic proportions."[4]

In their time, the stories discussed in this book were taken as routine, no harm meant. Today's readers find them embarrassing at the very least, and generally repugnant. Most of the stories feature a male character—Boskin called him generically Sambo—stripped of his manliness, derided, mocked, spoofed. Stories featuring Sambos (of either gender) "used humor as a device of oppression, and one of the most potent in American popular culture."[5]

Why, then, have I accumulated a shelf of these books for this study? Because their role in the repressive late segregation era in the United States should not be discounted. In the first half of the twentieth century, individuals of African heritage, or those even suspected of having a drop of Negro blood, were subjugated, bullied, isolated, minimally educated, shunned, legislated against, beaten, mocked, raped and killed. They were made to be substandard citizens. Civil rights legislation during Lyndon B. Johnson's presidency in the mid–1960s brought relief, but the United States yet grapples with lingering issues of race and social justice—witness the code words and winks and glances of some political candidates during recent congressional and presidential elections.

Occasionally acknowledged in academic writings and news stories of the day, the role of these selected popular short fiction writers in the decades up to and through World War II—such as Cohen, Roark Bradford and Hugh Wiley—is instructive not only of how blacks were portrayed, but of how white writers, purposely or unwittingly, fit into the pervasive Jim Crow paradigm.

This book looks at 101 writers and artists, twenty-two of them closely. Their work appeared in print and, often, other media. Eleven of these writers were represented in newspapers, twelve appeared in magazines. All but Arthur K. Akers turned up in books. Two were remarkably active in radio. Six of the writers' fictional characters appeared in motion pictures, seven were featured in plays and three in television shows. Four creators were cartoonists. The reach of this group, in short, was huge. Until now the writers' impact has not been tracked in the same way as has the output of mainstream hardcover authors of the time, much less performers on stage, radio, television and silver screen.

Writers black and white in the United States produced stories about black characters even before Harriet Beecher Stowe put ink to paper. Some depicted the horrors of plantation life, and some expounded on perceived benefits of slavery. A few were sincere in wanting to explore the black way of life, even as they distorted it. Others didn't care. These writers had a niche, particularly as the "local color" genre took hold. Local color, or regionalism of the sort Sarah Orne Jewett (coastal Maine) or Thomas Nelson Page (Virginia plantation) or Bret Harte (California frontier) wrote, flourished between the Civil War and 1900.

Three things changed in the early decades of the twentieth century:

- Periodicals for a mass audience, the *Saturday Evening Post* and its sisters, rose to unknown heights of circulation. The audience for a hardcover book was limited by access (bookstores were rare in rural parts of the country), awareness (not everyone read reviews), cost (these were depression years) and specific interest (did whites really want to buy a book just to read about black characters?). The *Post, Collier's, American* and other slick paper periodicals could be found on the remotest of newsstands, were affordable, carried broad offerings and from time to time comfortably included stories about nonwhites. An individual needn't purposely acquire a work of fiction about blacks to come across one in a magazine, become curious and read it.

- Regional newspapers enlarged their offerings through self-generated or syndicated fiction. The *Macon Telegraph* in Georgia ran Bridges Smith's Yamacraw stories in his regular column, for example. The *State* in South Carolina printed Ambrose E. Gonzales's Gullah tales. And the *Commercial Appeal* in Tennessee showcased James P. Alley's *Hambone Meditations* cartoon for a remarkable fifty-two years—until 1968.
- And the decades saw the advent of dozens and dozens of pulp paper magazines, from *Argosy* and *Munsey's* and *Adventure* to narrower-focus *Western Story Magazine* and *Black Mask* and *Startling Stories*. With brightly colored covers and illustrated stories, the pulps trace their origins to the earlier dime novels. The pulps came out on quarterly, monthly, even weekly schedules, and their editors had voracious appetites for stories. To relieve sameness, editors accepted "off-trail" yarns. For example, a western title would from time to time include one of James B. Hendryx's stories about Corporal Downey of the Yukon. *Popular Magazine* thus ran stories about a black character, Mister Fish Kelly, by Robert McBlair; E.K. Means's Skeeter Butts showed up in *All-Story Weekly;* and *Red Book* featured Akers's Bugwine Breck criminous misadventures.

The first half of the 20th century was a golden age for short-form fiction. The *Saturday Evening Post* was the acme of short story publication. It showcased innumerable series with white characters. Perhaps the best known is Norman Reilly Raine's towboat captain, Annie Brennan, savior of many a floundering freighter in Puget Sound. Tugboat Annie appeared in sixty-eight tales between 1931 and 1961. Another female character, Mary Roberts Rinehart's Tish Carberry, shared twenty-four adventures in the *Post* with her two unmarried women friends of a certain age, Aggie and Liz, between 1910 and 1937. British Author P.G. Wodehouse's foppish Bertie Wooster and his masterly manservant Jeeves, active in print from 1915 to 1971, carried on ten times in the *Post*; the rest of their myriad escapades went to other magazines.

Arthur Train, whose legal wizard Ephraim Tutt was as comfortable in the courtroom as he was at a lodge meeting or in an upstate New York trout stream, sold ninety-one stories to the *Post* between 1919 and 1951. The magazine ran four of Clarence Budington Kelland's rustic stories of Cold River hardware merchant Scattergood Baines, a meddler in everyone's affairs, in 1917 and 1918, before dropping the series; another 120 Scattergood entries showed up in *American Magazine* from 1919 to 1954. The *Post* liked Kelland, just not Scattergood. Kelland wrote twenty-one other series (none of great endurance) for the *Post*. His Scipio Mather stories, about an indefatigable horse trader, ran for thirty-one stories in the *Post's* sister magazine, *Country Gentleman*, from 1931 to 1955.

Almost catching up to Cohen in his output of *Post* stories was William Hazlett Upson, whose natural-born salesman Alexander Botts constantly exasperated his Earthworm tractor sales manager, Gilbert Henderson, in 123 stories between 1925 and 1974.

Some of the *Post's* series stars spoke in the vernacular. M.G. Chute's Sheriff Olsen, featured in twenty-seven stories between 1937 and 1953, had a distinct Minnesotan way of speaking. And Guy Gilpatrick's Colin Glencannon, engineer on the tramp freighter *Inchcliffe Castle*, swore (in a deep Scots brogue) by his Duggan's Dew in sixty-three stories between

1930 and 1950. Booth Tarkington's German-accented Mr. Rumbin went all out to make sure his gallery's works of art got into the right hands, or any hands, in a fifteen-story run in the *Post*, 1936–1945.

This is the tip of the iceberg in just the *Post*. Walter Brooks wrote stories about Mr. Ed the talking horse for the magazine in 1942 and 1943 (later moving to *Liberty*); Frank Leon Smith turned in McQuillan yarns for the *Post* from 1940 to 1943; and Erle Stanley Gardner wrote Pete Quint stories in 1941, soon gaining permanent welcome with his Perry Mason serials.

Further down the row of periodicals at the newsstands, Ellis Parker Butler's freight agent Mike Flannery first saw print in 1906 in *American Magazine*, when an unexpected shipment of guinea pigs arrived at his landing dock. James W. English wrote Tailbone Patrol stories for *Boy's Life* beginning in the 1950s. Arthur R. McDougal Jr. chronicled outdoorsman and fisherman Dud Dean's northern New England activities in *Field & Stream*. F. Scott Fitzgerald's Pat Hobby stories, about a down-and-out Hollywood talent agent, ran in *Esquire* from 1940 to 1942.

Some story series were vocationally specific. Marmaduke Surfaceblow, a six-foot marine engineer, figured out generator and compressor problems in Steve Elonka's stories for *Power* magazine beginning in 1948. Martin Bunn's Gus Wilson resolved transmission and brake puzzles in a series for *Popular Science*, 1925 to 1969.

These series characters also showed up in book collections.

The appeal of the stories is the richness of the characters and their ability to fall into a situation from which extraction seems impossible—followed by an unexpected resolution. Some situations are criminal (Tutt renders justice when the letter of the law fails), some are social (Tish and her pals go backpacking) or business-related (Botts outwits a Behemoth tractor salesman to land an important sale). Satisfying solutions often involve a comeuppance for a prickly antagonist (Annie beats rival Horatio Bullwinkle to a salvage). Protagonists are often secretly manipulative (Jeeves saves Bertie's skin countless times without Bertie's knowing it, Scattergood Baines pulls his neighbors' strings with the skill of a puppetmaster).

So it is in the landscape of these white series characters that the *Post* nurtured black series characters. Harris Dickson's Ole Reliable, Irvin S. Cobb's Jeff Poindexter, Cohen's Florian Slappey and Lawyer Chew and Wiley's Wildcat Marsden all had respectable runs in the Philadelphia-based magazine. Competing *Collier's* gave its readers Bradford's plantation episodes with the Widow Duck.

White writers with specialized (or who at least believed they had specialized) understanding of the black citizenry found markets for their tales. Examining their stories, it doesn't appear these writers had particularly strong literary ambitions. Many yarns were hastily written and it shows. The writers were looking to sell wordage. If one kind of story didn't work, they'd try another. When an editor asked for more black stories, they knew they had something going. The pay was a penny or five a word, not worth taking the time to polish language, shape character or work out logical stories.

These white writers persuaded readers they knew the black mind, character and ambition. Few blacks agreed.[6] However empathetic they might be, white writers never lived inside black skin. Only rarely did a writer—Cohen, for example, or Cobb—even acknowledge there existed two worlds, the white world and the Jim Crow world, for African Americans.

Black characters in Means's Tickfall tales interacted with a white sheriff, doctor and plantation owner, yes, but in a subservient way. Cohen avoided having his black characters have any but the most meaningless dealings with whites. His blacks lived in their own universe.

A promising black writer, Y. Andrew Roberson,[7] in 1922 offered aspiring writers sound advice on "Putting the Negro in Fiction":

> If you are a writer you will sooner or later be tempted to seize your pen, or grasp your typewriter, or take your pencil and dash off a negro tale. Because if you continue living in America—and writing—some day you will be struck by some phase of the black man's make-up. Maybe it will be his quaint philosophy of life, or his struggles, but more than likely it will be his, to you, humorous actions.
>
> "Yes," you will say, "darkies are so funny and a good story about them always pleases the reader by giving him a laugh. Besides, look at the money Cohen, Wiley and others are making out of them. The public likes good darky stories; therefore, I will do one." ...
>
> The black American is quite worthy of being written about, and wants to be put into print, but he desires to be correctly represented. Correct representation will do much to aid inter-racial feeling here in America, where he lives some twelve million strong. Fiction has done him more good and more harm than it has anyone else. All the good is summed up in the part "Uncle Tom's Cabin" played in the ending of slavery, but it is hard to sum up the harm because in all later fiction the Blacks have cut a sorry and most unnatural figure. So sorry a figure that the negro feels the effect in every part of the country, and knows his already heavy handicap has been added to by spreading this idea that his race is a race of buffoons, brutes, and old faithful servants who always sacrifice everything for the honor of the Peribrooks or young "Marse" Harry.[8]

Roberson, in giving an articulate and heartfelt plea for better stories about blacks, fingered many of the inconsistencies coming from white writers—who he thought bowed too easily to Jim Crow etiquette. He went on:

> One of the most common mistakes about the speech of the negro is to put poor grammar into the mouth of some character whose stated position in life would make such a possibility very unlikely. On one page we read that Ephraim Suggs is a negro lawyer, and on the next we have him saying, "Is you gwine," "Ain't it de truf," and so on. Negro lawyers have to pass just as hard a bar examination as white ones and are even more likely to have college diplomas. Why make them talk any differently from other educated persons? It is not needed to indicate color, for that you can state in a few words. This goes for all the professions except the ministry. ...
>
> Descriptions of Darktown society cause much and loud laughter as written by white writers, but the truth is that negro society differs only in degree, and not in kind, from white society. Yet we read that Amanda Jones, washerwoman to Colonel Billings, was a leader in Darktown social circles, or that Eustis Custardon, chauffeur to the mayor of Spiggotville, cut quite a dash among the colored elite. Anyone who took the trouble to look into the matter would find out that the persons in question will cut just about as wide a swath in negro life as people of their station do among whites. It is true that the sort of entertainments white writers describe are not far from what goes on, but the mistake is to call them the blow-outs of the elite, or of negro society, and give the reader the untruthful idea that colored people are a joke socially.[9]

Roberson saw differences among white writers. He allowed that Cohen gave his characters "feelings, aspirations, loves and hates like those of other people, while retaining all the little racial distinctions. His stories are very unlike those of E.K. Means or Hugh Wiley in more than one way. But the difference that makes the negro reader like Cohen best is that they never feel insulted or put upon after reading a tale by him, for he never uses the three or four words that are the pet aversions of negroes. The words are 'nigger,' 'darky,' 'shine,' 'coon' and 'boy.'"[10]

Note that the periodical that published the above excerpts used the term "negro" with a small *n*. One edition of Mark Twain's *Huckleberry Finn* was removed from a New York library in 1957, not for the use of "nigger" throughout, but for using "negro" and "negroes" without capital *N*'s. The edition in question, as it turns out, had been bowdlerized; Twain used neither word in his original manuscript, according to scholar Jonathan Arac.[11]

W.E.B. Du Bois,[12] editorial director of the National Association for the Advancement of Colored People (NAACP), wasn't overly concerned about terminology, in the right context: "My policy when I was editor of *The Crisis* was to let a writer use the word 'nigger' or 'darky' if it served an artistic purpose in his story. Of course I tried not to have this occur too often. The point is if an author is quoting a southern white man, and the white man is addressing a Negro, he will say 'nigger.' To make him say anything else would be rather a strain upon credulity."[13]

The low literature of the likes of Cohen, Wiley, Akers, Dickson, Smith and the others would barely fit Du Bois's criteria.

Sterling A. Brown[14] took the complaint about insufficient black characters to an academic level, writing about "Negro Characters as Seen by White Authors." Cohen, he griped, had his characters speak in a dialect never heard in real life. Akers resorted to "irate shrews and 'Milquetoast' husbands, with razors wielded at departing parts of the anatomy" and Wiley "another creator of the farce that negro life is too generally believed to be." Means, he wrote, "with obvious knowledge of Southern Negro life, is concerned to show in the main its ludicrous side." He allowed that Bradford could write good humor, but "he has a definite attitude to the Negro to uphold. His stories of the easy loves of the levee (frequently found in *Collier's*) concentrate upon the comic aspect of Negro life, another observer might well see the tragic."[15]

Professor Andre Esters[16] said there was no reason white writers couldn't write about blacks, though he suggested white writers generally had a poor grasp of what it meant to be black. But the contrary could work: "The interesting part about a black author writing from a white perspective is blacks historically have known more of whites and the intimacies and behaviors of their lives due to the roles Blacks played in their lives. Thus, blacks might be able to tell a more true and compelling story if they were given the task of telling a story of whites."[17]

Woe, particularly, to the northern writer who attempted black dialect. Booth Tarkington was a target of critics, including Sam W. Small[18]—himself white and a delineator of Negro dialect—who blasted the Indiana scribe in the *Atlanta Constitution* in 1913:

> He [Tarkington] has plugged a mulatto into his story of "The Flirt," current in *The Saturday Evening Post*,[19] and, as is usual with northern authors, he makes a miserable botch of the negro dialect.
>
> After more than forty years of critical attention to the particular thing, I cannot recall even one non-southern-bred writer who has made a passable success with the dialect of the negro. Those writers notoriously are unlearned in the psychology of his speech. The negro does not feel or reason in the conventional Caucasian ways. He does not express his sensations by the customary terms that accompany all-white association.
>
> A natural negro dialect is as a reflection in shallow, rippling water of the smooth and simple speech of the white people to whom the negro looks up for example, and whose customs and commandments he follows. His untutored mental grasp is that of a child. He learns the short

and simple words and phrases and often can express a rich or strong idea in terser and purer Anglo-Saxon than many ornately educated white men would phrase it...

Negro dialect is correctly written only when it is phonetically reproduced in letters. To do that with any skill and accuracy one must know negroes familiarly: in their daily life at home and at work, and study well their moods and manners when free from any artificial incitements.

When I first began to write negro dialect, in the "Old Si" papers for *The Constitution* some thirty-seven years ago, Colonel Henry Watterson paid me the compliment of saying that those articles contained "the best written and most characteristic negro dialect yet produced...."

Negro dialect that is not "nigger talk" at all is always absurd and aggravating to those who know and value the real article. The common stage negro minstrel and the northern-evolving fiction negro are both abominations. Like the dromedary in the menagerie was to the hayseed, "There ain't no sich animal."[20]

Whatever their abilities at recreating black dialect, from today's perspective one wants to point a finger at all white writers and accuse them of bigotry, of racism. And some of them would deserve it. We'll give the benefit of the doubt, though, and assume that most harbored moderate views of race relations and labored under Jim Crow etiquette. They had little choice, if they wanted to sell stories, but to resort to demeaning stereotype.

The tradition was a long one. John W. Lowe summarized, "The nineteenth century's appetite for 'Negro' folktales and folk humor proved insatiable, especially after the Civil War, when new cultural modes were sought to deal with whites' psychological fears caused by emancipation. But these needs were satisfied by white writers, performers, and artists. Collections of 'Negro humor,' plantation-tradition short stories and novels, and, above all, the minstrel show and popular stage productions, solidified the image of the 'comic darkie.'"[21]

Writers show occasional sparks of fondness for their characters. H.E.C. Bryant poked fun at his Rastus figure,[22] who is uneducated and apparently baffled by simple logic. But Rastus may be simply stringing an inquisitor along, so he can build to a zinger comeback. Cohen's Slappey Florian several times establishes a clever setup in order to best his antagonist. Likewise, Bradford's Widow Duck could be devilishly manipulative.

Jim Crow boundaries were strongly codified and ruthlessly enforced on all races in the South. For story series about blacks to have a chance, not only did they have to have cardboard characters, they also had to show the blacks as little-educated, superstitious, conniving, unreliable, lustful and lazy (not necessarily all in the same story). The stories had to be "funny." Funny, that is, to white readers. Black readers may have read them, may have tolerated them. But they found little funny in them.

As Margaret Just Butcher posited in *The Negro in American Culture*, "Frequently masking sorrow, and sometimes impotent resentment, the Negro's laughter was certainly more often contrived and artificial than natural and spontaneous, despite contrary Southern convictions."[23]

Further, she said, "Because the comic side of the Negro offered no offense or challenge to the South's tradition of the Negro's subordinate status, it richly colored southern local and regional culture, and eventually that of the whole nation."

Some white writers subtly positioned their black hero as a jester figure, seemingly making fun of his white betters, though as Boskin notes, the black figure "was denied the Fool's touch of wisdom and perspective—and thus the ability to manipulate humor for higher ends. While the Jester was often chosen for his acumen, Sambo was only occasionally accorded such a rational function."[24]

Here we resume discussion of dialect. Black characters in these stories universally spoke an exaggerated local lingo. Throughout this study, the word "dialect" will be used, sometimes inaccurately. "Dialect" should mean a form of language peculiar to a special region of the country, or to a social group such as the Gullah of Georgia. "Vernacular" might be a better word, or "colloquial." Many writers justify the use of strong idiom as a serious attempt to document a passing language. Even if their hearts are in the right place, the results still come off as distorted.

The *Nashville Banner* in 1912 began an interesting discussion about fictional black characters and their colloquial speech that disdained the "he am," "you am" school of writing. The *Macon Telegraph* picked up the thread: "The average writer ought to leave negro dialect absolutely alone. It is an art that few have mastered, and in the application of which only two have succeeded in any large measure. Eliminate Joel Chandler Harris and Thomas Nelson Page, and all the rest of the negro dialect in American literature is not, in the aggregate, worth the white paper on which it is written."[25]

This was written just before a rush of new white writers with Negro characters. After the rush, another commentator said the same thing: "After Joel Chandler Harris had introduced negro dialect into the field of literature, imitators leaped upon it as the latest literary novelty, whether they had ever heard a negro talk or not. This worthless imitation of Harris and other southern writers has not abated."[26]

In those days, newspapers exchanged issues with each other and freely printed from each other. The *Telegraph* disagreed that Harris was better than Page at replicating speech: "The average Southern negro never pronounces an 'r,' yet the 'r' is put into the mouth of Uncle Remus continually. For example, 'Brer' Rabbit," the exact sound being 'Buh' Rabbit," or very near it. Mr. Harris would have realized this himself if he had ever heard an 'r' rolling Northerner read 'Uncle Remus' aloud."[27]

There was more to it than that. White writers were inconsistent or anachronistic. Will N. Harben[28] in his 1900 collection *Northern Georgia Sketches*—an abolitionist view of lower southern society during antebellum times—in the story "The Sale of Uncle Rastus" has the ailing main character, hearing the approach of singing field workers, say: "I heer um—dat Nelse's tenor en Montague's bass; dey all comin'. I never heer sec her racket!'" Really? An illiterate slave would use words like tenor and bass?

Whatever the talents of the various replicators of dialect, it's obvious dialect is an accepted, even valued, aspect of stories featuring blacks. (The *Telegraph* went on to champion its hometown Macon writer, Bridges Smith, for his "accurate portraiture of the twentieth century negro of the police courts and back alleys of Southern towns.")

The *Charlotte Observer*, for its part, wrote: "All Southerners know perfectly well that negro dialect as produced by Northern writers and any other writers who may adopt the conventional forms to satisfy magazine editors was never heard in the South. It bears only a very remote resemblance to real negro dialect—hardly one capable of being recognized aside from conventional status and obvious intent. It hits the mark at one point along, namely, in forms like 'dat' and 'dey.' But the 'th' occurring in 'this,' 'they,' etc., is among the most peculiar and difficult sounds of any Aryan tongue, insomuch that here foreigners pronounce English just about as the negro does...."[29]

Which writers best reproduced the Negro tongue figures into the justification for this sub-literature; if it was seriously attempting to document a disappearing dialect (with so many southern blacks moving north or west), it was wholly worthwhile, even if it demeaned its subjects. As the *New York Times* observed of one writer, "Once in a while Miss [Ella Middleton] Tybout's dialect slips away from her—but after all the charm of dialect lies more in its pronunciation by the reader than in its spelling by the writer."[30]

An author's sympathy for his characters cannot necessarily be construed as sympathy for an entire race. Harry Stillwell Edwards, for one, wrote of his difficulty in accepting the newer generation of blacks, but he liked the older folks.

These writers sometimes approached black social issues. Just as often, they approached white issues under the guise of black characters. It was similar to how blackface stage performers hid behind burnt-cork personas: It could be liberating. And if a misstep were made, it would be soon be dismissed and forgotten.

Socially, one may be willing to give a little leeway to these local color writers.[31] But literarily it is more difficult. Just because dialect existed didn't mean it had to be used so constantly and so intensely, with no attempt to convey the white Southern lilt. Twain and Tarkington, of the writers discussed in this book, made perhaps the most skilled use of vernacular. Twain alone had his white hero, Huck Finn, sound like a southerner. Surely to the northern ear, any white inhabitant of Mississippi or Alabama had distinct vocal inflections. In the majority of these writings, none emerged.

Dialect was a Jim Crow etiquette necessity. As Michael Patrick Hearn observed, "Dialect was suitable only for humorous writing."[32] African American poet Paul Laurence Dunbar[33] created verses and stories using the vernacular. "William Dean Howells praised his work for the wrong reasons, setting a tone that other Dunbar critics would follow for years as they virtually ignored his standard English verse and his published experiments with Irish, German, and Western regional dialects," Joanne M. Braxton said.[34]

Later black writers Zora Neale Hurston[35] and Langston Hughes included dialect in their poems and stories—and were criticized for being "too racial" by whites who were offended and by blacks who saw dialect as a holdover of Jim Crow etiquette. However, just the fact that black writers have employed dialect—reaching for authenticity—suggests a legitimacy to using vernacular speech—if done right. Which, in the case of white writers, is always subject to debate.

Is there a value in these stories simply because they introduced blacks to the mainstream? Even through the Jim Crow filter, Bradford's Bugaboo Jones and Charles Correll and Freeman Gosden's Sam and Henry emerged as real people (as real as their fictional white contemporaries, that is).

Vernacular stories may serve some useful purpose to dialectologists and folklorists interested in regional Deep South speech patterns. But how trustworthy are the columnists and fictioneers? They may be familiar with colloquial speakers, but how qualified are they at recording it? How trustworthy are they, considering their writings aim first and foremost for humor?

Dialect and pathetic character, then, accounted for much of the humor in these stories. Fortunately, the better writers also showed an increasing ability to create situational humor, to weave their hapless fictional figures into interesting plots.

White writers of black characters had their value, suggests John Strausbaugh, when they took on the role of amateur ethnographers, and actually did some research before writing. Perhaps inspired by the Scotsman Robert Burns, who wrote in a thick Lowland Scots dialect, American authors set about incorporating indigenous speech patterns into their stories, poems and novels.

"Viewing negro-dialect literature in this broad context adds a level of perspective that lifts the best of it out of the knee-jerk presumption that it was all racist mockery or, at best, 'condescending ... literary slumming,'" Strausbaugh said. "The fact is, negro-dialect writing was used by both White and Black authors in work that arranged across the spectrum from loathsome vulgarity to some of the greatest American literature of the era."[36]

Writers in the late Jim Crow era might be considered transitional, establishing a bridge from the plantation apologists and Lost Cause defenders who were productive in the early Jim Crow era. Except that they transitioned to nothing.

By the 1950s, the pulp and general interest magazines were on the way out, replaced by paperback books and losing audiences to television, respectively. Newspapers had to economize, and stopped running fiction. Radio ceded its audience to television. Motion pictures, which mirrored this time period, followed a course that has been analyzed elsewhere in several book-length studies.

By the 1950s, short-form series fiction lost its markets and withered. Hughes is the most recent writer included in this book's main section; it was only by 1940 that he was able to find a home and produce short stories from a black voice. By then, only a handful of white writers were still writing their darky stories.

Space is inadequate here to document thoroughly the history of the Jim Crow era. Please accept this sparse overview. Southern whites, doubly shocked at losing the Civil War and being battered by Reconstruction carpetbaggers, weren't about to cede anything to sons and daughters of Africa who had so recently provided free domestic and field labor. There were some 347,525 enslaved blacks in the United States in 1850. One individual owned more than 1,000; nine individuals owned between 500 and 1,000. South Carolina accounted for a quarter of the slaves.[37] As historian David Brion Davis points out, "In 1860, the value of Southern slaves was about three times the amount invested in manufacturing or railroads nationwide."[38] The *Plessy v. Ferguson* case before the United States Supreme Court in 1897 sanctioned legal racial segregation under the doctrine of separate but equal treatment.

That decision is a good starting point for the late Jim Crow era, for our purpose. It would take blacks decades to muster the social and political power to fight back against the entrenched and institutionalized segregation. Du Bois, in writing *The Souls of Black Folk* (1903) and in convening the Niagara conferences, which led to creation of the NAACP, became the movement's intellectual leader.

As the country approached World War I, southern states and a few northern cities codified segregation. A reinvigorated Ku Klux Klan ran rampant, and indiscriminate beatings and lynchings terrorized the South. Some 370,000 blacks entered military service during the war, only to return home to oppressive conditions. Millions of blacks moved north and west in the 1920s and '30s in quest of better jobs and better social environments. So many left, in fact, that southern farmers became fearful they wouldn't have inexpensive labor to bring in their crops.

During this period, there were artistic renaissances in Harlem and Chicago. It was the jazz age. Yet Jim Crow etiquette bit hard. These were social rules, not spelled out in legislation. These were rules passed along by habit. Notably documented by Stetson Kennedy in his *Jim Crow Guide* in 1959, they covered everything from lighting cigarettes (under no circumstance should a black man ever light the cigarette of a white woman) to abiding lies (under no circumstance should a black man say a white person is lying) to driving a motor vehicle (white drivers have the right-of-way at intersections, no matter what).[39]

"It is a peculiar sensation, this double-consciousness, this sense of always looking at one's self through the eyes of others, of measuring one's soul by the tape of a world that looks on in amused contempt and pity," Du Bois wrote. "One ever feels his twoness,—an American, a Negro; two souls, two thoughts, two unreconciled strivings; two warring ideals in one dark body, whose dogged strength alone keeps it from being torn asunder."[40]

There were some 7 million individuals of African descent living in former Confederate states in 1910, 1 million blacks in the rest of the United States, 92 million people of all races in the country as a whole. Following World War II, in which blacks distinguished themselves in uniform, the United States realized Europeans increasingly felt that the country had as much to be ashamed of in its treatment of a minority. Yet, as historian Jerrold M. Packard points out, "Their backlash made this the last generation before blacks gained their due—the last two decades following the end of World War II—as bad as any time, perhaps even the worst of all times, since the end of slavery itself."[41]

Rosa Parks wouldn't give up her bus seat. Students refused to vacate a whites-only Woolworth lunch counter. The Rev. Martin Luther King, Jr. touched the emotional backbone. Momentum built for congressional adoption of the Civil Rights Act in 1965. The Jim Crow era was over—though of course it was never truly over.

Critics have justifiably maligned this late Jim Crow era's stereotypical literature, though few who have written critically about it can boast of a firsthand reading of the works. As will be seen, there are degrees of repugnance, and even an occasional bright light. None of the writing incites violence, for example. However, its passivity was hurtful to the Negro cause. Excerpts given in this text from selected short stories contain what today is considered racist language. There's no use censoring it.

Why weren't there more African Americans writing for these magazines? If humor and dialect were the requirements, most black writers found dialect condescending and the black experience had nothing amusing to write about.

Why aren't women writers represented in this book's core? Women writers were as active as men writers in depicting black society, and particularly took the lead in juveniles and children's books. But few worked in short form, and none wrote *humorous* stories in series in this time period. Thirty women writers are included in Part III.

White writers challenged for the way they depicted blacks fell back on the excuse "That's what everyone is doing." And decades later, we'll have to accept that reasoning in the absence of indications otherwise. Cartoonist Will Eisner, who otherwise was remarkably innovative and progressive, stumbles here. Beginning his Spirit comic stories as late as he did, when there were definite signs of change in the air, why did he make his young character Ebony White such a visual grotesque? He was doubtless locked in by tradition.

This isn't meant as a defense, but another point needs to be made. Short-form series fiction obliged fast-working writers to resort to stereotypes, white, black, Native American,

Hispanic, Asian. If readers already recognized the character's supposed traits, the writer could quickly get down to the business of the story. Earthworm tractor salesman Botts in Upson's stories in the *Post* is an unrestrained blowhard. Kelland's Scattergood Baines in *American Magazine* is an irksome manipulator. Gilpatric's seagoing Glencannon is virtually an alcoholic whose dense brogue can be challenging even when he's sober. Readers already expect that.

By the late Jim Crow era, the few black stereotypes from Harriet Beecher Stowe's day—the Uncle Tom, the mammy, the buck, the pickaninny—had bloomed to include the "high yellow"—a desirable biracial woman; the angry woman—the shrill wife (Correll and Gosden's Sapphire); the Sambo—an average man, an accommodationist (Correll and Gosden's Amos); the navigator—the Sambo in a lead role, but without the negative connotations, can be sympathetic, intuitive, creative, loving (Cohen's Slappey, Wiley's Wildcat, Hughes's Jesse B. Semple); the buck—a worldly man, more positive than the brute, but without the resources to become a navigator (Means's Butts, Bradford's Jones); the coon—a lazy, clownish man (Correll and Gosden's Lightning); the blowhard—a manipulator, often chubby (Correll and Gosden's Kingfish); the schemer—a greedy, plotting man less sympathetic than the Buffoon (Correll and Gosden's Calhoun); and the sidekick—companion to a leading character of a different race (Eisner's Ebony).

Ultimately, as has already been noted, these writers turned out these stories to earn a living. It was the decision of the editor whether to carry these stories, or to change them or drop them. A too-bold writer on racial issues might not find a home for his prose.

There's a last and primary perspective to consider. How do the writers emphasized in this book fit into the larger picture of African American literature? The short answer is, they nipped around the edges and did little to advance a real black literature.

If one were to eliminate the racist elements from the stories of Cohen, Bradford and others, take out the dialect and the stereotypes, what's left would be similar to what other white writers were writing about white characters. Exploring that angle is no path to redemption, however. We can't lose sight of what was going on, in racially tense times. Blacks were (and continue to be) apart because of their skin color, their ethnic origins. And that shouldn't be.

Introduction Notes

1. Page viii.
2. Page 13.
3. Page 1.
4. *Sambo*, 14.
5. Ibid. Boskin said the Sambo figure evolved, "the image reflecting time and place, eventually to crack and disintegrate. But through it all he was what he started out as: a comic performer *par excellence*," 4.
6. *The Nation* and the *Atlanta Constitution* debated, in 1890, what, exactly, Negro readers read. "The Nation says that the negroes, as a class, are devoting their attention to the most educational books. They are not reading Amelie Rives, nor Egar Saltus, and as for Rider Haggard and such writers, they simply would not look at them. They have, in short, eschewed fiction. They read Aristotle, Plato and Cicero. They are interested in the history of the Netherlands, the decline of Poland and the rise of theosophy and the tendency of modern opera. They consult Darwin and Spencer, and explore German poetry and philosophy and deplore the expositional tendency of French art. The Atlanta Constitution says that they read the New York story papers and the *Police Gazette*—that is if they read at all." See "What the Colored Brother Reads," *Omaha Daily World-Herald*, 2 May 1890, 4.

7. Roberson (1897–1922), a native of Louisiana, was city editor for the *New Age Dispatch* in Los Angeles. He wrote for the Associated Press and founded the Western Writers Association. His novel *Ashes* was in serial publication at the time of his death of pneumonia at age twenty-five. He never finished his manuscript for his Ethiopian novel, *Rhoda, Princess of Dawn*.
8. *The Editor*, 97.
9. Ibid, 98.
10. Ibid, 99.
11. *Huckleberry Finn as Idol and Target*, 64.
12. See Section III.
13. Letter to A.S. Pinkett, 11 March 1936. Du Bois also occasionally wrote fiction.
14. Brown (1901–1989), born in Washington, D.C., the son of a former slave who became a minister and college professor, graduated from Williams College and Harvard. He taught and wrote poetry and literary criticism. He is considered part of the Harlem Renaissance for his interest in folk culture and his use of jazz cadences in his works.
15. *Journal of Negro Education*, 179–202.
16. Esters taught English at Howard University.
17. As quoted in Chris Witherspoon, "From 'Uncle Tom' to 'The Help': Can white writers tell black stories?"
18. A brief profile of Small appears in Section III.
19. *The Flirt* was serialized in nine *Post* issues, beginning 21 December 1912.
20. "Negro Dialect Astray," 11 January 1913, 4.
21. "African American Humor," in *Comedy: A Geographic and Historical Guide*, Maurice Charney, ed. Westport, Conn.: Praeger, 2005.
22. The anecdote appears in the Bryant profile in the main section of this book.
23. Page 27.
24. *Sambo*, 9.
25. "Negro Character and Dialect," *Macon Telegraph*, 13 March 1912, 4.
26. "You-all," Laurel (Miss.) *Morning Call*, 17 June 1929, 4. Harris, it might be pointed out, wasn't the first at his craft to write for newspapers; he followed Sam W. Small as a contributor of dialect sketches at the *Atlanta Constitution*.
27. Ibid.
28. See Section III.
29. "Negro Dialect, Genuine and the Reverse," 16 March 1912, 4.
30. "In Darky Dialect," 24 December 1904.
31. Claude M. Simpson provides a good overview of the regionalists in *The Local Colorists: American Short Stories 1857–1900*.
32. *The Annotated Huckleberry Finn*, xci.
33. See Section III.
34. "Dunbar's Life and Career," Modern American Poetry, http://www.english.illinois.edu/maps/poets/a_f/dunbar/life.htm (viewed 9 November 2012).
35. See Section III.
36. *Black Like You*, 154.
37. "Statistics of Slave Owners," Pittsfield (Mass.) *Sun*, 31 January 1861, 1.
38. *Problem of Slavery in the Age of Revolution*, 174.
39. See Stetson Kennedy, *Jim Crow Guide: The Way It Was*.
40. *The Souls of Black Folk*, 9.
41. *American Nightmare: The History of Jim Crow*, 227.

Introduction Sources

Arac, Jonathan. *Huckleberry Finn as Idol and Target*. Madison: University of Wisconsin Press, 1997.
Boskin, Joseph. *Sambo: The Rise & Demise of an American Jester*. New York: Oxford University Press, 1986.
Braxton, Joanne M. "Dunbar's Life and Career," Modern American Poetry. http://www.english.illinois.edu/maps/poets/a_f/dunbar/life.htm (viewed 9 November 2012).
Brown, Sterling A. "Negro Characters as Seen by White Authors," *Journal of Negro Education*, Vol. 2 No. 2, April 1933.

Butcher, Margaret Just. *The Negro in American Culture*. New York: Alfred A. Knopf, 1956.

Craig, Terrence. *Racial Attitudes in English-Canadian Fiction 1905–1980*. Waterloo, Ontario: Wilfrid Laurier University Press, 1987.

Davis, David Brion. *Problem of Slavery in the Age of Revolution, 1770–1823*. Ithaca, N.Y.: Cornell University Press, 1975.

Du Bois, W.E.B. Letter to A.S. Pinkett, 11 March 1936. Special Collections and University Archives, University of Massachusetts Amherst Libraries, MS 312, W.E.B. Du Bois Papers.

_____. *The Souls of Black Folk*. Chicago: A.C. McClurg, 1903.

Gardner, Eric, ed. *Major Voices; The Drama of Slavery*. London: Toby Press, 2005.

Hearn, Michael Patrick, ed. *The Annotated Huckleberry Finn*. New York: W.W. Norton, 2001.

"In Darky Dialect," *New York Times*, 24 December 1904.

Kennedy, Stetson. *Jim Crow Guide: The Way It Was*. Tallahassee: Florida Atlantic University Press, 1959.

Lowe, John W. "African American Humor" in *Comedy: A Geographic and Historical Guide*, Maurice Charney, ed. Westport, Conn.: Praeger, 2005.

"Mrs. H.B. Stowe: Life and Work of a Great American Authoress," *Philadelphia Inquirer*, 16 February 1890.

"Negro Character and Dialect," *Macon Telegraph*, 13 March 1912.

"Negro Dialect, Genuine and the Reverse," *Charlotte (N.C.) Observer*, 16 March 1912.

Oliver, Paul. *Barrelhouse Blues*. New York: BasicCivitas Books, 2009.

Packard, Jerrold M. *American Nightmare: The History of Jim Crow*. New York: St. Martin's Griffin, 2002.

Roberson, Andrew. "Putting the Negro in Fiction," *The Editor*, Vol. 56, 1922.

"Y.A. Roberson, Editor, Dies," St. Paul, Minn., *Appeal*, 2 December 1922.

Silk, John, and Catherine Silk. *Racism and Anti-Racism in American Popular Culture: Portrayals of African-Americans in Fiction and Film*. Manchester, UK: Manchester University Press, 1990.

Simpson, Claude M., ed. *The Local Colorists: American Short Stories 1857–1900*. New York: Harper & Brothers, 1960.

Small, Sam W. "Negro Dialect Astray," *Atlanta Constitution*, 11 January 1913.

"Statistics of Slave Owners," Pittsfield (Mass.) *Sun*, 31 January 1861.

Strausbaugh, John. *Black Like You: Blackface, Whiteface, Insult & Imitation in American Popular Culture*. New York: Jeremy P. Tarcher/Penguin, 2006.

"What the Colored Brother Reads," *Omaha Daily World-Herald*, 2 May 1890.

Witherspoon, Chris. "From 'Uncle Tom' to 'The Help': Can White Writers Tell Black Stories?" The Grio, 22 February 2011. http://thegrio.com/2011/02/22/from-uncle-tom-to-the-help-can-white-writers-tell-black-stories/ (viewed 14 November 2012).

"You-all," Laurel (Miss.) *Morning Call*, 17 June 1929.

I

Writers of the Antebellum, Reconstruction and Early Jim Crow Era (1851–1899)

A black presence in American literature emerged only slowly, for several reasons. White readers were more interested in reading about white characters in their novels. Black writers were rarely allowed into the market, and when they were, it was only as curious poets or narrators of true stories of slavery and oppression.

To be the first to write poetry with black perspectives or stories with black characters was no guarantee of success, only a historical footnote. As is easily demonstrated, blacks had to struggle to break into print; they didn't even try for many years in fiction when so many nonfiction topics took precedent.

Before we meet in the main part of the book the white writers who dared (because they wanted to tap a fresh literary genre) to write about black characters in the years 1900 to 1955, we should consider earlier and simultaneous Negro character stories, mostly penned by white hands. Seven authors discussed here may be considered pacesetters, as the early Jim Crow literary era transformed into a later phase, when Americans emerged into a new century.

Harriet Beecher Stowe's *Uncle Tom's Cabin*, particularly the traveling road show abridgement, was still very familiar across the country. Mark Twain and Joel Chandler Harris were still in print, their folksiness widely popular with readers. Thomas Nelson Page and George Washington Cable were strong storytellers who were well known then, though they have fallen into obscurity today. Charles W. Chesnutt and Paul Laurence Dunbar were the most popular writers of the period who were of African descent.

There are at least four distinct historic segments of writings about blacks in the United States. The antebellum plantation stories; the postbellum Lost Cause stories; in the early 1900s, the late-period humorous Jim Crow stories; and finally the Harlem Renaissance–inspired truly black stories.

"I'se regusted," the Andy Brown would say. "Is you is, or is you aint?" Florian Slappey would ask. The use of dialect will become an important point as we look at this book's main subjects, therefore examples by these pacesetters are included. Some writers attempted accurate (if all but unreadable) re-creation of regional speech; others exaggerated it for amusing effect.

These authors only scratch the surface. Other contemporary writers, including a number of women, are included in the third section of the book. They range from Phillis Wheatley, who died in 1784, to Lorraine Hansberry, who died in 1965.

Harriet Beecher Stowe
(1811–1896)
Uncle Tom's Cabin (1851)

So you are the little woman who wrote the book that started this great war!
—*Abraham Lincoln*[1]

Connecticut-born Harriet Beecher was reared by her oldest sister, Catherine, following the death of their mother, Roxana Foote Beecher, in 1815, when Harriet was four. Her father, the noted Congregationalist preacher Lyman Beecher, enrolled Harriet at several private schools, where she demonstrated a knack for writing. She taught at Catherine's Western Female Institute in Cincinnati and began to sell her stories. She visited a plantation in Kentucky and saw firsthand the plight of slaves. Her friend Salmon P. Chase, later a governor, senator, cabinet member and Supreme Court chief justice, encouraged her antislavery activities. She married Calvin Stowe in 1836 and they raised seven children.

Harriet Beecher Stowe had a vision in 1851, from which came a compulsion to write about the plight of blacks and the evils of slavery and particularly damage it did to mother-child ties. Installments of *Uncle Tom's Cabin* appeared beginning on 5 June 1851 and in forty succeeding issues of the antislavery weekly *National Era* and were devoured by an estimated 50,000 readers. The work was revised for publication as a book (in two volumes). It sold an estimated 325,000 copies the first year.

"The novel's implicit message—that most slaves, like Uncle Tom, were docile, childlike, and imminently Christian; that slavery was an affront to families because it separated such and encouraged slaveholder adultery; and that freed slaves (like her characters George and Eliza) would be best off in Canada—were quite palatable to much of the white public, especially when wrapped in a sentimental framework," according to drama historian Eric Gardner.[2]

Stowe relied heavily on dialect, as this excerpt (from the *National Era* printing) of a conversation between Mrs. Shelby and the house servant Chloe from Chapter 43 demonstrates. They are in the dining room, anticipating the arrival of George Shelby:

"Didn't say nothin' 'bout my old man, s'pose?" said Chloe, still fidgeting with the tea-cups.

"No, he didn't. He did not speak of anything, Chloe. He said he would tell all when he got home."

"Jes like mass'r George—he's allers so ferce for tellin' everything hisself. I allers minded dat ar in mass'r George. Don't see, for my part, how white people gen'lly can bar to hev to write things much as they do, writin' 's such slow, oneasy kind o' work."

Mrs. Shelby smiled.

"I'm a thinkin' my old man won't know de boys and de baby. Lor'! she's de biggest gal now, good she is too, and pert, Polly is. She's out to the house, now, watchin' de hoe-cake. I's got jist de very pattern my old man liked so much, a bakin'. Jist sich as I gin him the mornin' he was took off. Lord bless us! how I felt dat ar mornin'!"

An 1899 poster depicts Topsy from Harriet Beecher Stowe's *Uncle Tom's Cabin* (Courier Litho Co./Library of Congress).

Uncle Tom's Cabin got away from its creator. It became a merchandising bonanza, but without Stowe's authorization. Minstrel show producers adapted the novel and reduced her characters to total caricature. The performers were whites in blackface.[3] Eliza's escape across the ice became a spectacle. Topsy became a slapstick figure. Tom became a submissive old man. George L. Aiken's 1852 adaptation, which Stowe saw in a theater, was popular on two continents for seventy-five years. H.J. Conway's *Uncle Tom's Cabin* (1853) was also popular. Stowe felt obliged to dramatize some of the story in *The Christian Slave* in 1855. But unauthorized "Tom Shows" toured well into the 1940s.

Stowe's novel was praised and castigated. It inspired upwards of thirty anti–Tom novels, such as *The Sword and the Distaff* (1852) by William Gilmore Simms, which depicted slave owners as paternalistic.

Novelist James Baldwin called *Uncle Tom's Cabin* a "very bad novel, having, in its self-righteous virtuous sentimentality, much in common with *Little Women*."[4] Baldwin considered Stowe a pamphleteer whose words did very little to change American attitudes, and in fact may have spurred racist attitudes.

"Beginning in the 1970s, however, the rise of feminist criticism provided an opportunity for new readings of *Uncle Tom's Cabin* and the study of Stowe as one of the major women writers of the United States," according to Susan Belasco. "As these scholars integrated *Uncle Tom's Cabin* into the canon of American literature, the novel became a part of the classroom experience of new generations of students and readers."[5]

In later years Stowe resided in Hartford, Connecticut, and Florida. She died in 1896.

Harriet Beecher Stowe Notes

1. Probably apocryphal.
2. *Major Voices*, page xxiv.
3. Actor, comedian, minstrel performer and former slave Sam Lucas (1850–1916) was the first man of African descent to play Uncle Tom on the stage (1878) and in film (1914).
4. "Everybody's Protest Novel," *Partisan Review* No. 16, 49, 578–579.
5. "Harriet Beecher Stowe in Our Time."

Harriet Beecher Stowe Selected Bibliography and Sources

NEWSPAPER SERIAL

"Uncle Tom's Cabin" (*The National Era*, 5 June 1851 to 1 April 1852)

SELECTED BOOKS

Uncle Tom's Cabin; or, Life Among the Lowly (1852) revised from the newspaper serial and issued 18 March 1852

A Key to Uncle Tom's Cabin; Presenting the Original Facts and Documents Upon Which the Story Is Founded Together with Corroborative Statements Verifying the Truth of the Work (1853)

The Christian Slave (1855) dramatization of *Uncle Tom's Cabin*

Dred: A Tale of the Great Dismal Swamp (1859)

SOURCES

Baldwin, James. "Everybody's Protest Novel," *Partisan Review* No. 16, 49, 578–579.

Belasco, Susan. "Harriet Beecher Stowe in Our Time," Stowe Center, http://nationalera.wordpress.com/ (viewed 26 October 2012).

"Harriet Beecher Stowe: Death of the Authoress of 'Uncle Tom's Cabin,'" *New York Times*, 2 July 1896.

"Uncle Tom's Serialization: The National Era Text," University of Virginia. http://utc.iath.virginia.edu/sitemap.html (viewed 20 November 2012).

Mark Twain
(1835–1910)
Nigger Jim (1876–1884)

> All modern American literature comes from one book by Mark Twain called *Huckleberry Finn*. American writing comes from that. There was nothing before. There has been nothing as good since.
> —Ernest Hemingway, *The Green Hills of Africa*

Samuel Langhorne Clemens was born in Florida, Missouri, in 1835, and grew up in Hannibal. Sam joined his brother Orion at the Missouri *Courier*. He traveled as an itinerant typesetter. He apprenticed as a pilot on a Mississippi steamboat in 1857, eventually becoming a journeyman pilot. He mustered out of the Confederate Army after two weeks and went with his brother to Nevada Territory, where he worked as a secretary, prospector and reporter. He became city editor of the *Enterprise* in Virginia City in 1862 and soon adopted the "Mark Twain" pen name for humorous writings. He gained considerable attention with publication of "The Celebrated Jumping Frog of Calaveras County" in a New York newspaper in 1865. A trip abroad furnished material for his first book, *The Innocents Abroad*. It also brought him a bride, Olivia Langdon, whom he married in 1870.

Clemens established himself as a popular humorist, travel writer and fiction writer. *The Adventures of Tom Sawyer* in 1876 derived from his Missouri boyhood, incorporated youthful adventure and introduced Nigger Jim. Jim appeared again in the more serious *Adventures of Huckleberry Finn* in 1884. *Huck* was a difficult book for Twain, who wrote part of the manuscript, put it away, then brought it out again and finished it at his home in Hartford, Connecticut.

Twain has his admirers and his critics. "What makes *The Adventures of Huckleberry Finn*[1] so brilliant," asserts A.D. Sullivan, "isn't its stand on slavery, although that is one very important part of its overall effect, but the voices and language used, and the sense of place Twain has managed to create within the pages of his book. We get a vision of America and the American male that people like [critic Jane] Smiley would have us deny, that primitive sense of ethics, mistaken loyalty and misguided systems of belief that is the center of most white, American males, and the heart of what built America."[2]

Jane Smiley was particularly critical of *Huck* in 1996, saying Harriet Beecher Stowe's *Uncle Tom's Cabin* was more deserving of worship. "No whitewash, no secrets, but evil, suffering, imagination, endurance, and redemption," she wrote in *Harper's*. "If 'great' literature has any purpose, it is to help us face up to our responsibilities instead of enabling us to avoid them once again by lighting out for the territory."[3]

Huck, retorted Justin Kaplan in *The New York Times Book Review*, "through its humor, lyricism and distinctive, even revolutionary narrative voice, not only [manages to] survive but to transcend its author's definition of a classic."[4]

Scholars in recent decades have reassembled Twain's *Huck* manuscript and restored Jim's "Ghost Story" and the Raftsmen's and the Pokeville Camp Meeting passages that the author dropped before book publication. Reading these sections, one can see Twain's care in shaping his final draft. (It's interesting to note that Booth Tarkington also excised—or his editors excised—the black boy Herman's rendition of a revival camp meeting from *Penrod*.)

This is an exchange between Huck and Jim:

"What's the matter with you, Jim? You been a drinking?"
"Drinkin'? Has I ben a drinkin'? Has I had a chance to be a drinkin'?"
"Well, then, what makes you talk so wild?"
"How does I talk wild?"
"*How?* Why, hain't you been talking about my coming back, and all that stuff, as if I'd been gone away?"
"Huck—Huck Finn, you look me in de eye; look me in de eye. *Hain't* you ben gone away?"[5]

Twain strove to re-create the rhythm and language of both Huck and Jim as they would have been heard. Many readers cringe at his use of "the 'n' word," to the extent that in 2011, a "cleaned-up" edition was brought out. Editor Alan Gribben said the expurgation was to shelter "the reader from a racial slur that never seems to lose its vitriol."[6]

To which critic Michiko Kakutani responded, "*Huckleberry Finn* actually stands as a powerful indictment of slavery (with Nigger Jim its most noble character), of using its contested language as an opportunity to explore the painful complexities of race relations in this country. To censor or redact books on school reading lists is a form of denial: shutting the door on harsh historical realities—whitewashing them or pretending they do not exist."[7]

Mark Twain Notes

1. E.W. Kemble (1861–1933) illustrated the first edition, also Stowe's *Uncle Tom's Cabin* and Joel Chandler Harris's *Uncle Remus*. He had a wide reputation for illustrating black characters, perhaps a little less exaggerated than some, though he was not without his detractors.
2. "No Easy Answers in Twain," *Scrap Paper Review* No. 21, August 1997. http://www.hourwolf.com/spr/spr0021.html (viewed 26 October 2012).
3. "Say It Ain't So, Huck," *Harper's*, January 1996, 69.
4. "Selling Huck Finn Down the River," 10 March 1996, 27.
5. *Adventures of Huckleberry Finn, The Only Comprehensive Edition*, 108.
6. Michiko Kakutani, "Light Out, Huck, They Still Want to Sivilize You," *New York Times*, 6 January 2011.
7. Ibid.

Mark Twain Selected Bibliography and Sources

SELECTED HUCK FINN AND TOM SAWYER BOOKS

(1) *Adventures of Tom Sawyer* (1876)
(2) *Adventures of Huckleberry Finn* (1884)
(3) *Tom Sawyer Abroad* (1894)
(4) *Tom Sawyer Detective* (1896)
(5) *Huck Finn and Tom Sawyer Among the Indians and Other Unfinished Stories* (1989)
(6) *Adventures of Huckleberry Finn: The Only Comprehensive Edition* (1996) ed. Victor Doyno, restored passages
(7) *Adventures of Huckleberry Finn: Mark Twain Library* (2001) ed. Victor Fischer, Lin Salamo, Harriet E. Smith and Walter Blair, restored passages
(8) *The Annotated Huckleberry Finn* (2001) ed. Michael Patrick Hearn and E.W. Kemble, restored passages
(9) *Adventures of Tom Sawyer and Huckleberry Finn: The New South Edition* (2011) ed. Alan Gribben, expurgated

Huck Finn and Tom Sawyer Stories in Periodicals

"Adventures of Huckleberry Finn" (*Century Magazine*, December 1884) chapters 17 and 18, and portion of 19, edited (2)
"Adventures of Huckleberry Finn" (*Century Magazine*, January 1885) "Speculatin' in Stock" and "King Sollerman" dialogues, edited (2)
"Adventures of Huckleberry Finn" (*Century Magazine*, February 1885) King and Duke, from chapters 19 to 28, edited (2)
"Tom Sawyer Abroad" (*Saint Nicholas*, November 1893 to April 1894) edited (3)
"Tom Sawyer's Conspiracy" (unfinished) (4)
"Schoolhouse Hill" (unfinished) (4)
"Huck Finn" (fragment) (4)
"Tom Sawyer Detective" (*Harper's*, August and September 1896) (5) (*Ellery Queen's Mystery Magazine*, August to October 1952, excerpt)
"Jim and the Dead Man" (*New Yorker*, 26 June 1995) (6) (7) (8)

Sources

Condon, Garret. "Yet Another Adventure in the Tale of Huck and Jim," *Hartford Courant*, 20 June 1995.
Ellison, Ralph. "Change the Joke and Slip the Yoke," *The Collected Essays of Ralph Ellison*. New York: Modern Library, 1995.
Gates, David. "Same Twain, Different Time," *Newsweek*, 20 July 1992.
Hornblow, Deborah. "Injun Joe's Creator," *Hartford Courant*, 14 January 2002.
Kaplan, Justin. "Selling 'Huck Finn' Down the River," *New York Times Book Review*, 10 March 1996.
Kenney, Michael. "The Further Adventures of Huck and Jim," *Boston Globe*, 8 May 1996.
Kakutani, Michiko. "Light Out, Huck, They Still Want to Sivilize You," *New York Times*, 6 January 2011.
Menaker, Daniel. "The Phoenix-like Manuscript of *Adventures of Huckleberry Finn*," *At Random*, December 1995.
Powers, Ron. *Mark Twain: A Life*. New York: Free Press, 2005.
Reif, Rita. "First Half of 'Huck Finn,' in Twain's Hand, Is Found," *New York Times*, 14 February 1991.
_____. "How 'Huck Finn' Was Rescued," *New York Times*, 17 March 1991.
_____. "Twain Manuscript Resolves Huck Finn Mysteries," *New York Times*, 26 February 1991.
Smiley, Jane. "Say It Ain't So, Huck," *Harper's*, January 1996.
Sullivan, A.D. "No Easy Answers in Twain," *Scrap Paper Review* No. 21, August 1997. http://www.hourwolf.com/spr/spr0021.html (viewed 26 October 2012).
Ulin, David L. "The Expurgated 'Huckleberry Finn,'" *Los Angeles Times*, 5 January 2011.

Joel Chandler Harris
(1848–1908)
Uncle Remus (1879)

> It needs no scientific investigation to show why [the Negro] selects as his hero the weakest and most harmless of all animals, and brings him out victorious in contests with the bear, the wolf, and the fox.
> —*Joel Chandler Harris*[1]

Joel Chandler Harris shaped his literary fame with publication in July 1879 of "Story of Mr. Rabbit and Mr. Fox as Told by Uncle Remus" in the *Atlanta Constitution*. The call was immediate and strong for more of these folksy stories, and his first book, *Uncle Remus, His Songs and His Sayings: Folklore of the Old Plantation*, came out the next year. Harris said he simply wanted to document the old stories he heard from rural blacks. Over time, he used them to make observations about black culture in the postbellum years.

Uncle Remus has "A Case of Measles" in Joel Chandler Harris's *Uncle Remus: His Songs and His Sayings*, illustrated by A.B. Frost (Grosset & Dunlap, 1880/1895/1908/1921).

Born in Eatonton, Georgia, in 1848, Harris was the illegitimate son of an Irish laborer—hence his red hair. He grew up in poverty, but with the generous financial help of neighbors. Shy as a youth, he developed a sense of humor as a remedy. He developed a fondness for the old plantations, which to him represented coziness and security.

Harris's exposure to plantation life came when he took a job as a typesetter's apprentice in 1861 for the weekly *Countryman*, published by Joseph Addison Turner. Turner nurtured Harris's modest education, and gave him liberty to use the library at his Turnwold plantation. With Turner's encouragement, Harris began to write for the newspaper: at first, wordplay and puns to fill spaces. Then Union Gen. William Tecumseh Sherman's troops plundered Turnwold and Turner's fortunes declined. All was a shock to Harris, who had only the southern press to rely on for news of the Civil War.

Harris married Esther LaRose in 1873 and they eventually had nine children. He moved on to other newspapers, joining the *Constitution* in 1876. Editor Evan P. Howell, having shed Sam W. Small as a columnist, urged Harris to write sketches in Negro vernacular. Uncle Remus showed up as a recurring character in 1879. Harris was praised for the authenticity of voice in his stories.

As popular as his stories were, Harris also had his critics, among them William Malone Baskervill, who said the tales belonged "to the class of [literature] which has nothing but pleasant memories of slavery, and which has all the prejudice of caste and pride of family that were the natural results of the system."[2]

Baskervill's disgust for Georgia writers was plain: "They seized the warm and palpitating facts of everyday existence, and gave them to the world with all the accompaniments of quaint dialect, original humor, and Southern plantation life."[3]

Harris, indeed, once voiced his belief that "primitive" blacks benefited from the civilizing effects of slavery and plantation life.

Among his contemporaries, Harris was, according to other sources, considered something of a progressive for advocating for public education for African Americans.

"Probably Mr. Harris is the only man living who could have embodied and put in print the old time plantation stories," a writer said in the *Macon Telegraph* in 1880, "which so delighted the young of all preceding generations of Southern children. Dialect, especially negro dialect writing, has been attempted by hundreds but successfully by only a few, foremost among whom stands 'Uncle Remus.'"[4]

In another *Telegraph* article written in defense of Harris, the writer said: "Mr. Harris is the first and only person who has succeeded in putting in cold type the lingo, the patois, or if you please, the dialect of the Southern negro."[5]

Here's an example of Harris's prose, from "Why the Negro Is Black":

> One night, while the little boy was watching Uncle Remus twisting and waxing some shoe-thread, he made what appeared to him to be a very curious discovery. He discovered that the palms of the old man's hands were as white as his own, and the fact was such a source of wonder that he at last made it the subject of remark. The response of Uncle Remus led to the earnest recital of a piece of unwritten history that must prove interesting to ethnologists.
>
> "Tooby sho de pa'm er my han's w'ite, honey," he quietly remarked, "en, w'en it come ter dat, dey wuz a time w'en all de w'ite folks 'uz black—blacker dan me, kaze I done bin yer so long dat I bin sorter bleach out."
>
> The little boy laughed. He thought Uncle Remus was making him the victim of one of his jokes; but the youngster was never more mistaken. The old man was serious. Nevertheless, he failed to rebuke the ill-timed mirth of the child, appearing to be altogether engrossed in his work. After a while, he resumed:
>
> "Yasser. Fokes dunner w'at bin yit, let 'lone w'at gwinter be. Niggers is niggers now, but de time wuz w'en we 'uz all niggers tergedder."[6]

"Interpreting the story is incredibly problematic for the modern reader," observed Melissa Murray and Dominic Perella. "On one hand, it can be interpreted as being extremely critical of contemporary southern society with its racial divisions. By having an elderly Negro man explain that at one time there was racial equality to a young white boy, shows a potential influence over the next generation—an influence that, perhaps, could lead to a future where there would again be no racial division. This version of racial evolution also negates the idea of the biological inferiority of African Americans by linking the origin of racial differences to a pool of water rather than to an innate disparity in the intellectual and biological capacities of whites and blacks.

"The text could also be interpreted as being extremely critical of Uncle Remus' intellect. In some of the earlier Uncle Remus texts that appeared in the *Atlanta Constitution* as commentaries on contemporary Atlanta society, Harris portrays Uncle Remus as technologically backward and incompetent. 'Why the Negro Is Black' could be read as a perpetuation of the stereotype of the backwards plantation Negro—a happy darky without any conception of the realities of the world around him."[7]

Calling Harris "one of slavery's most effective and influential apologists," Robin Bernstein noted he "seems to have been engaging in wishful thinking when he called Harriet Beecher Stowe's *Uncle Tom's Cabin* a 'wonderful a defense of slavery.' Harris registered this judgment in his 1880 introduction to his first book, *Uncle Remus: His Songs and His Sayings...* Harris used Stowe to introduce, frame, and thus define his first book, which he described as a 'supplement' to *Uncle Tom's Cabin*. Harris understood that Stowe intended to 'attack' the system of slavery, but in his interpretation, 'her genius took possession of her and compelled her, in spite of her avowed purpose, to give a very fair picture of the institution she had intended to condemn.'

"Harris did not simplistically misunderstand Stowe, nor did he merely impose or project his own proslavery politics onto her abolitionist novel," Bernstein went on. "Rather, Harris read Stowe with a warped genius for selectivity, and he crystallized his selective reading in the fictional relationship between Uncle Remus and the Little Boy. Joel Chandler Harris told the story of what could have happened if Uncle Tom had never left Kentucky."[8]

Harris resigned as editorial writer from the *Atlanta Constitution* in 1900; his son Julian was by then its managing editor, his son Everett its city editor.[9] He wouldn't give readings from his works. He visited President Theodore Roosevelt at the White House. Mostly he remained in Atlanta, where he died in 1908.

His sense of humor never diminished. "One day when Mrs. Harris was enjoying a twenty-handerkerchief-power cold she said to her husband: 'Tell de girls I can't wride today; by doze is stobbed ub.' Replied Harris: 'I hobe you don't wride wid your doze. I don't write wid bine.'"[10]

Joel Chandler Harris Notes

1. From introduction to *Uncle Remus, His Songs and His Sayings*.
2. As quoted in Joel Chandler Harris entry, *Contemporary Authors Online*.
3. *Southern Writers*, 41.
4. "Old Folks' Lore," 12 July 1880, 4.
5. "Brer Rabbit and Mr. Farmer Man," 31 March 1882, 4.
6. "Why the Negro Is Black" in *Legends of the Old Plantation*.
7. Introduction to online edition of *Legends of the Old Plantation*.
8. "Joel Chandler Harris's reading of Uncle Tom's Cabin." *Racial Innocence: Performing American Childhood from Slavery to Civil Rights*. New York: New York University Press, 2011.
9. "'Uncle Remus' Makes a Change," Macon (Ga.) *Telegraph*, 7 September 1900, 5.
10. "Joel Chandler Harris," *Dallas Morning News*, 23 November 1919, 3.

Joel Chandler Harris Selected Bibliography and Sources

NEWSPAPERS
Uncle Remus stories appeared in the *Atlanta Constitution* and others.

UNCLE REMUS BOOKS
Uncle Remus, His Songs and His Sayings: Folklore of the Old Plantation (1880)
Nights with Uncle Remus: Myths and Legends of the Old Plantation (1883)
Daddy Jake the Runaway, and Short Stories Told After Dark by "Uncle Remus" (1889)
Uncle Remus and His Friends: Old Plantation Stories, Songs and Ballads with Sketches of Negro Character (1892)

The Tar-Baby and Other Rhymes of Uncle Remus (1904)
Told by Uncle Remus: New Stories of the Old Plantation (1905)
Uncle Remus and Brer Rabbit (1907)
Uncle Remus and the Little Boy (1910)
Uncle Remus Returns (1918)
The Witch Wolf: An Uncle Remus Story (1921)
Walt Disney's Uncle Remus Stories (1947)
Seven Tales of Uncle Remus (1948), Thomas H. English, ed.
The Favorite Uncle Remus (1948), George Van Santfoord and Archibald C. Coolidge, eds.
The Complete Tales of Uncle Remus (1955), Richard Chase, ed.
Uncle Remus Tales (1974), John Tumlin, ed.
Uncle Remus, or Mr. Fox, Mr. Rabbit and Mr. Terrapin (1985)
The Classic Tales of Brer Rabbit (2008), Don Daily, ed.

Sources

Baskervill, William Malone. *Southern Writers: Biographical and Critical Studies*. Barbee & Smith, 1896.
Bernstein, Robin. "Joel Chandler Harris's Reading of *Uncle Tom's Cabin*." *Racial Innocence: Performing American Childhood from Slavery to Civil Rights*. New York: New York University Press, 2011.
"Brer Rabbit and Mr. Farmer Man," *Macon Telegraph*, 31 March 1882.
"Joel Chandler Harris," *Dallas Morning News*, 23 November 1919.
"Joel Chandler Harris," Contemporary Authors Online. http://gdc.gale.com/gale-literature-collections/contemporary-authors/. Detroit: Gale, 2007. Gale Biography in Context, 26 July 2012.
Lohmann, Bill. "Uncle Remus and His Home Are Sharing a New Image," *Springfield Republican*, 22 December 1985.
Murray, Melissa, and Dominic Perella. Introduction to online edition of *Legends of the Old Plantation*. http://xroads.virginia.edu/~ug97/remus/anablack.html (viewed 26 October 2012).
"Old Folks' Lore," *Macon Telegraph*, 12 July 1880.
"'Uncle Remus' Makes a Change," Macon (Ga.) *Telegraph*, 7 September 1900.

George Washington Cable
(1844–1925)
Ole Creole Days (1879)

> When it comes down to moral honesty, limpid innocence, and utterly blemishless piety, the apostles were mere policemen to Cable.
>
> —*Mark Twain*[1]

Born in New Orleans in 1844, George Washington Cable wore the gray during the Civil War, after which he became a reporter for the New Orleans *Picayune*. His *Old Creole Days* (1879) was a popular local color book, and some see an influence by his writings on later novelist William Faulkner. Cable displayed a sympathy for blacks and a disgust for racism and discussed civil rights issues in *The Silent South* (1885) and *The Negro Question* (1890). But he also played off black stereotypes; his characters Uncle Jube and Aunt Peggy were conjurers and manipulators.

Cable was fascinated with his native state, and *The Creoles of Louisiana* (1884) and *Lovers of Louisiana* (1918) were among his later works. Cable moved to Northampton, Massachusetts, and sometimes toured with his friend Samuel L. Clemens.

"In his career after *The Grandissimes* [1880] Cable was unable to reconcile his love for the South with his abhorrence of slavery and racism. The result was a split in his career—the polemical essays embody the spirit of reform and the New South, while the romances, beginning with *The Cavalier* (1901), attempt to retrieve an idyllic past, devoid of the problems of racism," in the view of Thomas J. Richardson.[2]

Cable made considerable use of dialect. This is an exchange between the parson and a black man in *Ole Creole Days*:

> The negro begged; the master wrathily insisted.
> "Colossus, will you do ez I tell you, or shell I hev' to strike you, saw?"
> "O Mahs Jimy, I—I's gwine; but"—he ventured nearer—"don't on no account drink nothin', Mahs Jimmy."
> Such was the negro's earnestness that he put one foot in the gutter, and fell heavily against his master. The parson threw him off angrily.
> "Thar, now! Why, Colossus, you must have been dosted with sumthin'; yo' plum crazy...."[3]

Cable was concerned about the situation of blacks, but he was also concerned about an influx of overseas immigrants. With the support of steel industrialist Andrew Carnegie, Cable founded Home Culture Clubs to help new arrivals become accustomed to American ways.

Cable died in Florida in 1925.

George Washington Cable Notes

1. Letter to William Dean Howells, 4 November 1882.
2. George Washington Cable, *Encyclopedia of Southern Culture*, as reprinted on Documenting the American South. http://docsouth.unc.edu/southlit/cablecreole/bio.html (viewed 26 October 2012).
3. Page 156.

George Washington Cable Selected Bibliography and Sources

SELECTED BOOKS
Ole Creole Days: A Story of Creole Life (1879)
The Grandissimes (1880)

SOURCES
Richardson, Thomas J. "George Washington Cable," *Encyclopedia of Southern Culture*, Charles Reagan Wilson and William Ferris, eds. Chapel Hill: University of North Carolina Press, 1989.
Twain, Mark. Letter to William Dean Howells, 4 November 1882.

Thomas Nelson Page
(1853–1922)

In Ole Virginia (1887)

> Universally, they [white Southerners] will tell you that while the old-time Negroes were industrious, saving, and when not misled, well-behaved, kindly, respectful, and self-respecting, and while the remnant of them who remain still retain generally these characteristics, the "new issue," for the most part, are lazy, thriftless, intemperate, insolent, dishonest, and without the most rudimentary elements of morality.... Universally, they report a general depravity and retrogression of the Negroes at large in sections in which they are left to themselves, closely resembling a reversion to barbarism.
> —*Thomas Nelson Page*[1]

Local color writer Thomas Nelson Page adored the plantation era in the Reconstruction and early Jim Crow days. Born in 1853 at Oakland Plantation in Hanover County, he was descended from two prominent Virginia families: the planter Pages (John Page was a Revolutionary War leader) and the importer and shipper Nelsons (Thomas Nelson was a governor of Virginia).

Thomas's world disintegrated in the antebellum South, his father's law career and sixty-slave farm gone. Page entered Washington College, and later completed his studies at University of Virginia. Entering the bar, he established a law practice in Richmond. He dabbled in writing for his local newspaper. His first fiction effort was "Uncle Gabe's White Folks," a poem for *Scribner's Monthly*'s April 1877 issue in the vernacular style favored by Irwin Russell.

Page was taken with a letter, shown him by a friend, found in a dead Confederate's pocket. The woman writer confessed her love for the soldier but told him that if he came home without a furlough, she would not marry him. Intrigued, Page drafted a story, showed it to friends, read it at gatherings, added and dropped material depending on the reaction. "Marse Chan" appeared in *Century Magazine* in April 1884.

In the published story, a former slave named Sam tells the story of Master Channing, whose beloved Anne, at her father's bidding, spurns his attentions. Her father and Chan's disagree on national politics. Anne comes to realize she truly loves Chan, and decides to wed. Unfortunately, by this time he has died in battle. Sam brings his former master's body home. Anne is distraught, and dies of a broken heart. The two are buried side by side. Through Sam, Page voices his love of the prewar South—a persuasive literary device that drew thousands of readers to the author's beliefs.

The story was included in *In Ole Virginia; or, Marse Chan and Other Stories* (1887). "It remains a classic of plantation fiction, or the so-called Moonlight and Magnolia school of southern writing that would find ultimate incarnation in Margaret Mitchell's *Gone with the Wind*," according to Taylor Hagood.[2]

Uncle Billy, a slave, is the hero of another story, "Meh Lady," in which Miss Ann feels obliged to betroth a northerner in order to save her family's failing plantation.

"Uncl' Edinburg's Drowndin" is about a young Marse George and his faithful slave, Uncl' Edinburg. George is making no headway in his romance with Miss Charlotte.

This is how Uncl' Edinburg describes a Christmas gathering:

"Well, after supper de niggers had a dance. Hit wuz down in de washhouse, an' de table wuz set in de carpenter shop jes' by. Oh, hit sutney wuz beautiful! Miss Lucy an' Miss Ailsy dee had superintend ev'ything wid dee own hands. So dee wuz down dyah wid dee ap'ons up to dee chins, an' dee had de big silver strandeliers out de house, two on each table an' some o' ole mistis's best damas' tablecloths, an' ole marster's gret bowl full o' egg-nog; hit look big as a mill-ond settin' dyah in de cornder; an' dee had flowers out de greenhouse on de table, an' some o' de chany out de gret house, an' de dinin' room cheers set roun' de room. Oh! Oh! Nuttin warn too good for niggers dem time; an'; de little niggers wuz runnin' roun' right 'stracted, squalin' an' peepin' an' gittin in de way under you foots; an' de mens dee wuz totin' in de wood—gret hickory logs, look like stock whyar you gwine saw—an' de fire so big hit look like you gwine kill hawgs, 'cause hit sutney wuz cold dat night. Dis nigger ain' nuver gwine forgit it!"[3]

"He was a sympathetic interpreter of Southern life," said the *Philadelphia Inquirer*. "He dealt with it both in the days before the Civil War and in the days after. There is no other writer, perhaps, who can compare with him in tales in negro dialect, except Joel Chandler Harris. He was in many ways a typical native of Virginia; but, like most of his class, he accepted the results of the war without bitterness, and of the genuineness of his patriotism there was never any doubt."[4]

As this newspaper story noted, Page explored various aspects of the Civil War in his prose. *Red Rock* (1898) looked at Reconstruction. *John Marvel, Assistant* (1909) looked at the New South in the early 1900s.

"Page's South, of course, was finer than any real place could ever be, but he satisfied the nostalgia of his readers for what might have been—a place where heroic men and women adhered to a code of perfect honor," according to Anne E. Rowe.[5]

Page also wrote history (*The Old South*), biography (Robert E. Lee) and political and literary criticism ("The Lynching of Negroes: Its Causes and Prevention"[6]). The last mentioned essay brought a scathing reply from Mary Church Terrell, an African American woman who called Page's essay "one of the most scurrilous attacks on colored men of this country which has ever appeared in print."[7]

He wrote a children's book, *Two Little Confederates* (1888). Page at various times lived in Washington, D.C., and Maine. His first wife, Anne Seldon Bruce, died in 1888. He married Florence Lathrop Field in 1893. He served as ambassador to Italy from 1913 to 1919, during Woodrow Wilson's presidency.

Page died in 1922 at the restored Oakland Plantation in Hanover, Virginia. His brother, Roswell Page, finished his last book, a novel about the Ku Klux Klan called *The Red Riders*.

Thomas Nelson Page Notes

1. "Thomas Nelson Page on the Negro," *Southern Workman*, Vol. 33 No. 6, June 1904, 326.
2. Thomas Nelson Page entry, *Encyclopedia Virginia*.
3. *In Old Virginia*, 67–68.
4. "Thomas Nelson Page," 3 November 1922, 12.
5. Thomas Nelson Page entry, *Encyclopedia of Southern Culture*.
6. *North American Review*, January 1904.
7. *A Colored Woman in a White World* (1940), 264.

Thomas Nelson Page Selected Bibliography and Sources

SELECTED BOOK

In Ole Virginia, Or, Marse Chan and Other Stories (1887)

SOURCES

Hagood, Taylor. "Thomas Nelson Page," Encyclopedia Virginia. http://www.encyclopediavirginia.org/Page_Thomas_Nelson_1853–1922 (viewed 28 October 2012).
Rowe, Anne E. "Thomas Nelson Page," *Encyclopedia of Southern Culture*, Charles Reagan Wilson and William Ferris, eds. Chapel Hill: University of North Carolina Press, 1989.
Terrell, Mary Church. *A Colored Woman in a White World*. New York: G.K. Hall, 1940.
"Thomas Nelson Page," *Philadelphia Inquirer*, 3 November 1922.
"Thomas Nelson Page on the Negro," *Southern Workman*, Vol. 33, No. 6, June 1904.

Charles W. Chesnutt
(1858–1932)
Uncle Julius McAdoo (1898–1899)

The author's work is "notable for the passionless handling of a phase of our common life which is tense with potential tragedy; for the attitude almost ironical, in which the artist observes the play of contesting emotions in the drama under his eyes; and for his apparently reluctant, apparently helpless consent to let the spectator know his real feeling in the matter."

—*William Dean Howells*[1]

Ohio-born, North Carolina–reared Charles Wadell Chesnutt rose from the slush pile at the *Atlantic Monthly* when his story about plantation life, "The Goophered Grapevine," caught an editor's attention in 1887.

Chesnutt had attended the Howard School, founded for black students during the Reconstruction era by the Freedmen's Bureau. He became a teacher and assistant principal in Fayetteville, North Carolina. He married Susan Perry in 1878 and moved to New York City. Six months later, they moved to Cleveland, where he passed the bar in 1887. He began writing, his first sale, as described, to the *Atlantic Monthly*.

More stories about the antebellum South followed, and Chesnutt approached the publisher Houghton Mifflin with a proposal. Though light-skinned and easily passing as white—his parents were "free persons of color" but his paternal grandfather was a white slaveholder—Chesnutt suggested the book publisher promote a proposed collection as the first venture into imaginative literature by someone of African descent. An editor finally said a book was possible if Chesnutt could provide more conjure stories. Chesnutt did, and the ones that didn't make it into *The Conjure Woman* (1898) showed up in *The Wife of His Youth and Other Stories of the Color-Line* (1899).

This brief exchange from "The Goophered Grapevine" shows the differences in language between the narrator and a black man he meets in central North Carolina:

> "Do you live around here?" I asked, anxious to put him at his ease.
>
> "Yas, suh. I lives des ober yander, behine de nex' san'-hil, on de Lumberton plank-road."
>
> "Do you know anything about the time when this vineyard was cultivated?"
>
> "Lawd bless yer, suh, I knows all about it. dey ain' na'er a man in dis settlement w'at won' tell yer ole Julius McAdoo 'us bawn an' raise' on dis yer same plantation. Is you denorv'n gemman w'at's gwine ter buy de ole vimya'd?"
>
> "I am looking at it," I replied; "but I don't know that I shall care to buy unless I can be reasonably sure of making something out of it."
>
> "Well, suh, you is a stranger ter me, en I is a stranger ter you, en we is bofe strangers ter one anudder, but 'f I 'uz in yo' place, I woudn' buy dis vimya'd."
>
> "Why not?" I asked.
>
> "Well, I dunner wh'r yo b'lieves in cunj'in er not,—some er de w'ite folks don't, er says dey don't,—but de truf er de matter is dat dis yer ole vimya'd is goophered."

"These stories tell with unquestionable accuracy some of the race superstitions of the Negroes in the South before the war of the rebellion and especially in North Carolina," said reviewer Charles Alexander.[2] The narrator of "The Goophered Grapevine" purchased the property despite McAdoo's advice. The narrator later learned McAdoo had been harvesting grapes from the vineyard for a modest profit, so had considerable self-interest in his advice.

"Showing that the narration did not spring from a mere foundation of faith in its truth, but from a motive of questionable selfishness," Alexander continued, "the stories are tinged with oriental color, and while extravagant, they present a study of Negro folklore that will continue to interest students of ethnology for centuries to come, for they commemorate traditions and events which pass from one generation to another from the earliest history of the race."

Chesnutt used humor to draw whites into accepting blacks. As he wrote in his journal, "But the subtle almost indefinable feeling of repulsion toward the negro, which is common to most Americans—and easily enough accounted for—, cannot be stormed and taken by assault; the garrison will not capitulate: so their position must be mined, and we will find ourselves in their midst before they think it."[3]

Tracy Wuster finds Chesnutt's low-key satire a little elusive. "Critics—both black and white—have found fault in Chesnutt (and with Paul Laurence Dunbar) for their relationship to the plantation tradition. To some, Chesnutt's decision to not directly attack or subvert the tradition might reinforce its ideology. I would caution against a belief that humor must satirize, attack, or assault in order to be effective."[4]

"Chesnutt maintained his literary relationship with the *Atlantic Monthly* for almost 20 years," according to Lucy Moore. "Over that time, he not only made a name for himself as an early voice in African American literature but also contributed to the magazine's reputation as a cultural space in which unknown and sometimes marginalized authors could explore some of America's most challenging issues of the day."[5]

Book sales were sufficient that Chesnutt left his legal secretary business to devote all of his energies to writing. He wrote a biography of Frederick Douglass. His new stories did well. His novels didn't. He was invited to Mark Twain's 70th birthday party in 1905. His play, *Mrs. Darcy's Daughter,* was a flop. He wrote only occasional short stories and essays after 1906, returning to his stenography business. Some of his writing appeared in the NAACP's *Crisis* magazine. Along with W.E.B. Du Bois and Booker T. Washington, he advocated for black rights.

Chesnutt died in Cleveland in 1932.

Charles W. Chesnutt Notes

1. "Mr. Charles W. Chesnutt's Stories," *Atlantic Magazine*, May 1900.
2. Indianapolis *Freeman*, 22 April 1899.
3. As quoted in Tracy Wuster, "The Subtle (and a little-less-than subtle) Humor of Charles Chesnutt."
4. Ibid.
5. "Crossing the Color Line," *The Atlantic*, January 2008.

Charles W. Chesnutt Selected Bibliography and Sources

UNCLE JULIUS STORIES

"The Goophered Grapevine" (*Atlantic Monthly*, August 1887) (1 expanded)
"Po' Sandy" (*Atlantic Monthly*, May 1899) (1)
"The Conjurer's Revenge" (*Overland Monthly*, June 1890) (1 revised)
"Dave's Neckliss" (*Atlantic Monthly*, October 1889) (2)
"Lonesome Ben" (*Southern Workman*, March 1900) (2)
"The Dumb Witness" (1/1993) (2)

BOOKS

(1) *The Conjure Woman and Other Conjure Tales* (1898/1993), Werner Sollors ed.
(2) *Charles W. Chesnutt: Stories, Novels, and Essays* (2001)

SOURCES

Alexander, Charles. *The Conjure Woman* review, Indianapolis *Freeman*, 22 April 1899.
Andrews, William L. "Charles Waddell Chesnutt," *Encyclopedia of Southern Culture*, Charles Reagan Wilson and William Ferris, eds. Chapel Hill: University of North Carolina Press, 1989.
Howells, William Dean. "Mr. Charles W. Chesnutt's Stories," *Atlantic Monthly*, May 1900.
Moore, Lucy. "Crossing the Color Line," *The Atlantic*, January 2008.
Terrell, Mary Church. *A Colored Woman in a White World* (1940).
Wuster, Tracy. "The Subtle (and a little-less-than subtle) Humor of Charles Chesnutt," HA! A blog about American humor and Humor Studies, 12 June 2012. http://humorinamerica.wordpress.com/2012/06/20/charles-chesnutt-subtle-humor-and-the-plantation-tradition/ (viewed 25 October 2012).

Paul Laurence Dunbar
(1872–1906)
Folks from Dixie (1899)

Paul Laurence Dunbar's work "is worthy of applause."
—James Whitcomb Riley

Poet, playwright and novelist Paul Laurence Dunbar was the best known black writer of his generation. He was born in Ohio in 1872. His parents had escaped slavery in Kentucky. His father served in two Massachusetts regiments during the Civil War. Editor of his high school's literary society, Paul sold his first poems to the *Dayton Herald* in 1888. He worked as an elevator operator. His first book collection, *Oak and Ivy*, came out in 1893. While giving a recitation at the World's Fair that year, Dunbar met abolitionist Frederick Douglass. Dunbar wrote some verses in standard English, some in black dialect. Another poet fond of dialect, James Whitcomb Riley, "The Hoosier Poet," took an interest in Dunbar's career.

Dunbar often wrote about the African American experience. His second book, *Majors and Minors*, solidified his reputation and brought praise from *Harper's Weekly* critic William Dean Howells.

Dunbar toured England, and upon his return, married Alice Ruth Moore, a supporter of equal rights for blacks and for women. Dunbar took a job with the Library of Congress, though prolonged contact with bookshelf dust may have instigated tuberculosis.

He sold nine pieces to the *Saturday Evening Post*, three to *Collier's* and ten to *Lippincott's* from 1900 to 1905.

Dunbar introduced one of his characters in "The Ordeal at Mt. Hope" in *Folks from Dixie* (1998) this way: "the Rev. Howard Dokesbury, as many already have been inferred, was a Negro,—there could be no mistake about that. The deep dark brown of his skin, the rich over-fulness of his lips, and the close curl of his short black hair were evidence that admitted of no argument. He was a finely proportioned, stalwart-looking man, with a general air of self-possession and self-sufficiency in his manner."

Dokesbury has accepted a pulpit in the South. In a story from *Folks from Dixie*, he asks directions of a man he meets:

"I reckon you's de new Mefdis preachah, huh?"
"Yes," replied Howard, in the most conciliatory tone he could command, "and I hope I find in you one of my flock."

"No, suh, I's a Babtist myse'f. I wa'n't raised up no place erroun' Mt. Hope; I'm nachelly f'om way up in Adams county. Dey jes' sont me down hyeah to fin' you an' to tek you up to Steve's. Steve, he's workin' to-day an' cou n't come down."[1]

Dunbar's use of black Southern language foreshadows how the pastor's going to make out in his new community. On the other hand, Dunbar's use of vernacular invited criticism. As Elaine Hedges and Richard Yarborough pointed out, "He has been viewed by some commentators as an artist who used negative stereotypes of his own people to satisfy a white audience, and there are still those who suggest that his work lacks substance."[2]

Dunbar's writings were often compared, not with mainstream literature, but with black literature of the time. Nevertheless he sufficiently appealed to both black and white readers that he became one of the most successful writers of his day, of either race. He thus felt secure enough to tackle the most controversial of topics, as in the short story "The Lynching of Jube Benson" (from *The Heart of Happy Hollow*, 1904).

Reviewer George Preston wrote in *The Bookman*: "It has claims on purely literary grounds. It is well written, it is better than well thought, it is most profoundly felt. The stories are firm, clear-cut, and interesting enough in themselves to lift the volume above the level of the books of the month.

"In addition to this, and beyond it, the work is notable as the first expression in national prose fiction of the inner life of the American negro.... Surely no one standing without could see and feel 'The ordeal at Mt. Hope' as the author sees and feels it."[3]

Dunbar eventually divorced. He became an alcoholic, but he continued to write. He died in Ohio in 1906.

Paul Laurence Dunbar Notes

1. Page 32.
2. "Paul Laurence Dunbar."
3. Review of New Books, June 1898, 348.

Paul Laurence Dunbar Selected Bibliography and Sources

SELECTED BOOKS

Folks from Dixie (1898)
The Complete Stories of Paul Laurence Dunbar (2006)

SOURCES

Hedges, Elaine, and Richard Yarborough. "Paul Laurence Dunbar (1872–1906)," *Instructor's Guide for The Heath Anthology of American Literature*. Ed. Judith A. Stanford. Lexington, MA: D. C. Heath, 1990. http://college.cengage.com/english/heath/syllabuild/iguide/dunbarp.html. (viewed 26 October 2012)
Preston, George. *Folks from Dixie* review, *Bookman*, June 1898.

II

Writers of the Late Jim Crow Era (1900–1955)

These writers of local color literature represent most of the former slave-holding Southern states. Three wrote series based in Georgia, another three in Louisiana. Two series were set in Mississippi, two in Tennessee, and one each in Kentucky, South Carolina, North Carolina, Virginia and Alabama. A few series took place in New York City, one in Indiana.

This section presents biographical information about the writers, looks at their running fictional characters and gives brief excerpts from their writings. Writers' feelings about their craft are included as available. The biographies include critical comments from contemporary and modern-day sources. Typically the former are favorable, the latter skeptical.

Don't overlook the story and book listings in the bibliographies: The sheer volume of stories by Cohen, Smith, Hughes and the others is remarkable and proves the point about their influence on American readers.

Richard F. Outcault
(1863–1928)
Pore Lil Mose

Dear Mammy
We went into a soda water store de yuther day,
But over looked de fact dat dey expected us ter pay.
I clean fergot I hadn't any money in my close
So we lined up befo' de bar where soda water grows.
It tasted awful beautiful, had ice cream in it too
He didn't say a word about de pay till we got froo.
And den I found I did n hab a penny to my name
So I commenced ter hum dat song 'aint dat a messly shame.
De man was jes' a gwin ter send a call fer de police
When some kind lady paid de bill and settled it in peace.
                                  Your Loving son, Mose
P.S. Please send some money.[1]

Richard Felton Outcault, the pioneering newspaper cartoonist best remembered for his *Hogan's Alley* (about Mickey Dugan, alias the Yellow Kid) and *Buster Brown* strips, drew

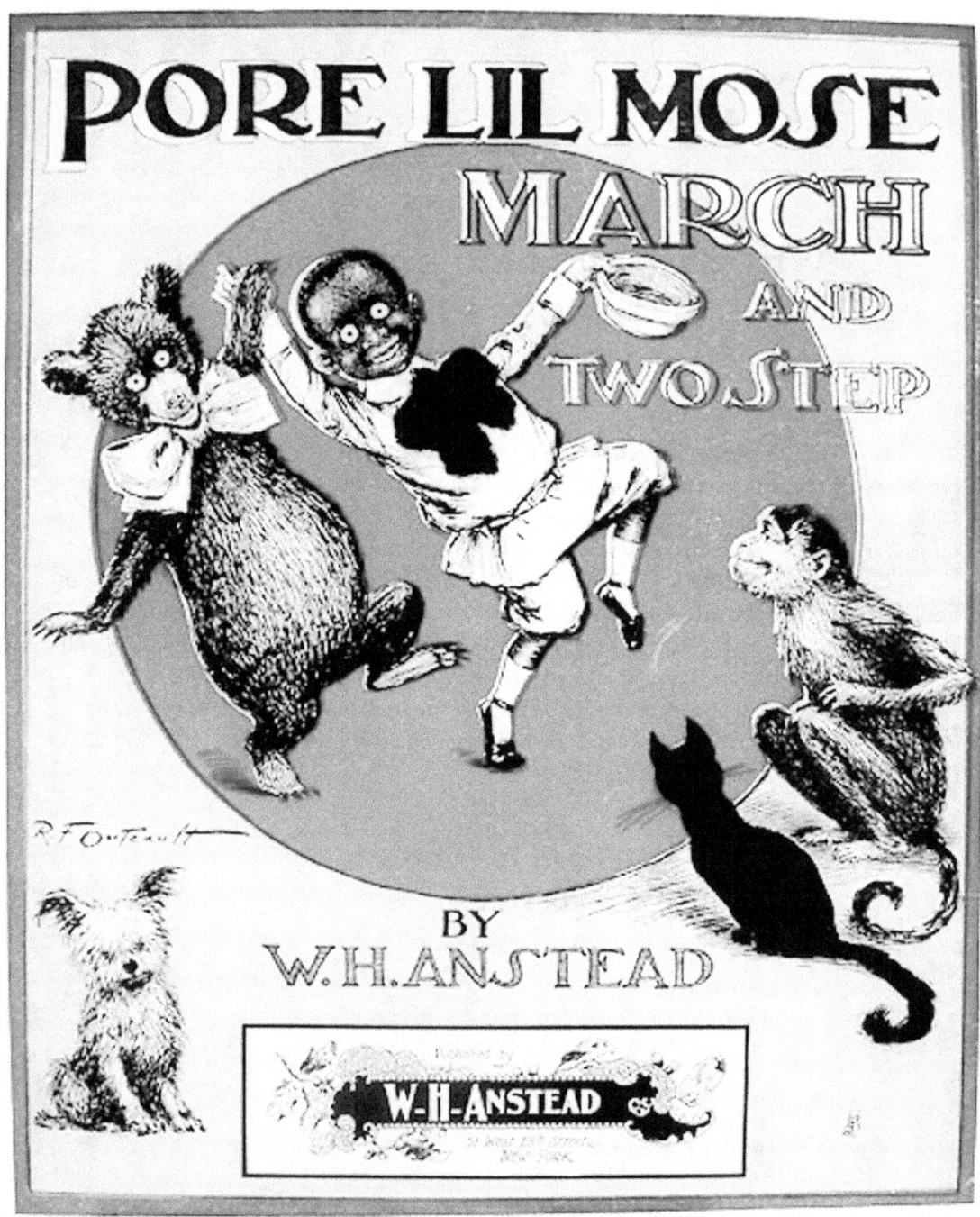

Pore Lil Mose inspired songwriter W.H. Anstead, whose march and two-step was issued as sheet music in 1902.

the first comic to feature a continuing black character. *Pore Lil Mose* ran for a year and a half in the *New York Herald*. Appearing in the period 1900–1902, it is the earliest work in the late Jim Crow era to fit this book's criteria for continuing, stereotyped, humorous series characters.

Outcault was born in Lancaster, Ohio, in 1863, the son of German cabinetmaker Jesse

P. Outcalt and his wife, Catherine Davis. Richard later added the second "u" to his last name. Richard had an early artistic outlet: He painted color landscape scenes on burglar-proof safes. He studied art at McMicken University in Cincinnati. Skilled at technical drawings, he went to Paris as official artist for Thomas A. Edison's traveling electric lighting exhibition.

When he settled in New York City in 1890, Outcault chummed with a reporter known for sensational stories, Nellie Bly[2]: "One of the stunts we pulled off together was begging on Fifth Avenue and making stories of the notables and millionaires when asked for help by two apparently starving people. Then we did slum stories, and it was then I stored the material which was to come to the front later with the Hogan's Alley series and the Yellow Kid," Outcault said.[3]

Outcault did technical drawings for *Electrical World* and humorous drawings for *Judge* and *Life*. By age twenty-two, he was delineating scenes of inner city slum life for the *New York World*, owned by Joseph Pulitzer. Pulitzer tested a four-color printing press using an Outcault drawing of a street urchin in a yellow nightshirt, yellow being a difficult color to manipulate.[4] The art was from an Outcault series originally printed in *Truth Magazine* in 1894 and 1895. Thus was born both the Yellow Kid, and the term "yellow journalism," descriptive of Pulitzer's feisty and often exaggerated news.

The hairless, toothy, slang-talking Yellow Kid became the star of the *Hogan's Alley* series of full four-color pages published in the newspaper beginning in 1895.[5] Pulitzer rival William Randolph Hearst lured Outcault and the Kid to his *New York Journal American* in October 1896.[6]

In 1902 Outcault began the adventures of Buster Brown and his sister Mary Jane and his bull terrier Tige.[7] In between, two black boys ran amok.

Outcault tried out an idea with *The Gallus Coon*, which had a very short run in the *New York World* from 10 June to 1 July 1900, less than a month.[8] "Gallus" is Scots slang for brash and self-confident. In one surviving example, "The Gallus Coon Shows Little Ah Dope How to Be a Flirt," the youthful main character, spiffily dressed, struts his moves before a Chinese boy, whose queue in the progressive sequence of panels spells out words: "What-a-great-masher-you-are [and as Gallus is slapped by a passing white girl] not." This could only have been printed in New York; in the South, the affront of the black lad trying to approach a white girl would have been a serious violation of Jim Crow etiquette.

Gallus Coon disappeared from the *World* and Moses Pryor appeared in the *Herald*. Pore Lil Mose, as he was called, was rustic and harmless. But his social messages were more informed than one might have expected.

"In his 'Mose' cartoons, Outcault presented a dual, somewhat contradictory, vision of blacks," Alan Havig said. "Some of the scenes which were set in rural Cottonville, or 'Coon town,' Georgia exploited the comic black image unmercifully: lazy, irresponsible, physically ugly 'niggers' ran from ghosts, stole watermelons, and botched plans to catch a hotel thief, among other schemes. But other rural, Southern-based vignettes contained no overt racism. In even greater contrast to the scenes which exploited race were the comic episodes which found Lil Mose and his animal cohorts visiting New York. Here the black child and friends were in an alien, though not hostile, environment. They explored and delighted in the wonders of a modern city—its streetcars, the amusement parks at Coney Island, and stores offering goods and services unknown to rural southern blacks."[9]

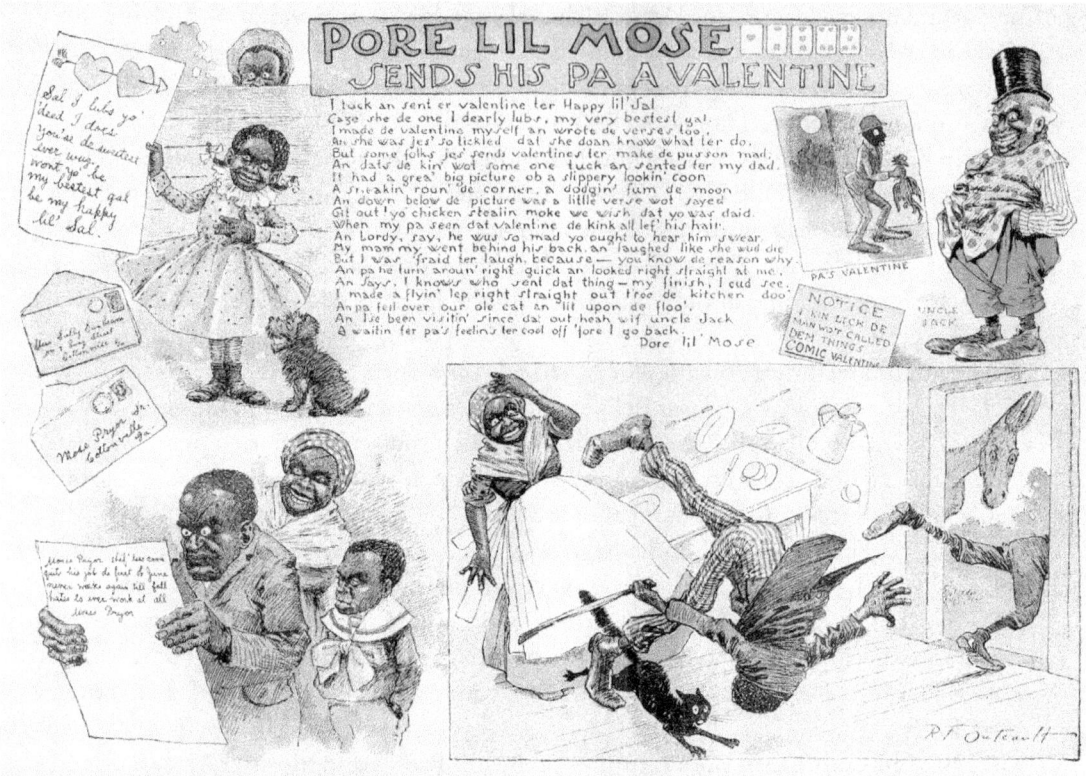

Pore Lil Mose was a traveling boy in Richard Outcault's comic strip for the *New York Herald*. His letters home were sometimes informative, sometimes insightful, always amusing. This sample is from February 10, 1901.

The seven-year-old pickaninny Mose and his companions Billy Bear, Mouse Houn', Pussy and Monkey visit the zoo or Baxter Street or Central Park. In one episode he calls on a painter, in another he sends his Pa a Valentine. The half-page strips—some appeared in color, some in black-and-white—typically had a narrative box surrounded by several vignettes. Some weeks were more visually daring than others. Some weeks the stories were set in sequential boxes. Some weeks' episodes were half-page, some weeks they were full-page.

With Mose, Outcault cast the hicks-in-the-big-town model for several writers to come: Irvin S. Cobb would send J. Poindexter to New York City; Octavus Roy Cohen would send Florian Slappey to New York City; Correll and Gosden would send Amos and Andy to New York City.

Outcault explained in the introduction to a book collection: "The author was standing at Broadway and 36th Street, one evening, when Pore Lil Mose presented himself. The first rhyme was composed and committed to memory then and there, because neither pencil nor paper were at hand. After the first appearance of Pore Lil Mose in the *Herald*, his kind disposition won for him many friends, among whom was the Managing Editor. Scores of children and many adults soon wrote letters addressed to him containing expressions of kind wishes. He soon gathered up his little group of friends and they started for New York where they have been ever since. Each week he has written to his Mummy and for all we know she has written to him. He doesn't seem to be afflicted with homesickness, though he left behind him a sweetheart."

This is the doggerel from "Pore Lil Mose Buys His Mammy a Hat," followed by "Pore Lil Mose Sends His Pa a Valentine":

> Dear Mammy,
> We took a walk de yuther day on de Fifth Avenue,
> An bought a lovely present mammy darling, just fer you.
> I knowed yo allus wears a plain bandana roun' yo' head,
> An dat yo nebber cares fo' style—yo bery often said.
> But when I saw doze lovely hats wif ribbons, flowers an lace
> I says to Billie Bear how nice dey'd look on mammy's face.
> I had a lot of money—an I'se got a bundle yet
> A horse had finished in a race de way dat I had bet.
> An so we went into de shop of Madame Caroline
> An looked at hats of every style—imported 'cross de brine.
> De one dat I picked out fer yo' I know yo'll think its sweet.
> It looks as though it might be almost good enuff to eat.
>
> Your Son, Mose
>
> P.S. Billie Bear sent one to his mother.[10]

> I tuck an sent er valentine ter Happy lil' sal
> Caze she de one I dearly lubs, my very bestest gal.
> I made de valentine myself an wrote de verses too,
> And she was jes' so tickled dat she doan know what ter do.
> But some folks jes' sends valentines ter make de pusson mad;
> An dats de kin' wot some one tuck an sented ter my dad.
> It had a grea' big picture ob a slipper lookin' coon
> A sneaking roun' de corner, a dodgin' fum de moon
> An down below de picture was a little verse wot sayed
> Git out! Yo chicken stealin moke we wish dat yo was daid.
> When my pa seen dat Valentine de kink all lef his hair.
> An Lordy, say, he was so mad you ought to hear him swear.
> My mammy went behind his back, an laughed like she wud die.
> But I was 'fraid ter laugh, because—you know de reason why.
> An pa he turn aroun' right quick an looked right strait at me,
> An says, I knows who sent dat thing—my finish, I cud see.
> I made a flyin' lep right straight out t'roo de kitchen doo'
> An pa fell over our old cat an lit upon de floo.'
> An I'se been visitin since dat out heah wif Uncle jack
> A waitin fer pa's feelin's ter cool off fore I go back.
>
> Pore Lil' Mose[11]

The strip appeared from 2 December 1900 to 24 August 1902, seventy episodes in all.[12] Thirty-six strips were collected and printed in four colors for the Grand Union Tea Co. edition of *Pore Li'l Mose: His Letters to His Mammy* (1902), a very rare book today.

Lil Mose had sufficient appeal in his short life that W.H. Anstead created and published the "Pore Lil Mose March and Two Step," cakewalk sheet music.

Mose was indicative of Outcault's evolution as an artist and writer. "Mose was an attractive pickaninny," said historian Coulton Waugh, "who did things like going out hunting with his animal friends and, in deference to their status, shooting at a target instead of living prey. It will be seen that a change had come over Outcault's ideas, a new motive of tenderness.

But this kind of thing was a bit of a strain on Outcault, who liked a good hot prank rather than a Sunday school lesson. Mose did not last long."[13]

Cultural historian Ian Gordon in *Comic Strips and Consumer Culture, 1890–1945* suggests Mose failed with a northern white audience because of the strongly depicted black characters. Later attempts to introduce minstrelsy to the comics worked only through the use of black animals, such as Felix and Krazy Kat, he suggested.

Outcault's mission was to entertain. Earlier cartoonists wanted to make political points. As an example, *Frank Leslie's Illustrated Newspaper* in March 1863 printed a full-page, six-panel cartoon, "Quashee's Dream of Emancipation," that portrayed blacks as lazy, rebellious and dumb. It was three months after the Emancipation Proclamation. One panel, as Cameron C. Nichels points out, suggests "the ultimate white (male) nightmare of free black men: not only do they want white women, but white women want them. The African American here is no laughable minstrel caricature, but a black man smoldering with unmistakable sexuality fueled by alcohol."[14]

Richard F. Outcault, a pioneering newspaper cartoonist, created two series with black characters but is best known for the Yellow Kid (author's collection).

It took decades for the country to get beyond that attitude.

"For over half a century *Pore Lil' Mose* was the only comic strip to have portrayed blacks as judges, teachers and other professionals," according to Donald W. Baker. "Outcault's characterizations of blacks were no more extreme than any of the other ethnic groups he drew and quite a bit less extreme than most other artists of the late 19th and early 20th centuries. When you look at the 70-plus *Pore Lil' Mose* strips, you see Outcault created a character in Mose who was polite, kind, generous, accepting, intelligent and at times a deeply profound thinker who loved his family and friends. A role model for every human being no matter what their color."[15]

Comics historian Don Markstein was also tolerant of Lil Mose. "Mose was depicted as pure stereotype, with big, white eyes and big, white teeth grinning out of his dark, fuzzy-topped face, from which a constant stream of grammatical solecisms flowed," he wrote in Toonopedia. "At least he wasn't colored solid black, like most of his brethren in the early decades of daily comics, but that's only because the Sunday pages he appeared in were printed in color, and thus offered greater scope for subtlety without the bother of stippling or cross-hatching. With black children in today's comics ranging from the completely ordinary Curtis Wilkins, who could just as easily be white, to the highly political Huey Freeman of *The Boondocks*, it's been a long time since a guy like Pore Lil Mose could be tolerated on the comics page.

"But that was only the first impression the reader got of Mose. Those who looked deeper saw a warm, loving, intelligent, morally upright little boy. He got into trouble from time to time, but then, so did Little Jimmy, Little Lulu and most of the other "littles" in comics. Outcault's portrayal of him may have conformed to the standards of the time, according to which that was simply how Negroes looked and sounded in the mainstream media, but there wasn't a drop of mean-spiritedness in it."[16]

Outcault abandoned Mose for Buster, poor black boy for upper-class white boy. Outcault "told one of his old friends that he lost most of the money he had made from 'The Yellow Kid' in Wall Street and that he created 'Buster Brown' to recoup his fortune," according to *Editor & Publisher*.[17]

Outcault liked drawing black characters. He provided four-color Koontown Kids images to the Ullman Manufacturing Co. postcard series in 1906. One, No. 76 in a series, shows three black girls tending two baby boys and a dog.

Outcault and his wife, Mary Jane Martin, had one son, Richard F. Outcault Jr., and one daughter, Mary Jane (Mrs. Frank E.) Pershing. Outcault retired in 1918, though he remained active with Outcault Advertising Co. of Chicago.

The artist died in Flushing, N.Y., in 1928, of cirrhosis of the liver.

Richard F. Outcault Notes

1. "He Treats His Friends to Soda Water," *New York Herald*, 6 April 1902.
2. Her real name was Elizabeth Jane Cochrane (1864–1922). She was known for exposing conditions in mental institutions and recreating Jules Verne's *Around the World in 80 Days*.
3. From an interview reproduced in Allan Holtz's Stripper's Guide, 3 October 2011.
4. In October 1894.
5. The first Yellow Kid appearance was 17 February 1895. The first *Down in Hogan's Alley* appeared 5 May 1895.
6. Pulitzer, meanwhile, owned the Hogan's Alley name, and hired another cartoonist, George Luks, to continue it. The Yellow Kid appearances overlapped in the two rival newspapers for about a year.
7. It began 4 May 1902.
8. Allan Holtz, *American Newspaper Comics*, 167.
9. "Richard F. Outcault's 'Poor Lil' Mose': Variations on the Black Stereotype in American Comic Art," 33.
10. *New York Herald*, 2 January 1902, 1.
11. *New York Herald*, 10 February 1901, 1.
12. Holtz, *American Newspaper Comics*, 318.
13. *The Comics*, 8.
14. *Civil War Humor*, 138.
15. Pore Lil Mose, Mastodon Studio website. Mastodon Studio has scanned and produced archival reprints of several of the comic strips.
16. "Pore Lil Mose," *Toonopedia*.
17. "R.F. Outcault, Father of Comic Strips, Dies," 29 September 1928. Newspaper rivalry reared again. Outcault created Brown for the *Herald Tribune* in 1902, but took it to Hearst's paper the *American and Journal* in 1906 for more money. Outcault called his strip "Buster and His Dog Tige" or "Buster and His Friends," and wrote and drew it until 1921, while William Lawler's version of "Buster Brown" continued in the *Herald* until 1911.

Richard F. Outcault Selected Bibliography and Sources

NEWSPAPER COMIC STRIP

Pore Lil' Mose (*New York Herald*, 2 December 1900 to 24 August 1902) Listed below are the episodes reprinted in the first book, with original newspaper dates.
"Ef I Wuz a Millionaire" (6 January 1901) (1)
"Why Pore Lil' Mose Left School" (13 January 1901) (1)
"Lil' Mose's Dog—Pore Lil' Dog" (20 January 1901) (1)
"De Burglar Brigade" (27 January 1901) (1)
"Poor Lil' Mose on the 7 Ages" (3 February 1901) (1)
"Pore Lil' Mose Sends His Pa a Valentine" (10 February 1901) (1)
"Pore Lil' Mose and His Hatchet" (17 February 1901) (1)
"Pore Lil' Mose Talks to the Animals" (24 February 1901) (1)
"Lil' Mose's Pet Chicken" (7 April 1901) (1)
"Happy Lil' Sal as Queen of the May" (21 April 1901) (1)
"A True Ghost Story by Pore Lil' Mose" (28 April 1901) (1)
"Pore Lil' Mose Entertains a Visitor" (12 May 1901) (1)
"Pore Lil' Mose, He Spends a Week on the Farm" (9 June 1901) (1)
"Pore Lil' Mose He Comes to New York" (16 June 1901) (1)
"Pore Lil' Mose at Coney Island" (23 June 1901) (1)
"Pore Lil' Mose at Central Park" (30 June 1901) (1)
"Pore Lil' Mose He Plays Golf" (7 July 1901) (1)
"Pore Lil' Mose He Takes a Ride on the Car" (21 July 1901) (1)
"His Pet Monkey Meets an Old Acquaintance" (28 July 1901) (1)
"He Takes a Sail" (4 August 1901) (1)
"Pore Lil' Mose, He Goes Bathing" (25 August 1901) (1)
"Pore Lil' Mose He Builds an Airship" (8 September 1901) (1)
"He Calls on Edison" (15 September 1901) (1)
"Pore Lil' Mose, He Has a Touch of Homesickness" (29 September 1901) (1)
"He Gets Mixed Up with a Painter" (6 October 1901) (1)
"On the Speedway" (13 October 1901) (1)
"He Tells His Mammy About a Football Game" (20 October 1901) (1)
"He Visits Baxter Street" (27 October 1901) (1)
"Pore Lil' Mose in Chinatown" (3 November 1901) (1)
"He Visits the Harlem Heights" (17 November 1901) (1)
"Too Busy to Write His Mammy" (24 November 1901) (1)
"Pore Lil' Mose He Buys His Mammy a Hat" (5 January 1902) (1)
"Pore Lil' Mose Still in New York, Writes His Weekly Letter" (12 January 1902) (1)
"He Visits the Wax Works" (26 January 1902) (1)
"Pore Lil' Mose Treats His Friends to Soda Water" (6 April 1902) (1)
"He Makes a Garden" (13 April 1902) (1)

BOOKS

(1) *Pore Li'l Mose: His Letters to His Mammy* (1902)
(2) *R.F. Outcault's Yellow Kid (with Pore Lil Mose)* (2009)

SHEET MUSIC

Pore Lil Mose March and Two Step (1902)

SOURCES

Baker, Donald W. "Pore Lil Mose," Mastodon Studio. http://mastodonstudio.com/index.html (viewed 15 November 2012).
"Footlight Flashes," *Philadelphia Inquirer*, 1 March 1908.
Gordon, Ian. *Comic Strips and Consumer Culture, 1890–1945*. Washington: Smithsonian Institution Press, 1998.
Grand Union Tea Co. advertisement. *Omaha World Herald*, 14 December 1902.

Havig, Alan. "Richard F. Outcault's 'Poor Lil' Mose': Variations on the Black Stereotype in American Comic Art," *Journal of American Culture*, Vol. 11 No. 1, spring 1988, 33–41.
Holtz, Allan. "News of Yore 1908: R.F. Outcoult in Los Angeles," Stripper's Guide. http://strippersguide.blogspot.com/2011/10/news-of-yore-1908-rf-outcault.html (viewed 14 November 2012).
Holtz, Allan. *American Newspaper Comics: An Encyclopedic Reference Guide.* Ann Arbor: University of Michigan Press, 2012.
Markstein, Don. "Pore Lil' Mose," Toonopedia. http://www.toonopedia.com/articles/p-l-mose.htm (viewed 21 November 2012).
Nichels, Cameron C. *Civil War Humor.* University of Mississippi Press, 2010.
Outcault, Richard F. *R.F. Outcault's The Yellow Kid: A Centennial Celebration of the Kid Who Started the Comics.* Northampton, MA: Kitchen Sink Press, 1995.
"Outcault Worsted," Fort Worth (Texas) *Star-Telegram*, 29 March 1906.
"R.F. Outcault, Father of Comic Strips, Dies," *Editor & Publisher*, 29 September 1928.
"Richard Outcault Dies," *Dallas Morning News*, 26 September 1928.
Waugh, Coulton. *The Comics.* New York: Macmillan, 1947.

Henry Edwards Cowen ("Red Buck") Bryant
(1873–1967)
Tar Heel Tales (1909)

> A prominent educator says of Mr. Bryant: "As a writer of negro dialect I do not place him next to Uncle Remus—Joel Chandler Harris—but absolutely his equal; his negroes do not use stage negro talk, but they talk, think and act like the niggers I knew as a boy on my father's farm."
> —Stone & Barringer advertisement for *Tar Heel Tales*

A newsman for seven decades, Henry Edward Cowen Bryant, "Red Buck" to readers of the *Charlotte Daily Observer*, was born in Mecklenburg's Providence Township, North Carolina, the son of Julia Parks and Henry Bryant. He wrote only a few books—including a biography of *Observer* editor J.P. Caldwell and a Presbyterian Church history—but his newspaper outpouring was enormous.

Bryant attended Agricultural and Mechanical College (now North Carolina State University) in Raleigh and earned a degree from the University of North Carolina at Chapel Hill. He taught in Alfordsville in 1894. But he yearned to become a reporter, and took his first news job at no pay.

Bryant was quickly assimilated into the *Observer* newsroom, and became popular with readers. "Mr. H.E.C. Bryant, our college friend, spent Thursday in Rockingham. Mr. Bryant is a clever gentleman, whose face, hair and talent shine on the *Charlotte Observer*. He is one of the State's brightest and most unique men and we shall not fool with the future by limiting the success which is certain to be his, nor the fame that is to crown his crimson head," the newspaper bragged.[1]

Bryant in 1896 briefly flirted with running his own newspaper when he acquired the *Charlotte Democrat*.[2] Within a dozen months, he was back as a correspondent with the *Observer*.[3] A year after that, he was again staff reporter.[4]

Caldwell in 1898 set Bryant to writing stories that promoted white supremacy. "Its [the newspaper's] actions helped lead to the overthrow of a duly elected and racially integrated government in the city of Wilmington and the disenfranchisement of the state's black voters," according to reporter Glenn Burkins.[5]

African Americans had been making considerable progress as property owners, business proprietors and public officials. They did particularly well in Wilmington. But a coalition of railroad executives, with state newspaper editors covering their eyes, campaigned vigorously to deprive blacks of the vote, so that only whites would again be in positions of authority. Bryant was assigned to write stories about black men as sexual predators. Bryant, called "Red Buck" because of his carroty hair and rosy complexion, handily turned in his racist assignments, written in his comfortable, folksy style. He traveled the state collecting information for "White Supremacy in Danger" and the ilk.

The upshot was that Jim Crow was vigorously asserted in Wilmington, and political power was restored to whites. Similar techniques were used by others elsewhere in North Carolina. (A state commission in 2006, according to Burkins, declared that the *Observer* and other newspapers "helped incite fear and damage democracy." *The Observer* published a special section in 2006 describing the entire affair, and apologizing.)

Years went by. Bryant wrote many more news stories, many of them portraying blacks in a positive light. He launched a column called "Tales of the Town and the Times" under his "Red Buck" nickname. Some columns contained stories (there's no clue as to whether they were presented as truthful or made up) with black characters. This is from 14 September 1908:

> "'Ef you ain't gwine to pray wid de sperit it ain't no use to pray,' declared Aunt Phoebe. 'De Lawd don't hear no half-way prayers. If you don't pray you can't look fur de Lawd to hep you when you git in a tight place.'
> "Aunt Phoebe is one of those rare creatures that Southern people like to call 'old-time darkies.' She's single, faithful and religious. I learned to like her on account of her clear-ringing, far-reaching, untamed voice, which can be heard throughout the house when she lets it out...."

Here's another example, from 17 October 1908:

> "Uncle Rastus," said the lawyer, cross-examining him, "how far is it from Washington to Alexandria?"
> "Yes, sir, boss, it's, it's—I don't know, sir, how fur it is, sir. I ain't never heered nobody say."
> "What would you say it was?"
> "I can't say, sir."
> "Forty miles?"
> "Yas sir, 'bout dat, sir."
> "Well, isn't it nearer twenty?"
> "Yas sir, I spec' it is, sir."
> "How about fifteen, ain't it more like that?"
> "Yas, sir, yas, sir, boss; I spec' dat's mo' lake it sir."
> "Well, Uncle Rastus, if it is fifteen miles from Washington to Alexandria, how far is it from Alexandria to Washington? Answer that."
> "Boss, dat's too much fur de ole man, he ain't much on figgers. No, sir, I ain't had no schoolin'."
> "Don't you know old man, if it's fifteen miles from Washington to Alexandria that it's fifteen from Alexandria to Washington?"
> "No, sir, I don't know as it's dat way. It 'mout be, sir, an' 'den agin it moutn't."
> "Don't you know that if it is a certain distance from one point to another, that it's the same distance back?"
> "Jedge, kin I axe him er question?" said Uncle Rastus.

"Yes, if you like," declared the court.

"Boss, how long is it frum Christmas to New Year's?"

"Seven days, of course."

"Cose it is, but it's er powerful long jump from New Year's back to Christmas ain't it? Dat argifyin' dat you's doin' won't wuk, sir."

"Tales of the Town and the Times" ran daily from mid–1908 to early 1909, after which the writer, given the Washington beat, produced instead "Tales of the Nation's Capitol" and "Gossip of the Capitol" (as Red Buck), "National Capital Gossip" and "Under the Capitol Dome" columns (as H.E.C. Bryant).

"Tales of the Town and the Times" columns plus some new material—eighteen chapters in all—comprised a book, *Tar Heel Tales,* published by Stone & Barringer of Charlotte in 1910. The book was illustrated with photographs of Uncle Ben, Aunt Matt and others.

Bryant dedicated the volume to Caldwell. Bryant's fellow journalist Harry Myrover is quoted in the preface: "I have been struck frequently at how the predominant mental characteristic sticks out in Mr. Bryant. His sense of humor is as keen as a razor. He sees a farce while other men are looking at a funeral, and this exquisite sense of humor is liable to break out at any time—even church.... I really think there is more individuality about his writings, than about those of any other writer in the state. Every page sparkles and bubbles with the humor of the man, and it is a clean, wholesome humor, there being nothing in it to wound, but everything to cheer and please."[6]

Caldwell chipped in: "His negro dialect stories are equal to those of Joel Chandler Harris—Uncle Remus."

Bryant's newspaper, announcing the book had gone on sale, said it was "indeed a work of art and forms a valuable acquisition to North Carolina literature. And it is strictly North Carolinian, for the author is a North Carolinian, the subject matter is North Carolinian and the publishing house is North Carolinian."[7]

Bryant once discussed black dialect:

> The old-time Negroes had a language all their own, founded on that of their owners. They took short cuts, snubbing the endings of words, or twisting them to suit their taste.
>
> I had often heard the same Negro use "goin'" for going, and in the next breath make it "gwine." I could see there was a distinction in the mind of the user, and I wanted to know what it was. At Reidsville one day, on the way from the old hotel to the station, I asked the porter, who carried my baggage to tell me why a few minutes before he had said "goin'" and then "gwine."
>
> "Well, boss, I ain't no scollard, but I kin splain it dis way," he responded. "You see Cap'n Albright on dat platform of de train? Now, sir, when it's time to go he'll retch up an' git dat bell cord, an' say: 'All erboard, de train's goin'. Now, dat's goin'. When de train gits down about Benaja, lickity-splittin', den she's 'gwine.'"
>
> To the Negro of the old school "goin'" was prosaic, and "gwine" indicated something finer with a swing to it.[8]

The *Observer* praised the dialect stories: "It is the colored brother that claims most of his attention, the Mecklenburg species being particularly prominent. Mr. Bryant, in common with most southerners, looks with a kindly eye upon the negro; in addition, however, to the kindliness there is in the brain behind the eye, a sense of humor which as has been said of it sees a farce where other men would behold only a funeral."[9]

The *Observer* of course reviewed the book, noting, "Far and wide has he journeyed in pursuit of 'news' that indefinite entity which is ever just ahead. In these various pilgrimages the auburn-topped youth has had many and varied opportunities for glimpses at odd sides of human nature, and these experiences are responsible for the volume of sketches just published."[10]

Bryant had a long career. He later wrote for the *New York Herald* and the *Boston Globe*. He was married to Eva Granbury Sumner of Austin, Texas. He enjoyed fox hunting.[11]

Bryant retired to Providence Township, where he died in 1967.

Henry Edwards Cowen ("Red Buck") Bryant Notes

1. "One of the Observer's Bright-Haired Young Men," *Charlotte Daily Observer*, 3 January 1896, 3.
2. "The Democrat Changes Hands," *Charlotte Daily Observer*, 6 March 1896, 4.
3. "Red Buck and His Travels," *Charlotte Daily Observer*, 28 February 1897, 4.
4. News item, *Charlotte Daily Observer*, 4 March 1898, 4.
5. "History Reflects Shame in Newspaper's Own Past," *Charlotte Observer*, 2 December 2012.
6. *Tar-Heel Tales*, unpaginated.
7. "Red Buck's Book on Sale," 19 January 1910, 11.
8. "Old-Time Negroes Knew Their Fine Points in Words," *Chapel Hill Weekly*, 27 January 1939.
9. "Red Buck's Book on Sale," op cit.
10. "Fine Record for New Book," 7 February 1910, 6.
11. He contributed to the book *The American Foxhound* (1905).

Henry Edwards Cowen ("Red Buck") Bryant Selected Bibliography and Sources

SELECTED TALES OF THE TOWN AND THE TIMES COLUMNS

"I Am Trying to Forget Denver" (*Charlotte Daily Observer*, 27 July 1908)
"Did You Have Any Rain?" (*Charlotte Daily Observer*, 28 July 1908)
"That's a Jolly Looking Girl Brown's With" (*Charlotte Daily Observer*, 3 August 1908)
"This Is a Great Country of Ours" (*Charlotte Daily Observer*, 5 August 1908)
"O. Henry!" (*Charlotte Daily Observer*, 9 August 1908)
"This Story Could…" (*Charlotte Daily Observer*, 16 August 1908)
"There Are Various Kinds of Humor" (*Charlotte Daily Observer*, 17 August 1908)
"Mrs. Humphrey Ward's New Novel" (*Charlotte Daily Observer*, 19 August 1908)
"Last Winter" (*Charlotte Daily Observer*, 20 August 1908)
"Bart Bledsoe" (*Charlotte Daily Observer*, 22 August 1908)
"You Are Always Talking About the Farm" (*Charlotte Daily Observer*, 24 August 1908)
"Fayetteville!" (*Charlotte Daily Observer*, 25 August 1908)
"The Season of Yarns Is at Hand" (*Charlotte Daily Observer*, 26 August 1908)
"Among the Most Interesting Characters" (*Charlotte Daily Observer*, 27 August 1908)
"Everyone Is Reading 'The Firing Line'" (*Charlotte Daily Observer*, 31 August 1908)
"The Old Man" (*Charlotte Daily Observer*, 1 September 1908)
"That Charming Story-Teller" (*Charlotte Daily Observer*, 2 September 1908)
"The Haunted House!" (*Charlotte Daily Observer*, 4 September 1908)
"I Spent Sunday Last…." (*Charlotte Daily Observer*, 11 September 1908)
"Billy Brown…" (*Charlotte Daily Observer*, 12 September 1908)
"I Spent Several Days of Last Week…." (*Charlotte Daily Observer*, 13 September 1908)
"Izzie's Lookin' for Me Now" (*Charlotte Daily Observer*, 14 September 1908)
"I Had an Odd Experience" (*Charlotte Daily Observer*, 16 September 1908)
"I Am in Salisbury" (*Charlotte Daily Observer* 17, September 1908)
"Lonesome Kate" (*Charlotte Daily Observer*, 18 September 1908)
"Ten Years Ago" (*Charlotte Daily Observer*, 19 September 1908)
"There Are More Cripples" (*Charlotte Daily Observer*, 20 September 1908)

"The Average North Carolina" (*Charlotte Daily Observer*, 22 September 1908)
"We Had Seen the Trail" (*Charlotte Daily Observer*, 23 September 1908)
"Night Riders" (*Charlotte Daily Observer*, 28 September 1908)
"The Man from Broadway" (*Charlotte Daily Observer*, 7 October 1908)
"Going to the Mountains" (*Charlotte Daily Observer*, 8 October 1908)
"The Boys and Girls" (*Charlotte Daily Observer*, 13 October 1908)
"The Hon. James Hamilton Lewis" (*Charlotte Daily Observer*, 17 October 1908)
"Those Two Grand Hydrographic Experts" (*Charlotte Daily Observer*, 28 December 1908)
"The Subject of This Yarn..." (*Charlotte Daily Observer*, 17 January 1909)
"The Most Versatile Man..." (*Charlotte Daily Observer*, 24 January 1909)

BOOKS

Tar Heel Tales (1910)

SOURCES

Burkins, Glen. "History Reflects Shame in Newspaper's Own Past," *Charlotte Observer*, 2 December 2012.
Bryant, H.E.C. "Old-Time Negroes Knew Their Fine Points in Words," *Chapel Hill Weekly*, 27 January 1939.
"Democrat Changes Hands," *Charlotte Daily Observer*, 6 March 1896.
"Fine Record for New Book," *Charlotte Daily Observer*, 7 February 1910.
H.E.C. Bryant Papers, 1737–1945. Southern Historical Collection, Louis Round Wilson Special Collections Library, University of North Carolina. http://www.lib.unc.edu/mss/inv/b/Bryant,H.E.C.html (viewed 2 December 2012).
News item. *Charlotte Daily Observer*, 4 March 1898.
"One of the Observer's Bright-Haired Young Men," *Charlotte Daily Observer*, 3 January 1896.
"Red Buck and His Travels," *Charlotte Daily Observer*, 28 February 1897.
"Red Buck's Book on Sale," *Charlotte Daily Observer*, 19 January 1910.
Tar Heel Tales advertisement. *Gates of Twilight* by Henry Elliott Harman (Charlotte: Stone & Barringer, 1910.

Bridges Smith
(1848–1930)
Yamacraw Stories

Bridges Smith was a "philosopher and a genial, kindly spirit that brightened the lives of countless thousands."—*Augusta Chronicle*[1]

Widely known throughout Georgia, Bridges Smith was stricken "while seated in the same big armchair that was used by Sarah Bernhardt and other notables of the stage when they appeared in Macon," according to the Augusta (Georgia) *Chronicle*.[2] "He had dropped into the historic chair, which had been salvaged from the old Academy of Music here years ago, and which occupied a prominent place in his bedroom 'den,' to listen to a radio program, his custom every night for years. He never regained consciousness after the attack."

That was in 1930. Smith had been born in 1848 in North Carolina, the son of James H. and Mary L. Smith. The father, a painter by trade, moved his family to Macon in 1858. Bridges Smith was three times married. The name of his first wife is elusive, but the second in 1886 was Katrina Goelz (they had three sons) and, after her death, the third in 1919 was her sister, Margaret Goelz.[3]

Smith in 1898 was elected to the first of four two-year terms as mayor of Macon, and at the same time continued as city clerk. After he retired in 1907, he returned to his first love, newspapering, and became city editor of the Macon *Telegraph*. He was mayor again for two terms, from 1914 to 1917.[4] Though he never studied law, he was judge of the Bibb County Juvenile Court from 1917, when it opened, and served until his death. Among other duties as judge, he performed some 100 marriages in the first two years, and refused to charge a fee to any soldiers tying the knot. In 1922, he agreed to be editor-in-chief of a centennial history of Macon.

"He was a counselor and friend of thousands and tens of thousands in his daily life and through a long career of activity he kept aloft high principles and majestic ideals that he tried to inculcate in the minds of the young, so that they might continue the chivalric record established by the old South," the *Chronicle* said at his death. "His knowledge and understanding of human nature was such as to give him that sympathetic touch which denominates the truly great. In sorrow and in suffering he was equally effective as in joy and gladness. He could enter into the spirit of the occasion with a versatility that was remarkable and everywhere he had friends."[5]

The newspaper called him "a soldier of the Confederacy." Actually, he had worked at the Confederate States Arsenal in Macon during the conflict.

Smith wrote newspaper columns under the headings "Lights and Shades," "Old Time Customs Are Vanishing," "Intimate Glimpses of Men and Things" and "Telegraphics." He concentrated on the doings of the black inhabitants of Yamacraw in Georgia in "Stories in Black" columns beginning in 1909.

Smith's first venture with the media had been in 1859, when he peddled copies of the *Telegraph*. The newspaper had begun publication in 1826, and purchased its competitors the *Journal* and *Messenger* in 1869.

Smith joined the *Telegraph*'s staff in the 1870s and soon made a name for himself. Newspapers in those days had a tradition of exchanging subscriptions, and freely using material from each others' columns. Thus the *Hawaiian Gazette* in Oahu ran this story with the credit line: "Bridges Smith's paper":

Struck a Bonanza

A Decatur street grocer took a sugar-cured ham from its yellow overcoat the other day, stuffed the canvas with saw-dust, and hung it temptingly before his door as a sign.

Yesterday short-legged Jim came along and seeing the decoy remembered that the old woman was out of meat, and concluded he'd appropriate what he termed the "big bonanza." Watching his chances he soon had the yellow fraud under his arm making for home.

Bridges Smith wrote Yamacraw stories from 1909 to 1918.

"Old woman hyar's a ham o' meat I fotched yer," he said, as he deposited his prize.

"Look hyar, niggar, whar in the name ob de Lam' did you fotch up wid all dat ham?"

"Ask me no queschuns an' I'll tell ye no lies," said Jim, evasively.

"Well, 't wud look sorter like old time ter see so much meat as did in de house. Clar to grashus dat man Haes ain't no slouch ob a presumdent—am he, Jim?"

"Shet yer fly trap, old woman, wot de dibbil you know 'bout Hayes? Fotch me dem scissors an le's sample dis ham."

"The scissors cut two or three stitches, and the sawdust began to pour out. There were two dark faces made darker by the revelation, and it flushed through Jim's mind that he hadn't struck a big bonanza after all.

"See hyar, Jim, 'pears to me dat 'f I couldn't steal a short nuff ham I wouldn't steal a bag ob sawdust!"

Then Jim wend down town fully satisfied that "all's not gold that glitters."[6]

This anecdote, maybe made up, maybe true, foreshadows Smith's later columns.

"Sitting in his office crowded with books, the majority of them enormous scrap books bulging with newspaper clippings on every subject from Fort Hawkins to the Georgia State Fair, he [Smith] received the question, 'Who are some of the great men you have interviewed?' with a wrinkling of the brow and a thoughtful expression. He leaned forward in his swivel chair and tapped with his fingers on the desk for several minutes...," wrote a reporter for the *Daily Telegraph*.[7]

"'Why, yes, I interviewed up to twenty years ago every man of note who visited Macon since '78, but I can't remember all of them just off-hand like this.'"

He was flustered at being interviewed at all, much less by a young woman named Willie A. Snow.

"I interviewed President Wilson when he came to Macon," Smith said. "Also Jefferson Davis on one of his visits here. Mr. Davis made several trips to Macon, but when I talked to him it was in '85, when he came here to attend the reunion. It was, I remember, on the balcony of the old union station just before he made a speech. I don't know what I asked him, but I suppose I inquired about his health...

"When William McKinley came here, I interviewed him on some current topic of the day. In honor of his visit, an arch made of cotton bales was built over Poplar street. While here, he also made a speech which I covered.'"

The interviewer provided some background. "It was during the civil war that Bridges Smith first broke into print. He was not a regular reporter in those days, but a contributing reporter, being engaged during the war in making ammunition for the Confederate army. His contributes were printed in the *Daily Citizen*, a little pioneer newspaper published in the exact place where the *Telegraph* is today.... In 1778 [*sic*] he came to the *Telegraph* as a local reporter and for ten years he filled that position of writing all the news that 'broke' in and around Macon. It was the business of one reporter to attend all the weddings in town, funerals, shows, entertainments, and everything else that 'turned up.'

"'In those days there was no such thing as a city editor,' he declared with a reminiscent look on his face. 'The one reporter was known as the local editor. I was that lone reporter and local editor for ten years. During those years I ran my life on a set schedule, leaving my home at 9 o'clock in the morning and working until after midnight every night.'"

In that decade, he was on duty all holidays. He only missed twenty-six days of work, sixteen due to illnesses, ten for a honeymoon.

Over the years he found time to manage a theatrical company, the Macon Minstrels; serve as secretary of a baseball club; promote a velocipede tournament; compose songs (including "Sweet Face in the Wind" and "Greeny Brown Eyes") and pen the libretto for an opera ("Dollie," with music by Arthur Wood[8]); and act and sing in various stage productions.

He completed his mayoral tenure in 1907, and after witnessing the new mayor being sworn in, he walked down the street from City Hall and "took the same seat I had left nineteen years before when I went into politics....

"'When I left the paper I was the only reporter and there was no city editor. When I returned that night there were five young fellows acting as reporters and a city editor. Nineteen years before the type had been set up by hand and when I returned it was set up by machinery.

"'Instead of the reporters handing in the copy in long hand they were writing it on typewriters. I realized at once that if I was going to keep up with those young fellows I must learn to write on the typewriter. Mr. [Charles R.] Pendleton, who was then at the head of the paper, bought me a machine and soon I was grinding out copy with the best of them. Ever since I have done practically all of my writing on the typewriter....'"

Smith met a young compositor at the newspaper, Joel Chandler Harris, who "talked but little, and at odd times when he was not busy with his work of taking proofs and aiding the foreman in his duties, he was either reading or writing."[9]

Smith recalled a horrendous train accident in Macon that severely injured two boys. He went to the depot. "'The little darkies had been wrapped up in blankets and brought to Macon for medical attention. When they were first taken off the train they were laid on the platform of the station until they could be taken to the hospital. Unconscious of their casualty, neither knowing that their legs had been cut off, the two laying out there under the stars began to sing, "In the Sweet Bye and Bye," and other melodies loved by the negro race. When they finished singing they talked, one saying that his toe itched and the other declaring that his leg hurt.

"'I stood there listening to them talking and singing realizing that I had a great human interest story,' the Judge said. 'I have always seized every opportunity to write the human things of life, and that is why I believe I have succeeded in my writings as well as I have. I write in my column the little human things that most people overlook.'"

Those overlooked people, mostly blacks, included Minerva Jackson, Slowfoot Sal, Harelip Pete, Banjo Bill, Dan the Dandy, Mittie Mills, Fatty Fan, Whispering Annie, Delia the Doper, Hog-Eye Jake, Precious Jackson, Henrietta and Dick Jackson, Foday and L'il Bit, all denizens of Yamacraw. All were made up from Smith's imagination.

The first "Stories in Black" column from the *Telegraph* for 27 January 1909 is "The Shine." It begins this way:

> It was evident to the bottblack [sic] when the stranger sat down in his chair to have his boots shined up, that the man was from away up north somewhere. The fact of his wearing boots was indisputable evidence, to say nothing of his inquisitiveness, and asking the price of the shine before he mounted the platform to get into the chair.
>
> "Any hard times around here, boy?"
>
> "Dat wot some uvvum say, but times is wot yer makkum, boss."
>
> "How are you colored people getting along in this country?"

"Dooz yer mean niggers boss?"

"I mean colored people like you. You don't like to be called niggers, do you?"

"Whar yer live, Mister, Noo Yawk?"

"I live up in Massachusetts, and I am on my way to Florida. Tell me something about you colored people."

"Dey is Yankees an norv'n peoples, aint dey?"

"I believe so. Why do you ask that?"

"Kase dey is cullud peoples an' niggers down hyere. Dem's cullud peoples, dat drive' de orterbeels an' wait on de table at da hotel an' de preachers an' dem wot bresh clo'es an; lay out de shuts for de w'ite men, but we al wot wuks furrer livin, some uvvum wuk in de brickyaad, some et de gwainner fac'ry, an' et de cotton compress, an' wuk on de railroad, wese niggers."

"How are you treated by the white people down here?"

"Ef twarnt fur de w'ite peoples de nigger pa'rsh ter deff. 'Spose datter 'pen on niggers shoo ter shine? Er sho would pairsh ter deff...."

Smith used the columns to work out social, religious, fashion and political ideas, filtered through the less-lettered, dialect-heavy language of Georgia blacks. He manipulated his characters to his purposes.

Smith landed a book contract in August 1909. A notice in the *Telegraph* said, "It is probable that there will be two books, one 'Stories in Black,' and the other 'Sermons in Black.' These dialect sketches are written hurriedly in the odd hours of daily work, and necessarily are imperfect. In book form they will probably be given a little more care and attention."[10]

Smith often titled his Sunday columns "Preaching in Yamacraw," thus the idea for the second book to focus on church matters. The second book never materialized, suggesting there were only modest sales of the first. The newspaper column itself, however, lasted nearly a decade. When Smith took a rare break, it invariably invited inquiries as to what was going on. "Only Taking a Needed Rest," an editor titled one such letter.[11]

Ogilvie Publishing Co. of New York collected 100 of the columns between book covers in July 1910.[12] The publisher wrote: "Not in years, if ever, have we seen or read anything which approaches the stories in this book for real, true depiction of character of the southern darkey of the present day. They are full of humor and entertainment, and absolutely true to the life both as to the incidents related, and the language used. The latter is so true, in fact, that our compositor who set the type for the book, said that he had never before seen anything like the diction and spelling."[13]

The *Augusta Chronicle* ventured that the stories were told "in a manner probably never before attempted by writers of negro dialect. There is an absence of the apostrophe which usually peppers this class of writing. Mr. Smith employing a peculiar method of spelling to produce the sounds that brings to the mind of the reader the exact words of the negro [*sic*]. To the Northern reader, perhaps, much of this would be Greek, but to the Southern reader, who has listened to the negro and who knows him, the dialogues are true to nature, as it were.

"The *100 Stories* are not exaggerations, but are like stenographic reports of conversations held by negroes, and of their sayings. A negro editor, who reads every story as it appears, paid the author a doubtful compliment when he said: 'You not only give the nigger talk, but you actually think like a nigger.' He meant by this that Mr. Smith had caught the negro's manner of expression of ideas."[14]

The reviewer was relentlessly upbeat. "The *100 Stories* are thoroughly enjoyable. Their reading carries the older citizen back to slavery days, when the reactions between master and slave were entirely different from those between the employer and the negro of these times. They give the younger readers the exact reproduction of street and police court scenes now enacted."

A reviewer in the *Racine Daily Journal* in Wisconsin opined of the book, "The color question has been before the people of the United States for the last 40 years. Some people think one way about it, others the opposite way, but there is one point upon which both sides unanimously agree, and that is the humor with which the colored race seems so naturally imbued, or else the particular way in which such humor as they may have, crops out."[15]

"Through some of the *100 Stories* there runs a tenderness, appreciated more, perhaps, by the older than the younger reader, and yet in each there is always the humor for the negro. The story of a little negro girl named 'Littlebit' brought tears to the eye of a Northern gentleman who read it, so he confessed in a letter to the author.

"Those who can appreciate the quaint and extravagant sayings and doings of the negro, well handled by one who has had abundant opportunities for knowing them, should by all means read the book. It cannot fail to bring many smiles, if not laughs."

Newspapers from Salt Lake City, Utah, to Springfield, Massachusetts, to, of course, Macon, praised the collection of stories.[16]

There was modest humor in the columns. The dialect was strong. But the characters weren't as exaggerated as some we will meet in this survey. In fact, they weren't particularly strong characters at all.

Smith was sympathetic in his vignettes. The pieces are short and don't always have a plot or resolution.

Not all views of Smith are positive. Andrew Michael Manis said he "regularly wrote derisive columns about blacks."[17]

News accounts suggest Smith as mayor, and later as judge, was appreciative of and sympathetic to blacks. In 1907, the Good Citizenship Club of Macon, "composed of the best element of the negro people of the city," according to the *Macon Telegraph*,[18] voted a resolution commending Smith for "having issued an order prohibiting the working of female prisoners upon the public highways"; and noted that "during his whole administration [he] sought to do justice to all classes of citizens in the conduct of his public office."

Smith addressed an African American conference at the Cotton Avenue A.M.E. Church in 1900[19] and he spoke to the 300 delegates at a statewide patriotic meeting of blacks in 1917.[20]

In between, in 1906, he and Macon had to grapple with a number of racial issues. Five hundred black delegates attended a conference, the Georgia Equal Rights Convention, that year to discuss school funding, prison conditions, Jim Crow travel rules, whites-only juries and the "white primary."[21]

He closed down a live dramatization of the racially controversial *The Clansman* in 1906, after it provoked outrage from blacks in other communities.

He often wrote regular news stories about blacks, albeit with a Lost Cause twinge, such as "Old-time Negro Sticks to Master of Secession Days,"[22] about a former plantation laborer named Bill, and "Capt. Simpson Tells About Negroes Who Went to War."[23]

Smith's columns were often dialogue driven. "A Chewing Gum Episode," as an example,[24] is about a "certain charming lady," white, who had the habit of leaving a wad of chewing gum in different places in the apartment, later picking it up to chew further. One day, Mandy, the maid, kept visiting the mantel and the woman asked why.

"'Er wuz lookin fur er piece er gum datter tol' dat nigger Jim ter lay up hyere on de mantelpiece, but dat nigger nevvy dun hit.'

"The lady felt the crimson glow in her face. Right then she was chewing Mandy's gum, but it would never do to let Mandy know it and she watched her chance to slip it out of her mouth. In the meantime Mandy was getting madder and madder with Jim. You could tell that by the vigorous manner in which she was striking the furniture with the duster.

"'Er ack de fool w'enner let dat nigger Jim chaw dat gum, but he jiss vowed he gwineter put hit right dar on dis mantel w'en he git thoo wid hit. Hit wuz gittin sorter crumly w'enner lowed him ter chaw it, anner speck he dun chawed hit ter pieces. Er nachly spice er low down nigger no how.'"

The woman of the house is distressed. She's chewing a piece of gum that has already been double-chewed!

The Jim in the story is Jim the drayman, who shows up in other stories including "Educated Fleas,"[25] in which he has a lunchtime chat with his friend Bill.

"Mer lil' gal reed in do paper lass night dat de whole town fuller fleas, evvy dog full and evvy house full, and deys keep en er comin'.

"'Ain dat de trufe,' said Jim, the cutrate drayman; 'er nevvy seed de lakker fleas sence er been bawnded. Dey sho lazer manyer flea in dis town, anner dunno whaar deys com fum.'

"'Dat wot deys the mer ol' comans,' said Pete, 'but fleas don bovver me. Er seed de ol' comans grub her frock and squat down an hunt fleas, but deys sho lemme lone.'"

The conversation turns to wise and smart fleas, and wise Simon finally expands the conversation to compare common and affluent blacks:

"'Hit de same wey wid dese eddicated niggers. Dey is de meanest niggers wot we got. Dese eddicated fleas we wusstist kiner fleas. Deys doan kyeer much fur de dog, lakker common flea wot jiss soon make he livin on de dog; but deys stay right dar in de house whar deys kin git all de good meat deys wants dout trav'llin round on er dog's back, and wukkin for deys livin. Dat de way dese eddicated niggers dooz. Deys donn wants ter be wukkin fur er livin. Deys wants ter stay round in de shade an look at de common niggers wuk....'"

In "The Yamacraw Cooking School,"[26] Evangeline Harris comes home from college fresh with ideas about education and broadening prospects. Her mother takes in laundry, her father works in the brickyard. She wants to do better. She wants those around her to do better. She appropriates the family's front room for a cooking school. She spreads the word and there is quick interest.

"There are plenty of good cooks who need no schooling, but here was an opportunity to do like the white folks. So on Friday afternoon there were many to hurry through with the cleaning up, and after the white folks' dinners, to hurry to Evangeline's house at the fur een er Dog Alley in Yamacraw.

"Evangeline had mounted a stove on a big box in the center of the big front room, and was surrounded with little tables containing various articles of food, flour, lard, meats, fish and other things. She was arrayed in white, with a white cap on, and greeted her guests effusively as they came in, exacting a nickel from each as an entrance fee. She waited until the room was filled and then she rapped for order.

"I want you ladies to know that there is fashion in cooking just as there is in clothes. People are tired of the old style of cooking and they want something new. If we ladies want to keep our places as cooks, we must keep up with the styles. For instance, fish is no longer fried—that's too common. We either bake, plank or boil fish—.'

"'Look hyere 'Vangeline Harris, how come deys doan fry fish,' said Melindy, who is fat and sassy: 'who sayes deys fry um no mo'?'

"'Up North, where I have been attending college, they regard fried fish as the dish of common people. They plank the shad and broil the bluefish and boil the bass and—

"'Wot deys doos wid de mullet?' asked Melindy."

Notice Evangeline speaks standard white English, her neighbors dialect. The Macon women don't like being talked down to. The whole cooking school, it's no surprise, deteriorates into failure.

Smith often waxed nostalgic about old-time Macon. He didn't mince words over racial attitudes of earlier times. "The negro figured but little in the town census of those days," he wrote in one article in 1914, "his habitat being the country, and he was a slave. His liberty on the streets was limited. Unless he had a pass written by his master he must be off the streets after 8 o'clock at night, or the 'patteroll' would get him."[27]

On another occasion, he explained how railroad conductors such as "Uncle Sandy" Matthews marked the shoulders of black passengers with chalk, to keep track of who had a ticket, "but later on they carried chalk themselves. Then he bought him a package of fishhooks, sticking a hook surreptitiously in the coat of the negro who paid his fare. In time they caught on to the hook business, and then was introduced the little red, blue and green slips of cardboard to be fastened in the hatbands, and used to this day."[28]

Bridges felt greater comfort with an older generation of blacks.

"You know my admiration for the old-timey negro. This comes from two causes: he belongs to the past, to the old days of the south when I was a boy and when the relationship between the negro and the child was of the most intimate and trusting nature; he is so superior to the present crop of superficially educated negro," he wrote in 1913.[29]

"Macon is fortunate in having some good negroes, plenty of them, and I am not talking about them. I have in mind the youngish kind, the purple-socked, cigarette-smoking kind, that make up the chauffeurs and proprietors of pressing clubs—not all of them, of course."

After 265 "Stories in Black"[30] columns, punched out seven days a week, Smith began to tire. In March 1910, he dropped back to Sunday-only columns, with an altered title, "Stories in Black and White." These columns would continue to 1918.

World War I brought temporary high employment. But what happens after the war is over? columnist Smith posed to the Rev. Wall-Eye Thomas, "the beloved pastor of the Fuss Meffodis Chu'ch er Yamacraw," who mows the lawns of white folks.

"'Yer knowed how de guv-ment spile de nigger her pain him three and four an five dollar er day furer jess common evvy-day han, an dat make him leave de farm and de shop an all uvver kiner wuk so he kin make dat much money er day. Dem niggers jess leave do country jess lak ey wuz running erway frum de small pox. Menyer plantation aint got er nigger on hit. Yer kaint git er nigger tergo ter de country. Evvy day farmers come ter town taking bout de farm gwine ter roonashun kase labor so skace. An hit sho did look bad, didn't hit, Mister?'"

Besides fomenting a migration to the cities, the war kept a lot of white men in uniforms. What now for the blacks?

"'Deys gwine back ter Afriky, dem dat kin git dar, dat whar deys gwine.how many milyun wite sojers in dis war? Aint evvy one er deys places in de shops and de stores and de banks and de railroads done been gi' ter somebody else, and wen all dem sojers come back deys bleege ter has wuk. Whar dem niggers gwineter wuk? Deys done quit de farm! Aint no mo' guv-ment wuk at four dollar er day! Deys sho in er bad fix atter de war.'

Smith as mayor in 1915, it should be noted, had strongly opposed a movement to replace blacks who had been employed as street cleaners by out-of-work whites.[31]

The column was titled "The Burning Question." Dated 18 August 1918, it was the last of some 427 "Stories in Black and White" columns in the *Telegraph*.[32] Interestingly, the column ended on the same note it had begun in 1909: An inquiry into the condition of the black population.

Smith wasn't tired of writing, he was just tired of "Stories in Black and White." He had created a new column, "Intimate Glimpses of Men and Things," in 1917, and continued to write another, "Just Twixt Us,"[33] until his death.

Bridges Smith Notes

1. 8 October 1930, 4.
2. "Prominent Macon Citizen Is Dead," 6 October 1930, 1.
3. "Mrs. Bridges Smith Dies of Apoplexy," *Macon Telegraph*, 27 December 1917, 10, and "Miss Goelz, Bride of Judge Bridges Smith," *Macon Telegraph*, 11 April 1919, 4.
4. "Wins for Fifth Time in Very Hot Campaign," Columbia, S.C., *State*, 28 September 1913, 16.
5. 8 October 1930, 4.
6. 16 May 1877, 4.
7. 19 October 1919, 12.
8. "Home Talent and 'Dollie,'" *Macon Telegraph*, 19 February 1882.
9. Smith, "Characteristic Little Letter from Joel Chandler Harris," *Macon Telegraph*, 6 July 1908, 5.
10. "Stories in Black to Be Published in Book Form," *Macon Telegraph*, 22 August 1909, 10.
11. 2 June 1909, 4.
12. The book is subtitled: "A Collection of Bright, Breezy, Humorous Stories of the Colored Race as Seen in the Sunny South." It was reprinted by Books for Libraries Press in 1972.
13. Promotional page in a reprint of the 1881 Street & Smith book *The Blunders of a Bashful Man* by Metta Victoria Fuller, 99.
14. 6 August 1910, 4.
15. 6 July 1910.
16. Respectively the *Tribune*, 10 July 1910; the *Union*, 24 July 1910; and the *Daily Telegraph*, 8 July 1910.
17. *Macon Black and White*, 43.
18. 29 July 1907, 4.
19. "Afro-American Meeting," *Macon Telegraph*, 27 September 1900, 8.
20. "Negroes Are Here for Big Meeting," *Macon Telegraph*, 25 May 1917, 7.
21. Copy of Georgia Equal Rights Convention Program, Special Collections and University Archives, University of Massachusetts Amherst Libraries.
22. *Macon Telegraph*, 28 October 1917, 8.
23. *Macon Telegraph*, 27 November 1916, 7.
24. *Macon Telegraph*, 6 July 1909, 4.
25. *Macon Telegraph*, 31 July 1910, 5.
26. *Macon Telegraph*, 4 December 1910, 5.
27. Smith, "Mayor Casts Retrospective Mind's Eye...," *Macon Telegraph*, 14 October 1914, 8.
28. Bridges, "Fish-Hooks and Chalk...," *Macon Telegraph*, 18 February 1917, 6.
29. Bridges, "The Old Versus the New...," *Macon Telegraph*, 23 March 1913.
30. As will be seen in the bibliography, there are a dozen chapters in the book for which corresponding columns could not be identified. Presumably they were retitled.

31. *Negro Migration During the War*, Emmet J. Scott (1919).
32. From time to time Smith reprinted an earlier column.
33. A five-days-a-week column.

Bridges Smith Selected Bibliography and Sources

STORIES IN BLACK

"The Shine" (*Macon Telegraph*, 27 January 1909)
"The Separation" (*Macon Telegraph*, 28 January 1909) (1)
"Old Acquaintances" (*Macon Telegraph*, 29 January 1909)
"The Wooing of Mary Jane" (*Macon Telegraph*, 30 January 1909)
"Cold Night for the Dog" (*Macon Telegraph*, 1 February 1909)
"How She Won Her Man" (*Macon Telegraph*, 2 February 1909) (1)
"The Clock That Didn't Go Off" (*Macon Telegraph*, 3 February 1909)
"The Card Party" (*Macon Telegraph*, 4 February 1909) (1)
"Mandy's Country Beau" (*Macon Telegraph*, 5 February 1909) (1)
"Skinny" (*Macon Telegraph*, 6 February 1909)
"The Dinner Hour" (*Macon Telegraph*, 7 February 1909) (1)
"The Delivery Boy's Mistake" (*Macon Telegraph*, 8 February 1909) (1)
"The Unwilling Witness" (*Macon Telegraph*, 9 February 1909) (1)
"The Engagement Ring" (*Macon Telegraph*, 10 February 1909) (1)
"Who Was Scared the Most" (*Macon Telegraph*, 11 February 1909) (1)
"The Plum-Colored Kimona" (*Macon Telegraph*, 12 February 1909) (1)
"Faith" (*Macon Telegraph*, 13 February 1909) (1)
"Valentine Party in Yamacraw" (*Macon Telegraph*, 14 February 1909) (1)
"Sump'n 'Bout Er Cow" (*Macon Telegraph*, 15 February 1909)
"The Unbadged Dog" (*Macon Telegraph*, 16 February 1909)
"Preaching in Yamacraw" (*Macon Telegraph*, 17 February 1909)
"Buying a Dog Badge" (*Macon Telegraph*, 18 February 1909)
"Aunt Liza" (*Macon Telegraph*, 19 February 1909)
"An Enoch Arden Case" (*Macon Telegraph*, 20 February 1909) (1)
"Preaching in Yamacraw" (*Macon Telegraph*, 21 February 1909)
"The Annexation of Tybee" (*Macon Telegraph*, 22 February 1909)
"A Domestic Near-Fuss" (*Macon Telegraph*, 23 February 1909)
"Politics in Yamacraw" (*Macon Telegraph*, 24 February 1909)
"John Henry" (*Macon Telegraph*, 25 February 1909)
"The Accusation" (*Macon Telegraph*, 26 February 1909) (1)
"Groundpea Ben" (*Macon Telegraph*, 27 February 1909)
"Preaching in Yamacraw" (*Macon Telegraph*, 28 February 1909)
"Mister Joe Brown" (*Macon Telegraph*, 1 March 1909)
"The Holt Pensioners" (*Macon Telegraph*, 2 March 1909)
"The Trainman's Revenge" (*Macon Telegraph*, 3 March 1909) (1)
"The Loiterer" (*Macon Telegraph*, 4 March 1909) (1)
"If I Were President" (*Macon Telegraph*, 5 March 1909) (1)
"The Skeleton in the Closet" (*Macon Telegraph*, 6 March 1909) (1)
"Preaching in Yamacraw" (*Macon Telegraph*, 7 March 1909)
"The Empire Gown" (*Macon Telegraph*, 8 March 1909) (1)
"Fatty Fan's Mistake" (*Macon Telegraph*, 9 March 1909) (1)
"The Burial of Shuffle-Toe Pete" (*Macon Telegraph*, 10 March 1909)
"The Fortune-Teller" (*Macon Telegraph*, 11 March 1909) (1)
"The Red Rat" (*Macon Telegraph*, 12 March 1909)
"Mame" (*Macon Telegraph*, 13 March 1909)
"The Waist-Line Party" (*Macon Telegraph*, 14 March 1909) (1)
"Preaching in Yamacraw" (*Macon Telegraph*, 15 March 1909)
"Aunt Ann" (*Macon Telegraph*, 16 March 1909)

"The Eagle and the Buzzard" (*Macon Telegraph*, 17 March 1909) (1)
"The Spotter" (*Macon Telegraph*, 18 March 1909) (1)
"Chloroforming Criminals" (*Macon Telegraph*, 19 March 1909)
"Old Miss and Aunt Lou" (*Macon Telegraph*, 20 March 1909) (1)
"Preaching in Yamacraw" (*Macon Telegraph*, 21 March 1909)
"The Bridal Trip" (*Macon Telegraph*, 22 March 1909)
"Mind-Reading in Yamacraw" (*Macon Telegraph*, 23 March 1909) (1)
"Uncle Isom's Star" (*Macon Telegraph*, 24 March 1909) (1)
"The Tybee Debating Society" (*Macon Telegraph*, 25 March 1909) (1)
"A Type of Witness" (*Macon Telegraph*, 26 March 1909)
"The Serenade" (*Macon Telegraph*, 27 March 1909) (1)
"Amanda's Ninth Wedding" (*Macon Telegraph*, 28 March 1909) as A Wedding in Tybee (1)
"The Invalid" (*Macon Telegraph*, 30 March 1909) (1)
"The Sign of Death" (*Macon Telegraph*, 31 March 1909) (1)
"Talking About Dogs" (*Macon Telegraph*, 6 April 1909)
"The Humming Bird Society" (*Macon Telegraph*, 7 April 1909) (1)
"Why He Was Happy" (*Macon Telegraph*, 8 April 1909)
"Cupid" (*Macon Telegraph*, 9 April 1909) Cupid on Matrimony (1)
"The Lovers' Quarrel" (*Macon Telegraph*, 10 April 1909) (1)
"Preaching in Yamacraw" (*Macon Telegraph*, 11 April 1909)
"The Left Foot" (*Macon Telegraph*, 12 April 1909)
"The Wireless Telephone" (*Macon Telegraph*, 13 April 1909)
"What the Nurses Said" (*Macon Telegraph*, 14 April 1909) (1)
"Niggers and Poor White Trash" (*Macon Telegraph*, 15 April 1909)
"Peliagra" (*Macon Telegraph*, 16 April 1909)
"Old Jim" (*Macon Telegraph*, 17 April 1909)
"Preaching in Yamacraw" (*Macon Telegraph*, 18 April 1909)
"Compulsory Education" (*Macon Telegraph*, 19 April 1909)
"The Black Hand Letter" (*Macon Telegraph*, 20 April 1909)
"The Pastor's Surprise Party" (*Macon Telegraph*, 21 April 1909)
"Tag Day in Tybee" (*Macon Telegraph*, 22 April 1909)
"Eli the Peddler" (*Macon Telegraph*, 23 April 1909)
"Talking About the Doctors" (*Macon Telegraph*, 24 April 1909)
"Preaching in Yamacraw" (*Macon Telegraph*, 25 April 1909)
"Miss Jackson Hypnotised" (*Macon Telegraph*, 26 April 1909) (1)
"Beauty Spots" (*Macon Telegraph*, 27 April 1909)
"Talking of the Gatling Gun" (*Macon Telegraph*, 28 April 1909)
"Swallowed a Lightning Bug" (*Macon Telegraph*, 29 April 1909) (1)
"His Faith in Marsa John" (*Macon Telegraph*, 30 April 1909)
"The Pure Food Law" (*Macon Telegraph*, 1 May 1909) (1)
"Preaching in Yamacraw" (*Macon Telegraph*, 2 May 1909)
"Registration" (*Macon Telegraph*, 3 May 1909)
"Mosquitoes and Flies" (*Macon Telegraph*, 4 May 1909)
"Just Talking" (*Macon Telegraph*, 5 May 1909)
"A Case of Loitering" (*Macon Telegraph*, 6 May 1909)
"The Odd Couple" (*Macon Telegraph*, 7 May 1909) (1)
"The Slim Girl" (*Macon Telegraph*, 8 May 1909) (1)
"Preaching in Yamacraw" (*Macon Telegraph*, 9 May 1909)
"A Fair Exchange" (*Macon Telegraph*, 10 May 1909) (1)
"The Wrong Color" (*Macon Telegraph*, 11 May 1909)
"The Burnt Child" (*Macon Telegraph*, 12 May 1909)
"In a Tybee Backyard" (*Macon Telegraph*, 13 May 1909) (1)
"A First-Class Funeral" (*Macon Telegraph*, 15 May 1909) (1)
"Preaching in Yamacraw" (*Macon Telegraph*, 16 May 1909)
"The Tissue Paper Ball" (*Macon Telegraph*, 16 May 1909) (1)
"The New Law" (*Macon Telegraph*, 18 May 1909)

"What Fools These Husbands Be" (*Macon Telegraph*, 19 May 1909) (1)
"Merely Comments" (*Macon Telegraph*, 20 May 1909)
"Overheard Among the Draymen" (*Macon Telegraph*, 21 May 1909)
"A Tybee Trick" (*Macon Telegraph*, 22 May 1909) (1)
"Preaching in Yamacraw" (*Macon Telegraph*, 23 May 1909)
"Preaching in Yamacraw" (*Macon Telegraph*, 30 May 1909)
"Preaching in Yamacraw" (*Macon Telegraph*, 6 June 1909)
"A Groundless Claim" (*Macon Telegraph*, 7 June 1909)
"Poor Emma" (*Macon Telegraph*, 8 June 1909) (1)
"Another Claim Case" (*Macon Telegraph*, 9 June 1909)
"The Cocaine Sniffer" (*Macon Telegraph*, 10 June 1909) (1)
"Sleep Sickness" (*Macon Telegraph*, 11 June 1909) (1)
"Nut-Grass" (*Macon Telegraph*, 12 June 1909)
"Preaching in Yamacraw" (*Macon Telegraph*, 13 June 1909)
"Memories" (*Macon Telegraph*, 14 June 1909)
"The Bribe" (*Macon Telegraph*, 15 June 1909) (1)
"A Typical Case" (*Macon Telegraph*, 16 June 1909) (1)
"African Watermelons" (*Macon Telegraph*, 17 June 1909)
"Precious Jackson's Last Beau" (*Macon Telegraph*, 18 June 1909) (1)
"The Plain Truth" (*Macon Telegraph*, 19 June 1909)
"Preaching in Yamacraw" (*Macon Telegraph*, 20 June 1909)
"His First Ride in an Automobile" (*Macon Telegraph*, 21 June 1909)
"All Mothers Are Alike" (*Macon Telegraph*, 22 June 1909) (1)
"Dinner Hour Discussion" (*Macon Telegraph*, 23 June 1909)
"The Old Grass-Cutter" (*Macon Telegraph*, 24 June 1909)
"Disappointment" (*Macon Telegraph*, 25 June 1909)
"Why the Board Was Raised" (*Macon Telegraph*, 26 June 1909) (1)
"Preaching in Yamacraw" (*Macon Telegraph*, 27 June 1909)
"Just Talking" (*Macon Telegraph*, 28 June 1909)
"The Little Boy" (*Macon Telegraph*, 29 June 1909) (1)
"Warm Days" (*Macon Telegraph*, 30 June 1909)
"Cross Alley Conversation" (*Macon Telegraph*, 1 July 1909) (1)
"Loitering" (*Macon Telegraph*, 2 July 1909)
"The Linen Shower" (*Macon Telegraph*, 3 July 1909) (1)
"Preaching in Yamacraw" (*Macon Telegraph*, 4 July 1909)
"The Human Stump" (*Macon Telegraph*, 5 July 1909)
"A Chewing Gum Episode" (*Macon Telegraph*, 6 July 1909) (1)
"The Tybee Flea" (*Macon Telegraph*, 7 July 1909)
"Cotton-Eye Joe" (*Macon Telegraph*, 8 July 1909)
"Stormy Talk" (*Macon Telegraph*, 9 July 1909) Alley Talk (1)
"Slowfoot Sal's Outing" (*Macon Telegraph*, 10 July 1909) (1)
"Preaching in Yamacraw" (*Macon Telegraph*, 11 July 1909)
"When the President Comes" (*Macon Telegraph*, 12 July 1909) (1)
"The Fight" (*Macon Telegraph*, 13 July 1909) (1)
"Liberia" (*Macon Telegraph*, 14 July 1909)
"Reconciliation" (*Macon Telegraph*, 15 July 1909) (1)
"Larceny After Trust" (*Macon Telegraph*, 16 July 1909) The Larceny of the Rose (1)
"Cupid on Matrimony" (*Macon Telegraph*, 17 July 1909) (1)
"Preaching in Yamcraw" (*Macon Telegraph*, 18 July 1909)
"The Sunshine Club" (*Macon Telegraph*, 20 July 1909)
"The Compromise" (*Macon Telegraph*, 21 July 1909)
"Discussing the Tariff" (*Macon Telegraph*, 22 July 1909)
"Wrestling with the Devil" (*Macon Telegraph*, 23 July 1909)
"The Preacher in Prison" (*Macon Telegraph*, 24 July 1909)
"Preaching in Yamacraw" (*Macon Telegraph*, 25 July 1909)
"The Loiterers" (*Macon Telegraph*, 25 July 1909)

"Marriage Licenses Marked Down" (*Macon Telegraph*, 26 July 1909)
"Spiders" (*Macon Telegraph*, 27 July 1909) (1)
"Jim's Dream" (*Macon Telegraph*, 28 July 1909)
"Discussing Drinks" (*Macon Telegraph*, 29 July 1909)
"The Star Boarder" (*Macon Telegraph*, 30 July 1909) (1)
"How He Got Even" (*Macon Telegraph*, 31 July 1909)
"The Honeysuckle Sewing Circle" (*Macon Telegraph*, 1 August 1909)
"The Tybee Sunshine Club" (*Macon Telegraph*, 2 August 1909)
"The Mary Jane Gown" (*Macon Telegraph*, 3 August 1909) (1)
"Mosquitoes" (*Macon Telegraph*, 4 August 1909)
"Parting of the Ways" (*Macon Telegraph*, 5 August 1909) (1)
"Summer Vacations" (*Macon Telegraph*, 6 August 1909)
"Watermilyuns" (*Macon Telegraph*, 7 August 1909)
"The Honeysuckle Sewing Circle" (*Macon Telegraph*, 8 August 1909)
"Talk of the Draymen" (*Macon Telegraph*, 10 August 1909)
"Minerva's Sister in Chicago" (*Macon Telegraph*, 11 August 1909) (1)
"The Legislature" (*Macon Telegraph*, 12 August 1909)
"Fall Styles" (*Macon Telegraph*, 13 August 1909) (1)
"Slowfoot Sal's Ride" (*Macon Telegraph*, 14 August 1909)
"Rev. Wall-Eye in Trouble" (*Macon Telegraph*, 15 August 1909)
"Taking the Census" (*Macon Telegraph*, 16 August 1909) (1)
"Foday and Li'l'bit" (*Macon Telegraph*, 17 August 1909) as Before Day and Little Bit (1)
"Haslit Pete" (*Macon Telegraph*, 18 August 1909) (1)
"Wireless Street Cars" (*Macon Telegraph*, 19 August 1909)
"The Fortune Teller" (*Macon Telegraph*, 20 August 1909) (1)
"Society Emblems" (*Macon Telegraph*, 21 August 1909)
"Preaching in Yamacraw" (*Macon Telegraph*, 22 August 1909)
"The Tybee Sunshine Club" (*Macon Telegraph*, 23 August 1909)
"Talking About Moving" (*Macon Telegraph*, 24 August 1909)
"The Ex-Slave's Reunion" (*Macon Telegraph*, 25 August 1909)
"The Hook Worm" (*Macon Telegraph*, 26 August 1909) (1)
"A Scene in Yamacraw" (*Macon Telegraph*, 27 August 1909) (1)
"The Funeral" (*Macon Telegraph*, 28 August 1909)
"Preaching in Yamacraw" (*Macon Telegraph*, 29 August 1909)
"The Sunshine Club" (*Macon Telegraph*, 30 August 1909)
"For Sale: One Goat" (*Macon Telegraph*, 31 August 1909) (1)
"The Flying Machine" (*Macon Telegraph*, 1 September 1909)
"Odorless Whiskey" (*Macon Telegraph*, 2 September 1909)
"What the Doctor Took" (*Macon Telegraph*, 3 September 1909)
"The North Pole" (*Macon Telegraph*, 4 September 1909) (1)
"The Prodigal Son" (*Macon Telegraph*, 5 September 1909)
"The Tybee Sunshine Club" (*Macon Telegraph*, 6 September 1909)
"Labor Day" (*Macon Telegraph*, 7 September 1909)
"The Thermos Bottle" (*Macon Telegraph*, 8 September 1909)
"Back-Boneless Mullet" (*Macon Telegraph*, 9 September 1909) (1)
"The Manicure Artist" (*Macon Telegraph*, 10 September 1909) (1)
"The Rise in the Price of Meat" (*Macon Telegraph*, 11 September 1909)
"Preaching in Yamacraw" (*Macon Telegraph*, 12 September 1909)
"The Sunshine Club" (*Macon Telegraph*, 13 September 1909)
"The President's Breakfast" (*Macon Telegraph*, 14 September 1909) (1)
"The Pardoned Convict" (*Macon Telegraph*, 15 September 1909)
"Cotton Pickers and Things" (*Macon Telegraph*, 16 September 1909)
"Matt Henson" (*Macon Telegraph*, 17 September 1909)
"Littlebit" (*Macon Telegraph*, 18 September 1909) (1)
"Preaching in Yamacraw" (*Macon Telegraph*, 19 September 1909)
"The Sunshine Club" (*Macon Telegraph*, 20 September 1909)

"The Horned Snake" (*Macon Telegraph*, 21 September 1909)
"The Dopester" (*Macon Telegraph*, 22 September 1909)
"Watermelon and Microbes" (*Macon Telegraph*, 23 September 1909)
"Halley's Comet" (*Macon Telegraph*, 24 September 1909)
"Buttermilk" (*Macon Telegraph*, 25 September 1909)
"Preaching in Yamacraw" (*Macon Telegraph*, 26 September 1909)
"The Club Discusses Politics" (*Macon Telegraph*, 27 September 1909)
"Old Ben" (*Macon Telegraph*, 28 September 1909)
"The World-Enders" (*Macon Telegraph*, 29 September 1909)
"The President Preached" (*Macon Telegraph*, 30 September 1909)
"Modernized Watermelons" (*Macon Telegraph*, 1 October 1909)
"Slowfoot Sal's Fight" (*Macon Telegraph*, 2 October 1909) (1)
"Preaching in Yamacraw" (*Macon Telegraph*, 3 October 1909)
"The Club Discusses the New Mayor" (*Macon Telegraph*, 4 October 1909)
"Pictures of the Loafers" (*Macon Telegraph*, 5 October 1909)
"Bill Is Worried" (*Macon Telegraph*, 6 October 1909)
"Election Expenses" (*Macon Telegraph*, 7 October 1909)
"A Chance Meeting" (*Macon Telegraph*, 8 October 1909) (1)
"Bill's Ghost" (*Macon Telegraph*, 9 October 1909)
"Preaching in Yamacraw" (*Macon Telegraph*, 10 October 1909)
"The Sunshine Club" (*Macon Telegraph*, 11 October 1909)
"[Two little negro boys]" (*Macon Telegraph*, 12 October 1909)
"The Hurricane" (*Macon Telegraph*, 13 October 1909)
"The Riff-Raff" (*Macon Telegraph*, 14 October 1909)
"A Wedding in Tybee" (*Macon Telegraph*, 16 October 1909)
"Preaching in Yamacraw" (*Macon Telegraph*, 17 October 1909)
"The Sunshine Club" (*Macon Telegraph*, 18 October 1909)
"The Tourist Hotel" (*Macon Telegraph*, 19 October 1909)
"The Cooking School" (*Macon Telegraph*, 20 October 1909)
"The Broken Engagement" (*Macon Telegraph*, 21 October 1909) (1)
"A Typical Fight" (1)
"The Rival Societies" (1)
"The Educated Daughter" (1)
"The Belated Groom" (1)
"Out with the Church" (1)
"The Ministering Angels" (1)
"The Disagreement" (1)
"The Vags" (1)
"A Friend in Court" (1)
"The Matrons' Club" (1)
"Aunt Ann" (1)
"Slowfoot Sal's Ride" (1)
"Sugar Babe" (1)
"Reconciliation" (*Macon Telegraph*, 22 October 1909)
"Preaching in Yamacraw" (*Macon Telegraph*, 24 October 1909)
"The Sunshine Club" (*Macon Telegraph*, 25 October 1909)
"Gal Babies" (*Macon Telegraph*, 26 October 1909)
"The Circus" (*Macon Telegraph*, 29 October 1909)
"Preaching in Yamacraw" (*Macon Telegraph*, 31 October 1909)
"The Educated Fleas" (*Macon Telegraph*, 2 November 1909)
"The President's Breakfast" (*Macon Telegraph*, 5 November 1909)
"Preaching in Yamacraw" (*Macon Telegraph*, 7 November 1909)
"Preaching in Yamacraw" (*Macon Telegraph*, 14 November 1909)
"Preaching in Yamacraw" (*Macon Telegraph*, 21 November 1909)
"Preaching in Yamacraw" (*Macon Telegraph*, 28 November 1909)
"The Left and the Right" (*Macon Telegraph*, 5 December 1909)

"Preaching in Yamacraw" (*Macon Telegraph*, 12 December 1909)
"Preaching in Yamacraw" (*Macon Telegraph*, 19 December 1909)
"Preaching in Yamacraw" (*Macon Telegraph*, 26 December 1909)
"The Sunshine Club" (*Macon Telegraph*, 2 January 1909)
"Preaching in Yamacraw" (*Macon Telegraph*, 9 January 1910)
"Preaching in Yamacraw" (*Macon Telegraph*, 16 January 1910)
"Preaching in Yamacraw" (*Macon Telegraph*, 23 January 1910)
"Preaching in Yamacraw" (*Macon Telegraph*, 30 January 1910)
"Preaching in Yamacraw" (*Macon Telegraph*, 6 February 1910)
"Preaching in Yamacraw" (*Macon Telegraph*, 13 February 1910)
"Preaching in Yamacraw" (*Macon Telegraph*, 20 February 1910)
"Preaching in Yamacraw" (*Macon Telegraph*, 27 February 1910)

STORIES IN BLACK AND WHITE

"John and His Teeth" (*Macon Telegraph*, 6 March 1910)
"Unwept, Unhonored, Unsung" (*Macon Telegraph*, 13 March 1910)
"Taft and Teddy" (*Macon Telegraph*, 20 March 1910)
"Mammy's Foolish Boy" (*Macon Telegraph*, 27 March 1910)
"The Wrong Number" (*Macon Telegraph*, 3 April 1910)
"The Systematic Man" (*Macon Telegraph*, 10 April 1910)
"A Yawp from Yamacraw" (*Macon Telegraph*, 17 April 1910)
"Preaching in Yamacraw" (*Macon Telegraph*, 1 May 1910)
"Cal's Dollar" (*Macon Telegraph*, 8 May 1910)
"It Made a Difference" (*Macon Telegraph*, 15 May 1910)
"Mame and Florrie" (*Macon Telegraph*, 22 May 1910)
"The Comet Party" (*Macon Telegraph*, 29 May 1910)
"Mame's Engagement" (*Macon Telegraph*, 5 June 1910)
"Household Economy" (*Macon Telegraph*, 12 June 1910)
"The Aviators" (*Macon Telegraph*, 19 June 1910)
"Singing Sam" (*Macon Telegraph*, 26 June 1910)
"The Pizened Dog" (*Macon Telegraph*, 3 July 1910)
"A Home at Last" (*Macon Telegraph*, 10 July 1910)
"The Black Hand Letter" (*Macon Telegraph*, 17 July 1910)
"Bacteria" (*Macon Telegraph*, 24 July 1910)
"Educated Fleas" (*Macon Telegraph*, 31 July 1910)
"Compulsory Baths" (*Macon Telegraph*, 7 August 1910)
"Preaching in Yamacraw" (*Macon Telegraph*, 14 August 1910)
"Punishing the Pastor" (*Macon Telegraph*, 21 August 1910)
"Miss Sallie's Scheme" (*Macon Telegraph*, 28 August 1910)
"Good Old Barbecue" (*Macon Telegraph*, 4 September 1910)
"In the Dining Car Ahead" (*Macon Telegraph*, 11 September 1910)
"Graft" (*Macon Telegraph*, 18 September 1910)
"The Boosters" (*Macon Telegraph*, 25 September 1910)
"The Tybee Debaters" (*Macon Telegraph*, 2 October 1910)
"The Soul Kiss" (*Macon Telegraph*, 9 October 1910)
"The Tybee Debaters" (*Macon Telegraph*, 16 October 1910)
"Preaching in Yamacraw" (*Macon Telegraph*, 23 October 1910)
"Preaching in Yamacraw" (*Macon Telegraph*, 30 October 1910)
"A Tybee Thanksgiving Prayer" (*Macon Telegraph*, 20 November 1910)
"Preaching in Yamacraw" (*Macon Telegraph*, 27 November 1910)
"The Yamacraw Cooking School" (*Macon Telegraph*, 4 December 1910)
"The Partners" (*Macon Telegraph*, 11 December 1910)
"The Tybee-Yamacraw Musicale" (*Macon Telegraph*, 18 December 1910)
"A Christmas Sermon" (*Macon Telegraph*, 25 December 1910)
"A New Year Sermon" (*Macon Telegraph*, 1 January 1911)
"The Draymen Discourses" (*Macon Telegraph*, 8 January 1911)

"The Experience Meeting" (*Macon Telegraph*, 15 January 1911)
"Current Comment" (*Macon Telegraph*, 22 January 1911)
"Preaching in Yamacraw" (*Macon Telegraph*, 29 January 1911)
"The Dreamers" (*Macon Telegraph*, 5 February 1911)
"Preaching in Yamacraw" (*Macon Telegraph*, 12 February 1911)
"A Valentine Ball in Tybee" (*Macon Telegraph*, 19 February 1911)
"Preaching in Yamacraw" (*Macon Telegraph*, 25 February 1911)
"The Tybee Waterworks" (*Macon Telegraph*, 5 March 1911)
"The Personal License" (*Macon Telegraph*, 12 March 1911)
"Henry Turned the Tables" (*Macon Telegraph*, 19 March 1911)
"Preaching in Yamacraw" (*Macon Telegraph*, 26 March 1911)
"The Wedding" (*Macon Telegraph*, 2 April 1911)
"The Dog Fight" (*Macon Telegraph*, 9 April 1911)
"An Easter Sermon" (*Macon Telegraph*, 16 April 1911)
"Yamacraw's New Hotel" (*Macon Telegraph*, 23 April 1911)
"Government by Commission" (*Macon Telegraph*, 30 April 1911)
"Preaching in Yamacraw" (*Macon Telegraph*, 7 May 1911)
"The Coronation" (*Macon Telegraph*, 14 May 1911)
"Preaching in Yamacraw" (*Macon Telegraph*, 21 May 1911)
"What Is a King?" (*Macon Telegraph*, 28 May 1911)
"The Tybee Debating Club" (*Macon Telegraph*, 4 June 1911)
"Preaching in Yamacraw" (*Macon Telegraph*, 11 June 1911)
"Preaching in Yamacraw" (*Macon Telegraph*, 18 June 1911)
"The Draymen Are Sore" (*Macon Telegraph*, 25 June 1911)
"Preaching in Yamacraw" (*Macon Telegraph*, 2 July 1911)
"The Tybee Playground" (*Macon Telegraph*, 9 July 1911)
"Preaching in Yamacraw" (*Macon Telegraph*, 16 July 1911)
"Preaching in Yamacraw" (*Macon Telegraph*, 23 July 1911)
"Tybee Police Court" (*Macon Telegraph*, 30 July 1911)
"Preaching in Yamacraw" (*Macon Telegraph*, 6 August 1911)
"The Tybee Foot Race" (*Macon Telegraph*, 13 August 1911)
"Wall-Eye Takes a Vacation" (*Macon Telegraph*, 20 August 1911)
"[And a man there...]" *Macon Telegraph*, 27 August 1911)
"The Story of the Prodigal Son" (*Macon Telegraph*, 3 September 1911)
"The Story of Lazarus 9" (*Macon Telegraph*, 10 September 1911)
"The Story of Belshazzar's Feast" (*Macon Telegraph*, 17 September 1911)
"The Story of Samson" (*Macon Telegraph*, 24 September 1911)
"Daniel in the Lion's Den" (*Macon Telegraph*, 1 October 1911)
"The Story of Jonah" (*Macon Telegraph*, 8 October 1911)
"Story of Esau and Jacob" (*Macon Telegraph*, 15 October 1911)
"The Pastor's Return" (*Macon Telegraph*, 22 October 1911)
"Moving Pictures in Yamacraw" (*Macon Telegraph*, 29 October 1911)
"The Pastor Sees the Pictuers" (*Macon Telegraph*, 5 November 1911)
"Yamacraw's First Newspaper" (*Macon Telegraph*, 12 November 1911)
"Whar Is We Gwine?" (*Macon Telegraph*, 19 November 1911)
"The Busted Tire" (*Macon Telegraph*, 26 November 1911)
"Thanksgiving Sermon" (*Macon Telegraph*, 3 December 1911)
"The Yellow Paper Ball" (*Macon Telegraph*, 10 December 1911)
"Organising the Cooks' Union" (*Macon Telegraph*, 17 December 1911)
"Tybee's Christmas Tree" (*Macon Telegraph*, 24 December 1911)
"The Day of Good Beginning" (*Macon Telegraph*, 31 December 1911)
"Littlebit's Revenge" (*Macon Telegraph*, 7 January 1912)
"The Wooing of the Widow Watts" (*Macon Telegraph*, 14 January 1912)
"The Third Degree" (*Macon Telegraph*, 21 January 1912)
"The Preacher's Dog" (*Macon Telegraph*, 28 January 1912)
"Studies in Natural History" (*Macon Telegraph*, 4 February 1912)

"Natural History Continued" (*Macon Telegraph*, 11 February 1912)
"The Great White Way" (*Macon Telegraph*, 19 February 1912)
"The Sayings of Wall-Eye" (*Macon Telegraph*, 25 February 1912)
"More Sayings of Wall-Eye" (*Macon Telegraph*, 3 March 1912)
"The Evils of the Suit Case" (*Macon Telegraph*, 10 March 1912)
"The Tybee Tea Room" (*Macon Telegraph*, 17 March 1912)
"Preaching in Yamacraw" (*Macon Telegraph*, 24 March 1912)
"The Piddler" (*Macon Telegraph*, 31 March 1912)
"The Food Famine" (*Macon Telegraph*, 7 April 1912)
"White Way in Yamacraw" (*Macon Telegraph*, 14 April 1912)
"The Lady and the Tiger" (*Macon Telegraph*, 21 April 1912)
"The Queen of Tybee" (*Macon Telegraph*, 28 April 1912)
"The Liquor Situation" (*Macon Telegraph*, 5 May 1912)
"Religion with the Lid Off" (*Macon Telegraph*, 12 May 1912)
"The Oil of Goodness" (*Macon Telegraph*, 19 May 1912)
"The Passing of the Womanly Woman" (*Macon Telegraph*, 26 May 1912)
"Littlebit and Trouble" (*Macon Telegraph*, 2 June 1912)
"Silent Night in Yamacraw" (*Macon Telegraph*, 9 June 1912)
"Widow Walker's Wad" (*Macon Telegraph*, 16 June 1912)
"The Tybee Beauty Parlor" (*Macon Telegraph*, 23 June 1912)
"The World Is Too Full of Beggars" (*Macon Telegraph*, 30 June 1912)
"The 5-C Club's First Party" (*Macon Telegraph*, 7 July 1912)
"Abolishing the Market" (*Macon Telegraph*, 14 July 1912)
"There Is No Hell" (*Macon Telegraph*, 21 July 1912)
"The Steam Roller" (*Macon Telegraph*, 28 July 1912)
"A Yamacraw Wedding" (*Macon Telegraph*, 4 August 1912)
"No Reforms for Tybee" (*Macon Telegraph*, 11 August 1912)
"The Pint Bottle" (*Macon Telegraph*, 18 August 1912)
"The Man Higher Up" (*Macon Telegraph*, 25 August 1912)
"A Kind of Detective Story" (*Macon Telegraph*, 1 September 1912)
"The Umbrella Menders" (*Macon Telegraph*, 8 September 1912)
"A Farewell to Summer" (*Macon Telegraph*, 15 September 1912)
"Playing Possum" (*Macon Telegraph*, 22 September 1912)
"The Corkscrew Straightener" (*Macon Telegraph*, 29 September 1912)
"All on Account of the Cook" (*Macon Telegraph*, 6 October 1912)
"Post Mortem Flowers" (*Macon Telegraph*, 13 October 1912)
"Hack No. 40-11" (*Macon Telegraph*, 20 October 1912)
"The Reformation of Slowfoot Sal" (*Macon Telegraph*, 27 October 1912)
"The Sunny Side of the Street" (*Macon Telegraph*, 3 November 1912)
"The Runaway Marriage" (*Macon Telegraph*, 10 November 1912)
"Is Marriage a Failure" (*Macon Telegraph*, 17 November 1912)
"The Trouble with the Cooks" (*Macon Telegraph*, 24 November 1912)
"A Thanksgiving Sermon" (*Macon Telegraph*, 1 December 1912)
"Christmas in Yamacraw" (*Macon Telegraph*, 22 December 1912)
"Littlebit and Didhebiteyou" (*Macon Telegraph*, 29 December 1912)
"A New Year Sermon" (*Macon Telegraph*, 5 January 1913)
"The Angel of Paradise Alley" (*Macon Telegraph*, 12 January 1913)
"The Possum Post" (*Macon Telegraph*, 19 January 1913)
"The Town of Highball" (*Macon Telegraph*, 26 January 1913)
"Why He Was Not Discouraged" (*Macon Telegraph*, 3 February 1913)
"Trusts" (*Macon Telegraph*, 9 February 1913)
"Yamacraw Suffragettes" (*Macon Telegraph*, 16 February 1913)
"Swing Low Sweet Chariot" (*Macon Telegraph*, 23 February 1913)
"The Joint Debate" (*Macon Telegraph*, 2 March 1913)
"The New President" (*Macon Telegraph*, 9 March 1913)
"Chatting with the Cook" (*Macon Telegraph*, 16 March 1913)

"The Reformation of Limping Lige 9" (*Macon Telegraph*, 23 March 1913)
"The Initiation of Sam" (*Macon Telegraph*, 6 April 1913)
"The Bon Ton Beauty Parlor" (*Macon Telegraph*, 13 April 1913)
"Bedelia's Beaux" (*Macon Telegraph*, 20 April 1913)
"Groundpea Ben" (*Macon Telegraph*, 27 April 1913)
"Aunt Sue's Observations" (*Macon Telegraph*, 4 May 1913)
"Liza's Lawn Party" (*Macon Telegraph*, 11 May 1913)
"The Yamacraw Dentist" (*Macon Telegraph*, 18 May 1913)
"The Yamacraw Mothers' Congress" (*Macon Telegraph*, 25 May 1913)
"The Dancing School" (*Macon Telegraph*, 1 June 1913)
"Psalm-Singing Sam" (*Macon Telegraph*, 8 June 1913)
"The Hoodooed Alarm Clock" (*Macon Telegraph*, 15 June 1913)
"Law Enforcement" (*Macon Telegraph*, 22 June 1913)
"The Coroner's Jury" (*Macon Telegraph*, 29 June 1913)
"The Japs in Georgia" (*Macon Telegraph*, 6 July 1913)
"[The draymen had assembled...]" (*Macon Telegraph*, 13 July 1913)
"Dreams at So Much Per" (*Macon Telegraph*, 20 July 1913)
"A Committee of the Whole" (*Macon Telegraph*, 27 July 1913)
"The Depot Situation" (*Macon Telegraph*, 3 August 1913)
"A Case of Appendicitis" (*Macon Telegraph*, 10 August 1913)
"Delia's Dope Dream" (*Macon Telegraph*, 17 August 1913)
"Humorous Troubles" (*Macon Telegraph*, 24 August 1913)
"The Yamacraw Developers" (*Macon Telegraph*, 31 August 1913)
"Labor Day for Yamacraw" (*Macon Telegraph*, 7 September 1913)
"Discussing Divorces" (*Macon Telegraph*, 14 September 1913)
"Peliagra and the Chinch" (*Macon Telegraph*, 21 September 1913)
"An Election in Yamacraw" (*Macon Telegraph*, 28 September 1913)
"The Mother's Aid Society" (*Macon Telegraph*, 12 October 1913)
"Closed by Injunction" (*Macon Telegraph*, 19 October 1913)
"In the Matter of Teeth" (*Macon Telegraph*, 26 October 1913)
"Winter Time in Yamacraw" (*Macon Telegraph*, 2 November 1913)
"The Income Tax" (*Macon Telegraph*, 9 November 1913)
"The Rival Restaurants" (*Macon Telegraph*, 16 November 1913)
"Is Beer Intoxicating?" (*Macon Telegraph*, 23 November 1913)
"A Thanksgiving Sermon" (*Macon Telegraph*, 30 November 1913)
"Chawin' Terbacker" (*Macon Telegraph*, 14 December 1913)
"Christmas in Yamacraw" (*Macon Telegraph*, 21 December 1913)
"A Too Hurried Affair" (*Macon Telegraph*, 28 December 1913)
"Suit Case vs. Carpet Bag" (*Macon Telegraph*, 4 January 1913)
"Yamacraw Philosophy" (*Macon Telegraph*, 11 January 1913)
"The Disownment of Lou" (*Macon Telegraph*, 18 January 1913)
"Aunt Dinah Discourseth" (*Macon Telegraph*, 25 January 1913)
"Dreams of Avarice" (*Macon Telegraph*, 1 February 1913)
"Gossip of the Alleys" (*Macon Telegraph*, 8 February 1913)
"The Reasonable Bank" (*Macon Telegraph*, 15 February 1913)
"The Prince of Lobelia" (*Macon Telegraph*, 22 February 1913)
"Athletics in Yamacraw" (*Macon Telegraph*, 1 March 1913)
"Wall-Eye's Philosophy" (*Macon Telegraph*, 8 March 1913)
"The High Cost of Salvation" (*Macon Telegraph*, 15 March 1914)
"Precious Pet's Party" (*Macon Telegraph*, 22 March 1914)
"The Wonders of Modern Surgery" (*Macon Telegraph*, 29 March 1914)
"Sweet Memories" (*Macon Telegraph*, 5 April 1914)
"A Game in the Rain" (*Macon Telegraph*, 12 April 1914)
"The Undertaker's Mistake" (*Macon Telegraph*, 19 April 1914)
"Thoughts on Marriage" (*Macon Telegraph*, 26 April 1914)
"How Liza Got Even" (*Macon Telegraph*, 10 May 1914)

"The Soft Drink Stand" (*Macon Telegraph*, 17 May 1914)
"If There Was No Liquor" (*Macon Telegraph*, 24 May 1914)
"The Rabbit Foot" (*Macon Telegraph*, 31 May 1914)
"Better Babies in Yamacraw" (*Macon Telegraph*, 7 June 1914)
"Hit Sho Is Hot!" (*Macon Telegraph*, 14 June 1914)
"Littlebit's Joy Ride" (*Macon Telegraph*, 21 June 1914)
"Grub and Grub-Time" (*Macon Telegraph*, 28, June 1914)
"Back to the Farm" (*Macon Telegraph*, 5 July 1914)
"An Angel—Good or Bad" (*Macon Telegraph*, 12 July 1914)
"The New Cook" (*Macon Telegraph*, 26 July 1914)
"Modern Marriages" (*Macon Telegraph*, 2 August 1914)
"Old Nig" (*Macon Telegraph*, 9 August 1914)
"Where Education Fails" (*Macon Telegraph*, 16 August 1914)
"The European War" (*Macon Telegraph*, 23 August 1914)
"Doing Away with Santa Claus" (*Macon Telegraph*, 30 August 1914)
"To Wear Cotton Goods" (*Macon Telegraph*, 6 September 1914)
"Labor Day in Yamacraw" (*Macon Telegraph*, 13 September 1914)
"Slowfoot Sal Learns the News" (*Macon Telegraph*, 20 September 1914)
"The Civil Service Commission" (*Macon Telegraph*, 27 September 1914)
"Poor Pay, Poor Preach" (*Macon Telegraph*, 4 October 1914)
"The Abolition of Cooks" (*Macon Telegraph*, 11 October 1914)
"The Go-to-Church Movement" (*Macon Telegraph*, 18 October 1914)
"What Is Loitering?" (*Macon Telegraph*, 25 October 1914)
"Yamacraw's Cotton Ball" (*Macon Telegraph*, 1 November 1914)
"How Susan Excused Herself" (*Macon Telegraph*, 8 November 1914)
"Yamacraw Bridal Shower" (*Macon Telegraph*, 15 November 1914)
"A Sermon on Charity" (*Macon Telegraph*, 22 November 1914)
"How to Take Up a Collection" (*Macon Telegraph*, 29 November 1914)
"Funerals and Weddings" (*Macon Telegraph*, 6 December 1914)
"Simple Gifts in Yamacraw" (*Macon Telegraph*, 13 December 1914)
"[For years and years...]" (*Macon Telegraph*, 20 December 1914)
"Compulsory Military Service" (*Macon Telegraph*, 27 December 1914)
"[Dawson was holding....]" (*Macon Telegraph*, 3 January 1915)
"The Loaded Grip" (*Macon Telegraph*, 10 January 1915)
"A Retarded Reformation" (*Macon Telegraph*, 17 January 1915)
"New Line of Cussin'" (*Macon Telegraph*, 24 January 1915)
"The Story of a Chicken Pie" (*Macon Telegraph*, 31 January 1915)
"A Sermon on Rain" (*Macon Telegraph*, 7 February 1915)
"You Can't Please Everybody" (*Macon Telegraph*, 14 February 1915)
"The Alabama Law" (*Macon Telegraph*, 21 February 1915)
"The Cause of Hard Times" (*Macon Telegraph*, 28 February 1915)
"When Sister Lou Kicked" (*Macon Telegraph*, 7 March 1915)
"Bundle Day in Yamacraw" (*Macon Telegraph*, 14 March 1915)
"Dandy and His Dad" (*Macon Telegraph*, 21 March 1915)
"Charity's Loss" (*Macon Telegraph*, 28 March 1915)
"The End of the War" (*Macon Telegraph*, 4 April 1915)
"Yamacraw's Queen O' May" (*Macon Telegraph*, 11 April 1915)
"Yamacraw Backyards" (*Macon Telegraph*, 18 April 1915)
"Mrs. Rockefeller's Millions" (*Macon Telegraph*, 25 April 1915)
"A Question of Weather" (*Macon Telegraph*, 2 May 1915)
"The Jitney Bus" (*Macon Telegraph*, 9 May 1915)
"The Sunday Closing Movement" (*Macon Telegraph*, 16 May 1915)
"The Melting Pot" (*Macon Telegraph*, 23 May 1915)
"A Chaw Er Terbacker" (*Macon Telegraph*, 30 May 1915)
"A Perplexing Question" (*Macon Telegraph*, 6 June 1915)
"In Ol' Virginny" (*Macon Telegraph*, 13 June 1915)

"The Color Line Above" (*Macon Telegraph*, 20 June 1915)
"Just a Miracle" (*Macon Telegraph*, 27 June 1915)
"The New Governor" (*Macon Telegraph*, 4 July 1915)
"Dropping Bombs" (*Macon Telegraph*, 11 July 1915)
"When the World Goes Dry" (*Macon Telegraph*, 18 July 1915)
"The Yamacraw Suffragist" (*Macon Telegraph*, 25 July 1915)
"The Story of the Rose" (*Macon Telegraph*, 1 August 1915)
"Delia the Doper" (*Macon Telegraph*, 8 August 1915)
"Seedin' de Speed Limit" (*Macon Telegraph*, 15 August 1915)
"Bob the Bobber" (*Macon Telegraph*, 22 August 1915)
"The Uncertain Son-in-Law" (*Macon Telegraph*, 29 August 1915)
"Up for Loitering" (*Macon Telegraph*, 5 September 1915)
"Gratitude with a Little G" (*Macon Telegraph*, 12 September 1915)
"The House Party" (*Macon Telegraph*, 19 September 1915)
"The One-Gallon Allowance" (*Macon Telegraph*, 26 September 1915)
"The Deadly Germ" (*Macon Telegraph*, 3 October 1915)
"Dress Up Week in Yamacraw" (*Macon Telegraph*, 10 October 1915)
"The 'Possum Trail" (*Macon Telegraph*, 17 October 1915)
"The Midnight Pass" (*Macon Telegraph*, 24 October 1915)
"A Yamacraw Sermon" (*Macon Telegraph*, 31 October 1915)
"Bad News for Yamacraw" (*Macon Telegraph*, 7 November 1915)
"The Land of Canaan" (*Macon Telegraph*, 14 November 1915)
"If She Had Her Way" (*Macon Telegraph*, 21 November 1915)
"Another Products Dinner" (*Macon Telegraph*, 28 November 1915)
"No End of Trouble" (*Macon Telegraph*, 5 December 1915)
"Babies" (*Macon Telegraph*, 12 December 1915)
"July—A Christmas Story" (*Macon Telegraph*, 19 December 1915)
"Abolishing the Market" (*Macon Telegraph*, 26 December 1915)
"New Year Resolutions" (*Macon Telegraph*, 2 January 1916)
"The President's Marriage" (*Macon Telegraph*, 9 January 1916)
"Mule Steak" (*Macon Telegraph*, 16 January 1916)
"Billie" (*Macon Telegraph*, 23 January 1916)
"A Pig in Court" (*Macon Telegraph*, 30 January 1916)
"Alimony" (*Macon Telegraph*, 6 February 1916)
"A Terrible Affliction" (*Macon Telegraph*, 13 February 1916)
"1916 Fashions" (*Macon Telegraph*, 20 February 1916)
"Disappointment" (*Macon Telegraph*, 27 February 1916)
"The Negro in the Movies" (*Macon Telegraph*, 5 March 1916)
"The Straw That Broke" (*Macon Telegraph*, 12 March 1916)
"The New Way" (*Macon Telegraph*, 19 March 1916)
"Teaching Dancing in Yamacraw" (*Macon Telegraph*, 26 March 1916)
"Back to the Farm" (*Macon Telegraph*, 2 April 1916)
"The Shadow in the Door" (*Macon Telegraph*, 9 April 1916)
"The Eye of the Needle" (*Macon Telegraph*, 16 April 1916)
"Slowfoot Sal's Return" (*Macon Telegraph*, 23 April 1916)
"Compulsory Education" (*Macon Telegraph*, 30 April 1916)
"A Sot Sermon" (*Macon Telegraph*, 7 May 1916)
"['Miss Calline...]" (*Macon Telegraph*, 14 May 1916)
"Thrift" (*Macon Telegraph*, 21 May 1916)
"The Anti-Tobacco Crusade" (*Macon Telegraph*, 28 May 1916)
"Joy Dreams" (*Macon Telegraph*, 4 June 1916)
"Sons-in-Law" (*Macon Telegraph*, 11 June 1916)
"June Brides" (*Macon Telegraph*, 18 June 1916)
"A Matter of Alimony" (*Macon Telegraph*, 25 June 1916)
"War" (*Macon Telegraph*, 2 July 1916)
"De Foter July" (*Macon Telegraph*, 9 July 1916)

"Growing Old" (*Macon Telegraph*, 16 July 1916)
"Henrietta's Complaint" (*Macon Telegraph*, 23 July 1916)
"As to Marriages" (*Macon Telegraph*, 30 July 1916)
"A Spell o' Sickness" (*Macon Telegraph*, 13 August 1916)
"Gossip of the Alley" (*Macon Telegraph*, 20 August 1916)
"In the Mayor's Office" (*Macon Telegraph*, 27 August 1916)
"In the Mayor's Office" (*Macon Telegraph*, 3 September 1916)
"In the Mayor's Office" (*Macon Telegraph*, 10 September 1916)
"In the Mayor's Office" (*Macon Telegraph*, 17 September 1916)
"Lady Lawyers" (*Macon Telegraph*, 24 September 1916)
"Watch Yer Step!" (*Macon Telegraph*, 1 October 1916)
"The Negro Exodus" (*Macon Telegraph*, 8 October 1916)
"A Yamacraw Mass Meeting" (*Macon Telegraph*, 15 October 1916)
"Othello's Occupation Gone" (*Macon Telegraph*, 22 October 1916)
"Discussing Politics" (*Macon Telegraph*, 29 October 1916)
"You Can't Always Tell" (*Macon Telegraph*, 5 November 1916)
"Does Prohibition Prohibit" (*Macon Telegraph*, 12 November 1916)
"The Prodigal's Return" (*Macon Telegraph*, 19 November 1916)
"Breakfast Table Talk" (*Macon Telegraph*, 26 November 1916)
"A Misplaced Switch" (*Macon Telegraph*, 3 December 1916)
"Expensive Eating" (*Macon Telegraph*, 10 December 1916)
"Chrismus Gif'" (*Macon Telegraph*, 17 December 1916)
"Old New Year' Days" (*Macon Telegraph*, 24 December 1916)
"The Story of a Benefit" (*Macon Telegraph*, 31 December 1916)
"On Baby Boulevard" (*Macon Telegraph*, 7 January 1917)
"If I Were King" (*Macon Telegraph*, 21 January 1917)
"This Wicked World" (*Macon Telegraph*, 28 January 1917)
"Dreams of Dryness" (*Macon Telegraph*, 4 February 1917)
"It Is to Dodge" (*Macon Telegraph*, 11 February 1917)
"Mullet, Mackerel and Molasses" (*Macon Telegraph*, 18 February 1917)
"A Night at Millie's" (*Macon Telegraph*, 25 February 1917)
"The Length of the Skirt" (*Macon Telegraph*, 4 March 1917)
"The Chocolate Chauffeur" (*Macon Telegraph*, 11 March 1917)
"In the Matter of Cooks" (*Macon Telegraph*, 18 March 1917)
"The Charity Society" (*Macon Telegraph*, 25 March 1917)
"A Burnin' Shame" (*Macon Telegraph*, 1 April 1917)
"Henrietta at the Phone" (*Macon Telegraph*, 8 April 1917)
"T'Other Side of the Mount'in" (*Macon Telegraph*, 15 April 1917)
"Pigs Is Pigs" (*Macon Telegraph*, 22 April 1917)
"The Five Foolish Virgins" (*Macon Telegraph*, 29 April 1917)
"Conscription" (*Macon Telegraph*, 6 May 1917)
"Henrietta's Prophecy" (*Macon Telegraph*, 13 May 1917)
"Dominicker Joe" (*Macon Telegraph*, 20 May 1917)
"The Hold-up" (*Macon Telegraph*, 27 May 1917)
"The Lil Cote" (*Macon Telegraph*, 3 June 1917)
"Henrietta's Dilemma" (*Macon Telegraph*, 10 June 1917)
"The Rotary Club" (*Macon Telegraph*, 17 June 1917)
"Did You Register?" (*Macon Telegraph*, 24 June 1917)
"A Summer Diet" (*Macon Telegraph*, 1 July 1917)
"Troubles of the Ice Man" (*Macon Telegraph*, 8 July 1917)
"Old Lice Ruminates" (*Macon Telegraph*, 15 July 1917)
"Henrietta's Surprise" (*Macon Telegraph*, 22 July 1917)
"Gossip of the Alley" (*Macon Telegraph*, 29 July 1917)
"The Aviators" (*Macon Telegraph*, 5 August 1917)
"The Cooks' Convention" (*Macon Telegraph*, 12 August 1917)
"A Sot Sarmon" (*Macon Telegraph*, 19 August 1917)

"What Shall We Eat?" (*Macon Telegraph*, 26 August 1917)
"Dr. Passmore Gives Up" (*Macon Telegraph*, 2 September 1917)
"Henrietta Is Worried" (*Macon Telegraph*, 9 September 1917)
"Maria's Birthday Party" (*Macon Telegraph*, 16 September 1917)
"Slowfoot Sal's Last Exploit" (*Macon Telegraph*, 23 September 1917)
"Wall-Eye Out of a Job" (*Macon Telegraph*, 30 September 1917)
"Old Hackman's Lament" (*Macon Telegraph*, 7 October 1917)
"Henrietta at the Circus" (*Macon Telegraph*, 14 October 1917)
"Things So Is Riz" (*Macon Telegraph*, 21 October 1917)
"The New Fall Fashions" (*Macon Telegraph*, 28 October 1917)
"Dark Red Cross" (*Macon Telegraph*, 4 November 1917)
"Wall-Eye Speeds Up" (*Macon Telegraph*, 11 November 1917)
"Slowfoot Sal's Disgust" (*Macon Telegraph*, 18 November 1917)
"Jay-Walking" (*Macon Telegraph*, 25 November 1917)
"Down at Shorty Sam's" (*Macon Telegraph*, 2 December 1917)
"The Charity Club" (*Macon Telegraph*, 9 December 1917)
"The Pan-Toters' Union" (*Macon Telegraph*, 16 December 1917)
"A Hooverized Supper" (*Macon Telegraph*, 23 December 1917)
"The Old New Year" (*Macon Telegraph*, 30 December 1917)
"The Passing of Dilsey" (*Macon Telegraph*, 6 January 1918)
"Henrietta Was Late" (*Macon Telegraph*, 13 January 1918)
"Precautionary Measures" (*Macon Telegraph*, 20 January 1918)
"Wussun Wusser" (*Macon Telegraph*, 27 January 1918)
"Henrietta's Husband" (*Macon Telegraph*, 3 February 1918)
"Freezing Him Out" (*Macon Telegraph*, 10 February 1918)
"Henrietta on the Fashions" (*Macon Telegraph*, 17 February 1918)
"Henrietta and the Children" (*Macon Telegraph*, 24 February 1918)
"The War Food Schedule" (*Macon Telegraph*, 3 March 1918)
"Littlebit's Revenge" (*Macon Telegraph*, 10 March 1918)
"A Mean Trick" (*Macon Telegraph*, 17 March 1918)
"Josephine's Luck" (*Macon Telegraph*, 24 March 1918)
"Up in the Air" (*Macon Telegraph*, 31 March 1918)
"The Ku Klux" (*Macon Telegraph*, 7 April 1918)
"War Bread and Gardens" (*Macon Telegraph*, 14 April 1918)
"Henrietta's Clock" (*Macon Telegraph*, 21 April 1918)
"Wall-Eye Returns" (*Macon Telegraph*, 28 April 1918)
"Henrietta Befuddled" (*Macon Telegraph*, 12 May 1918)
"A Yamacraw Reception" (*Macon Telegraph*, 19 May 1918)
"Emmeline's Brat" (*Macon Telegraph*, 26 May 1918)
"Work or Fight" (*Macon Telegraph*, 2 June 1918)
"Just Like a Woman" (*Macon Telegraph*, 9 June 1918)
"The Beauty Parlor" (*Macon Telegraph*, 16 June 1918)
"Henrietta Puzzles" (*Macon Telegraph*, 23 June 1918)
"Slowfoot Sal's Homecoming" (*Macon Telegraph*, 30 June 1918)
"Waffles" (*Macon Telegraph*, 7 July 1918)
"The Elevator Boy" (*Macon Telegraph*, 14 July 1918)
"Rents and Blue Laws" (*Macon Telegraph*, 21 July 1918)
"The Juvenile Court" (*Macon Telegraph*, 28 July 1918)
"The Burnin' Question" (*Macon Telegraph*, 11 August 1918)

BOOKS

(1) *100 Stories in Black: A Collection of Bright, Breezy, Humorous Stories of the Colored Race as Seen in the Sunny South* (1910, reprinted 1972)

SOURCES

"Afro-American Meeting," *Macon Telegraph*, 27 September 1900.

"Bridges Smith Is Judge of New Court," *Macon Telegraph*, 21 November 1917.
"Bridges Smith, Noted Georgia Journalist, Dies in Macon Sunday," *Thomasville Times-Enterprise*, 6 October 1930.
"Bridges Smith, Philosopher," *Augusta Chronicle*, 8 October 1930.
"'Clansman' Is Suppressed," *Macon Telegraph*, 26 September 1906.
"Darky Humor," *Macon Telegraph*, 11 August 1910.
"Dialect Stories," *Macon Telegraph*, 9 August 1910.
"Ex-Mayor Bridges Smith and Bride Honored in Savannah," *Macon Telegraph*, 19 April 1919.
"From the pages of history: Looking back at 185 years of the *Telegraph*," *Macon Telegraph*, 5 November 2011.
Georgia Equal Rights Convention Program, 1906. Special Collections and University Archives, University of Massachusetts Amherst Libraries.
"Home Talent and 'Dollie,'" *Macon Telegraph*, 19 February 1882.
"Is Now Mayor Smith," *Macon Telegraph*, 14 December 1899.
Manis, Andrew Michael. *Macon Black and White: An Unutterable Separation in the American Century*. Macon: Mercer University Press, 2004.
"Miss Goelz Bride of Judge Bridges Smith," *Macon Telegraph*, 11 April 1919.
"Mrs. Bridges Smith Dies of Apoplexy," *Macon Telegraph*, 27 December 1917.
"Negroes Are Here for Big Meeting," *Macon Telegraph*, 25 May 1917.
"Negroes Thank Mayor Smith," *Macon Telegraph*, 29 July 1907.
100 Stories in Black, review. *Macon Telegraph*, 8 July 1910.
100 Stories in Black, review. *Racine Daily Journal*, 6 July 1910.
"Only Taking a Needed Rest," *Macon Telegraph*, 2 June 1909.
"Prominent Macon Citizen Is Dead," *Augusta Chronicle*, 6 October 1930.
Smith, Bridges. "Capt. Simpson Tells About Negroes Who Went to War," *Macon Telegraph*, 27 November 1916.
_____. "Characteristic Little Letter from Joel Chandler Harris," *Macon Telegraph*, 6 July 1908.
_____. "Fish-Hooks and Chalk Used by Conductors in Old Days to Keep Tab on the Negroes," *Macon Telegraph*, 18 February 1917.
_____. "Mayor Casts Retrospective Mind's Eye Over the Macon of Fifty Years Ago," *Macon Telegraph*, 4 October 1914.
_____. "Old-Time Negro Sticks to Master of Secession Days," *Macon Telegraph*, 28 October 1917.
_____. "Old Versus the New Negroes Change with the Times, but Not for Better," *Macon Telegraph*, 23 March 1913.
_____. "Struck a Bonanza," *Hawaiian Gazette*, 16 May 1877.
"Stories in Black to Be Published in Book Form," *Macon Telegraph*, 22 August 1909.
Snow, Willie A. "Bridges Smith, After Fifty Years of Newspaper Work, Interviewed for First Time by Girl Reporter," *Macon Telegraph*, 9 October 1919.
"Son of Judge Smith Now with the Protectograph," *Macon Telegraph*, 26 April 1919.
"To Edit Macon History," *Macon Telegraph*, 20 July 1922.
"228 Children Are Taught to Do Right," *Macon Telegraph*, 26 October 1918.
"Unique Contribution to South's Literature," *Macon Telegraph*, 6 August 1910.
"Wins for Fifth Time in Very Hot Campaign," *Macon Telegraph*, 28 September 1913.

Harris Dickson
(1868–1946)
Ole Reliable

> Harris Dickson [is] perhaps the greatest living authority on negro dialect and the portrayal of negro character.—*Augusta Chronicle*[1]

Harris Dickson was born in Yazoo City, the son of Thomas H. and Harriet E. Hardenstein Dickson, and grew up in Mississippi. He studied at the University of Virginia in

1891. He learned shorthand and established a court-reporting firm. With proceeds from a particularly lengthy case, he traveled to see the Paris Exposition. When he returned, he became secretary to Congressman Andrew Price of Louisiana.

Dickson's first book, *The Black Wolf's Breed*, a romance of France during the reign of Louis XIV, came out in 1899. Three years later, his *The Siege of Lady Resolute* offered more scenes in historic France, and a few in North America. Other novels followed. One biographer said of his prose, "The word-painting of his Nature descriptions is of fine tone, original and rhythmical. His analytical arrangement of events is systematic and strong, while the burden of his narrative proper is carried along with a splendid swing."[2] This was before he turned to the light humor of his Ole Reliable stories.

While living in Washington, D.C., Dickson earned a law degree from Columbia University. He opened a practice in Vicksburg, Mississippi, where he became a municipal court judge in 1905, serving two years. In 1907, a year before he built a new home in which he would live the rest of his life,[3] he began submitting short stories to the *Saturday Evening Post*.

"He was at heart a belated Local Colorist with a natural gift for dialect and the creation of Negro character in the tradition of Irwin Russell and Joel Chandler Harris. 'Old Reliable' became a central figure in a number of his stories—easy going, jovial, and naturally lazy, but quick to take advantage of any situation that comes his way, with a member of his own race, the Colonel, or the visiting Yankee contractor.... Dickson loved and understood the intricacies of black and white relations in his day and falls easily into irony and humor, strangely lacking in his other work," according to Elmo Howell.[4]

The periodical published more than twenty tales featuring Ole Reliable, a black man of modest ambition. The stories were gathered in *Old Reliable* (1911), published by Bobbs-Merrill and illustrated by Emlen McConnell and H.T. Dunn.

The running character is a grey-haired, creaky villager named Zack Foster, once enslaved to Ole Judge Foster but now a free man. He went to war alongside Marse Robert, wearing a Confederate uniform. "We fit side by side. He jes' couldn't make me stay back in de camp." Only Zack came back. "Everybody, white an' black, calls me Old Reliable," he says. In the first story, he tells his wife, Selina, he can't cut firewood.

Harris Dickson wrote stories about Old Reliable for the *Saturday Evening Post* from 1910 to 1923.

"I got de rheumatiz."

"Rheumatiz!" the huge woman tightened the cord around her middle, like a warrior girding his loins. "Rheumatiz don't hinder you from eatin' up de vittle fast as I tote 'em from de white folks' house. Put on yo' clothes an' git dat az; I ain't gwine to leave dis house till I sees you started tode de ribber for dat driftwood.[5]

Zack aims for the river, but is waylaid when young Doctor Gray sets him to looking for a runaway roan. Then the maiden Trevelyan sisters, Savannah and Betsy, ask for help extracting the dog Edward from the cistern. Ole Reliable then agrees to become their gardener, and takes occupancy of the gardener's house that goes with it. A quarter for retrieving the doctor's horse, fifty cents for moving expenses, it's Zack's lucky day. Then he gets a job grading some land for the northerner, John Stampley. Pay is $4 for the use of Zack, two mules and a scraper. Except that Colonel Spottiswoode wants him to saddle his horse. The colonel needs a yard man. As if that isn't enough, Alec Brown and Nathan Hooter try to rope him into helping them pick cotton. For six weeks. When he returns home, naturally he hasn't cut any wood.

"I ain't had no time; I been too busy tendin' to white folks' bizness to cut wood fer wimmen."

"Git out o' here; you'se too busy to eat dinner wid wimmen."[6]

The Times-Picayune for February 8, 1923, carried this illustration of Salina berating Old Reliable, in a Harris Dickson short story, "Old Reliable Weathers a Storm and Enjoys His Breakfast."

A reviewer in the *Idaho Statesman* commented on Ole Reliable: "Zack is fond of proclaiming that he 'works kin and can't'—as soon as he can see and until he can see no longer—but as a matter of fact he only works when he must and when his vigorous wife, Aunt Selina, makes him. He is as untruthful as he is humorous, as dishonest as he is shiftless. And yet, in the end, Uncle Zack is made out something of a hero, though the glory wherewith he is clothed is worse than unearned."[7]

Dickson told a newspaper reporter his first Ole Reliable story was based on an experience in his household: "Our Old Reliable had been neglecting his work and we needed extra servants so I asked him if he knew of a couple that would be honest and reliable and he said he did, just the pair I needed. Olive and her husband Mathew. He stopped work at once and went out to engage the treasures and when by the following day he had not returned it was very inconvenient, my wife was young, inexperienced and all that. And, well it annoyed her greatly. So I went down to his house and saw his wife. Old Reliable was still away on his mission. 'Law,' said Betsy, 'you ain't aimin' to hire Olive! She's been gone away from dis town five years, an' Mathew, dey ain't nobody knows where he is!' So to clear the air at home I wrote the first Old Reliable."

Ole Reliable was "a mouthpiece for Dickson's satire of both whites and blacks."[8]

Edward C. Reilly found Dickson's humor comfortable: "In the first volume, one of the most entertaining episodes results when Reliable rescues a bulldog floating on a piece of driftwood in the Mississippi and which he names Drif. After much care and feeding, Drif becomes a vicious pit bull, and Old Reliable make easy money by traveling around matching Drif with other dogs. One day Drif is soundly beaten by a scraggly dog belonging to a traveling salesman and refuses to fight anymore."[9]

Dickson shaped his Zack material into a play. The Playhouse in Hudson, New York, mounted the production in 1914.[10] "Betty Spottiswoode, niece to Colonel Beverley Spottiswoode, fell in love with Murray Duncan, a young Mississippi planter who inherited many acres and a temper which is constantly getting him into trouble. Now, it would be quite impossible to write a story or a play about the Spottiswoode family without bringing in something about 'Old Reliable,' and it was just here that Mr. Dickson ran up against a difficulty. Try as he would he could not bring 'Old Reliable' on the stage without having him do what actor describe as 'hogging the scene.' No amount of remonstration would make 'Old Reliable' behave himself and, as usual, he won the point. The play was being written for presentation by Henry W. Savage and a consultation between Messsrs. Savage and Dickson resulted in the announcement that Willis P. Sweatman would be presented in the title role of the new play and that the play would be called 'Old Reliable,'"[11] according to a newspaper report.

The road show was in Hudson for a Wednesday. It was in Washington, D.C., that Saturday, at the Columbia.[12] Sweatman, by the way, "that well-known delineator of darky characters,"[13] played another black character from the *Post*, Irvin S. Cobb's Jeff Poindexter, on Broadway the next year. He was of African descent.

The second book, a 1920 novel published by Frederick A. Stokes & Co., took the black houseman and the colonel and his friend Lord Meadowcroft overseas to investigate the activities of the British Cotton Growers' Association. Zack nearly misses boarding the S.S. *Trojan* as *Old Reliable in Africa* opens:

> "'Cunnel,' [Zack] panted, 'I never stopped a minute, 'cept jes to git dis orange; whole bunch o' trunks got me blocked off. Reckon dey don't know I'm gwine over to larn dem niggers at Africky Landin.'"
> "'Get aboard, Zack!' the Colonel gave him a shove, 'unless you want to swim.'"[14]

"Jovial tales of the doings of an old school darky servant who goes to Africa with his Colonel. His adventures are as queer as they are funny," said a reviewer in *The Outlook*.[15]

Dickson had a system for writing his stories. "He uses a Dictaphone, probably because he has been accustomed to public speaking all his life. Into this he tells his story—to you, invisible reader. His stenographer transcribes it and brings him the copy. Then he goes at it hammer and tongs, or more delicately, by hand. Again and again he re-writes, revamps until to his fastidious sense the patient product is finished."[16]

He said he wrote in spurts. "Last week, I shut myself up for four days, and the result was one short story, two articles and a one-act play." "And you went in without an idea?" "I went in with nothing but ideas. But across the infinite, arid, acrid, sand-burned acre of my brain there may not come another idea for four years."[17]

Dickson circulated a dozen later Ole Reliable stories through the *Chicago Tribune*'s syndicate in 1923. Zack hadn't changed his ways any. In one story, for example, he hopes Selina will give him breakfast:

"What makes you hungry?" she whirled and glared. "Answer me dat. You's too lazy for yo' vittles to taste good. Po' ole fool, can't study nothin' 'cept dat Grand Lodge peerade. Now lissen to me, Zack Foster, next time I sees you gallivantin' round dese streets wid dem wuthles niggers, when you oughter be diggin' taters, I'm goin' to grease yo' head, pin yo' ears back, an' swaller you whole. Hear me?"

Could he have two bits? Zack asks.

"Two bits! Two bits! Didn't I give you two bits last week, den seed you nigh de Hot Cat Eatin' House, wid yo' hat cocked over yo' left ear, makin' eyes at dat yaller wench what jes got out o' jail?" Selina bounced up, and Zack ducked just in time to dodge a knockout.[18]

Dickson wrote other stories for the *Post*, as well as for *Metropolitan, Popular, Everybody's, Complete Stories, Ladies Home Journal* and *Red Book*. His play, *Nigger in the Woodpile*, without Zack Foster, had a brief run in Hartford, Connecticut's, Parson's Theatre in 1917.[19]

The author was a World War I correspondent for *Collier's* and a technical advisor to the Works Projects Administration in Mississippi. He wrote a series of stories about early New Orleans for *Collier's* in the 1930s. His nonfiction book, *The Story of King Cotton*, was published in 1937. The next year, *Collier's* serialized his novel, *Marse Jeff Davis*, in six parts.

Dickson married Madeleine Metcalf of Louisville, Kentucky, in 1906. They had two daughters. He died in Vicksburg in 1946.

Harris Dickson Notes

1. "A Successful Georgia Writer," 10 July 1931, 4.
2. Edwin Anderson Alderman, Joel Chandler Harris, eds., *Library of Southern Literature*, Vol. 3, 1387.
3. At 1306 Mulvihill St., Vicksburg, "Surrounded by a pasture and stables," according to Patti Carr Black and Marion Barnwell, *Touring Literary Mississippi*, 64–65.
4. *Mississippi Home-Places; Notes on Literature and History*, 243.
5. "The Job Hunter," *Saturday Evening Post*, 8 January 1910, 2.
6. Page 26.
7. 13 August 1911, 4.
8. "Harris Dickson—An Interview," *Times-Picayune*, 28 February 1915, 11.
9. *Lives of Mississippi Authors, 1917–1967*, 131.
10. Advertisement and "'Old Reliable' Wednesday Night, *Hudson Evening Register*, 3 January 1914, 4.
11. "'Old Reliable' Wednesday Night," *Hudson Evening Register*, 3 January 1914, 4.
12. "Columbia—'Old Reliable,'" *Washington Herald*, 8 January 1914, 9.
13. "Chicago News," *New York Clipper*, 4 April 1920, 18.
14. "The Ocean Gamblers," *Old Reliable in Africa*, 3.
15. "The New Books," 17 November 1920, 515.
16. "Harris Dickson—An Interview," op cit.
17. Ibid.
18. "Old Reliable Weathers a Storm and Enjoys His Breakfast," *Times-Picayune*, 8 July 1923, 4.
19. "Harris Dickson Play Produced," Biloxi, Miss., *Daily Herald*, 24 February 1917, 6.

Harris Dickson Selected Bibliography and Sources

OLE RELIABLE STORIES

"The Job Hunter" (*Saturday Evening Post*, 8 January 1910) as "A Busy Day" (1)
"With Luck Agin Him" (*Saturday Evening Post*, 2 April 1910) as "He Finds a Job—For Somebody Else" (1)
"The Drift of the Golden Dog" (*Saturday Evening Post*, 16 April 1910) (1)
"A Dead-Game Sport" (*Saturday Evening Post*, 11 June 1910) as "He Entertains an Angel and Catches the Devil" (1)
"Bogus Twenties" (*Saturday Evening Post*, 30 July 1910) as "He Helps a Worthy Young Man and Wins the Long-Distance Liar Medal" (1)
"The J'iner" (*Saturday Evening Post*, 10 September 1910) as "He J'ines the Army, J'ines the Jail and J'ines the Cotton Pickers" (1)
"The Cheerful Swearer" (*Saturday Evening Post*, 1 October 1910) as "He Plays a Lone Hand, Discards a Tan Overcoat and Draws a Frizzly Wig" (1)
"Elopement—Personally Conducted" (*Saturday Evening Post*, 22 October 1910) as "He Fills In and Has a New Wife Thrust Upon Him" (1)
"The Locked Door" (*Saturday Evening Post*, 17 December 1910) as "He Gets on the Good Side of the White Folks and the Bad Side of the Negroes" (1)
"When Luck Was with Him" (*Saturday Evening Post*, 24 December 1910) as "He Saves the Country and Reaps His Just Reward" (1)
"The Beast of Buckshot Ridge" (*Saturday Evening Post*, 6 May 1911) (1)
"The Crooked Deal" (*Saturday Evening Post*, 30 December 1911)
"The Capsule" (*Saturday Evening Post*, 16 March 1911)
"The Expected One" (*Saturday Evening Post*, 13 April 1912)
"The Prophet Who Slipped" (*Saturday Evening Post*, 18 May 1912)
"The Tricky Traders" (*Saturday Evening Post*, 27 July 1912)
"The Most Important Donkey" (*Saturday Evening Post*, 10 August 1912)
"The Colonel's Chance" (*Saturday Evening Post*, 7 September 1912)
"The Incendiary" (*Saturday Evening Post*, 5 October 1912)
"Suspicion" (*Saturday Evening Post*, 29 May 1915)
"The Truth and the Corpus Delicti" (*Saturday Evening Post*, 30 December 1916)
"Old Reliable and the Colonel Give Views on Beverages" (*Times-Picayune*, 6 May 1923)
"Old Reliable Negotiates for an Extravagant" (*Times-Picayune*, 13 May 1923)
"Old Reliable Gets Pestered with Kinfolks' Children" (*Times-Picayune*, 20 May 1923)
"Old Reliable Takes a Nip of Chicken Whiskey" (Portsmouth, Ohio, *Daily Times*, 23 May 1923) (*Times-Picayune*, 27 May 1923)
"Old Reliable Considers Po' White Trash" (*Times-Picayune*, 10 June 1923)
"Old Reliable Knocks Out the Darwinian Theory" (Portsmouth [Ohio] *Daily Times*, 8 June 1923) as "Old Reliable Discusses Darwin's Idea" (*Times-Picayune*, 17 June 1923)
"Old Reliable Secures a Tenant" (*Times-Picayune*, 24 June 1923)
"Old Reliable Takes Up Fat Reducing" (*Times-Picayune*, 1 July 1923)
"Old Reliable Weathers a Storm and Enjoys His Breakfast" (*Times-Picayune*, 8 July 1923)
"Old Reliable on Kinks and Curl Papers" (New Orleans *Times-Picayune*, 15 July 1923)
"Old Reliable on the Folly of Saving" (*Times-Picayune*, 22 July 1923)

BOOKS
(1) *Old Reliable* (1911)
(2) *Old Reliable in Africa* (1920)

PLAY
Old Reliable (1914) with Henry W. Savage

SOURCES
Alderman, Edwin Anderson, and Joel Chandler Harris, eds. *Library of Southern Literature*. New Orleans: Martin & Hoyt, 1907.

Black, Patti Carr, and Marion Barnwell. *Touring Literary Mississippi*. University Press of Mississippi, 2002.
"Chicago News," *New York Clipper*, 4 April 1920.
"Columbia—'Old Reliable,'" *Washington Herald*, 8 January 1914.
Dickson (Harris) Papers. Mississippi Department of Archives & History. http://mdah.state.ms.us/manuscripts/z0124.html (viewed 1 November 2012).
"Harris Dickson—An Interview," *Times-Picayune*, 28 February 1915.
"Harris Dickson Play Produced," Biloxi, Mississippi, *Daily Herald*, 24 February 1917.
"Harris Dickson, Southern Writer, Dies in Vicksburg," *Greenville Delta Democrat Times*, 18 March 1946.
Howell, Elmo. *Mississippi Home-Places; Notes on Literature and History*. Memphis: Howell, 1988.
Newman, Daisy. *The Negro in the Writings of Harris Dickson*. Master's thesis, George Peabody College for Teachers, August 1938.
Reilly, Edward C. "Harris Dickson," *Lives of Mississippi Authors, 1917–1967*, James B. Lloyd, ed. Oxford: University of Mississippi, 1981.
"Old Reliable Wednesday Night," *Hudson Evening Register*, 3 January 1914.
Old Reliable review, with Authors and Books. *Idaho Statesman*, 13 August 1911.
Old Reliable in Africa review. "The New Books," *The Outlook*, 17 November 1920.
Playhouse 1912 advertisement for *Old Reliable* play. *Hudson Evening Register*, 3 January 1914.
"Successful Georgia Writer," *Augusta Chronicle*, 10 July 1931.

Irvin S. Cobb
(1876–1944)
Jeff Poindexter

> I suppose I have been reading your stories ever since you have been writing for "The Saturday Evening Post." I am a colored man, born and reared and more or less educated in the South. I have also spent some time in the North in various capacities. I have had an opportunity to come in touch with all classes of people, white and colored, both North and South. I have known, in perhaps a half dozen different localities, a Judge Priest, a Jeff Poindexter and Aunt Sharley, and numerous others of your splendid characters. Anyone who reads your stories, if he has lived in the south, can realize that your characters are not creatures of your imagination alone but the portraits of persons to be found in every community. I read all of the so-called "negro" stories that come my way, and some of them really give me a pain on account of what the writers do not know about my people. Your writings show a wonderful knowledge of the people you write about.
>
> —W.R. Coles, Winston-Salem, N.C.[1]

Horse-faced, burly Irvin S. Cobb in his day was one of the most recognized authors in the United States because of his huge output, but also because of a modest career in motion pictures.

Irvin Shrewsbury Cobb was born in Paducah, Kentucky, in 1876, one of four children of Joshua Clark Cobb and Marie Saunders. The father, a Confederate Army veteran, was a tobacco trader, steamboat investor,[2] manager of a steamship supply store—and an alcoholic.[3] Irvin grew up at the end of the radical Reconstruction and the beginning of the Jim Crow laws that severely restricted individuals of African descent.

"In my youth, I was the younger Bohemian set of Paducah," he said.[4]

Paducah was to Cobb as Hannibal was to Mark Twain, in the view of biographer Wayne Chatterton: "Cobb lived so rich a childhood and was so profoundly affected by the people he knew and the things he did that in the years of his literary fame there was some speculation about the possibility of his being considered the legitimate successor to Mark Twain."⁵

Though he once aspired to enter the law, Irvin quit school at age sixteen to write for his hometown newspaper. He free-lanced comic essays to weeklies on the side. By age nineteen, he was editor of the *Paducah News*, but he quickly outgrew the position. After a tenure with the *Louisville Evening Post*, he sought employment in the North's largest city in 1904.

"A funny letter to all the New York editors of daily papers ended a long search for work by landing him a job on the *Evening Sun*. A break gave him a murder story that got him a better position on another paper, and a first-class job of reporting at the Russo-Japanese conference at Portsmouth, N.H., set him definitely on the way up in newspaperdom," summarized a writer in the *Dallas Morning News*.⁶

Cobb's Russo-Japanese conference reportage was widely syndicated and landed him a new job with Joseph Pulitzer's *New York World*.

Irvin S. Cobb's Jeff Poindexter started out as a secondary character in the Judge Priest stories, and graduated to his own 1922 novel.

Cobb later bemoaned not moving to New York sooner. "It is one place where you seem to get your real measure quick in contrast with a world market for literary work as well as pumpkins and potatoes," he told interviewer Joe Mitchell Chappel.⁷ At the time, Cobb lived at Rebel Ridge, on the Hudson River.

Cobb wrote more than 300 short stories (many for the *Saturday Evening Post*) and 60 books (*Cobb's Anatomy*, *A Laugh a Day Keeps the Doctor Away* and *Many Laughs for Many Days* among them). One of his last works, *Exit Laughing*, a biography by a writer on the wane, garnered glowing reviews.

Cobb became so famous that the Yorkana Cigar Co. of Pennsylvania put his face on boxes of its prime tobacco product in the 1920s.

The author considered himself firmly in the southern literary tradition. In compiling an imagined list of fictional dinner guests in 1924, he included Tristam Shandy, Ma Pettingill and Becky

Sharp, Robinson Crusoe and Huck Finn. And: "As a Southerner I'd want Uncle Remus. Naturally we might not want him as a guest since we still draw the color line in some respects. But at least he could wait on the table. He'd give a real American tone to the proceedings by reason of the fact that he is an authentic, black-skinned American and so utterly different from the average popular conception today of what a real negro is."[8] Cobb, it seems, wasn't prepared to wholeheartedly challenge that color line, even for a character created by a white author.

Newspaper trained, Cobb angled his talents to handle fiction. "I consider myself a reporter and stick to what seems to me to be reporting fiction," he said in the *Reno Evening Gazette* in 1912. "When I have a story in my mind I think it all out, what the people are, what they do, and where they do it, and then sit down at a typewriter and pound it out rapidly. Striking words from a typewriter is exactly like striking sparks from a flint of steel, and the high lights of ideas and impressions come out in the writing. It's reporting—that's what it is; it's newspaper rewrite work. I would not do it a bit differently, except in the 'intro.'"[9]

Cobb's southern local color fiction, laden with vernacular speech, was configured to paint a different portrait from the stereotypical bitter Kentucky colonel and downcast Lost Cause holdovers. It caught the attention of film director John Ford.

Cobb devised his fiction character Judge William Pitman Priest, who appeared in stories and even one detective novel, as a rustic sage, the epitome of a genteel southerner who holds a lingering yearning for the days before the Civil War. Some of the stories include a sidekick of sorts, a black servant named Jefferson Davis Poindexter. Poindexter affords humor to most of the stories he appears in, and takes center stage in his own novel, *J. Poindexter, Colored*.

At about the same time Judge Priest made his first appearance in print, Cobb made his first showing in the movies, taking small roles in John W. Noble's *Our Mutual Girl* (1914) and Cecil B. DeMille's *The Arab*. Cobb incorporated aspects of the world of movie studios in the novel *J. Poindexter, Colored*.

Cobb met *Saturday Evening Post* editor George Horace Lorimer and joined the weekly's staff in 1911, taking a number of overseas reportage assignments. *Cosmopolitan* editor Ray Long, and publisher William Randolph Hearst's deep pockets, brought Cobb to that magazine in 1924.

Cobb had already written a Judge Priest play in 1915, called *Back Home*.[10] Featuring John W. Cope as the judge and Willis P. Sweatman as Jeff, it closed in New York after two weeks. The next year, Cobb wrote another play, based on his first short story (non–Priest), *The Escape of Mr. Trimm*.[11] When another play, *Boys Will Be Boys*, came to the stage in 1921, Will Rogers appeared in the role of Peep O'Day.[12]

Cobb wrote movie scenarios and dialogue titles for silent films. John Ford directed two movies based on Cobb stories, *Judge Priest* (1934), starring Will Rogers, and *The Sun Shines Bright* (1953), featuring Charles Winninger. Cobb himself had a walk-on in the first film. But the writer died in 1944, nearly a decade before the second picture went into release. By that time, many of the values embraced in the characters and stories were being knocked head over heels by new legislation and Supreme Court decisions.

Cobb in 1934 signed a contract with Hal Roach Studios, not as a scenarist, but as an actor. He played a captain in *Steamboat Around the Bend* (1935). Cobb laughed off his new career: "Just the end of a misspent life, and an eagerness to try something new. I've been a war correspondent, a writer, a radio performer and pretty near everything but never an actor and I always like to try something once."[13]

Will Rogers latched onto Cobb's character Judge Priest, calling him "a grand old fellow and I am proud to play him."[14] The movie *Judge Priest* is jarring to view on YouTube today. In an opening courtroom scene, the condescending judge asks questions of a whiny coon character played by Stepin Fetchit (Lincoln Perry). Fetchit's Jeff is on trial for stealing chickens. As the prosecutor makes his case, the judge reads a newspaper and the defendant sleeps on the bench.

"Come here, boy," beckons the judge. "What's your name?"

"Jeff Poindexter."

The groveling black man says he was given his name by Major Randolph Poindexter of Pine Bluffs, a hero of Kennesaw Mountain. Or was it Chickamauga? Everyone in court is soon arguing and reminiscing about the heroics of Major Poindexter. The prosecutor objects. What's the defendant's answer to the charges? He says he was fishing. When Poindexter reveals he uses beef liver as bait to catch catfish in the Sleepy River, he has the judge's attention. The scene cuts to the judge and Jeff walking down a country road, fishing poles over their shoulders.

Judge Priest was based on real-life Kentucky people, Cobb told reporter Chapel in 1923, "a composite of a circuit judge I knew in Paducah, Judge Bishop, a little of my father and a little of other characters in old Kentucky. All just seem to naturally blend in my friend, Judge Priest, who is ever with me."[15]

William Sutton Bishop (1837–1902), a lawyer by training, a Confederate soldier by enlistment, a teacher by necessity and a court of common pleas judge by appointment in 1873, later served as circuit judge in Paducah, where he became good friends with Cobb.[16] Biographer Chatterton characterized the real judge as "an arbiter of legal entanglements, a confessor to the poor, and in times of trouble, a source of sympathy and homely wisdom."[17]

"There has not been so perfect a picture of the old Confederate as that presented in the person of Judge Priest," said a *Lexington Herald* reviewer of *Back Home*. "The name is significant. Judge, Priest and friend to all the people to whom he represented the controlling power of the universe, for in the smaller southern towns the

Irvin S. Cobb was a humor writer who became a film actor.

judge was a potentate indeed, his honor upheld by public confidence, that confidence inspired by his honor."[18]

Judge Priest had an interesting and subtle relationship with his houseman, Jeff Poindexter. From Cobb's perceptions of the complexities of whites and blacks in society together "comes the devotion that prevails indissolubly between Jeff Poindexter and Old Judge Priest," in Chatterton's view. "Out of this awareness come also the vivid tales that depict the precarious subtleties whereby Jeff and the other 'darkies' of the community manage their own affairs and whereby they keep their private things to themselves."[19]

Cobb's estimate of a world within a world, a black sphere within a white one, is not far afield from the assessment of civil justice activist W.E.B. Du Bois, who described the oppressive "veil" behind which blacks must live and function.[20]

The prolific Cobb had a sounding board for his writing. "He always talks over his story plots here at home," Laura Spencer Baker, who became Cobb's bride in 1900,[21] told an interviewer, "and usually the day before he begins to write a story he tells it to me from beginning to end. In this way he learns how the story will sound if read aloud."[22]

Mrs. Cobb said her husband never kept story notes more than a few key words, jotted in a red notebook. She said she "had never known him to write a story until he has worked it over in his mind for a couple of months or more. He tells her that he has always a hundred germs developing at a time, and that he will not live long enough to write all his stories."

And, "When he was writing 'The County Trot' Mrs. Cobb marveled at his lifelike pictures of the Kentucky characters, all of whom he had really known. She asked him how it was possible for him to remember their faces and mannerisms after a lapse of so many years. He said: 'Why, I can close my eyes and see the knotholes that were in the fence around that fairground.'"[23]

That story is a good candidate for a closer look.

Published in the *Saturday Evening Post* in 1911, the third Judge Priest story, it was collected in *Back Home*. It is Saturday, the last day of the county fair. Crowds order barbecue from Uncle Isom Woolfolk's kitchen, run by "two negro women of his household." It's the fair's busiest day, with scads of old Confederates and their wives and families on hand for the County Trot horse race. Contenders in the harness race include a small red gelding, Flitterfoot, the only local entry and at the bottom of the odds.

A small man makes a wager. "This intruder handled himself so deftly and so nimbly as not to jostle by one hair's breadth the dignity of any white gentleman there present, yet was steadily making progress all the while and in ample time getting down a certain sum of money on Flitterfoot to win at odds," we read.

"'Ain't that your nigger boy Jeff?' inquired Doctor Lake of Judge Priest, as the new comer, still boring deftly, emerged from the group and, with a last muttered 'Scuse me, boss—please, suh—scuse me!' darted away toward the head of the stretch, where others of his race were draping themselves over the top rail of the fence in black festoons.

"'Yes, I suppose 'tis—probably,' said Judge Priest in that high singsong of his. 'That black scoundrel of mine is liable to be everywhere—except when you want him, and the he's not anywhere. That must be Jeff, I reckin.' And the old judge chuckled indulgently in appreciation of Jeff's manifold talents."

Thus we are introduced to Poindexter, "a small, jet-black person, swift in his gait and wise in his generation. He kept his wool cropped close and made the part in it with a razor.

By some subtle art of his own he could fall heir to somebody else's old clothes and, wearing them make them look newer and better than when they were new."

At the fair, Jeff meanders to the stables in time to witness Van Wallace, owner of the mare Minnie May, and Jackson Berry, owner of Blandville Boy, go into a huddle in a feed shed. Jeff is curious and squats by the shed "on a pile of stable scrapings, where a swarm of flies flickered above an empty pint flask and watermelon rinds were curled up and drying in the sun like old shoesoles." Cobb's descriptions are masterful.

Jeff hears the rival horse owners hatch a plot. When they peer around to see if anyone is listening, he feigns sleep. "'Just some nigger full of gin that fell down there to sleep it off,' said Van Wallace. And he would have gone on; but Berry, who was a tall red-faced, horsy man—a blusterer on the surface and a born coward inside—booted the sleeper in the ribs with his toe.

"'Here, boy!' he commanded. 'Wake up here!' And he nudged him again hard.
"The negro only flinched from the kicks then rolled farther over on his side and mumbled through a snore.
"'Couldn't hear it thunder,' said Berry, reassured."

And they go on with their scheming to tilt the race away from the favorite and toward the horse with the best odds.

Jeff races to find Judge Priest, but first blurts his discovery to Captain Buck Owings. Jeff and Owings find the judge and tip the plot. The bookmaker is in on it, Jeff relates. It's too late to do much, the race bell is about to ring. Owings pleads for action. Most of the fair attendees have put their money on Minnie May. But the judge cautions against revealing the ruse after the race, when it might be seen in the wrong light.

"'Tryin' to declare the result off afterward wouldn't do much good. It would be—'" the judge said.
"'The word of three white men against a nigger—and nobody would believe the nigger,' added Captain Buck Owings, finishing the sentence for him."

In a remarkable orchestration, Priest directs Jeff and Captain Buck to station themselves one at the base of a tree, the other at a certain gate on the race course infield. On signal, the captain fires off an old musket he swiped from one of the visiting veterans. Jeff opens the gate, and the lead racer Berry's Blandville Boy takes a wrong turn. Wallace's Minnie May wins.

It's a Judge Priest signature. Things may not be done in precisely the right way. But they turn out right.

There was a third regular character in the Judge Priest stories, the housekeeper Aunt Dilsey Turner. She was based on Aunt Minerva Victoria Machem, who worked for the Cobb family, and confided in Cobb's mother (and not necessarily Cobb himself) some of the goings-on in the black community. Hattie McDaniel played Aunt Dilsey stereotypically but wonderfully in the movie *Judge Priest*.

A writer in the *Daily Herald* assessed Cobb's writing: "The keynote of his career like all of the literati has been hard work, an infinite capacity for taking pains. He is not satisfied with simply dashing off a story in a few minutes, but there is much painstaking thought behind his every work. This, too, is in line with the work of many of the world's great geniuses."[24]

As Cobb himself told the reporter, "I plug away at the machine about four hours a day. If I turn out 2,500 words in that time, I feel good about it. I can't dash off stuff. I guess the guys who talk about dashing off a masterpiece don't dash more than an inch at a time."

The reporter found Cobb's journalism background vital to his large output. Newspaper training "enables one trained to write until the cows come home about the simplest of things, provided space is one of the requisites required. Take an ordinarily trained newspaper writer and he could write three columns about a peanut, if needs be, which would be readable, too."[25]

Cobb transformed Priest's black houseman for the novel *J. Poindexter, Colored*. It was a rare Cobb attempt at a longer writing form (he did it again, less successfully, in *Judge Priest Turns Detective* in 1936). "I can't write a story more than 10,000 words in length. I suppose that is a part of the reporter in me, too," the author said in 1912.[26]

J. Poindexter, Colored opens with the main character's self-introduction: "My name is J. Poindexter. But the full name is Jefferson Exodus Poindexter, colored. But most always in general I has been known as Jeff, for short. The Jefferson part is for a white family which my folks worked for them one time before I was born, and the Exodus is because my mammy craved I should be named after somebody out of the Bible."

The judge has retired from the bench. He's annoyed that once in a while a Republican wins an election. He's decided Prohibition is too much, and at the invitation of a niece, moves to Bermuda, where he can drink to his heart's content. Poindexter agrees to look after the place in Kentucky, but the offer from dandy Dallas Pulliam of a trip to New York City to serve as his valet is too much to pass up. Particularly as Dallas Pulliam is generous in recycling his wardrobe.

> "And lessen twenty-four hours from that time we is both all packed up and on our way, New York bound, me wearing one of Mr. Dallas' suits of clothes which I figures he ain't had it on his back more than five or six times before altogether. It's a suit of a most pleasing pattern, too. And cut very stylish, with a belt in the back."

Cobb was bold in making Poindexter the main character of a novel. In 1922, he was the first of his reputation to do so. Bridges Smith's *Stories in Black* in 1910 had limited regional interest. Hugh Wiley's *Wildcat* beat Cobb by two years and E.K. Means's Skeeter Butts stories merited three collections starting in 1918. But none had Cobb's reputation, nor did Robert McBlair, whose *Mister Fish Kelly* would come out in a book 1924. Only Octavus Roy Cohen, who gave Epic Peters his own volume in 1930, enjoyed as wide a readership as Cobb.

In fact, it was Cobb's intention from the start of the Judge Priest series in 1911 to make Jeff the stronger character, saving the hides of the judge or other whites from seemingly inextricable situations. As biographer Chatterton explains, Judge Priest didn't want to play second fiddle. He emerged more and more as a full-blown, fascinating character to Cobb.

"I just couldn't keep that lazy nigger on the job," Cobb said inelegantly.[27]

"Negroes as heroes of novels are rare," the *Kansas City Star* said of *J. Poindexter, Colored*, published by the George H. Doran Company, "but Cobb's power of portrayal makes this one seem natural enough. He is made to display a native shrewdness and ingenuity, when confronted by strange conditions in new surroundings, that overcome many obstacles confronting his patron and employer, and that extricate the latter from the intrigues of the sharpers into whose hands he has fallen."

Poindexter, by the way, was based on another Paducah denizen, Connie Lee, a chiropodist.

Richard A. Lupoff was taken with *J. Poindexter, Colored*, saying Cobb "alone had the audacity and the astonishing courage for his time, to make the wealthy fool a white southerner and his far cleverer savior a black man. And while Jeff Poindexter speaks and writes in seemingly ignorant dialect, his thoughts are deep and moving."[28]

Cobb's feelings about race seem mixed. On the one hand, he railed against the Ku Klux Klan in a guest editorial in the *Paducah News-Democrat* in 1922. On the other hand, as related in Anita Dawson's biography of Cobb, he was reluctant to recommend that the publisher Doran accept a manuscript from Walter White, an NAACP staff member, that described the racial tribulations of a black physician, unless the violence was toned down.[29]

One thing Cobb was particular about was the matter of death. He wanted a burial with no mourning, no ceremony, per instructions left in a sealed envelope.

"In death I desire that no one shall look upon my face and once more I charge my family, as already and repeatedly I have done, that they shall put on none of the bogus habiliments of so-called mourning. Fields of black crepe never ministered to the memory of the departed, they only made the wearers unhappy and self-conscious."[30]

There's no humor in those directions.

Cobb's widow interred his ashes beneath a dogwood tree.[31]

Irvin S. Cobb Notes

1. Letter to Irvin S. Cobb, reprinted in Hilda Jackson's "Shop Talk," *New York Tribune*, 16 July 1922, 5.
2. Charles Kerr, *History of Kentucky*, v. 4, 497.
3. Wayne Chatterton, *Irvin S. Cobb*, 5.
4. "Irvin Cobb Writes New Comic Story About Kentucky Negroes," *Dallas Morning News*, 14 March 1935, 4.
5. *Irvin S. Cobb*, op cit, 4–5.
6. Ibid.
7. "Flashlights of Famous People: Face to Face with Irvin Cobb," *Portsmouth Herald*, 26 December 1923, 4.
8. Cobb, "Fiction Characters, Irvin Cobb's Week-End Guests," *San Antonio Express*, 24 February 1924, 15.
9. "Cobb Tells Secrets," 2 November 1912.
10. "Cobb Turns Dramatist," *Oregonian*, 4 July 1915, 9.
11. "Cobb Determined to Try Drama Again," *Duluth News-Tribune*, 27 August 1916, 6.
12. At the Theatre, *Olympia Record*, 28 May 1921, 8.
13. "Cobb Wants to Do Everything Just Once," *Springfield Sunday Union and Republican*, 13 May 1934, 39.
14. "Rogers in Irvin Cobb's Favorite Role Makes Bet Picture of Series," *Dallas Morning News*, 7 October 1934, 4:1.
15. "Flashlights of Famous People," op cit.
16. "History of Judge William S. Bishop…," Lexington Herald, 4 December 1921.
17. *Irvin S. Cobb*, op cit., 87.
18. "Current Book Review," 10 November 1912.
19. *Irvin S. Cobb*, op cit., 14.
20. *The Souls of Black Folk* (1903), chapter 1: "The Negro is a sort of seventh son, born with a veil,

and gifted with second sight in this American world, a world which yields him no true self-consciousness, but only lets him see himself through the revelation of the other world. It is a peculiar sensation, this double consciousness, this sense of always looking at one's self through the eyes of others."

21. They had one daughter, Elisabeth, who wrote *My Wayward Parent* about her father in 1945.
22. "Through Mrs. Cobb's Eyes," *Kansas City Star*, 5 October 1916.
23. Ibid.
24. "Literary Methods," 30 December 1914.
25. Ibid.
26. "Cobb Tells Secrets," op cit.
27. Sloane Gordon, *The Story of Irvin S. Cobb*, 279.
28. "Secret Feelings of Our Own."
29. H.L. Mencken, on the other hand, overtly opposed to southerners black and white, suggested the novel would be viable, and Knopf brought out the fire in the Flint in 1924, according to Dawson, *Irvin S. Cobb*, 179.
30. "Cobb Bequeaths Himself a Burial Without Mourning: No Tail-Coat and White Tie," Cleveland *Plain Dealer*, 11 March 1944, 3.
31. "Mrs. Cobb Covers Husband's Grave," *Augusta Chronicle*, 9 October 1944, 1. There's a marker in Oak Grove Cemetery in Paducah.
32. Charles E. Ford purchased screen rights to the Judge Priest property in 1940 and planned to make films starring Bob Burns, according to Richard E. Hays, "Along Film Row," 27.

Irvin S. Cobb Selected Bibliography and Sources

JUDGE PRIEST STORIES

Note: Jeff Poindexter is not a character in all of the stories.

"Judge Priest—Murder Witness" (*Saturday Evening Post*, 28 October 1911) as "Words and Music" (1) (12) (15) (*Saint Mystery Magazine,* January 1955) (32)
"A Judgment Comes to Daniel" (*Saturday Evening Post*, 11 November 1911) (1)
"The County Trot" (*Saturday Evening Post*, 9 December 1911) (1)
"The Mob from Massac" (*Saturday Evening Post*, 10 February 1912) (1) (14)
"Stratagem and Spoils" (*Saturday Evening Post*, 6 April 1912) (1)
"Ermine and Money" (*Saturday Evening Post*, 27 April 1912)
"When the Fighting Was Good" (*Saturday Evening Post,* 15 June 1912) (1)
"A Dogged Under Dog" (*Saturday Evening Post*, 3 August 1912) (1)
"Black and White" (*Saturday Evening Post*, 7 September 1912) (1)
"Five Hundred Dollars Reward" (*Saturday Evening Post*, 19 October 1912) (1) (*Argosy* UK, January 1929) (33)
"Up Clay Street" (1)
"To the Editor of the Sun" (2, 1913) as "The Thunder of Silence" (2, 1918) as "A Beautiful Evening" (3)
"Sergeant Jimmy Bagby's Fleet" (*Saturday Evening Post*, 4 October 1912) (3)
"Judge Priest Comes Back" (*Saturday Evening Post*, 7 August 1915) (3) (22)
"A Blending of the Parables" (*Saturday Evening Post*, 28 August 1915) (3)
"The Lord Provides" (*Saturday Evening Post*, 9 October 1915) (3)
"Last Charge of Forrest's Cavalry" (*Saturday Evening Post*, 13 November 1915) as "Forrest's Last Charge" (3)
"According to the Code" (*Saturday Evening Post*, 15 January 1916) (3)
"A Chapter from the Life of an Ant" (*Saturday Evening Post*, 11 March 1916) (3) (20)
"Double-Barreled Justice" (*Saturday Evening Post*, April 8, 1916) (3) (20)
"The Cure for Lonesomeness" (*Saturday Evening Post*, 4 November 1916) (4)
"Ex-Fightin' Billy" (*Pictorial Review*, June 1917) (4)
"Mr. Felsburg Gets Even" (4)
"Hark! From the Tombs" (4)
"A Kiss for Kindness" (4)
"Boys Will Be Boys" (*Saturday Evening Post*, 20 October 1917) (5) (6) (21) (*Argosy* UK, October 1938) (29) (30)

"The Ravelin' Wolf" (*Saturday Evening Post*, February 21, 1920) (8)
"The Cater-Cornered Sex" (*Saturday Evening Post*, September 24, 1921) (8)
"J. Poindexter, Colored" (serialized *Saturday Evening Post*, 10, 17 and 24 June and 1 July 1922) (7)
"—That Shall He Also Reap" (*Saturday Evening Post*, 15 July 1922) (9)
"Snake Doctor" (*Cosmopolitan*, November 1922) (9) (10) (13) (17) (25) (28) (31)
"One Block from Fifth Avenue" (*Cosmopolitan,* January 1923) (10) (*Golden Book Magazine*, May 1925) (*Argosy* UK, September 1927)
"The Last of the Bourbons" (11)
"Judge Priest's Funeral" (*Cosmopolitan*, June 1930)
"The Dark Horse" (*Cosmopolitan*, July 1930) (13) (16)
"Treeful of Hoot Owls" (*Cosmopolitan*, August 1930) (16)
April Fool (17)
"Great Day in the Morning" (*Cosmopolitan*, November 1930) (16)
"The King of the Liars" (16)
"Br'er Fox and the Briar Patch" (16)
"Ole Miss" (*Cosmopolitan*, December 1930) (16)
"The Sun Shines Bright" (*Cosmopolitan*, April 1921) (16)
"A Colonel of Kentucky" (*Cosmopolitan*, June 1931) (16) (18)
"Uncle Sam Collaborating" (16)
"Judge Priest Goes Fishing" (*Cosmopolitan*, August 1931)
"An Incident of the Noble Experiment" (*Cosmopolitan*, October 1931) (16)
"Aged Local Vets Hold Final Rally" (*Cosmopolitan*, November 1931) (16)
"Bird in the Hand" (*Cosmopolitan*, December 1931) (19) (23)
"Judge Priest Turns Detective" (serialized New York *Sunday News* beginning 23 August 1936) (*Oregonian* beginning 25 October 1937) (20)
"Judge Priest and the Widow" (*American Magazine*, August 1936) (*Saint Detective Magazine* UK, February 1959) as "The Widow Arrives" (*Saint Detective Magazine* Australia, December 1958)
"The Darkest Closet" (1936) (*Ellery Queen's Mystery Magazine,* February 1951) (34)

JUDGE PRIEST BOOKS

Note: Jeff Poindexter is not a character in all of the books.

(1) *Back Home, Being the Narrative of Judge Priest and His People* (1912)
(2) *The Escape of Mr. Trimm: His Plight and Other Plights* (1913/1918)
(3) *Old Judge Priest* (1916)
(4) *Those Times and These* (1917)
(5) *The Best Short Stories of 1917* (1918)
(6) *From Place to Place* (1920)
(7) *J. Poindexter, Colored* (1922)
(8) *Sundry Accounts* (1922)
(9) *O. Henry Memorial Prize Stories 1922* (1923)
(10) *Snake Doctor, and Other Stories* (1923)
(11) *Pros and Cons* (1926)
(12) *The World's 100 Best Short Stories, Vol. 8, Men*, Grant M. Overton, ed. (1927)
(13) *Modern American Short Stories*, Thomas R. Cook, ed. (1929)
(14) *Significant Contemporary Stories*, Edith Ronald Mirrieless, ed. (1929)
(15) *Stories of the Old South, Old and New* (1931)
(16) *Down Yonder with Judge Priest and Irvin S. Cobb* (1932)
(17) *20 Best Short Stories in Ray Long's 20 Years as an Editor*, Ray Long and R.R. Smith, eds. (1932)
(18) *O. Henry Memorial Prize Stories 1932*, Blanche Colton Williams, ed. (1933)
(19) *Faith, Hope and Charity* (1934)
(20) *Judge Priest Turns Detective* (1937)
(21) *50 Best American Short Stories 1915–1939*, Edward Joseph Harrington O'Brien, ed. (1939)
(22) *Favorite Humorous Stories of Irvin S. Cobb* (1941)
(23) *World's Great Mystery Stories; American and English Masterpieces*, Will Cuppy, ed. (1943)
(24) *World's Greatest Books* (1944) includes (3)
(25) *For Men Only: A Collection of Short Stories*, ed. James M. Cain (1944)

(26) *Cobb's Calvacade* (1945) includes (13)
(27) *The Best of Irvin S. Cobb* (1945) includes (3)
(28) *The Pocket Book of O. Henry Prize Stories*, Herschel Brickell, ed. (1947)
(29) *The Best American Short Stories, 1915–1950*, Martha Foley, ed. (1952)
(30) *Fiction Goes to Court: Favorite Stories of Lawyers and the Law Selected by Famous Lawyers*, Albert P. Blaustein, ed. (1954)
(31) *Treasury of Snake Lore*, Brandt Aymar, ed. (1956)
(32) *Favorite Trial Stories: Fact and Fiction*, A.K. Adams, ed. (1966)
(33) *Consider the Evidence: Stories of Mystery and Suspense*, Phyllis R. Fenner and Charles Geer, eds. (1973)
(34) *Masterpieces of Mystery: The Golden Age, Part 2*, Ellery Queen, ed. (1977)

FILMS

Boys Will Be Boys (1921)
Judge Priest (1934), based on "Words and Music"
The Sun Shines Bright (1953), based on the title story and "The Mob from Massac" and "The Lord Provides."[32]

PLAYS

Sergeant Jimmy Bagby (1913)
Back Home (1915)

RADIO

"A Bird in the Hand," episode of Mutual Network's *Murder Clinic*, 12 September 1943

TELEVISION

"Boys Will Be Boys," episode of *Kraft Television Theater*, 26 January 1955

SOURCES

"At the Theatre," *Olympia Record*, 28 May 1921.
"Back Home," Current Book Review, *Lexington Herald*, 10 November 1912.
Chapple, Joe Mitchell. "Flashlights of Famous People: Face to Face with Irvin Cobb," *Portsmouth (N.H.) Herald*, 28 December 1923.
Chatterton, Wayne. *Irvin S. Cobb*. Boston: Twayne, 1986.
"Cobb Bequeaths Himself a Burial Without Mourning; No Tail-Coat and White Tie," *Plain Dealer*, 11 March 1944.
"Cobb Determined to Try Drama Again," *Duluth News-Tribune*, 27 August 1916.
"Cobb Tells Secrets," *Reno Evening Gazette*, 2 November 1912.
"Cobb Turns Dramatist," *Oregonian*, 4 July 1915.
"Cobb Wants to Do Everything Just Once," *Springfield Sunday Union and Republican*, 13 May 1934.
Cobb, Elizabeth. *My Wayward Parent*. Bobbs-Merrill, 1945.
Cobb, Irvin S. *Exit Laughing*. Bobbs-Merrill, 1941.
Coles, Irvin S. Letter from W.R. Coles, Winston-Salem, N.C., reprinted in Hilda Jackson's Shop Talk, *New York Tribune*, 16 July 1922, 5.
"Fiction Characters, Irvin Cobb's Week-End Guests," *San Antonio Express*, 24 February 1924.
Hays, Richard E. "Along Film Row," *Seattle Daily Times*, 4 October 1940.
Gordon, Sloane. "The Story of Irvin S. Cobb," *Pearson's Magazine*, March 1915.
"History of Judge William S. Bishop; Who Was Irvin S. Cobb's 'Old Judge Priest,' Is Recalled in Paducah Newspaper Story," *Lexington Herald*, 4 December 1921.
"Irvin Cobb Writes New Comic Story About Kentucky Negroes," *Dallas Morning News*, 14 March 1935.
"Irvin Cobb's Address," *Macon Telegraph*, 26 July 1916.
"Irvin S. Cobb Is Guest of Crumit," *Springfield (Mass.) Republican*, 24 January 1933.
"Irvin S. Cobb Story Due on 'TV Theater,'" *Springfield (Mass.) Union*, 23 January 1955.
Kerr, Judge Charles. *History of Kentucky*. Vol. 4. Chicago: American Historical Society, 1922.
Lawson, Anita. *Irvin S. Cobb*. Bowling Green, OH: Bowling Green State University Popular Press, 1984.
"Literary Methods," *Biloxi Daily Herald*, 30 December 1914.
Logsden, Katherine. *Irvin S. Cobb and the Judge Priest Stories*. Bowling Green, Ky., 1936.

Lupoff, Richard A. "Secret Feelings of Our Own: An Introduction." http://www.ramblehouse.com/jpoindexterchapter.htm (viewed 19 September 2012).
"Mrs. Cobb Covers Husband's Grave," *Augusta Chronicle*, 9 October 1944.
"Rogers in Irvin Cobb's Favorite Role Makes Best Picture of Series," *Dallas Morning News*, 7 October 1934.
"Through Mrs. Cobb's Eyes," *Kansas City Star*, 5 October 1916.
Van Dover, J.K., and John F. Jebb. *Isn't Justice Always Unfair? The Detective in Southern Literature*. Bowling Green, OH: Bowling Green State University Popular Press, 1996.
"What Is New in Literature," *Morning Olympian*, 20 August 1922.

E.K. (Eldred Kurtz) Means
(1878–1957)
Skeeter Butts and "Tickfall"

Surely these chronicles of Tickfall, of Skeeter Butts and Vinegar Atts and their contemporaries, became classic in the very moment of their inception. Portrayals of postbellum negro life in the South we have had galore, good, bad and indifferent. But these sketches are something more. They are the actual life itself. You can hear the darkeys sing and laugh and sometimes weep. You can see their faces and their actions as clearly as though you were at the door of the Shoo Fly Church or the Hen Scratch saloon.

—Book reviewer, *New York Tribune*[1]

E.K. Means didn't leave much of a biographical trail.

Born Eldred Kurtz Means in Taylor, Kentucky, in 1878, he was the son of George H. Means and Teresa Virginia Lively. He married Ella Q. Crebbin in Monroe, Louisiana. And he wrote short stories with black characters for *All-Story Weekly* and other Frank A. Munsey pulp magazines.

Maine-born Munsey (1854–1925) published *The Golden Argosy*, later called *The Argosy*, for younger readers beginning in 1882. He rethought the title in 1896, and began to feature short and serialized longer fiction for an adult audience. Munsey also published *All-Story Magazine* (which carried early Edgar Rice Burroughs and Max Brand), later to merge with sister publications to become *All-Story Cavalier* (1914), then *All-Story Weekly* (1916), then *Argosy and Railroad Man's Magazine*, then *Argosy All-Story Weekly* (1920). After a while, it was called simply *Argosy* again, and was published until 1978, by which time it concentrated on male-oriented nonfiction.

Munsey in 1905 printed his magazines on high-speed presses using roll-fed newsprint, or pulpwood paper. The affordably priced magazines found a mass audience. Heavier stock glossy-paper covers had lavish full-color illustrations. Competitors such as Street & Smith (*Popular*) and Story Press (*Red Book* and *Blue Book*) quickly entered the same field.

Pulps had a voracious appetite for stories. Among thousands of writers was E.K. Means.

In discussing his favorite stories, humorist Irvin S. Cobb in 1924 selected Means's "darky stories," and told newspaper readers the author "is at his home in Jackson, Miss., the Rev. E.K. Means, pastor of Galloway Memorial M.E. Church, South. He is a zealous clergyman, a gifted speaker and a fluent writer, but being, as befits a clergyman, a truthful man also, Mr. Means would be the last to lay claim to great personal beauty."[2]

Means also served the pulpits of the Erlanger Methodist Episcopal Church, South, in Kentucky, and the Travis Street Methodist Church of Sherman, Mississippi.

For his Munsey stories Means developed a broad cast of fictional characters who lived in an area of Louisiana he called Tickfall. Skeeter Butts, proprietor of the Hen-Scratch Saloon, shows up the most often, but we see a lot of the Rev. Vinegar Atts, who is "pasture" of Shoofly Church; Hitch Diamond, a boxer; Figger Bush and Mustard Prophet, all black. Among white characters are Sheriff John Flournoy, Doctor Moseley and Colonel Tom Gaitskill, the generally benevolent owner of a plantation.

The first Tickfall story, "Gabe Shrunk, Hog Thief," appeared in *Cavalier's* 14 June 1913 issue. There were nine more stories in that magazine before it changed its name to *All-Story Cavalier*, for which Means wrote three Tickfall stories. Stories also appeared in *All-Story Weekly*, which became *Argosy All-Story Weekly*. But Means's longest association was with *Munsey's*, from 1919 to 1929. The last story was "A Tickfall Hero" for the October 1929 issue.

Supremely egotistic? Or was he really that well known? Eldred Kurtz Means did not title his three books of black stories issued from 1919 to 1921, he only gave his byline.

The stories were collected in three G.P. Putnam's books with improbable titles. Actually, they had no titles. The first, in 1918, bore only the words *E.K. Means* and the depiction of Skeeter Butts on the front cover. On the title page it said, "Is this a title? It is not. It is the name of a writer of negro stories, who has made himself so completely the writer of negro stories that his book needs no title."

In a foreword, Means said the stories "were written simply because of my interest in the stories themselves and because of a whimsical fondness for the people of that Race to whom god has given two supreme gifts,—Music and Laughter.

"For the benefit of the curious, I may say that many of the incidents of these tales are true and many of the characters and places mentioned actually exist.

"The Hen-Scratch saloon derived its name from the fact that many of its colored habitués played 'craps' on the ground under the chinaberry trees until the soil was marked by their scratching finger-nails like a chicken-yard."

Means said he used real names of black settlements, such as Dirty-Six, Hell's-Half-Acre, Shiny and Tinrow.

He said Skeeter Butts's real name was Perique, and that he acquired the name Butts for his small stature. That is, butt rather than a full cigar. Pastor Atts, who wore a Prince Albert coat and stove-pipe hat, was, Means purported, based on a real preacher in northern Louisiana.

While many of his black characters can read, their language—and it may have basis as dialect—keeps them apart from the whites.

Readers of *All-Story Weekly* found his stories amusing, Means said in his introduction, "Nevertheless, I hold that a story containing dialect must necessarily have many depressing and melancholy features. But dialect does not consist of perverted pronunciations and phonetic orthography. True dialect is a picture in cold type of the manifold peculiarities of the mind and temperament. In its form, I have attempted to give merely a *flavor* of the negro dialect by making these stories contain a true idea of the negro's shrewd observations, curious retorts, quaint comments, humorous philosophy, and his unique point of view on everything that comes to his attention."

He further justified his stories as preserving a way of life about to vanish. All that said, he was liberal in his writings in describing his black characters in the most grotesque, sensational ways, even as he might ultimately be sympathetic to their plights. His solicitude came through in curious ways.

Although she ultimately becomes a most sympathetic person, the black giantess in "Diada, Daughter of Discord" (*All-Story Weekly*, 4 September 1915) is given remarkably rude treatment: "Her head was covered with a mat of coarse hair growing down on a sloping forehead almost to her eyebrows; her eyes were immensely large and protruding, and had the wolf's vicious glint and surly shifting glance; her nose was no longer adorned, according to the custom of her native land, by having long thorns and splinters of bone thrust through it, but it had suffered grievously from this devotion to fashion, and was now a battered daub of a snout which looked as though it had been run through a sausage-grinder before it was smeared on her face; her ears had been so deformed by carrying heavy iron rings that the lobes hung down nearly to her shoulders and flapped at every motion of her head like the loose-hung ears of the hound; and her mouth was a cavernous monstrosity—great, horrid, horse-like teeth protruding outward, and covered with thick, repulsive lips which curled back when she spoke or grinned until the blue gums of the upper teeth were revealed."

Diada was a black woman rescued from certain death at the hands of Pacific Ocean cannibals by plantation owner Gaitskill's friend Captain Lemuel Manse, who brought her to Louisiana for her own safety. Manse had an errand to do in further up the Mississippi River. Could Gaitskill watch her for a couple of weeks?

"If the Christian missionaries in the Pacific Islands are engaged in saving the immortal souls of she-baboons like that,' Gaitskill snorted, pointing to Diada, 'I'll never give 'em another cent—not a dang cent!'

"Diada was made in the image of God, Tom,' Manse snickered."

Gaitskill reluctantly takes responsibility for the native woman, handing her care to his employee Hitch Diamond and his wife Hopey. There ensue a series of misadventures as the Louisiana blacks are unable to communicate with the curious, light-fingered, wandering woman. In the culmination, Gaitskill sends for Manse to come back immediately. Sheriff Flournoy and a posse are in hot pursuit of Diada, who keeps intoning something that sounds like "Whoosh!"

It isn't "whoosh," Manse explains at the last. She was saying "Whu atch," which, the captain explained, translated as "Help! I am in trouble!"

A reviewer for the *Duluth News Tribune* said of the first book, "The negroes of this volume as the author points out are the sons of the old slaves, a passing type also for 'Ethiopia is stretching out her hands after art, science, literature and wealth and when the sable sons of laughter and song grasp these treasures, all that remains of the southern village negro of today will be a few faint sketches in fiction's beautiful temple of dreams.'

Specifically, the reviewer said Means in his eight stories "has preserved for future generations much of the quaint humor, the shrewd observations, the superstitious philosophy of the American negro. In keeping with the text are the excellent illustrations by [Edward Windsor] Kemble."[3]

Excellent perhaps in some eyes, and yes, relatively realistic, but certainly sensational.

Means ran the same foreword in *More E.K. Means* ("Is this a title? It is not. It is the name of a writer of negro stories, who has made himself so completely the writer of negro stories that this second book, like the first, needs no title") in 1919.

Means is blunt in his depictions of blacks, and remindful of their social obligations.

"Sugar Sibley, the dusky belle of the Tickfall Parish Fair, sat in the Jim Crow section of the grand stand, clothed in all the colors of the rainbow, posing with all the indolence and insolence of an African princess lavishing her charms upon the yellow-faced barkeeper of the Hen-Scratch saloon," we read in "Owner of Doodle-bug" (*More E.K. Means*).

"'Whut hoss we gwine bet on next, Skeeter?' she inquired.

"'Dunno,' Skeeter answered anxiously. 'I hopes it'll be a winner.'"

Men are no less objects of Means' mean assessments. We read in "The Gift of Power" (*More E.K. Means*):

"At the end of the table sat the Reverend Tucky Chew Sipe, a tall, black, think-faced, ladder-headed negro, whose clothes were so loud that they proclaimed the man a block and a half away."

In the same story, Vinegar Atts "sat in the shade of a chinaberry tree in the rear of the Hen-Scratch saloon, his gorilla-like hands nursing his fat knees, his fat stomach resting upon his lap, his moonlike baby face twisted into countless wrinkles as if he were just turning up to cry."

Atts is at a loss to retain his pastorate at the Shoofly Church. The elders want to replace him. Until Atts orchestrates a remarkable séance. How did he manipulate the séance? Thanks to a few tricks he learned from Marse Gaitskill and Captain Manse, Atts confides to Skeeter Butts. Descriptions and characterizations and superstitions aside, it's a typical comeuppance story of the time period.

A *San Jose Mercury News* reviewer gushed over the second book: "The negroes whose language and peculiarities are described in 'More' are not the negroes of the old plantation life in the south before the Civil War, but the children of the old slaves. Those who echoed their owner's prejudice of caste and pride of family have been succeeded by others who reflect many changes of character, mind and temperament which have taken place in the last half century, through the influence of freedom and education."[4]

Yes, some of Means's black characters can read and hold regular jobs. They also call Gaitskill "Marse Tom" and Flournoy "Marse Flournoy," and keep their distance from white doings. Nevertheless, there can be testy moments, as in the previously mentioned Diada story, when the entire black community assembles. Means writes:

> The negroes of Tickfall and the neighboring plantations outnumbered the whites by ten thousand. Having a natural respect and generally a true friendship for the white people, following the peaceable pursuits of agriculture, raising cotton, cotton, and then more cotton; music-loving, laughter-loving, care-free as children and inoffensive as a bird, the negroes of Tickfall lived quietly with their white neighbors and employers.
>
> But any unusual movement among them always awakened the white man's suspicions and brought him forth full-armed, grim as death, white-faced and keen-eyed, to search the matter to the very bottom.

Well, that's frank. There's more:

> "'Thunderation!' Gaitskill bawled in a mighty voice. 'What's the matter with you damnation niggers?'"

Yes, there's a status quo, but Gaitskill runs things.

Surely Means's stories appealed to a southern white audience, as the relationship between Marse Gaitskill and the single-generation-freed blacks was alien to northerners.

There's probably truth to the lack of interest of blacks, come cotton-picking time. Witness this rude exchange:

"'What are you doing here, nigger?' Colonel Tom Gaitskill's voice cracked like a whip beside the ear of Pap Curtain," we read in "The Art of Enticing Labor" (*All-Story Weekly*, 18 September 1915).

> The challenge startled Curtain. "'Fer Gawd's sake, Marse Tom,' he chattered, speaking under a visible strain, his eyeballs nearly popping out of his head. 'I shore didn't soupspicion dat you wus snoopin' aroun' here nowheres.'
>
> "Gaitskill's face grew red with annoyance. The veins in his neck swelled and his eyes snapped.
>
> "'Where are all those other coons?' he demanded. 'Did they run off too?'
>
> "'Yes, suh; dey said dar wus plenty time to pick dat cotton an' de trouts wus bitin' fine down in de bayou, so dey all hauled off and went fishin'....'"

A *Dallas Morning News* reviewer said Means was not as skilled a writer as Joel Chandler Harris or Thomas Nelson Page, yet their characters "belong in the past. E.K. Means is perhaps the only living writer who really knows the life of the typical Southern negro of today. The average negro of today is no more like his ancestor of the days of slavery than the modern merchant is like the old Southern gentleman. All this Mr. Means thoroughly understands. His negroes have not the conventional earmarks that we all know; they are real."[5]

The writer went on, "The adventures which they experience recall the rogue stories that were popular in the days of Henry Fielding and Daniel Defoe. No one else seems to have undertaken to describe this phase of the life of the free negro, who has never been a popular subject in fiction."

Critic Gene Andrew Jarrett didn't hesitate to lump Means with Thomas Dixon—who seems to be in a category by himself when it comes to incitefulness and fearmongering:

"The black characters found in the novels of Thomas Dixon elicited anxiety from white readers over the perceived insolence of postbellum blacks toward white superiority. Eldred Kurtz (E.K.) Means's short stories also sought to amuse readers within the grotesque and comic traditions of blackface minstrelsy."[6]

The concluding volume was *Further E. K. Means (Is this a title? It is not. It is the name of a writer of Negro Stories, Who Has Made Himself So Completely the Writer of Negro Stories That This Third Like the First and Second, Needs No Title")* in 1921.

A reviewer in the Portland *Oregonian* called Means one of the more entertaining of writers of black characters. He said of *Further*, "In these seven tales, we are treated to amazing, laughable and pathetic pictures of the Louisiana negroes, written by a kindly author who knows these colored citizens apparently as intimately as they know themselves. He is a clever master of negro dialect."[7]

Finally, a *New York Times* reviewer said of the book, "The crass lack of good taste, and worse than crass conceit shown by the title of this volume, are not-redeemed by any remarkable quality in its content."[8]

The reviewer continued, "The opening tale of the new volume, 'The Left Hind Foot,' is concerned with the adventures of a small colored boy known as Little Bit, his white chum, Orren Randolph Gaitskill, generally called Orrie, an alligator, a mule, a rabbit's foot mounted in silver and the guardian thereof, one Mustard Prophet. How all these and a number of other persons became mixed together in a manner which produced great excitement in Tickfall and eventually brought about a most desirable wedding the story tells at excessively great length."

Means in this short story, originally in *All-Story Weekly* for 17 January 1920, tries his best to put forth sympathetic child characters, one white, one black. Ultimately, the tale about a missing rabbit's foot good-luck piece becomes convoluted; one roots for the rampant alligator.

Orren Gaitskill, called Orrie, has come to Tickfall from California. He's never experienced black folk before.

"'I never saw many colored persons in my life,' Orrie explained.

"'You ain't had no eyes ef you ain't seed no niggers,' Little Bit chuckled. 'Niggers is eve'y whar. Gawd made 'em in de night, made 'em in a hurry an' fergot to make 'em white. Dar's niggers in heaven, an' dars even plenty niggers in hell.'"

If that revelation of creation isn't distasteful enough, Orrie goes into a panic when he and Little Bit go skinny dipping—and Orrie realizes black kids have black skin over their whole bodies, not just on their heads.

Jim Crow is very evident in the stories. A white man, for instance, asks for a drink in the Hen-Scratch Saloon in "The Ten-Share Horse" (*Munsey's*, May 1920).

> "'Us ain't sellin' no drinks to white men, boss,'" Skeeter Butts tells him. "'enduring' of de barroom time, it wusn't allowed. De law made us hab sep'rate barrooms fer de whites an' blacks. Dar ain't no saloons no mo', but—'"
>
> The white man, Dick Nuhat, claims poverty. "'I'm worse off than a nigger... More is expected of my race than yours.'
>
> "'Dat's right,' Skeeter agreed. 'Dey lets us blacks down easy; but neither de whites nor de blacks is up to expectations.'"

The blacks don't always come out on the bottom. For example, little does Marse Tom know that when he's away, Hopey and Mustard Prophet entertain other blacks in the big house, as we see in "The 'Fraid Cat" (*Further E.K. Means*).

Means can be playful in his stories, and nearly entertaining but for the racism. As did Joel Chandler Harris, Means justified his depictions on the rapid disappearance of "authentic" blacks. "The central trope of the movement, the 'disappearing Negro,' was serviceable on several levels," pointed out Michael North. "It functioned as wish fulfillment, revealing the barely submerged hope that the freed slave would simply die off. It served as a metaphor of the temporal reversal of the post–Reconstruction period, taking readers imaginatively back in time as the south was being taken politically back in time. And it fed nostalgia for a time when racial relationships had been simple and happy, at least for white, suggesting that they might be simple and happy again if southern white were simply left alone to resolve things themselves."[9]

A 1931 novel by Means, *Black Fortune*, also featured a Gaitskill and had a Tickfall setting, though none of the other regular characters appeared.

The last thing we know about Means is he died in 1957.

E. K. Means Notes

1. "The Iliad of Tickfall," *New York Tribune*, 13 July 1918, 5.
2. "My Favorite Stories," *Fort Worth Star-Telegram*, 24 October 1924.
3. 25 January 1920, 9.
4. 8 June 1919, 8.
5. 26 October 1919, 6.
6. *Deans and Truants: Race and Realism in African American Literature*, 77.
7. Review of *Further*, 20 February 1921, 3.
8. 8 February 1921.
9. *The Dialect of Modernism: Race, Language and Twentieth-Century Literature*, 22.

E. K. Means Selected Bibliography and Sources

SKEETER BUTTS STORIES

"Gabe Shrunk, Hog Thief" (*Cavalier*, 14 June 1913)
"Itching for Bear Meat" (*Cavalier*, 5 July 1913)
"Two Gentlemen of Good Fortune" (*Cavalier*, 9 August 1913)
"Ricky-shay-boom-da-ay" (*Cavalier*, 13 September 1913)
"A Matrimony Sign" (*Cavalier*, 4 October 1913)
"A Gentleman of the New South" (*Cavalier*, 1 November 1913)
"Acting Brave" (*Cavalier*, 29 November 1913)
"Courting Goldie Curtain" (*Cavalier*, 3 January 1914)
"Trying Out Vinegar Atts" (*Cavalier*, 24 January 1914)
"In Search of a Wife" (*Cavalier*, 2 May 1914)
"One Rosy Day for Rosie" (*All-Story Cavalier Weekly*, 12 September 1914)
"Luck in Old Clothes" (*All-Story Cavalier Weekly*, 3 October 1914)
"Very Raw Recruits" (*Munsey's*, November 1914)
"Courting a Highbrow" (*All-Story Cavalier Weekly*, 12 December 1914)
"A Matrimonial Mishap" (*Munsey's*, January 1915)
"Diada, Daughter of Discord" (*All-Story Weekly*, 4 September 1915) (2)
"The Art of Enticing Labor" (*All-Story Weekly*, 18 September 1915) (1)
"A Mascot Jinx" (*All-Story Weekly*, 30 October 1915) (2)
"The Love Scrape" (*All-Story Weekly*, 29 January 1916)

"Every Pose a Picture" (*All-Story Weekly*, 29 April 1916) (2)
"The Lucky Number" (*All-Story Weekly*, 26 August 1916)
"The Squeeze Wheel" (*All-Story Weekly*, 5, 12, 19 May 1917)
"Snapshots" (*All-Story Weekly*, 15 September 1917)
"The Girls He Left Behind Him" (*All-Story Weekly*, 18 August 1917)
"Light-Foot Lady" (*All-Story Weekly*, 5 January 1918)
"D.D." (*All-Story Weekly*, 9 February 1918) (2)
"The Tombstone Test" (*All-Story Weekly*, 22 June 1918)
"The Best Policy" (*All-Story Weekly*, 13 July 1918)
"The Late Figger Bush" (1)
"Hoodoo Eyes" (1)
"The Cruise of the Mud Hen" (1)
"Two Sorry Sons of Sorrow" (1)
"Monarch of the Manacle" (1)
"All Is Fair" (1)
"Hoodoo Face" (1)
"The Consolation Prize" (*All-Story Weekly*, 22 February 1919) (3)
"Rebellion" (*All-Story Weekly*, 20 September 1919)
"A Chariot of Fire" (*All-Story Weekly*, 1 November 1919) (3)
"Getting Ready to Die" (2)
"Messing with Matrimony" (2)
"A Corner in Pickaninnies" (2)
"Idle Dreams" (2)
"The Gift of Power" (2)
"Owner of Doodle-Bug" (2)
"Family Ties" (*Munsey's*, September 1919) (3)
"The Left Hind Foot" (*All-Story Weekly*, 17 January 1920) (3)
"The Ten-Share Horse" (*Munsey's*, May 1920) (3)
"Keeper of the Grave Clothes" (*All-Story Weekly*, 15 May 1920)
"Prize-Money" (*All-Story Weekly*, 26 June 1920)
"Proof of Holy Writ" (*Munsey's*, September 1920)
"A Head for Business" (*Munsey's*, November 1920)
"Who's Who and Why" (*Munsey's*, February 1921)
"Poisoned Pugilism" (*Munsey's*, June 1921)
"The Hoodoo Sermon Text" (*Munsey's,* October 1921)
"The 'Fraid Cat" (3)
"The Trouble Scooter" (*Munsey's*, March 1922)
"Rags" (*Argosy All-Story Weekly*, 4 July 1920)
"First Aid for Skeeter Butts" (*Argosy All-Story Weekly*, 12 December 1925)
"A Dress Affair" (*Munsey's*, December 1925)
"In Memory of the Past" (*Munsey's*, February 1926)
"The Inevitable Answer" (*Munsey's*, March 1926)
"The Gospel Wagon" (*Munsey's*, April 1926)
"That Old Southern Feeling" (*Argosy All-Story Weekly*, 17 April 1926)
"A Trifling Opening" (*Munsey's*, September 1926)
"Smoke Without Fire" (*Munsey's*, October 1926)
"A Big Four Failure" (*Munsey's*, November 1926)
"A Farewell Tour" (*Munsey's* December 1926)
"At the End of the Rope" (*Munsey's*, January 1927)
"Number Five" (*Munsey's*, February 1927)
"The Misery Medicine" (*Munsey's*, March 1927)
"By Aid of the Donkey" (*Munsey's*, April 1927)
"Domestic Relations" (Munsey's, May 1927)
"The Ninth Time" (*Munsey's*, June 1927)
"The Hot Cat Cook" (*Munsey's*, July 1927)
"Gift Garments" (*Munsey's*, August 1927)

"The Buck Stone" (*Munsey's*, September 1927)
"The Graveyard Club" (*Munsey's*, October 1927)
"A Hot One" (*Munsey's*, November 1927)
"The Great Tickfall Cotton Gamble" (*Munsey's*, December 1927)
"The Way of a Witness" (*Munsey's*, January 1928)
"A Matrimony Fixer" (*Munsey's*, February 1928)
"A Royal Road to Fortune" (*Munsey's*, March 1928)
"Slaughter in the Smoke House" (*Munsey's*, April 1928)
"Matrimonial Finals" (*Munsey's*, May 1928)
"For President—Skeeter Butts" (*Munsey's*, June 1928)
"The Last Act" (*Munsey's*, July 1928)
"Grave Clothes" (*Munsey's*, August 1928)
"The Faith Healer" (*Munsey's*, September 1928)
"Saving Sinners" (*Munsey's*, October 1928)
"Music Money" (*Munsey's*, November 1928)
"One Kind Deed" (*Munsey's*, December 1928)
"The Gunman of Tickfall" (*Munsey's*, January 1929)
"Uplift of Sugar" (*Munsey's*, February 1929)
"The Widow Inconsolable" (*Munsey's*, March 1929)
"His Secret Sorrow" (*Munsey's*, April 1929)
"Author, Author!" (*Munsey's*, May 1929)
"Home Again" (*Munsey's*, June 1929)
"A Life Job" (*Munsey's*, July 1929)
"The Fatal Picnic" (*Munsey's*, August 1929)
"The Great Farm School" (*Munsey's*, September 1929)
"A Tickfall Hero" (*Munsey's*, October 1929)

BOOKS

(1) *"Is this a title? It is not. It is the name of a writer of negro stories, who has made himself so completely the writer of Negro stories that his book needs no title"* (1918)
(2) *More E.K. Means "Is this a title? It is not. It is the name of a writer of negro stories, who has made himself so completely the writer of negro stories that this second book, like the first, needs no title"* (1919)
(3) *Further E. K. Means. Is this a title? It is not. It is the name of a writer of negro stories, who has made himself so completely the writer of negro stories that this third like the first and second, needs no title* (1921)
(4) *Black Fortune* (1931)

REFERENCES

E.K. Means review. *Duluth News Tribune*, 15 January 1920.
Further review. Portland, Ore., *Oregonian*, 20 February 1921.
"Iliad of Tickfall," *New York Tribune*, 13 July 1918.
Jarrett, Gene Andrew. *Deans and Truants: Race and Realism in African American Literature*. Philadelphia: University of Pennsylvania Press, 2007.
More review. *San Jose Mercury News*, 8 June 1919.
"More Negro Stories from the Pen of E.K. Means," *Dallas Morning News*, 26 October 1919.
"My Favorite Stories," *Fort Worth Star-Telegram*, 24 October 1924.
North, Michael. *The Dialect of Modernism: Race, Language and Twentieth-Century Literature*. New York: Oxford University Press, 1998.

Booth Tarkington
(1869–1946)
Herman and Verman

"Herman," said Penrod, in a weak voice, "you wouldn't honest of cut his gizzard out, would you?"

"Who? Me? I don't know. He mighty mean ole boy." Herman shook his head gravely, and then, observing that Vermin was again convulsed with unctuous merriment, joined in laughter with his brother.
—Booth Tarkington, *Penrod*[1]

Booth Tarkington, asserts biographer James Woodress, was "an amiable humorist, a shrewd psychologist, and a skillful storyteller: in short, a writer whose best works ought not to be left unread."[2]

Newton Booth Tarkington was born in Indianapolis, Indiana, in 1869, the son of John S. Tarkington and Elizabeth Booth. He was named for his mother's brother, the governor of California. Booth's father was a lawyer, soldier, politician and judge.

As a boy, Booth and his neighborhood buddies staged amateur theatrics that he would later fictionalize in *Penrod*.[3] Booth attended Shortridge High School in his hometown and Phillips Exeter Academy in Massachusetts. He studied for two years at Purdue University and later accepted an honorary degree from that institution. He attended Princeton University, where he was active in the drama club and The Triangle Club, which he cofounded. But he failed to take the required course in classics, and did not graduate. Nevertheless, the university bestowed honorary master's and doctoral degrees on him years after. He briefly held public office as an Indiana state legislator. He married Laurel Louisa Fletcher in 1902. They divorced in 1911 and he married Susanah Robinson in 1912.

Tarkington became a best-selling crafter of Midwest regional prose, and earned two Pulitzer Prizes in fiction, in 1919 for *The Magnificent Ambersons* and 1922 for *Alice Adams*.

Winning no notable awards, but hugely popular, and at times controversial, was a trio of novels about a boy named Penrod and his good friend Sam Williams and their frequent playmates including two black boys, Herman and Verman.

Penrod (1914), a sequence of short stories from *Everybody's* and the *Saturday Evening Post* strung into a book, depicts the adventures and misadventures of 11-year-old Schofield in the years before World War I. Tarkington's wife Susanah gave him the nudge to write about young characters. He based his stories on his own memories and on observations of his three nephews. *Penrod and Sam* followed in 1916 (with stories that appeared in *Cosmopolitan*) and *Penrod Jashber* came more than a decade later in 1929. All of the

Indiana scribe Booth Tarkington wrote popular stories of America's Midwest.

tales—with exceptions to be noted—were gathered in *Penrod: His Complete Story* (1931). All told the Penrod stories sold some 586,000 copies through 1945.[4]

Penrod became a minor phenomenon.

"Tarkington was in full mastery of his literary medium when he wrote Penrod," in the view of Woodress. "His style, which is supple, articulate, witty, is equal to all the demands he makes of it and succeeds simultaneously in entertaining children and delighting adults."

Woodress described Tarkington as a writer of detail, rather than plot. Indeed, the Penrod books, the Orvie book and others are gathered vignettes. In writing about young people in these books and in *Seventeen*, the biographer said, he was diverting from, rather than imitating, Mark Twain, who, he once said, imbued Tom Sawyer and Huck Finn with realistic character then bestowed with outrageous and unlikely adventure. Tarkington was happy with slight exaggeration.

Edward E. Rose adapted *Penrod* for the New York stage in 1918, and Penrod and his mates enjoyed a run in black-and-white movies, starting with silent—*Penrod* in 1922 starring "Freckles" Barry[5] and *Penrod and Sam* in 1923 with Ben Alexander. Leon Janney played the young hero Penrod in two movies in 1931, the first of the sound pictures, then Billy Hayes assumed the part for eight movies in 1931 and 1932. Billy Mauch took over for three pictures, his brother Bobby also appearing during the period 1932–1938.[6]

The black boys were integral to the series. Ernest "Sunshine Sammy" Morrison (who had a long career in films and television) was Herman and his sister Florence Morrison (in her only movie role) was Verman in the 1922 *Penrod*. Joe McGray and Eugene Jackson played Herman and Verman in the 1923 sequel. James Robinson and Robert Dandrige played the parts of Herman Washington and Verman Washington in the 1931 sound film. Uncredited, Ed Edwards was "Vermin" and Paul White was Herman in *Snakes Alive*, *One Good Deed* and *Batter Up* in 1931, *Detectives*, *His Honor—Penrod*, *Hot Dog* and *Penrod's Bull Pen* in 1932. Philip Hurlick was Verman Diggs in *Penrod and Sam* (1937). As Philip Hurlic, he was Vermin in *Penrod and His Twin Brother* (1938) and Verman in *Penrod's Double Trouble* (1938).

Some found Tarkington's Penrod offensive. What were the objections? The lad's antics, his occasionally mildly vulgar language and his treatment of the two young African Americans.

Penrod is delighted on the day (in Chapter 15) he and his dog Duke discover a new family has moved into his neighborhood, albeit the poor section of town. Pursuing an unusual odor, boy and dog encounter a raccoon on a leash. A black boy is at the other end of the leash.

> "What's that 'coon's name?" Penrod asked, intending no discourtesy.
> "Aim gommo mame," said the small darky.
> "What?"
> "Aim gommo mame."
> *"What?"*
> The small darky looked annoyed. "Aim gommo mame, I hell you," he said impatiently.

An older black boy shows up to explain that his brother has a speech impediment. That's the best he can talk. Penrod is intrigued.

> "Talk some more," he begged eagerly.
> "I hoe you ackoom aim gommo mame," was the prompt response, in which a slight ostentation was manifest. Unmistakable tokens of vanity had appeared upon the small, swart countenance.

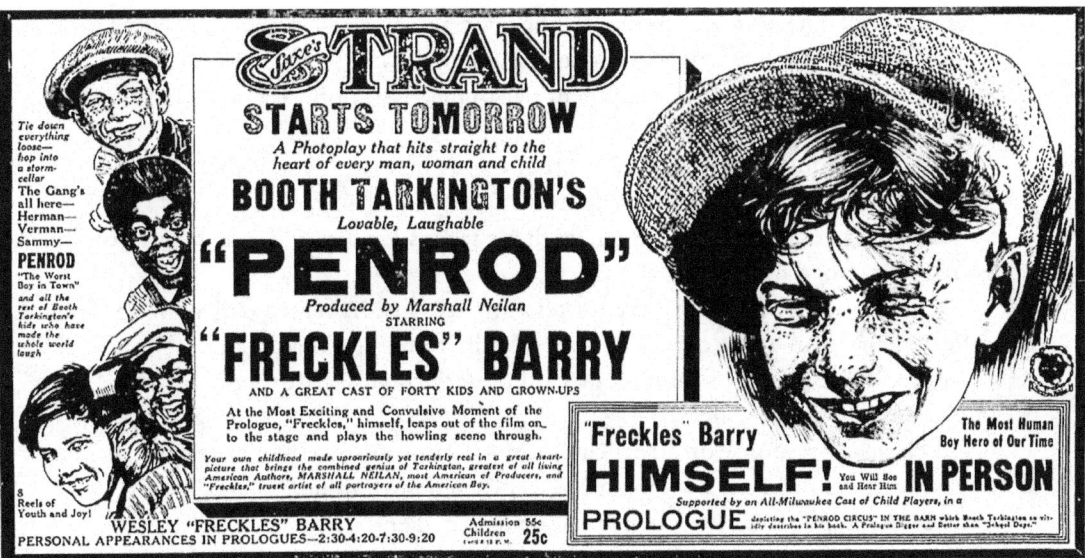

Wesley "Freckles" Barry played Penrod in a 1922 eight-reeler (Advertisement, *Milwaukee Journal*, February 24, 1922).

"What's he mean?" Penrod asked, enchanted.
"He say he tole you 'at 'coon ain' got no name."
"What's *your* name?"
"I'm name Herman."
"What's his name?" Penrod pointed to the tongue-tied boy.
"Verman."
"What!"
"Verman. Was three us boys in ow fam'ly. Ol'est one name Sherman. 'N'en come me; I'm Herman. 'N'en come him; he Verman. Sherman dead. Verman, he de littles' one."

Thus are friendships made. Ever an opportunist, Penrod immediately enlists Verman to be a sideshow attraction in his backyard circus. This, some critics attest, is mean-spirited. One can only respond, read the whole book. Penrod at times treats most of his friends—including girls such as Marjorie Jones, even good old Sam—meanly. The important point is, Herman and Verman are adopted into the regular gang.

But black children are "never invited to a social function," complains critic Dorothy M. Broderick,[7] who found Tarkington's two black boys "among the most unrelentingly negative.... Tarkington's bias was ingrained."[8]

The *Penrod* chapter "Coloured Troops in Action" was found offensive by one editor, and was retitled "Troops in Action" in some editions, notes Robert S. Sargent Jr., who opined, "Like history, fiction cannot be judged by today's standards."[9]

Critic Paul Fussell was outraged at changes made for a Tempo paperback edition: "Text has been slyly manipulated throughout to purge the evidence of Tarkington's characteristic affectionate condescension towards Negroes. And as the evidence has been secretly destroyed, so have Tarkington's wit and vigour. The text has been reduced to insipidity: we have now ... *Penrod* constant with our day."[10]

Fussell further ventured, "Tarkington's point, here and elsewhere, is Twain's: dogs,

Negroes, and white boys occupy essentially the same universe, one happily distant from that peopled by adult whites like policemen, dancing and music masters, school teachers, parents, barbers, the clergy, and other Establishment personnel. This point is effectively blunted by the expurgator."[11]

Fussell found quite a few changes in the text, as in when Sam Williams declares he's going to hire a couple of colored waiters to swing him in a hammock.

Herman is irate: "Ain' nobody goin' hiah me whens *I'm* a man. Goin' be my own boss. I'm goin' be a rai'road man."

That's the original. In the paperback revision, it's this: "Ain't nobody goin' to hire me when I'm a man. Goin' to be my own boss. *I'm* goin' to be a rai'road man."

The original sequence of bully Rupe Collins declaring, "Chase them nigs out o' here!" became "Chase them out o' here!"

And Herman's response of "Don' call me nig. I mine my own biznuss. You let 'em boys alone" turns into "I mine my own buznuss. You let 'em boys alone."

Some paragraphs from the exchange were dropped entirely.

"The past is not the present: pretending it is corrupts art and thus both rots the mind and shrivels the conscience," Fussell steamed.

To which Thomas Mallon replied, "Herman and Verman, mumbling in dialect, are presented like sideshow exhibits.... In *The Gentleman from Indiana*, Tarkington—having grown up the son of a southern-mannered father in a copperhead state—writes with a condescension that's less affectionate than outright romantic, giving us glimpses of 'happy negroes' out of Thomas Nelson Page. Like many Roosevelt Progressives, he got off the train of reform before TR's distant cousin turned the square deal into something entirely New."[12]

This may be reading too much into Tarkington's prose, but what if the author was really exaggerating stereotypes on purpose? Herman and Verman aren't just kids speaking vernacular. Verman's speech limitation makes him impossible to understand—a mocking statement on the propensity of popular fiction writers to include dialect for dialect's sake, for amusement, not for literary purposes.

Herman has a further distinction. He's missing a finger.

"*I* mum map," said Verman, with egregious pride.
"*He* don 'at," interpreted Herman, chuckling. "Yessuh; done chop 'er spang off, long 'go. He's a playin' wif a ax an' I lay my finguh on de do'-sill an' I say, 'Verman, chop 'er off!' So Verman he chop 'er right spang off up to de roots! Yessuh."
"What *for*?"
"Jes' fo nuthin'."

Tarkington could be poking fun at other writers for making black characters so exotic, so pathetic. Jes' fo nuthin'.

In the opinion of Robin Bernstein, "Today, this episode is shocking, but in 1914, no critics remarked on the story's allegations that dismemberment does not pain black children and that violence is a 'nothing' that pickaninnies comically visit upon each other. Indeed, Penrod was perceived as a novel that reproduced the carefree innocence of boyhood.... Penrod could be celebrated as 'innocent fun' because by the time the novel was published, the pickaninny, defined by insensitivity to pain, was among the most common libels against

African Americans.... The repetitious ubiquity of the insensate pickaninny itself desensitized white readers and other consumers to African American pain."[13]

If you locate a *Penrod* first edition, first or second state, illustrated by Gordon Grant, it includes five chapters that were omitted in later editions, particularly as Grosset & Dunlap brought the stories to market for young readers. Three of those chapters, 26 to 28, "The Quiet Afternoon," "Conclusion of the Quiet Afternoon" and "Twelve," were orphaned, while two others, 29 and 30, "Fanchon" and "The Birthday Party," after a while found a new home in *Penrod Jashber*.

One chapter never appeared in a book. "Sam's Beau" (*Cosmopolitan*, April 1917) was inconsequential and very insensitive. Sam Williams and Mable Miles and Penrod engage in a verbal back-and-forth with repeated use (seventeen times) of "nigger."

Why were some chapters dropped sometime after 1915? Some speculate it was because the first two chapters, at least, centered on the two black characters, Herman and Verman. A more likely reason is that the book's page count needed to be harnessed for secondary publishers. And "The Quiet Afternoon" and "Conclusion of the Quiet Afternoon" not only included modest bashing of the annoyingly saintly character Georgie Bassett, they featured Herman's rousing replication of a revivalist preacher praising the Lord, so sincere and emotional that Penrod and Sam and mates (including a Jewish boy) became true believers, however fleetingly.

Here's a sampling from the repugnant chapters. Young masters Schofield and Williams, on a scrap metal and glass collecting excursion, link with their friends and play a one-upboyship game of "When I become a man." Penrod will be a senator or general, he says. Maurice Levy will own a store. Sam wants to be a policeman, so no one can force him to marry a girl. Georgie Basset has holier aspirations.

"I am going to be," said Georgie, consciously, "a minister."
This announcement created a sensation so profound that it was followed by silence. Herman was the first to speak.
"You mean preachuh?" he asked incredulously. "You go' PREACH?"
"Yes," answered Georgie, looking like Saint Cecilia at the organ.
Herman was impressed. "You know all 'at preachuh talk?"
"I'm going to learn it," said Georgie simply.
"How loud kin you holler?" asked Herman doubtfully.
"He can't holler at all," Penrod interposed with scorn. "He hollers like a girl. He's the poorest hollerer in town!"
Herman shook his head. Evidently he thought Georgie's chance of being ordained very slender. Nevertheless, a final question put to the candidate by the coloured expert seemed to admit one ray of hope.
"How good kin you clim a pole?"
"He can't climb one at all," Penrod answered for Georgie. "Over at Sam's turning-pole you ought to see him try to—"
"Preachers don't have to climb poles," Georgie said with dignity.
"GOOD ones do," declared Herman. "Bes' one ev' I hear, he clim up an' down same as a circus man. One n'em big 'vivals outen whens we livin' on a fahm, preachuh clim big pole right in a middle o' the church, what was to hol' roof up. He clim way high up, an' holler: 'Devil's got a hol' o' my coattails; devil tryin' to drag me down! Sinnuhs, take wawnun! Devil got a hol' o' my coat-tails; I'm a-goin' to hell, oh Lawd!' Nex', he clim up little mo', an' yell an' holler. 'Done shuck ole devil loose; goin' straight to heavum agin! Goin' to heavum, goin' to heavum, my

Laud!' Nex' he slid down some mo' an' he holler, 'Leggo my coat-tails, ole devil! Goin' to hell agin, sinnuhs! Goin' straight to hell, my laud! An' he clim an' he slide, an' he slide, an' he clim, and' all time holler: "Now 'm a-goin' to heavum; now 'm a-goin' to hell! Goin' to heavum, heavum, heavum, my Lawd!' Las' he slide all a-way down, jes' a squalin'; and a-kickin' an' a-rarin' up an' squealin', 'Goin' to hell. Goin' to hell! Ole Satum got my soul! Goin' to hell! Goin' to hell! Goin' to hell, hell, hell!"

Herman possessed that extraordinary facility for vivid acting which is the great native gift of his race, and he enchained his listeners. They sat fascinated and spellbound.

"Herman, tell that again!" said Penrod, breathlessly.

Herman, nothing loath, accepted the encore and repeated the Miltonic episode, expanding it somewhat, and dwelling with a fine art upon those portions of the narrative which he perceived to be most exciting to his audience. Plainly, they thrilled less to Paradise gained than to its losing, and the dreadful climax of the descent into the Pit was the greatest treat of all!

The effect was immense and instant. Penrod sprang to his feet.

"Georgie Bassett couldn't do that to save his life," he declared. "I'm goin' to be a preacher! I'd be all right for one, wouldn't I, Herman?"

"So am I!" Sam Williams echoed loudly." I guess I can do it if YOU can. I'd be better'n Penrod, wouldn't I, Herman?"

"I am, too!" Maurice shouted. "I got a stronger voice than anybody here, and I'd like to know what—"

The three clamored together indistinguishably, each asserting his qualifications for the ministry according to Herman's theory, which had been accepted by those sudden converts without question.

How many offenses can you find in that passage? That tour-de-force from young Herman? Actually, there's more. Young Georgie, insisting he can "climb," climbs a tree outside his folks' home and begins to orate, at the same time his mother is entertaining her church's minister. Oops.

Greg Wright defended the scene, noting, "Tarkington's grandfather was a Methodist circuit rider. I'm sure he must have also been well aware that such antics were not unknown on the Great White frontier."[14]

Jonathan Yardley conceded Herman and Verman were portrayed "in antiquated and occasionally offensive ways." But, "A good deal of evidence indicates that Tarkington is more respectful and sympathetic to his black characters than first impressions suggest. Penrod and Sam play with their black friends Herman and Verman pretty much as equals, and Tarkington invests them with a certain dignity. When Verman is insulted by Georgie Bassett with a racial slur, Sam quickly and emphatically comes to his defense, making plain that Verman "won't let *anybody* call him that."[15]

Interestingly, though long dropped from newer print editions, the Herman preacher impersonation made it (although of necessity abbreviated) into a 1949 *NBC Theatre* radio production of "Penrod," adapted by Robert Gray.[16]

Booth Tarkington Notes

1. Page 77.
2. *Booth Tarkington: Gentleman from Indiana*, 8.
3. Ibid., 37.
4. Ibid., 331.
5. Gordon Griffith played Penrod's friend Sam Williams.
6. When Tarkington learned the movie producer Warner Brothers was ignoring his plots in favor of

The Prince and the Pauper, for *Penrod and His Twin Brother*, he sued to regain his movie rights. Gray sang the lead in two final films, *On Moonlight Bay* (1951) and *By the Light of the Silvery Moon* (1953), based on Tarkington's books, but not using the Penrod character names.

7. *Image of the Black in Children's Fiction*, 150.
8. Ibid., 100.
9. "Booth Tarkington and Penrod."
10. "The Strange Case of 'Penrod' Revised," *Encounter*, April 1970, 76–80.
11. *The Boy Scout Handbook*.
12. "Hoosiers: The Lost World of Booth Tarkington," *The Atlantic*, May 2004.
13. *Racial Innocence: Performing American Childhood and Race from Slavery to Civil Rights*. New York: New York University, 2011, 53.
14. "Scandalous Penrod."
15. "Attaboy! Booth Tarkington's Rascals," C1.
16. The program was previously known as NBC University Theatre. "Penrod" was the first of a series of thirty-five adaptations of American novels. The "Penrod" cast, according to radio historian J. David Goldin, included Anne Whitfield Kane, Florence Ravenal, Gail Bonney, GeGe Pearson, H. B. Barnum, Jeffrey Silver, Jerry Farber, Johnny McGivern, Junius Matthews, Margie List, Marion Richman, Theodore Von Eltz and Tom Charlesworth. With intermission commentary by J. Donald Adams. The episode streams at http://www.podfeed.net/episode/nbc+university+theatre+penrod+09251949/2957199 (heard 3 October 2012).

Booth Tarkington Selected Bibliography and Sources

PENROD SCHOFIELD STORIES

"Penrod and the Pageant" (*Everybody's Magazine*, June 1913) (syndicated in *Oregonian*, 7 February 1915; Biloxi *Daily Herald*, 1 May 1915; Belleville, Ill., *News-Democrat*, 7 September 1915, etc.) (1A and 1B, chapters 1 to 6, A Boy and His Dog, Romance, the Costume, Desperation, The Pageant of the Table Round, Evening) "The Pageant of the Table Round" (13) (24)

"Talleyrand and Penrod" (*Saturday Evening Post*, 21 June 1913) (1A and 1B, chapters 12 to 14) Miss Rennsdale Accepts, The Smallpox Medicine, Maurice Levy's Constitution (13)

"A Boy in the Air" (*Cosmopolitan*, October 1913) (syndicated *Oregonian*, 14 February 1915, etc.) (1A and 1B, chapters 7 to 11, Evils of Drink, School, Soaring, Uncle John, Fidelity of a Little Dog) (13) Soaring, Uncle John (34) The Evils of Drink (38)

"An Overwhelming Saturday" (*Cosmopolitan*, November 1913) (syndicated *Oregonian*, 21 February 1915, etc.) (1A and 1B, as chapters 15 to 17, The Two Families, The New Star, Retiring from the Show Business) "Retiring from the Show Business" (syndicated *Baltimore Sun*, 3 December 1914 etc.) (13)

"Brothers of Angels" (*Cosmopolitan*, December 1913) (syndicated *Oregonian*, 28 February 1915, etc.) (1A and 1B, as chapters 18 to 20, Music, The Inner Boy, Brothers of Angels) (13)

"Little Gentleman" (*Cosmopolitan*, January 1914) (syndicated *Oregonian*, 7 March 1915, etc.) (1A and 1B, chapters 14 and 15) (7) (9) (10) (12) (13) (21) (25) (27) (31) (32)

"The Fall of Georgie Bassett" (*Cosmopolitan*, February 1914) (syndicated *Oregonian*, 14 May 1915, etc.) (1A, as chapters 26 and 27, The Quiet Afternoon, Conclusion of the Quiet Afternoon) (1B, omitted) "The Quiet Afternoon" (32)

"Twelve!" (*Cosmopolitan*, March 1914) (1A, chapters 23 to 31, Twelve, Fanchon, The Birthday Party, Over the Fence) (11) (13) condensed (25) Twelve (40)

"Rupe Collins" (*Metropolitan*, April 1914) (syndicated, *Oregonian*, 28 March 1915 etc.) (1A, chapter 21) (13) (20) (27)

"Penrod—Zoologist" (*Metropolitan Magazine*, May 1914) Zoologist (syndicated *Oregonian*, 4 April 1915, etc.) (11, as chapter 22, New Stars Arise)

"The Empty House" (*Metropolitan*, June 1914) (syndicated, *Oregonian*, 11 April 1915 etc.) (never collected)

"The Imitator" (1A and 1B, chapter 22)

"Coloured Troops in Action" (1A and 1B, chapter 23)

"Bing!" (*Cosmopolitan*, January 1915) (2, chapters 3 and 4, The Militarist and Bingism) (*Indianapolis Star*, 20 May 1917) "Bingism" (11) (13, omitted) (19)

"Munchausen Penrod" (*Cosmopolitan*, February 1915) (3, as chapters 3 and 4, Prophylaxis, Munchausen) (13, omitted)

"The Bonded Prisoner" (*Cosmopolitan*, March 1915) (2 and 13, chapters 1 and 2, Penrod and Sam, The Bonded Prisoner) (*Indianapolis Star*, 13 May 1917)

"The In-or-In" (*Cosmopolitan*, April 1915) (2 and 4, chapters 5 and 6, The In-or-in, Georgie Becomes a Member) (*Indianapolis Star*, 27 May 1917)

"Penrod's Busy Day" (*Cosmopolitan*, May 1915) (2, chapter 17) (8) (15) (16) (17) Penrod's Day (18) "Penrod's Busy Day" (28) (35)

"Reward of Merit" (*Cosmopolitan*, July 1915) (2 and 13, chapters 7 to 9, Whitey, Salvage, Reward of Merit) (22) "Reward of Merit" (4) (14)

"Part Panther or Something; Penrod Stages a 'Movie' Show" (*Cosmopolitan*, September 1915) (2, chapters 12 to 14, Gipsy, Concerning Trousers, Camera Work in the Jungle) "Gipsy" (5)

"The Heart of Marjorie Jones; Penrod Learns Something of the Ways of Love" (*Cosmopolitan*, October 1915) (2 and 13, chapters 23 and 24, The Party, The Heart of Marjorie Jones) "The Party" (36)

"Wednesday Madness; Penrod Gets into a Pack of Trouble" (*Cosmopolitan*, December 1915) (2 and 13, chapters 15 and 16, A Model Letter to a Friend, Wednesday Madness) "A Model Letter to a Friend" (37)

"Penrod's Little Cousin" (*Cosmopolitan*, January 1916) (11 and 13, chapters 7 and 8, Jashber Is Interrupted, Little Ronald)

"Penrod's Nervous Breakdown" (*Cosmopolitan*, April 1916) (2 and 13, chapters 10 and 11, Conscience, The Tonic)

"On Account of the Weather" (*Cosmopolitan*, September 1916) (2 and 13, chapters 18 to 20, On Account of the Weather, Creative Art, The Departing Guest)

"The Horn of Fame" (*Cosmopolita*n, October 1916) (2, chapters 21 and 22, Yearning, The Horn of Fame) (13, omitted)

"Penrod and Sam" (syndicated *Kansas City Star, News-Democrat,* etc.) (2) (13)

"Sam's Beau" (*Cosmopolitan*, April 1917) (never collected)

"Marjorie Jones's Picnic" (*Nash's Pall Mall Magazine*, May 1917)

"Walter John Penrod and Sam Plan a New Career" (*Cosmopolitan*, November 1917) (11 and 13, chapters 1 and 2, The New Pup, Bad Influence of Walter-John) "The New Pup: A Penrod Story" (7)

"Penrod Jashber: His Career as a Detective, Part 1, George B. Jashber" (*Cosmopolitan*, January 1918) (11 and 13, chapters 5 and 6, Beginnings of Jashber, Jashber Develops)

"Penrod Jashber: His Career as a Detective, Part 2, The Scoundrel's Den" (*Cosmopolitan*, February 1918) (11 and 13, chapters 10 and 11, Ways of Knowing Things, The Scoundrel's Den)

"Penrod Jashber: His Career as a Detective, Part 3, Herman and Verman Join" (*Cosmopolitan*, March 1918) (11 and 13, chapters 12 and 13, Herman and Verman Are Allowed to Join, The Man with the False Whiskers)

"Penrod Jashber: His Career as a Detective, Part 4, The Pursuit of Dade" (*Cosmopolitan*, April 1918) (11 and 13, chapters 15 to 17, The Pursuit of Dade, A Sundy Stroll, The Pursuit Continues)

"Penrod Jashber: His Career as a Detective, Part 5, The Superboy" (*Cosmopolitan*, May 1918) (11 and 13, chapters 28 and 29, Two Return to Private Life, Disaster)

"Miss Herman Misses a Treat" (11) (13)

"Impressing Marjorie" (11) (13)

"Protective Coloration" (11) (13)

"Inquisition" (11) (13)

BOOKS

(1A) *Penrod* (1914)

(1B) *Penrod* (1914 revised) omits chapters 26 to 30 The Quiet Afternoon, Conclusion of the Quiet Afternoon, Twelve, Fanchon and Over the Fence; chapters 28 to 30 were later included in (11); chapters 26 and 27 were orphaned

(2) *Penrod and Sam* (1916)

(3) *The Boy Scouts Book of Stories* (1919) Franklin K. Mathiews and Walt Louderback, eds.

(4) *Short Stories of Various Types* (1920) L.F. Freck, ed.

(5) *Lords of the Housetops: Thirteen Cat Tales* (1921) Carl Van Vechten, ed.

(6) *Short Stories by Present-Day Authors* (1922) R.W. Pence, ed.

(7) *Short Stories by Present-Day Authors* (1922) Raymond Woodbury Pence, ed.
(8) *Short Stories* (1925) H.C. Schweikert, ed.
(9) *Little Gentleman* (1926)
(10) *Short Stories for College Classes* (1929) B.C. Williams, ed.
(11) *Penrod Jashber* (1929)
(12) *The Bedside Book of Famous American Stories* (1936) Angus Burrell and Bennett A. Cerf, eds.
(13) *Penrod, His Complete Story* (1931)
(14) *The Treasure Chest of Literature for Seventh Year—First Half* (1935) Charles G. Eichel, Edward J. Kehoe, Ignus D. Hornstein and Floyd R. Smith, eds.
(15) *Interest Trails in Literature Book Three* (1936) Helene W. Hartley, ed.
(16) *Notable Short Stories* (1937) Raymond McFarland, ed.
(17) *Beacon Lights of Literature, Grade Eight* (1927) Rudolph W. Chamberlain, ed.
(18) *The Great American Parade* (1935)
(19) *Twenty-Two Short Stories of America* (1937) Edith Mirrieless ed.
(20) *Children's Literature by Grades and Types* (1938) Ollie Depew ed.
(21) *A Junior Anthology: Book One* (1938) Blanche Wellons, Lawrence McTurnan and Henry L. Smith, eds.
(22) *Stories About Boys and Girls*, Vol. 6 (1938) Mabel Williams and Marcia Dalphin, eds.
(23) *A Subtreasury of American Humor* (1941) E.B. White and Katharine S. White, eds.
(24) *The Children's Anthology* (1941) William Lyon Phelps, ed.
(25) *Joy in Reading, Catholic High School Literature Series, Book One* (1941) Roy J. Deferrari, Sister Mary Theresa Brentano and Brother Edward P. Sheekey, eds.
(26) *Challenge to Understand: Adventures in Literature, Book Three* (1942) Luella B. Cook, Walter Loban, George W. Norvell and William A. McCall, eds.
(27) *As You Were: A Portable Library of American Prose and Poetry Assembled for Members of the Armed Forces and the Merchant Marine* (1943) Alexander Woollcott, ed.
(28) *Literature: A Series of Anthologies—Types of Literature* (1944) E.A. Cross and Neal M. Cross, eds.
(29) *The Best American Humorous Short Stories* (1945) Robert N. Linscott, ed.
(30) *Time to Be Young; Great Stories of the Growing Years* (1945) Whit Burnett, ed.
(31) *The Family Reader* (1946) Marjorie Barrows, ed.
(32) *A Treasury of Laughter* (1946) Louis Untermeyer, ed.
(33) *Pageant of American Humor* (1948) Edwin Seaver, ed.
(34) *Unseen Harvests* (1947) Claude M. Fuess and Emory S. Basford, eds.
(35) *Craft of the Short Story* (1948) Richard Summers, ed.
(36) *The Home Book of Laughter* (1948) May Lamberton Becker, ed.
(37) *Worlds of People* (1951) Matilda Bailey and Ullin W. Leavell, eds.
(38) *Eyes of Boyhood* (1953) Clyde Brion Davis, ed.
(39) *Our Wonderful World* (1956) Herbert S. Zim, ed.
(40) *An Anthology of Indiana Writers* (2000) James A. Huston, ed.

Plays

Penrod (1918) adapted by Edward E. Rose, staged in New York City
Penrod: The Pageant (1978)

Silent Films

Penrod (1922)
Penrod and Sam (1923)

Sound Films

Penrod and Sam (1931)
Snakes Alive (1931)
One Good Deed (1931)
Batter Up! (1931)
Detectives (1932)
His Honor—Penrod (1932)

Hot Dog (1932)
Penrod's Bull Pen (1932)
Penrod and Sam (1932)
Penrod and His Twin Brother (1938)
Penrod's Double Trouble (1938)
On Moonlight Bay (1951)
By the Light of the Silvery Moon (1953)

Radio

"Penrod" (NBC, 30 July 1946)
"Penrod" (*NBC University Theatre*, 25 September 1949)

Sources

Adcock, John. "Unexpurgated Penrod," Yesterday's Papers. http://john-adcock.blogspot.com/2009/07/unexpurgated-penrod.html (viewed 20 September 2012).
Bernstein, Robin. *Racial Innocence: Performing American Childhood and Race from Slavery to Civil Rights*. New York: New York University, 2011.
"Booth Tarkington '93," *The Princeton University Library Chronicle*, Vol. 16, No. 2, winter 1955.
Broderick, Dorothy M. *Image of the Black in Children's Fiction*. New York: R.R. Bowker, 1973.
Fussell, Paul. *The Boy Scout Handbook and Other Observations*. New York: Oxford University Press, 1985.
_____. "The Strange Case of 'Penrod' Revised," *Encounter*, April 1970.
Goldin, J. David. *NBC University Theatre*, episode log, http://radiogoldindex.com/cgi-local/p2.cgi?ProgramName=The+NBC+University+Theatre (viewed 3 October 2012).
Mallon, Thomas. "Hoosiers, the Lost World of Booth Tarkington," *The Atlantic*, May 2004.
Russo, Dorothy R., and Thelma L. Sullivan. *A Bibliography of Booth Tarkington, 1869–1946*. Indianapolis: Indiana Historical Society, 1949.
Sargent, Robert S., Jr. "Booth Tarkington and Penrod," Enter Stage Right, 14 June 2004. http://www.google.com/search?source=ig&rlz=1G1GGLQ_ENUS293&q=Sargent+%22Booth+Tarkington+and+Penrod%22 (viewed 20 September 2012).
Small, Sam W. "Negro Dialect Astray," *Atlanta Constitution*, 11 January 1913.
Woodress, James Leslie. *Booth Tarkington, Gentleman from Indiana*. Greenwood Press, 1969.
Wright, Greg. "Scandalous Penrod," *Booth Tarkington: The Final Word*, 22 July 2009. http://dramatic-insights.org/tarkington/index.php/2009/scandalous-penrod/ (viewed 20 September 2012).
Yardley, Jonathan. "Attaboy! Booth Tarkington's Rascals," *Washington Post*, 7 August 2004.

James P. Alley
(1885–1934)

Calvin Alley
(1915–1970)

Hambone

"Sto-keepuh say he sol' me dese heah shoes at less'n cost—en at dat I be dawg-gone ef we didn't boff git tricked!!"—Hambone[1]

James Pinckney Alley was the first staff editorial cartoonist for the Memphis, Tennessee, daily newspaper the *Commercial Appeal*, hired in 1915 by editor C.P.J. Mooney. Mooney had recognized Alley's talents when Alley worked for Bluff City Engraving. His ability to quickly shape political beliefs to line drawings would be credited with helping the newspaper win a Pulitzer Prize for a crusade against the Ku Klux Klan in 1923.

Born at Sidel, near Benton, Arkansas, in 1885, James was the son of John Pinckney Alley and Malinda Catherine Everett. Alley clerked in a grocery store. He submitted drawings to the *Arkansas Democrat* and *Southern Breeze*, and took a job as a commercial artist with Cronk & Foster Engraving in 1908. A year later, he moved to Bluff City Engraving, which was quartered in the same Memphis building as the *Commercial Appeal*.

Alley drew a black man in some of his political cartoons,[2] and in 1915 he developed a single-panel cartoon that would run on the newspaper's front page for a half century. McClure Syndicate, and later Bell Syndicate and Agnes A. Kelleher, distributed the cartoons to other newspapers. Mooney wrote text for many of the cartoons in early years, according to historian Allan Holtz.[3]

Political cartoonist James P. Alley developed *Hambone's Meditations* for the *Memphis Commercial Appeal* and Bell Syndicate circulated it to other newspapers (LouJane Adams Wills/ www.FindaGrave.com).

Hambone's Meditations featured a roughly sketched, diminutive (so he would fit the small box) man who shared a daily aphorism. "Dey's a nigguh tellin' me mah white folks ain' payin' me 'nough wages, but da's all right bout dat— hit's nough t'spile a fool nigguh lak him," Hambone said, for example. Or, "Somebody wanter know is me en de boss gwine hab enny aigg-nogg dis Chris-mus—ah don' know bout de boss but me' en de boss aint apt t' hab none!!" These cartoons are accompanied by depictions of the character carrying a tub and washboard[4] and sawing firewood,[5] respectively.

Alley was inspired by another cartoonist, Kin Hubbard,[6] who had created a rustic sage for the Mansfield, Ohio, *News* in 1904. The lean, whiskered, bow-tie-wearing Abe Martin shared such wisdom as: "If ther's anything a dentist hates it's a droopin' mustache" or "Miss Germ Williams says peroxide blondes ort t' be tagged jist like oleomargarine."

Alley kept his character folksy but made him a Negro, and based him on a former slave named Tom Hunley. Hunley told a Works Progress Administration interviewer how he had come to know the cartoonist:

> "Upstairs, dat was where Mr. J.P. had his office—leastways his li'l room where he did his drawin' at. Twan't no regular office. I cleant up that place in dem days, an' I come trompin' up de stairs wit my mot an' bucket de fust time Mr. J.P. ever seed me. He cotch one glimpse of me, an' he jump an' holler: 'Bless goodness, uncle! You stand right there 'til I can git yo' picture.' Den he hole up his fingers like dis and squinch he eye at me, and fus' thing I knowed he had my picture. 'Now,' he says, 'I got to get a name for you.' And sho nuff, I'se comin' up de stairs one day a-gnawin' on a big ham-bone what a white lady had guv me. 'I got it!' he hollers, 'Hambone! From now on yo' name is Hambone!' An' dats what I been ever since, wit my picture in de *Commercial Appeal* ever' morning."[7]

Alley's Hambone struck a chord. Everyone knew a Hambone. Eighty-year-old Jesse Paschal, who in 1928 had worked for the Georgia railroad for fifty-four years, was Hambone personified, in the view of an *Augusta Chronicle* reporter. "He looks like Hambone, he trudges about the railroad shops with a broom on his shoulder, much in the same manner as the original Hambone, and, furthermore, he philosophizes exactly like the newspaper character."

Hambone actually owes something to a tradition even older than Hubbard's cartoons. House servants in the southern slavery era actually passed along advice to their outdoor mates in the form of aphorisms for good behavior; maybe, young people were told, they could move into the big house someday too. Literary historian William Schechter suggests these tidbits of advice in pre–Civil War days were a means of "maintaining law and order according to genteel white standards." Slaves were protective of their status, and urged others to good behavior. "The propaganda value of his 'satisfaction' with slave life was fully exploited by his former master after the Civil War and extends to the racists of this day," Schechter wrote.[8]

Hambone reached deeper than the daily panels. In 1929, Alley, working with his manager, Hugh J. Mooney (son of C.P.J. Mooney), came up with a merchandising idea.

"The plan, already under way in Memphis and several other cities where the comic character 'Hambone' is used editorially, has a contest angle and presents advertising selling talk through the subtle and philosophical utterances of the darkey. Advertisements, of which there may be a dozen or 50, and six cartoons are packed in a page, to be run weekly for 30 weeks by the newspaper using the series," *Editor and Publisher* said.[9]

"Under the plan, each advertiser is represented in a cartoon one or more times during the series, depending on his position and space on the page."

Readers were encouraged to hand-color and submit the cartoons for a prize drawing.

Blatantly commercial, a typical cartoon in this package shows Hambone standing in front of a Southern Motor Car Company showroom, admiring a Cadillac LaSalle. "Shucks! W'en you buys one dem good cyars you jes' natcherly gits hoss power and mule endurance," he says.

"Neither Mr. Alley nor myself feel he is prostituting his talents in any way," Mooney told *Editor and Publisher*.

Hambone lent his image to two cigar manufacturers, and Hambone box labels are handily found on eBay to this day.

Alley had to give up the comic strip in April 1934, for health reasons.

"For years Hambone has been one of the standbys of the paper, said the *Augusta Chronicle*, which carried the panel in syndication. "In recent months he has moved from this [editorial] page to the front page and some of our subscribers tell us that they look first to see what Hambone has to say about the world and its ways, then consider what the headlines bring them to ponder."[10]

Front page of *The Commercial Appeal* and the *Augusta Chronicle*—that was a hefty audience for a rude depiction of a black temporizer by a white cartoonist. "It was Hambone, we believe, who first enunciated the magnificent opinion of a gift 'Massah' had presented him. It was 'jes' right,' for if it had been any better it wouldn't have been given him, and if it had been any worse, he couldn't have 'done nuffin' with it.' Such a philosophy is perhaps not in accord with teachings of the academicians—for Hambone knows nothing, praise goodness, about nominalism and realism—but it goes a long way in guiding us toward an acceptance of things as they are."[11]

The newspaper's editor went on, "Nor is Hambone a traditionalist. Modern inventions and their results have not escaped his notice. The other day, as he was about to take a sip from the well bucket, he reflected, 'Mah old mule got a ride in a truck yistiddy, en de fus' thing he done w'en dy on-load him was try to kick me!!' but he was not daunted by such a demonstration that our humble friends become 'uppity' the first time they start rising in the world. Nor should we be. Nor, we hope, will Mr. Alley become faint of heart in his struggle for health. For he is greatly needed. We simply couldn't get along without Hambone, and Mr. Alley, having spoiled us, must continue supplying us with good-tempered observations of the world and its ways."

Hambone was not the only racist cartoon panel, by any means. Gumps cartoonist Sidney Smith created Ching Chow for the *Chicago Tribune/New York Daily News* syndicate in 1927, and, continued by Stanley Link in 1935, Will Henry in 1957 and, after a four-year lapse from 1971–1975, by Rocco Lotto and Will Levinson from 1975–1980. A stereotypically delineated Chinese with round face and long queue, he shared such thoughts as "It has been truly said—he who stumbles twice over the same stone deserves to break his shins."[12]

There were also sexist panels, such as Ethel Hays' Flapper Fanny for Newspaper Enterprise Association. The heroine, in a typical 1926 cartoon, raises her

Hambone's Meditations was syndicated from 1916 to 1968. This sample is from June 15, 1933.

skirt so she can admire a pair of shoes, as a clerk stands by with a dozen boxes in his arms. "The shoe clerk is often successful because he starts at the foot," is the caption.

Hambone had sufficient following that collections of the cartoons were brought out in 1917 and 1919. A 1934 retrospective included appreciations by Irvin S. Cobb and Roark Bradford, white authors who specialized in black fiction.

J.P. Alley died in spring 1934.

"His few words each day have been clipped and have found place in the scrap-books of philosophers and business men," an *August Chronicle* editor lamented.[13] "His homely common sense has found response in lives tempted to stray into impractical dreams. His sure basis of approach to life has given strength, and his apparent unconcern for the artificial has drawn thousands to a finer and better way of living. This has been done without one word of critical bitterness. Always there has been a humor which appeals to the clean heart of every man. Thousands of newspaper men who never had the opportunity of knowing the creator of 'Hambone' recognized in him one who made the craft to attract the best men."

An Augusta reader, W.E. Rainwater, wrote the newspaper to say he had clipped and collected the Hambone panels since the beginning, and had corresponded with the artist, receiving a reply in which Alley "stated that if 'Hambone's Meditations' had attained any measure of success he was well rewarded for his efforts as he was deeply interested in the portrayal of a type he had known intimately and loved since his boyhood plantation days."[14]

Hambone was not long orphaned. J.P. Alley's son, Calvin Lane Alley, took over the Meditations, with the assistance of his brother, James P. Alley Jr. (1912–1990),[15] who according to Holtz alternated weeks in drawing the panel. Their mother, Nona Alley, wrote for the panels.

Born in 1915, Cal Alley trained as an artist in Memphis and Chicago. He was an editorial cartoonist with the *Kansas City Journal* from 1939 to 1942, when it folded. He had brief experience there working on a comic strip titled "Shadow Grabbers," about a newspaper photographer and his reporter girlfriend. He then went to work for the *Nashville Banner*. Three years later he joined the *Appeal*.

How long did it take Alley to produce one of Hambone's Medita-

Hambone's rustic comments were collected in three books. This was the first, published by the *Commercial Appeal* in 1917.

tions? Ten hours and 20 minutes, he said. Ten hours to come up with the idea, 20 minutes to draw it.[16]

"Alley was best known for editorial cartoons that won him six awards from the Freedom Foundation and numerous citations from groups such as Sigma Delta Chi, the professional journalism society," according to the *Trenton Evening Times*.[17] He developed the family comic strip *The Ryatts*, distributed by Hall Syndicate beginning in 1954, and continuing (after his death, by other hands) until 1994. The strip was easy for the artist to illustrate; he and his wife, Sissy Jehl, had five children and a dog at home.

"Alley is one of the few cartoonists who uses pen and ink exclusively instead of grease pencil or lithograph crayon," according to one account.[18]

When he settled into *The Ryatts,* Cal Alley ceded Hambone to James. Cal Alley retired in 1965. When he died five years later, of cancer, he was 54. Cal Alley was inducted into the Tennessee Newspaper Hall of Fame in 1979.

By then, Hambone had also retired, unwillingly. Many thought the anachronism should have disappeared long before, but a major 65-day garbage hauler strike in Memphis in 1968 prompted a plea from municipal authorities to lay off the hackneyed, racist cartoons. Pickets were heard to chant, "Hambone just go." The Rev. Martin Luther King, Jr., speaking in Memphis a day before he was assassinated, lamented Hambone's overtones of African American subservience.

Historian Michael K. Honey described how galling the caricature Hambone and his homilies were in the 220,000-circulation daily: "The grinning simpleton Hambone, through his exaggerated lips, spoke in dialect, saying such things as, 'Ef tomorrow evuh *do* come, I reck'n Ole Tom gwine be de busies' man in de *whole worl*'!!!' Judge Benjamin Hooks related this image to 'total and colossal indifference to negroes and their achievements.'"[19]

The *Commercial Appeal*, which according to Honey considered itself progressive, finally backed down and in announcing Hambone's removal on 1 May 1968[20] said, "As with many other hallowed traditions, Hambone was not for the computer-space age.

"Nona Lane Alley, widow of the 'Hambone creator,' quoted one of the earlier sayings of the smiling negro philosopher: 'Dry dem tears. You cain't see de road wid you' eyes full o' cryin'. De Lawd leads de way fuh de folks what's a tryin'. Dry dem tears.'"[21]

Still, Clayton Rand in the *Times-Picayune* rued Hambone's expulsion: "This scribe has lost another old and dear friend, in the passing of Hambone, whose Meditations, rustic humor and surpassing wisdom charmed a generation of readers."[22]

He went on, "Hambone's Meditations and philosophic observations, exposing the follies and foibles of people, both black and white, personified the character of the colored race at its very best, when its members lived close to the soil. No other breed has contributed so much humor to our bi-racial society. One reason humor is dying out is that the races, creeds, and breeds of men have become supersensitive—they no longer want to be laughed at."

In a backward way, that writer was correct: blacks no longer wanted to be laughed at.

James P. Alley and Calvin Alley Notes

1. 22 March 1938.
2. "James P. Alley," Memphis History.
3. *American Newspaper Comics*, 181.

4. 15 December 1921.
5. 17 December 1919.
6. Cal Alley paid artistic tribute to Hubbard in a cartoon, "His Last Trestle Board," seen in, among other papers, the *Trenton Evening Times*, 7 January 1931, at the time of Hubbard's death.
7. Interview, Slave Narratives, WPA.
8. *The History of Negro Humor in America*, 54.
9. "New Hand-Coloring Stunt...," 23 March 1929.
10. "To Hambone's Biographer," 4.
11. Ibid.
12. 20 October 1928.
13. "Forward March! Hambone," 18 April 1934, 4.
14. "Deplores Death of Mr. Alley," *Augusta Chronicle*, 23 April 1934, 4.
15. Two sources, "Cartoonist Hurt in Auto Accident," *Times-Picayune*, 14 June 1945, 1, and Clayton Rand, "Dear Friend Is Lost," *Times-Picayune*, 22 May 1968, 42, suggest J.P. Alley Jr. also drew Hambone Meditations.
16. "Cal Alley," Memphis History.
17. "Calvin 'Cal' Alley, Editorial Cartoonist," 11 November 1970, 10.
18. "Five Children, Pup Play Big Part in Life of Alley," *Times-Picayune*, 10 October 1954, 22.
19. *Going Down Jericho Road*, 128.
20. Holtz in *American Newspaper Comics*, 181, indicates the strip ended in the *Florence Morning News* on 30 November 1968.
21. As reported in "Newspaper Drops Old Cartoon in Negro Dialect," *Corpus Christi Times*, 1 May 1968.
22. "Dear Friend Is Lost," 22 May 1967, 42.

James P. Alley and Calvin Alley Selected Bibliography and Sources

HAMBONE NEWSPAPER COMIC STRIP

Hambone's Meditations (1915–1968) originated in the Memphis *Commercial Appeal*, distributed by McClure Syndicate and later Bell Syndicate

BOOKS

Hambone's Meditations (1917)
The Meditations of Hambone (1919)
Hambone's Meditations (1934)
Hambone's Meditations (1972) with Elizabeth Alley Ahlgram
The Lively Art of J.P. Alley, 1885–1934 (1973)
Cal Alley (1973)

SOURCES

Alley, J.P. "His Last Trestle Board," *Trenton Evening Times*, 7 January 1931.
Bosman, Erwin. "Hambone," Blues Junction. http://bluesjunctionproductions.com/hambone (viewed 21 September 2012).
"Cal Alley," Memphis History. http://memphishistory.com/Politics/Newspapers/CalAlley.aspx (viewed 21 September 2012).
"Cal Alley," Tennessee Newspaper Hall of Fame. http://www.cci.utk.edu/jem/tn-newspaper-hall-fame/cal-alley (viewed 21 September 2012).
"Calvin 'Cal' Alley, Editorial Cartoonist," *Trenton Evening News*, 11 November 1970.
"Cartoonist Hurt in Auto Accident," *Times-Picayune*, 14 June 1956.
"Ching Chow," The Saturday Comics. http://bmj2k.com/2011/08/27/the-saturday-comics-ching-chow/ (viewed 21 September 2012).
Deas, Allen. "Negro Employee at Georgia R.R. Hambone's Image," *Augusta Chronicle*, 24 September 1928.
"Ching-Chow," Toon Encyclopedia. http://www.umich.edu/~csie/comicart/StripArt/chingchow/chingchow.html (viewed 21 September 2012).
Crawford, Charles W., ed. *Cal Alley*. Memphis: Memphis State University Press, 1973.

"Deplores Death of Mr. Alley," letter, *Augusta Chronicle*, 23 April 1934.
"Five Children, Pup Play Big Part in Life of Alley," *Times-Picayune*, 10 October 1954.
"Forward March! Hambone," *Augusta Chronicle*, 18 April 1934.
Holtz, Allan. *American Newspaper Comics: An Encyclopedic Reference Guide*. Ann Arbor: University of Michigan Press, 2012.
_____. "Ethel, Great Female Cartoonist," *Hogan's Alley* No. 13.
Honey, Michael K. *Going Down Jericho Road; The Memphis Strike, Martin Luther King's Last Campaign*. New York: W.W. Norton, 2007.
Hunley, Tom. Interview, slave narratives, Federal Writer's Project of the Works Progress Administration for the State of Mississippi. http://msgw.org/slaves/hunley-xslave.htm (viewed 21 September 2012).
Hyman, Tony. "Hambone Fantasies & Fakes," National Cigar Museum, http://cigarhistory.info/Frauds-Fakes-Fantasies/Hambone_fakes.html (viewed 21 September 2012).
"J.P. Alley, Memphis Cartoonist, Expires," *Dallas Morning News*, 17 April 1934.
"James P. Alley," Memphis History. http://memphishistory.com/Politics/Newspapers/JPAlley.aspx (viewed 21 September 2012).
Kelly, Fred. *The Life and Times of Kin Hubbard, Creator of Abe Martin*. New York: Farrar, Straus & Young, 1952.
"New Hand-Coloring Stunt Sold FULL Pages for Thirty Weeks in Commercial Appeal—Prizes Offered—Originated by Jim Alley and Hugh J. Mooney," *Editor & Publisher*, 23 March 1929.
"Newspaper Drops Old Cartoon in Negro Dialect," *Corpus Christi Times*, 1 May 1968.
Rand, Clayton. "Dear Friend Is Lost," *Times-Picayune*, 22 May 1968.
Schechter, William. *The History of Negro Humor in America*. New York: Fleet Press, 1970.
"To Hambone's Biographer," *Augusta Chronicle*, 4 April 1934.

Ambrose E. Gonzales
(1857–1926)
Black Border (1922)

"Witch mus' be pit bad mout' 'puntop Betsey. I 'spec' 'e done cunjuh."
"Pa, is you pit any powduh een dat gun?"
"Who? Me? Wuh gun? Betsey? C'ose I pit powduh een um."
—Boysie, in "Simon the 'Squerril' Hunter"[1]

Ambrose E. Gonzales was a journalist by profession, an anthropologist by aspiration. He was intrigued by the Gullah, descendants of slaves on coastal South Carolina and Georgia who spoke in a lilting mash of English, Creole and other tongues. He wrote about them often.

Born on a Paolo Parish, South Carolina, plantation in 1857, Ambrose Elliott Gonzales was the son of an exiled Cuban patriot and Confederate Army chief of artillery for Gen. P.G.T. Beauregard, Ambrosio José Gonzales, and his wife, Harriet Rutledge Elliot. Though his parents had come from wealth, Ambrose grew up in increasingly poor circumstances during Reconstruction. He attended a private school but not college, though he was bestowed an honorary doctor of laws degree by the University of South Carolina in 1923.[2]

Gonzales and his younger brother, Narciso Gener Gonzales (1859–1903), learned the newspaper trade with the Charleston *News and Courier*. Narciso was the Columbia, South Carolina, bureau chief during the Tillman political days, Ambrose was assigned the agriculture beat. The two men in 1891 started a newspaper in Columbia, *The State*, to which Ambrose from time to time contributed black dialect sketches under the column heading Silhouettes. Fourteen appeared in 1892, a fifteenth in 1895.

The State was a respected newspaper, and Ambrose the "most capable and constructive of the three brothers [William E. Gonzales was also active with the newspaper] who made the Columbia *State* a newspaper of commanding usefulness. It is the product of the union of old Cuban and South Carolina families, the forbears of the Gonzales branch being distinguished patriots in the early struggles for Cuban independence," according to the Springfield *Republican*.[3]

The State emerged in the dregs of recovery from Reconstruction. "*The State* from the first has been free from sensation, free from yellowness, free from all selfish ends," the *Republican* went on. "It has been the sort of paper that Editor Mooney told the editors at Asheville last week the South must have to serve this day and generation—a paper that printed the news and contained 'courageous editorials.'"

The State through N.G. Gonzales's sharply worded editorials was staunchly in favor of the old-guard Bourbons who elected Gen. Wade Hampton III as governor and, later, U.S. Senator. It opposed particularly Lt. Gov. James H. Tillman, nephew of South Carolina Gov. Benjamin R. "Pitchfork" Tillman, both members of the Farmer's movement. Tillman called Gonzales "the Cuban pony." Gonzales called the lieutenant governor "Tillman the Little." The Tillmans were voted out in the 1902 election. The next January, Tillman killed N.G. Gonzales with a Luger pistol, in a confrontation outside the South Carolina statehouse. Following a sensational trial held in another county, Tillman was found not guilty—the likely tainted jury concluded he was the victim of an outrageous crusade and entitled to take justice in his own hands.[4] Gonzales became a martyr.

Ambrose was "a man of real literary taste and talent, but he was also the practical director of the business." He took over the company. The third brother, William, who under President Woodrow Wilson served as ambassador to Cuba and Peru, later became editor of *The State*. (A fourth brother had died in the fight for Cuban freedom.)

Gonzales suffered a stroke that impeded his movements and restricted his speech. He lost his "remarkable baritone voice,"[5] in which he frequently sang opera. While recovering, he assembled forty-two of his Gullah pieces for a book, *The Black Border* (1922). The State Company, his own corporation, issued the volume. The stories replicated the Gullah tongue of the 1890s, which the writer had heard from slaves while growing up on his family's rice plantation. Despite Gonzales's interest in preserving the way these people talked, by modern standards, the stories are demeaning and racist.

A reviewer in the *Charleston News and Courier* praised Gonzales's stories: "If Ambrose Gonzales had been free to devote his talents to literature no one who has read the stories he has written in the past three or four years will question that he would have made a place for himself with the greatest creative writers this country has produced. With his fine imagination, his mastery of words, his sure and discriminating grasp of character and his rich dramatic instinct he was preeminently the man to have interpreted imperishably the period which marked the passing in South Carolina of the old regime and the coming of the new."[6]

A.W. Brabham in a letter to *The State* lauded Gonzales's grasp of the vernacular: "The real rice field dialect is passing away. The younger generation is thrown more with the whites, is being educated to some extent, and the dialect spoken by their ante-bellum ancestors will soon be a thing of the past. Hundreds of writers have tried to write this dialect, but they have all made miserable failures. Of all the dialect writers, Mr. Gonzales is the only one who writes it as it was spoken."[7]

The writer went on to explain that Gullah is a combination of English, French and Spanish "and not less than three tribal dialects, Yemassee, Cherokee and tribal African. It is likely that it contains parts of several African dialects for the importation of slaves came from several districts of the black belt of Africa. In each district a different dialect is spoken even to this day."[8]

In contrast, Brabham said, "The purest English spoken outside of England could be heard among the rice planters of South Carolina. This can be accounted for easily. The planters educated their children in England."

Others wrote in the Gullah dialect, notably William Gilmore Simms (1806–1870), who anticipated Gonzales with his story "A Scene of the Revolution" in *The Book of My Lady* in 1833.

Gonzales once said the Gullah lingo fell on the ear as pleasantly as the Irish brogue. He included a glossary in the first book. A reader today needs not only a glossary, but at least a familiarity with the sound of Gullah. Gonzales's replications are slow reading.

This next excerpt is lawyer Hacklus Manigo speaking in "A Short Cut to Justice," from *Tales of the Black Border*. Manigo is providing a defense for Paul Harris, a free mulatto who has been charged with assault on the black slave who belonged to a wealthy white man:

> "De debble! Punkin skin' nigguh fuh beat black nigguh en' black nigguh ent fuh beat'um back, enty? Oonuh ebbuh yeddy 'bout shishuh t'ing since you bawn? Me fuh 'low yalluh nigguh fuh knock me en' me yent fuh knock'um back! No, man! Uh knock'um ef uh dead!"
>
> "Yaas, man, *knock'um, knock'um*!" came the cries of approval...
>
> "Uh yent fuh wait 'tell 'e knock me fus'. Uh gwine knock'um befo' 'e hice 'e han'! Uh knock-'um een 'e yeye, uh kick'um on 'e shin, alltwo one time. Den uh butt'um een 'e belly. Uh double'um up 'cause 'e too swonguh, 'e too 'laagin'! Cap'n, who dis yalluh nigguh nyuse to blonx to een slabery time?" he asked the foreman.
>
> "To nobody [the foreman replied]. He was free. He belonged to himself."
>
> "Great Gawd! Cap'n, all dese'yuh mans blonx to quality! ... En' da' yalluh t'ing wuh blonx to nigguh tek 'to'ruhty 'puntop 'eself fuh knock nigguh wuh blonx to juntlemun, en bex w'en de nigguh knock'um back! No, suh, 'e mus be fool! Leh we tu'n Bredduh Paul loose!"
>
> "*Yaas, man, tu'n'um loose, tu'n'um loose*!" came the chorus...

In short, Harris was defending himself and why should he be convicted just because he struck a rich man's Negro?

Gonzales's first book did well enough that he followed it with three more: *The Captain: Stories of the Black Border, Laguerre: A Gascon of the Black Border* and *With Aesop Along the Black Border*, all in 1924. The last title included folk tales such as "De Fox en de Crow," about a clever fox who tricks a crow into dropping her piece of meat stolen from a white man. The fox reasons the crow, liking to talk, will open her beak to respond to him, and let loose her prize.

> Fox call to de Crow: "Mawnin tittuh," e say. "Uh so glad you tief da meat fum de buckruh, cause him bin fuh trow-um-way pan de dog.... E mek me bex fuh see man do shishuh ting lukkuh dat."

Gonzales described the origin of the Gullah dialect this way in the introduction to his first book: "Slovenly and careless of speech, these Gullahs seized upon the peasant English used by some of the early settlers and by the white servants of the wealthier Colonists, wrapped their clumsy tongues about it as well as they could, and, enriched with certain expressive African words, it issued through their flat noses and thick lips as so workable a form of speech that it was gradually adopted by the other slaves and became in time the accepted Negro speech of the lower districts of South Carolina and Georgia. With characteristic laziness, these Gullah Negroes took short cuts to the ears of their auditors, using as few words as possible, sometimes making one gender serve for three, one tense for several, and totally disregarding singular and plural numbers. Yet, notwithstanding this economy of words, the Gullah sometimes incorporates into his speech grotesquely difficult and unnecessary English words; again, he takes unusual pains to transpose numbers and genders."[9]

"Mr. Gonzales' gullah is as perfect as it can be written, and he is easily the first honor man in that school. The low-country negro's description of a jackass to a negro who had never seen a jackass: 'E look same like mule, only mo' so,' is almost true of Mr. Gonzales' gullah," adored J.W.H. Dyches in a letter to *The State*'s editor in 1922.[10]

Gonzales thumped his own drum in *The Black Border* introduction. His stories, he said with modestly, were better than those of Thomas Nelson Page, who wrote well enough about the family man servant of the old days who was forever tied to his master, but "as to the younger Negro, Negro life before and since the war, and the relations of Negroes to one another, it is to be regretted that he has contributed little or nothing."[11] Harry Stillwell Edwards, Gonzales said, only touched on the Gullah dialect. And, "The genius of Joel Chandler Harris, who, with Judge Longstreet and his 'Georgia Scenes,' fixed Georgia firmly upon the literary map of the world, embalmed the Negro myths and folk-tales of the South so subtly in the amber of his understanding that 'Uncle Remus' is known and loved by the children of half the civilized world. There was little creative work in 'Uncle Remus.'"[12]

A *New York Evening Post* reviewer, Herschel Brickell, lamented that the stories might go unnoticed: "It is unfortunate that the majority of negro dialect stories may be dismissed as utterly worthless. Inaccurate in the representation of the speech of the negro, they are equally as faulty in their efforts to catch his fresh humor and quaint spirit. But Mr. Gonzales knows his Gullah negro, he knows the life of the rice plantations, '"puntop Cumbre,' and added to this intimate knowledge, which arises from his recognition of the camber of an unusual dialect, he has a pleasing style of his own."[13]

W.C.B., a reviewer, chimed in, *The Black Border* "is a contribution to good literature and it will live as long as other good books live."[14] And John Bennett added, "Not since Wilson's day, unless in Twain's 'Roughing It,' have we had such stout exuberance of naïve, rustic humor, wholehearted jocularity, and broad, ironic mirth."[15]

Gonzales enjoyed the praise, and he made sure it was reprinted in *The State*.

Gonzales never married. He died in 1926, following a sudden seizure.

Ambrose E. Gonzales Notes

1. From *Black Border*.
2. "Ambrose E. Gonzales Had Most Remarkable Career," *Augusta Chronicle*, 13 July 1926, 4.
3. "Three Gonzales Brothers," 19 July 1926, 6.
4. See "Editor Shot Down," *Dallas Morning News*, 16 January 1903, 1, and "Gonzales Is of Fighting Stock," *Fort Worth Star-Telegram*, 19 January 1903, 1.
5. "Ambrose E. Gonzales Had Most Remarkable Career," op cit.
6. 1 January 1922, 7.

7. "Rice Field Dialect," *The State*, 15 December 1917, 4.

8. The writer said the tidewater section of North Carolina was held for a time by the French and the Spanish, and had previously been home to the two Indian tribes.

9. Page 9.

10. "Mr. Gonzales' Gullah," Columbia (S.C.) *State*, 2 February 1922, 4.

11. Ibid., 12.

12. Ibid.

13. "Gullah Stories Show Unique Negro Type," reprinted in Columbia (S.C.) *State*, 29 October 1922, 29.

14. Review, Columbia (S.C.) *State*, 26 November 1922, 12.

15. "'Comedie Humaine' of the Gullah Darkey," Columbia (S.C.) *State*, 17 December 1922, 26.

Ambrose E. Gonzales Selected Bibliography and Sources

SILHOUETTES COLUMNS

1. "Issue missing from archive" (Columbia, S.C., *The State*, 21 February 1892)
2. "The Cat Was Crazy" (Columbia *State*, 28 February 1892)
3. "A Congaree Water Color" (Columbia *State*, 6 March 1892)
4. "Waiting till the Bridegroom" Comes (Columbia *State*, 13 March 1892)
5. "A Gullah's Tale of Woe" (Columbia *State*, 20 March 1892)
6. "The Doctor Didn't Exceed" (Columbia *State*, 27 March 1892)
7. "The Lady Couldn't 'Specify'" (Columbia *State*, 3 April 1892)
8. "A Question of Privilege" (Columbia *State*, 10 April 1892)
9. "Conductor Smith's Dilemma" (Columbia *State*, 17 April 1892)
10. "One Was Taken—the Other Left" (Columbia *State*, 24 April 1892)
11. "Egg-Zactly" (Columbia *State*, 1 May 1892)
12. "An Interrupted Offertory" (Columbia *State*, 8 May 1892)
13. "Old Wine—New Bottles" (Columbia *State*, 15 May 1892)
14. "A Flaw in the 'Eenditement'" (Columbia *State*, 22 May 1892)
15. "De Fuss' Lick" (Columbia *State*, 17 March 1895)

SELECTED LATER COLUMNS

"Pon Pon Echoes" (Columbia *State*, 21 April 1918)
"Sam Dickerson" (Columbia *State*, 26 May 1918)
"My Maussa" (Columbia *State*, 23 June 1918)
"The Yellow Jacket" (Columbia *State*, 21 December 1920)
"Riever of the Black River" (Columbia *State*, 31 December 1922)

BOOKS

The Black Border: Gullah Stories of the Carolina Coast (1922)
The Captain: Stories of the Black Border (1924)
Laguerre: A Gascon of the Black Border (1924)
With Aesop Along the Black Border (1924)
Two Gullah Tales: The Turkey Hunter and at the Cross Roads Store (1926)

SOURCES

"Ambrose E. Gonzales, Author and Publisher, Died Early Yesterday," Augusta (Ga.) *Chronicle*, 12 July 1926, 1.
"Ambrose E. Gonzales Had Most Remarkable Career," Augusta (Ga.) *Chronicle*, 13 July 1926.
"Ambrose Gonzales Dies," Portland *Oregonian*, 12 July 1926.
"'Comedie Humaine' of the Gullah Darkey," Columbia (S.C.) *The State*, 17 December 1922.
"Editor Shot Down," *Dallas Morning News*, 16 January 1903.
Gonzales, Ambrose E. *Rumbling of the Chariot Wheels, Doings and Misdoings in the Barefooted Period of a Boy's Life on a Southern Plantation*. Columbia, S.C.: The State, 1918.
"Gonzales Is of Fighting Stock," Fort Worth (Tex.) *Star-Telegram*, 19 January 1903.
"Gullah Stories Show Unique Negro Type," Columbia *State*, 29 October 1922.

"Mr. Gonzales' Gullah," Columbia *State*, 2 February 1918.
"Our Silhouette Artist," Columbia *State*, 8 April 1892.
"Returned," Columbia (S.C.) *The State*, 17 November 1898.
"Rice Field Dialect," Columbia *State*, 15 December 1917.
"Those Sunday Silhouettes," Columbia *State*, 30 March 1892.
"Three Gonzales Brothers," Springfield (Mass.) *Republican*, 19 July 1926.
"Volume We Miss," Columbia *State*, 1 January 1922.
W.C.B., *The Black Border* review, Columbia *State*, 26 November 1922.

Robert McBlair
(1888–1976)
Mister Fish Kelly

A mouse poked its sharp gray head from a hole in the corner, then ran out with quick tiny steps, stopped, sat up on its haunches, and regarded him with black friendly eyes, turning its head from side to side and wiggling its infinitesimal nose and whiskers. Fish grinned companionably at the mouse, and got up, feeling in his bosom that something wonderful was about to happen.

—*Mister Fish Kelly*[1]

Pulp writer Robert McBlair may have been born in 1888 and died in 1976. He may have come from Virginia. He may have been a wholesale lumberman in New York City and secretary to the Lumberman's Bureau in 1911. He may have married Gretchen Frick of Wisconsin.

He may have written a little poetry for *Bookman* and a little humor for *Gaiety* from 1921 to 1927. He may have written short fiction such as "One of the Beautiful Few" for *The Midlands* January 1922 number and "Murder in the Death House" for *Detective Fiction Weekly*'s 4 May 1935 issue. He may have written four stories for *Munsey's* from 1926 to 1928 and one short story, "A Seeing Eye," for *Collier's* in 1932. He may have written for *Dynamic Adventure* and *Five-Novels Monthly* and *Western Adventure* and *The Smart Set* and *Complete Stories*. He may have written stories syndicated to newspapers such as "Mr. Simkin Pays His Income Tax" in 1918 and "The Ghost of Broadway" and "Love Takes a Hand" in 1947.

But definitely he, or someone with his name, wrote a dozen short stories for *Popular Magazine*, from June 1918 to March 1927, featuring a black character named Mr. Fish Kelly.

"Stories featuring stereotypical characters like McBlair's Mr. Fish Kelley and Cohen's Florian Slappey helped to spread the image of the Negro as an inferior buffoon," Leon Coleman said.[2]

Street & Smith published *Popular Magazine* from 1903 to 1931. In its heyday it came out twice a month and included the fiction of well-known authors such as Rafael Sabatini, Zane Grey, Arthur B. Reeve, Sax Rohmer and Edgar Wallace. Editor Charles Agnew MacLean purchased the Kelly stories, ten of which were strung together in an eponymously titled book in 1924 from D. Appleton and Company.

Robert McBlair was familiar to pulp magazine readers, and apparently to consumers of the *Saturday Review*, whose editor in 1932 included a McBlair poem, "Hangman's Holiday," in his "The Phoenix's Nest" column, with the remark the "individual poem by our old friend, Robert McBlair, seems to us well worth quoting."[3]

Robert McBlair's Mister Fish Kelly held a piece of information that was key to his future success, in stories that appeared in *Popular Magazine* from 1918 to 1927. This illustration, from the D. Appleton book, is by an unidentified artist.

Not a huge stone in the rambling wall of black characters created by white writers in the Jim Crow era, but a stone nevertheless, and a stone who left virtually no biographical trail except for this scrap from a Helena, Montana, newspaper, the *Independent*: "Robert McBlair, author of the new novel, 'Mister Fish Kelly,' has joined the McDowell Colony at Peterborough, N.H., where he expects to do much writing. 'Mister Fish Kelly' is a humorous story of a negro character in his native southern environment."[4]

The *Mister Fish Kelly* book, issued by D. Appleton, garnered a praising review in the *Times-Picayune* for showing "his negro characters in their native Southern Environment. Mr. Fish Kelly is an ebony gentleman who struggles under the despotic domination of a lazy individual who depends upon Fish to extricate his chestnuts from the fire. Freedom dawns for Fish it seems through a marital connection; but he awakens to find a father-in-law can be a task of unparalleled severity. Yet there comes a day when the triumphant Mr. Fish Kelly can turn the tables on his persecutors—an event which is the climax of this hilarious volume."[5]

The Syracuse (N.Y.) *Herald* reviewer found the book a pleasing story of "the occasionally rainied incidents in the life of as funny, no-account, shiftless, yet profound and crafty bacon-colored gentleman as ever figured in any tale, short or long. Fish is the saddest darky in the world with a philosophy that stirs a white man to mirth. For a time he barely lives by carrying out the schemes of the domineering 'reverend' alias 'Lawyer Little,' of the same complexion of race and morals, a well smoked Solomon among his tribe and ever like the lilies of the field. Fish does the toiling and the spinning. Then he rebels. How he schemes to emancipate himself by marrying the glorious Miss Macedonia Clinton, then find a father-in-law worse than his former tyrant, is diverting and his turn of tables in the climax unexpected and hilarious. Evidently McBlair knows his Southland; the darky environment is his forte, and the unconscious humor of the darky mind is to him an open book. The welding of the separate tales has made a very amusing novel.[6]

The Davenport *Democrat and Leader's* reviewer observed, "The young colored gemman who gave the title to this book is in hard luck thru most of its progress. Domineered by 'Lawyer' Little, another gentleman of color who lives solely by his wiles, he falls also under the heel of a father-in-law when he marries the lovely Macedonia Clinton. Unwittingly, however, he stumbles upon the secret of the older Clinton's life—the skeleton that resides in his close—and the tables are turned. Fish's triumph is a delightful termination of a really humorous tale of Southern Negro Life."[7]

All that's left is to look at some of the stories, which to this reader are rather leaden in plot movement, dull in character, and pained in dialogue. As one reviewer noted, Kelly is just out to keep life simple. He hopes marriage is his path to happiness.

To win the heart of his desired bride, how about a gift? A clock, perhaps, from Moses Greenberg's store:

> "How much one dese clocks, Mr. Mose?" Fish inquired, brightening as he pictured how Miss Macedonia would smile to receive one.
> Macedonia giggled. "What you want wid one of dem clocks?"
> "Gimme dat one, Mr. Mose."
> "Where's your money, Fish?"
> "You kin take it out my pay."
> "Nothing doing," replied Mr. Moses Greenberg decidedly. "Not till you clean up that eight dollars coming to me."
> "When you ain't got no money you needn't come around!" sang a rich baritone, and Ted Harpy pushed his burly frame in front of the showcase, elbowing Fish out of place. His gold tooth fairly scintillated in his round brown grinning face. His sharply pressed mustard-colored suit, his striped silk shirt, and his apple-green cravat fastened with a diamond as large as a pigeon's egg, were aptly calculated to catch the feminine eye.
> "At nigger ain't gwine never buy you nothing.' He jes' talkin'," said he to Miss Clinton, whose white teeth were showing self-consciously at the appearance of competition.

"Who ain't gwine buy her sumpin'? I got money."

"Yeah. You got money like a fish got hair," retorted the driver of Mr. Greenberg's delivery wagon. "You don't know how to take care of no little brown. Whyn't you go 'way an' leave a man's job to a man?"

Fish took in awfully the big thews of Ted Harpy's shoulders, but he would have faced death itself, at any rate conversationally, if Miss Clinton were looking on."[8]

The story and characters have the easygoing gait of the later Correll and Gosden Sam and Henry, or early Amos and Andy, but without the wit.

Mr. Fish Kelly's literary career in *Popular Magazine* didn't last much beyond the book's issue. McBlair's later publications included "Philosophy," a poem in *New Republic* in 1928; a romance novel, *Black Gold*, in 1929; and *A Modern Version of the Night before Christmas* in 1932.

Robert McBlair Notes

1. Page 97.
2. "Carl Van Vechten and the Harlem Renaissance: A Critical Assessment."
3. 8 October 1932, 168.
4. "Authors and Their Books Seen in a Casual Manner," 27 July 1924.
5. 20 April 1924, 83.
6. 11 May 1924.
7. 24 June 1924.
8. *Mr. Fish Kelly*, 150–151.

Robert McBlair Selected Bibliography and Sources

MISTER FISH KELLY STORIES

"Never Irritate a Lion" (*Popular Magazine*, 7 June 1918) (1)
"Anybody in the Audience" (*Popular Magazine*, 20 January 1019) (1)
"Read 'Em and Weep" (*Popular Magazine*, 7 October 1920) (1)
"'Fish' Kelly, Jonah" (*Popular Magazine*, 7 March 1921) (1)
"Apology Accepted" (*Popular Magazine*, 20 June 1921) (1)
"Love Powders and Dragon's Blood" (*Popular Magazine*, 7 February 1922) (1)
"A Man What Stirs Up Trouble" (*Popular Magazine*, 7 August 1922) (1)
"Settin' Pretty" (*Popular Magazine*, 20 January 1923) (1)
"Luck" (*Popular Magazine*, 7 April 1923) (1)
"Natural Methods" (*Popular Magazine*, 20 July 1926) (1)
"The Ace of Spades" (*Popular Magazine*, 20 December 1926)
"Mr. Kelly's Corpus" (*Popular Magazine*, 20 March 1927)

McBlair wrote 11 more stories for Popular Magazine, the characters not yet identified.

BOOK

Mister Fish Kelly (1924) The book rearranges magazine stories in 24 chapters.

SOURCES

"Authors and Their Books Seen in a Casual Manner," Helena, Mont., *Independent*, 27 July 1924.
Coleman, Leon. "Carl Van Vechten and the Harlem Renaissance: A Critical Assessment," in *Studies in African American History and Culture*. Graham Russell Hodges, ed. New York: Garland, 1998.
Mr. Fish Kelly review. *Davenport Democrat and Leader*, 15 June 1924.
Mr. Fish Kelly review. *Times-Picayune*, 20 April 1924.
Mr. Fish Kelly review. *Syracuse Herald*, 11 May 1924.
"Phoenix's Nest," *Saturday Review*, 8 October 1932.

Octavus Roy Cohen
(1891–1959)

*Florian Slappey, Lawyer Chew, Epic Peters,
Midnight Film Corp. and Birmingham's Darktown*

> I think humorists, for the most part, are an extremely intelligent crowd. It is much easier to interpret life darkly than to present it cheerfully, in its brighter phases, just as it is much easier to be gloomy about living than it is to be happy about it.
> —*Octavus Roy Cohen*[1]

Octavus Roy Cohen was a capable, prolific, entertaining mid-twentieth-century fiction writer who sold more short stories to the *Saturday Evening Post* than any other writer, yet he is not only largely forgotten today, he's actively disdained. The *Post* brought out book collections of Tugboat Annie and Colin Glencannon and Alexander Botts stories—but none of Florian Slappey, the smart-dressing, jive man-about-Birmingham. Nor should it have. The stories are considered highly derogatory today.

Cohen was both a product and a victim of his times. A product, in that he was encouraged to write his dialect ethnic tales of city blacks and found a receptive audience; a victim because, had his editors discouraged his direction, or toned back his ridicule, his talent and drive would have assured him success with other subjects, as happened years later.

Octavus Roy Cohen—he pronounced his first name Ock-tave-us—came from a line of southern Jewish Cohens prominent in Charleston, South Carolina, and environs for two centuries. He was descended from Moses Cohen, who emigrated from London, England, in 1815 and was among those to build the first place of Jewish worship in the South. It was also the second synagogue in North America.

The author's great-great-grandfather, Jacob Cohen, son of the rabbi, served as an officer in the Continental Army. His great-grandfather, also Jacob Cohen, was a soldier in the War of 1812 and the Mexican War. His grandfather, Joseph Cohen, was a civil engineer and officer in the Confederate Army.

His father, Charleston native Octavus Cohen (1860–1927), the son of Joseph Cohen and Sarah Barrett, was a veteran of World War I. He was a syndicate editor and later assistant managing editor of the American Press Association in New York City. His play *Santee* was produced in Brooklyn in 1897. He returned to Charleston in 1880 to edit the *Charleston World*. Later he went back to New York, and then he settled permanently in Charleston in 1906 to practice law.[2] He was one-time candidate for lieutenant governor in South Carolina.

The author's mother, Rebecca Florence Ottolengui (1856–1928), also a Charleston native, was the daughter of Israel Ottolengui and Rosalie Cecile Moise. In 1910 she was president of the Charleston Section of the Council of Jewish Women and delivered an address on "The Observance of Mother's Day."[3]

Octavus Roy Cohen was born in June 1891 in South Carolina. He attended Porter Military Academy (now Porter-Gaud School) and Clemson Agricultural College (now University), where he studied civil engineering.[4] Some sources indicate he graduated in 1908, but Cohen himself said he "took three-quarters of an engineering degree at Clemson College, South Carolina.[5] Following a series of disagreements with the faculty relative to my desirability as a student, I departed suddenly and completely from the zone of higher learning and went to shoveling coal in Alabama. Lovely existence shoveling coal. Romance of the mining camps, and all that sort of thing."[6]

He worked for Tennessee Coal, Iron and Railroad Co. in 1909 and 1910. That was the extent of his career as an engineer.

"I was the world's lousiest engineer, but bad," he told a reporter, "with the emphasis on 'bad.'"[7]

In an autobiographical essay for *Our American Humorists*, Cohen said there ensued "a series of misadventures, each embarked upon with the idea of securing the wherewithal for the next meal. I wound up as a newspaper reporter on the Birmingham (Ala.) *Ledger*, now happily defunct. That was in 1910. I continued in newspaper work principally as a sport writer in Charleston, South Carolina; various New Jersey papers ... with a bit of a space assignment, now and then, from New York journals."

Octavus Roy Cohen produced nearly 400 stories featuring black characters (author's collection).

After the *Ledger*, Cohen was with the Charleston *News and Courier* then he was editor and general manager for the *Bayonne Times* and assistant city editor and feature writer for the *Newark Morning Star*, both in New Jersey

He returned to South Carolina to clerk in his father's law office until he was sufficiently versed in law to take the state's bar exam in 1913. He practiced in Charleston for two years. But he still yearned to write.

"I started writing while I was studying law—and I sold my first stories just when I was about to be admitted to the bar—I continued with the writing in preference to law," he said.[8]

His father had written, among other things, sports and arts stories for a syndicate. Octavus Cohen's theatrical review of Rice's burlesque *1492* and Heinrich's Grand Opera Company's season, as an example, appeared in the *Lewiston Evening Journal*.[9] He discussed Amelia Bingham's appearance in *Hearts Aflame*, as another example, in a column that appeared in, among other papers, the *Mansfield Daily Shield*.[10]

The law office became drudgery for the son. "For many long and dreary months, I puzzled over legal phrases and legal forms. During that period I amused myself by hammering a typewriter. I judge that I amused a good many editors, too," he said.[11]

Octavus Roy Cohen sent out manuscripts of fiction. Editors set back notes of rejection. He finally made a $25 sale to *Blue Book*, an early pulp-era fiction magazine, in 1913. It was an engineering story.[12]

"I lifted plot material from five other previously rejected yarns and fashioned them into one thriller," he said.[13] "The *Blue Book* bought another story a few days later, and although my check for it was only $15, I was content. At last I was writing stuff that somebody would print and pay for."

Cohen fell in love.

As he explained, "In 1913 I became engaged. In 1914 I married the girl to whom I was engaged, Miss Inez Lopez [1892–1953] of Bessemer, Alabama. She is now the mother of one child, to wit: Octavus Roy Cohen, junior, age five [in 1922], and persistently growing older."[14]

Cohen's bride was the daughter of Edward Hinton Lopez and Cecile Ottolengui. The couple's son Octavus Jr. (1916–1974) would marry Katherine Van Allen Tallman (1911–2008).[15] He would also write, under a yet-to-be-revealed pen name beginning in 1937,[16] before taking up a career in real estate in New Jersey in 1950.[17]

> "At the time of my marriage, I made a momentous decision," Cohen Sr. said. "Coming to the conclusion that no hazard was quite so desperate as matrimony, I dropped my law practice and dedicated myself to a writing career. The first month after that marriage my total receipts from the literary field amounted to $15. I had just about decided that a mistake of judgment had been made when the stories—I had seventy of them in circulation—commenced to sell.
>
> "Since then I've been pretty fortunate. But it was hard sledding for awhile.
>
> "For several years I tried to make up in story-quantity what I lacked in story-quality. And finally, back in 1918, I conceived the idea of fictionizing the ultra-modern city negro of the South.
>
> "I started something when I did that particularly as that first attempt and all that have followed it up to the date of this writing sold to the *Saturday Evening Post*. And I suspect that, because the negro lends himself so readily to a humorous portrayal, I have taken a sort of rank as a humorist. Certainly, if that doesn't explain the inclusion of this autobiography in this book, then nothing can.
>
> "And so, for three years, I have devoted myself to negro stories, to an occasional outside short story that demanded to be writ, and, by way of variety detective novels. And plays of various sorts."[18]

While most pulp writers aspired to higher status, Octavus Roy Cohen didn't think it untoward to start low and work his way up.

"The pulps are the finest training ground in the world," Cohen said in an interview with David W. Hazen for *The Oregonian*. "Instead of looking down, I look up to them. Those who serve a novitiate in the pulps, when they do break into the big magazines usually will keep going for many, many years.

"They get a training that serves them in good stead throughout their professional life," Cohen went on. "Nearly all of the successful writers today once wrote for the pulps and they were highly elated whenever they received checks from these magazines. Among the very successful novelists who started on the pulp road to fame are Sinclair Lewis and Mary Roberts Rinehart."[19]

Cohen said he churned out a million words a year, using three pen names. "I was one of the most prolific pulp writers there ever was, from sport stories in the United States to South Sea island love mysteries." He wrote for *Top-Notch*, *Argosy*, *Sports Story*, *Detective Magazine*, *All-Story Weekly*, *Operator 5*, *Fight Stories* and *Pioneer Tales*.

"I had no illusions about what I was doing," the author told William Whitman. "I tried to do good work, the best that I could. I wasn't paid much, but I figured it was like working my way through college. I was learning how to write, and the only way to learn how to write is to write, and that takes a long time."[20]

His first story published in a major periodical was for *Collier's* in 1915.²¹ Acceptance came, the author told the *Kansas City Times*,²² after 130 other stories had been tossed back. With the *Collier's* success, he reworked and sold many of those earlier rejects.

There's another telling of how he started out.

"Authorship is said to have been an accident with Octavus Cohen," the *Augusta Chronicle* said in 1937.²³ "Having been seized with the writing fever to such an extent that it interfered with his law business, he decided to give it a fling and let discouragements and rejection slips restore him to normal again—but such is the contrariness of fate, enough checks came instead of the expected rejections to make authorship win over the legal profession."

He took up writing full time, and eventually published fifty-six books—humorous novels, mysteries, science fiction and short-story collections—and, at a guess, 2,000 short stories.²⁴ As the *Chronicle* told its readers, "his métier is the Southern darky story."

"Cohen is a small, unassuming young man with blue eyes, a shock head and a soft musical voice with a slight southern twang," the *Kansas City Times* said.²⁵ "He says he is 28 years old, but should occasion demand he could easily pass for four years younger. He talked of himself only when urged and then reservedly. All in all, he is just what one would expect from his stories that scintillate with wit and humor, but with never a touch of the questionable."

The writer credited his newsroom background for helping him write fiction. "'I wouldn't take anything for the time I spent on the Bayonne, N.J., *Times*,' he said. 'In the morning I wrote editorials, then I covered police and hurried back to the office to read copy, and often I found my linotype operator under the influence of demon rum. Under such circumstance there was nothing for me to do but to operate the machine, and I did. I am firmly convinced the machine in that office was the one that drove Mr. Mergenthaler, the inventor, insane.'"

Cohen once described his writing routine: "I always keep two stories going. I write two stories, two rough drafts. Then I polish one. Put that aside, and write another rough draft. Polish the second, then back to the first until it is finished. Writing is a business. Of course, speaking of talent, genius, inspiration, whatever you call it, we have it in a measure in all we do. But not always in the same measure. A great violinist is not always exalted, but he is always a master technician."²⁶

The author said he tried sports and other genres, then determined to find something no one else was doing.²⁷

"Cohen, who was born and has always lived in the south, conceived the idea of the modern negro story," the *Kansas City Times* said. "His first was accepted immediately and in the year since that day he has written twenty-three of the same kind for the same magazine. It was with these stories he 'broke into' the leading publications, where they are now in demand."²⁸

"There were two types of people he [thought he] would never write about, detectives and negroes," columnist Whitman wrote in 1929. "So said Octavius [sic] Roy Cohen. 'And all the real success I've had,' he declared recently, 'has come from these two sources.'"²⁹

"The negro had long been a prominent character in literature," Hollywood columnist Robin Coons noted in 1929, "but no author had written of him as a social entity in city life—so Cohen did. The result was that publishers' estimates of the cash value of all his works multiplied about 25 times in three months."³⁰

Cohen's second Birmingham story, "Pool and Genuine,"[31] finds dapper Florian Slappey out of sorts. The horses won't win for him, the morning (Pool) and afternoon (Genuine) lotteries sneer at him, his creditors are getting pesky and his honey, Blossom Prioleau, is talking marriage. Desperation takes him to hefty Sally Crouch, proprietress of the Cozy Home Hotel for Coloured, his aim to borrow funds. Blossom abruptly leaves town, but Florian continues his attentions on Sally. If nothing else, she offers financial stability. Sally is elected Grand Exalted Princess of the Sons and Daughters of I Will Arise lodge, and begins to plan her wedding. The day of, she owns up to Florian as how she's broke, the hotel is losing money, what should she do? She hopes he will support her.

Come time of the betrothal, the Rev. Plato Tubb of the first African M.E. Church has only one contestant. Florian's a no-show. He sends a note from his doctor saying he "seems to have acute articular rheumatism: indigestion; a slight fever and symptoms of neuritis, on account of which this is to certify that he is unable to attend his wedding tonight and should be excused." The next time Florian sees Sally, he admits he's broke. She shrugs. He goes to the Genuine—and that day wins $2,500. He takes the next train to Nashville to find Blossom—who is now Mrs. Zekiel Rothwell! "Well, anyway," he murmured philosophically, "'reckon I ain't got no call 'specting ev'thing to break my way!'"

At least one Cohen supporter was Andrew Roberson, who wrote in the *Editor* in 1922: "Octavus Roy Cohen has done more to let the public know that we are neither a race of beggars nor paupers than any other story writer. He was the first to dare to write about negroes who, while acting like human beings, were quite as funny as those who acted like jackasses. He gives his characters feelings, aspirations, loves and hates like those of other people, while retaining all the little racial distinctions."[32]

His success changed Cohen, in the opinion of Louis Decimus Rubin, who wrote of his Uncle Dan, a Cohen contemporary: "His boyhood friend Octavus Roy Cohen had meanwhile begun producing his Florian Slappey stories, which the *Saturday Evening Post* was publishing regularly. The stories, which caricatured black life in what nowadays would be outrageously unacceptable fashion, were widely popular. Cohen's commercial success, Dan found, had gone to his head. At the sessions of the writing group 'he was like a king holding court.' Dan dropped out."[33]

On the other hand, travel writer Larry Nixon blossomed under Cohen's tutelage: "Octavus Roy Cohen saw several articles on freighter travel Larry had done," according to columnist George Tucker, "and told Larry he should do a book on the subject. Larry said no. Cohen said yes. That went on until Cohen locked Larry in his apartment, threw a batch of paper at him and said 'write.' Larry wrote. *Vagabond Voyaging* went into more than half a dozen editions and still is selling after four years."[34]

Cohen studied for a literature degree from Birmingham-Southern College in 1927. That year he was a member in good standing of the Birmingham Loafers Club, made up, despite its name, of hard-working professional writers.[35]

Cohen for many years golfed at the Roebuck Country Club in Birmingham.[36] In 1930, he participated in the Artists and Writers Annual Winter Golf Tournament, with his wife staying at the Royal Poinciana Hotel.[37]

Cohen had a lifelong interest in athletics, particularly football and boxing, also tennis. He was a member of the national Olympic Games committee in 1924 and chaired the South-eastern Amateur Athletic Union's boxing committee. He was a member of the National A.A.U. boxing committee.

The writer told the *Cass City Chronicle* in 1933 that "he takes pride in the fact that he probably is the most enthusiastic and worst saxophone player in the world; that he collects postage stamps and has a general collection of about 300,000 major varieties; that he is an enthusiastic, though not very expert, tennis player; that he has broken 90 on a golf course; that he plays a fairly good game of contract; and that he has, at one time or another, indulged in most forms of athletics including football, baseball, hockey, boxing, swimming, etc."[38]

Cohen said he was rejected for World War I military service sixteen times, though he served in the U.S. Naval Reserve from 1930 to 1940. He achieved the rank of lieutenant.

Cohen became a household name as a writer. Improbable as it may seem, Cohen's vernacular stories were a feature in at least one society gathering in Tuscaloosa in 1929, when Mrs. I.N. Hobston "gave in her own splendid style a negro dialect number by Octavus Cohen" at a meeting of the Estes Embroidery Circle.[39]

He knew he was well known, but Cohen was caught by surprise during a visit with an Idaho friend, Courtney Ryley Cooper.[40] They learned that he, Cohen, was the advertised guest speaker at a men's luncheon club in Denver. It was the first he knew about it. He went to the luncheon without revealing who he was and watched a fake give a "splendid literary talk." Also on the program was a surprise second author, Edna Ferber. Cohen had long hoped to meet Ferber, but he held back, not wanting to embarrass the club president, not exposing the imposter until after the meeting. By then it was too late to catch up with Ferber. The next time he was in New York, Cohen phoned Ferber. "I'm Octavus Roy Cohen," he said, "the man you *thought* you met recently in Denver"—"What are you talking about?" came the reply. "I haven't been in Denver in years."[41]

It was a low rumble, but contemporaneous doubts arose about the purity of Cohen's writing. A Florida newspaper columnist was dubious as to the legitimacy of the characters or their dialects in Cohen's stories, until, he said, he had a particular encounter: "Recently at a shoe-shining stand here in St. Petersburg a negro pulled a good one. The conversation was about a Marathon dance held in Detroit, and it was stated by a white man present that one couple had danced for four months. The negro, shining a shoe, looked up and said: 'Danced a month? My goodness, lazy as I am I could not sleep for four months.'"[42]

Cohen was a master of gobbledy-speak. This is an exchange, from "Chocolate Grudge,"[43] between Florian and Semore Mashby, to whom he owes money:

"Is you gwine pay me them moneys you owe me—or ain't you?"
"Now, Semore, tha's what I is come to argify 'bout."
"Ain't no argifyin' roun' hah. You pays that note when it's due or you gits yo'se'f in mo' trouble than what you has ever in yo' whole mis'able lfe got out of."
"But I ain't got no money."
"Says which?"
"Says I'se broke. Absolutely an' ontirely busted."
"Then," counseled Semore grimly, "you had better go git you a lawyer."

A Georgia newspaper writer doubted the dialect's authenticity. "We don't say Birmingham negroes do talk the way Octavus Roy Cohen has them talking in the *Saturday Evening Post*; all we say is, we've been around B'ham quite a bit off and on and we've never heard any of them talking that way. Nor did we ever meet anyone who has."[44]

The author and his family lived in a large home in the Highlands neighborhood of Birmingham for two decades (with a sojourn in Los Angeles in the early 1920s). Artemus S. Calloway was for a time Cohen's secretary.[45]

Cohen decided to move to New York in 1935. He sold the Charleston office building he and his late father owned in Moncks Corner. "Many of the author's short stories were written in these rooms and no doubt some of his characters were drawn from Berkeley folks," the *News and Courier* noted at the time.[46]

"The Octavus Roy Cohens have moved to New York, bag and baggage," Rienzi E. Lemus wrote in *Afro-American*,[47] "intend to stay, and what's more, Mr. Cohen announces in an interview in an afternoon daily his intention to find in Harlem counterparts of Lawyer Evans Chew, Pullman Porter Epic Peters, Brother Probable Huff, Miss Melissa Cheese, Sis Callie Flukers, Spokane G. Washington, to compose a setting for Florian Slappey there."

The reporter continued, "As quoted by Irene Kuhn, in the *World-Telegram*, Mr. Cohen is on record thus: 'I want to do some stories with the Harlem background because Harlem has never been done lightly. I am not going to touch the cultured Negro class in Harlem,' he hastily added, 'nor am I going to try to re-write Carl Van Vechten.'[48]

"'One thing has struck me with great force already in my journey to Harlem for material,' he continued. 'There is no marked difference between the Harlem Negro and the Southern Negro. I'm excepting the educated, cultured Harlem Negro, of course.

"'The Savoy dance hall here, for instance, is merely a deluxe counterpart of the deluxe negro dance halls in Birmingham. I see no difference between Florian Slappey's moving to Harlem and my moving to New York.'"

The reporter doubted Harlem was anything like Birmingham: "One who read the above noted that while Cohen may see in the endless Sunday parades of various societies through Harlem a reminder of the Sons and Daughters of I Will Arise, there certainly is nothing to remind him of a Birmingham dance hall at the Savoy in Harlem, whose patronage is sixty percent white, the whites mostly mixing with the colored folks on terms of amity, concord and equality....

"Now, he has picked the Harlem locale, with its clown-like street corner oracles to make more money, while colored writers neglect the field to poke fun at each other or belittle successful colored men with who they disagree."

Literary critic John Strausbaugh considers Cohen's venture into Harlem blasphemous. "You have to wonder whether Cohen understood what an extraordinary affront it was to launch his Jazz age Zip Coon into the heart of the Harlem Renaissance, where he never seems to encounter a Langston Hughes or an Arna Bontemps,[49] but only characters straight out of *Amos 'n' Andy* ... with names like Caesar Clump, Forcep Swain and Orifice R. Latimer."[50]

Reporter Carol Bird, to quiz Cohen about his philosophy of humor, visited his New York office. "If you expect a humorist to 'look the part' and appear a droll, funny fellow with merry eyes, quirked-up corners to his lips and a blithe, laughing manner you will be a bit surprised when you meet Octavus Roy Cohen," she wrote for newspaper syndication.[51] "He is a slender, serious-appearing man, kindly learned, modest and looks much too young to have a grown son at Harvard....

"Although Mr. Cohen, who has made his livelihood chiefly because he possesses in rich measure this inherent character quality or temperamental asset, a sense of humor, and who has caused millions of persons to laugh in sympathy with the doings of all the characters he writes about, he nevertheless is not, in superficial outward appearance and manner at any rate, a jocose man. His humor is of the quiet, subtle, droll kind, and its only indicator, so far as his own personality is concerned, is his quick and lively mind, his keen, observant eye."

What's humor? Cohen responded to Bird, "Humor is a form of translation. It is something that comes from within, direct from the person capable of indulging in it, not from any outside source. It is all in the way the individual interprets life, people, happenings. One person will see an event as, basically, a tragedy. Another will, so long as it does not involve a death or anything else really macabre, see it lightly.... The person in whom humor is born sees something funny where other persons will not detect it. A sense of humor is not an acquired thing. It is something that comes into the world with a man."

Cohen upended Florian Slappey to Harlem for a few stories in the late 1930s, but was more comfortable in Birmingham. ("Mr. Florian Slappey diagnosed his own condition in pessimistic fashion. 'I got ambition,' he reflected, 'but it seems awful puny up heah in Harlem,'" he said in "Personal Appearance."[52]) The Harlem stories were enough for a collection, *Florian Slappey*, which according to a Pittsburgh reviewer was his "most hilarious book."[53]

The reviewer elaborated:

"The weather is cold and the sidewalks hard when Mr. Slappey arrives in Harlem, but the familiar sights of pork stores and beauty parlors specializing in straightening of hair gives him courage that here in Harlem he would find the counterparts of his gullible friends in Birmingham.

"After a one-day stand as a banker in the policy racket, a deal in raccoon coats and attendance at a Harlem rent party, Mr. Slappey is convinced that Birmingham is the only place for him.

"So he sends word that he is coming back South and is met at the station by the cream of dusky society, a brass band and an oration of welcome. He has exactly two thin dimes in his pocket, but he has brought home an idea—that of a Social Register for 'cullud' society.

"Few know that he has been whipped by Harlem and fewer suspect that even back in Birmingham, Mr. Slappey suffers another reverse from Harlem. However, he pulls his Social Register out of the fire in true Slappey style and goes on to open up a private detective agency and to solve the first mystery of stolen laundry. Later he opens a swank night club, becomes a prize fight manager, wins a male beauty contest by strategy and outslicks a champion dice cajoler."

Cohen knew more about the South.

"I lived in Birmingham, Ala., a long time, and there I saw a great deal of Negro life," Cohen told writer Hazen.[54] "I made Birmingham my home for 25 years, but I had to come to New York often. It came to be that I was commuting here, and that was pretty hard on me and took up a lot of time. So two years ago I moved up here. I hated to leave Birmingham, I have a large number of friends there, and I enjoyed living there. But New York is a good town, too."

The Cohens moved to Los Angeles when the writer contracted again to write screenplays. His credit appeared on thirty motion pictures. He wrote a few scripts for radio's *Amos 'n' Andy* in 1945 and 1946.

"He writes about eighty short stories a year and has also written movies and plays," according to one source.[55]

Cohen earned between $80,000 and $100,000 a year from writing, the *Seattle Daily Times* said at the time of his death in Los Angeles on 6 January 1959, from a stroke.[56]

Cohen wrote the first of a decades-long series of short stories about blacks in Birmingham's "Darktown" for *The Saturday Evening Post* in 1918. The stories often featured hip Florian Slappey, but Lawyer Evans Chew, Pullman porter Epic Peters (who also owns the Broadway Tavun), money lender Semore Mashby and country boy Jasper De Void sometimes dominated the action. There was a long sequence of stories featuring movie mogul Orifice R. Latimer, director J. Caesar Clump and others of the Midnight Pictures Company, also Forcep Swain, Willie Plush, Edwin Boscoe Fizz, Dr. Brutus Herring, Andiron Smith, Dr. Lijah Atchison, the Rev'end Wesley Luther Thigpen, Ollie Waters and various members of Sons and Daughters of I Will Arise lodge, the Amalgamated Order of Laboring Ladies and the Over the River Burying Society benevolent group. And more. Lots more.

A cast of more than 100 characters threaded in and out of his stories. You can tell Cohen was looking in the medicine cabinet the day he named Iodinah Jones, Callous Deech, Quinine Clott, Magnesia Jones and Vapor Jackson, Neuritis Mapes and Jim Colic. He thought of the garden in naming Magnolius Ricketts, William Sodd, Jasper Pruney, Samuel Lime and Casaba Hyson; of travel in naming Ethiope Wall and Sicily Clump; of the dictionary when coming up with Thesis Pratt and Opus Randall.

And the business names: Sally Crunch's Hotel for Colored and Sis Callie Fluke's Boarding House (Florian Slappey and Epic Peters stay there); Yeast and Sneed's Tailoring Emporium, Exotic Hines' Artistic Photograph Gallery, Gold Crown Ice Cream Parlor, Keefe Gaines' Mortuary Emporium, Acey Upshaw Taxicab Company, Penny Prudential Bank (Slappey has an office there for a time), Bud Peaglar's Barbecue Lunch Room and Billiards and the Shining Stars Country Club for Colored.

And the musicians: Professor Aleck Champagne's Jazzphony Orchestra and the street musicians, Yodel Harris and Rancid Johnson.

Cohen wrote 166 Birmingham stories for the *Post*, one play and 151 more Birmingham stories for *Photoplay* or *This Week* or for newspaper syndication or for book collections.

There were at least 324 Birmingham tales. And maybe a few more that have eluded this bibliographer's search; the *Los Angeles Times* in 1940 put the number at 400.[57]

Cohen wrote twenty Birmingham stories for the *Post* in the first fourteen months of his association with the periodical. Then, whether the *Post* backed off or Cohen decided it, only six stories ran in the *Post* between April 1920 and March 1921. After which, Florian Slappey et al were once again *Post* regulars.

Where was Slappey in the interim? In the newspapers. Cohen tested the waters with "The Guvment Quits Controllin'," an opinion piece that appeared under the tagline "Florian Slappey the Dooley Darkey,"[58] when it ran in papers in late March 1920.[59] United Features Syndicate marketed Cohen's short columns twice weekly for a year.

One of the subscribers, the *Fort Worth Star-Telegram,* boasted Cohen's arrival on is pages: "Cohen is the boy who has made the Nation roar with his delightful stories of negro life. He has been the sensation of the year. His stories have appeared in a certainly weekly magazine with a regularity seldom equaled by any writer."[60]

Cohen's busy years were 1924, 1925, 1926 and 1927, with sixteen, seventeen, nineteen and seventeen stories each year, respectively. After fourteen stories in 1930, there was a gradual slowing. Only three appeared in 1934, one in 1940, one in 1952, the Birminghammers' last year with the magazine.

"Cohen knows the negro, the common everyday negro of the South and the sporty negro of the city," the *Star-Telegram* said. "Better still he knows how to write about them: his stories ring true and his dialect is the real dialect of the Southern negro. Cohen's stories have been gems of negro humor, tinctured with a little of the negro philosophy.

"One of the central characters in all Cohen's magazine stories has been Florian Slappey, the Beau Brummell of the negro colony. Florian is the social arbiter of the colony, the dictator in all things. Work and Florian are enemies. He lives by his wits and the work of the less educated darkeys. Florian has views on life; he has schemes of all sorts, some clever, others weird, but all amusing."[61]

Appearing in the newspapers on Wednesdays and Sundays, Florian soapboxed on everyday topics, starting with government control. Selecting a column at random, "Dancin' Fools" from the *Star-Telegram* for 26 December 1920, finds Florian demonstrating a new dance step, the Shimmytang, to his friend Lawyer Chew. Chew at first scoffs at Slappey's invention, then wants to learn how to do it himself. Why? Florian asks. Won't your wife find it indecent? "A slow grin expanded Lawyer Chew's lips. 'She's visitin' down to Montgomery, Florian—an' I is got me a ticket to that picnic tonight! C'mon—how do that dance commence?'"

The newspaper syndication experiment lasted a year, 106 columns. Then the Birmingham gang was back regularly on Saturday evenings in the *Post*.

Let's look at a typical story.

In "The Law and the Profits,"[62] Florian Slappey commiserates with Lawyer Evans Chew, who has just been notified by Grand Magnificent High Potentate Isaac Gethers that his retainer as counsel to the Sons and Daughters of I Will Arise has been terminated. It hurt his ledger. It also hurt his pride. Tight-fisted financier Semore Mashby was behind the move; Mashby holds a mortgage on the lodge's new rooms. Chew just won a major case against Mashby, and Mashby holds a grudge.

Meanwhile, Dr. Elijah Atcherson has proposed the lodge enter a competition of sorts with another lodge, the Gleaming Torchbearers of Divinity. The lodges will compare fundraiser results. Whichever is the higher will keep 60 percent of the total, the lesser lodge receiving 40 percent. The idea is, members will work doubly hard to come out on top. Chew happens to belong to both organizations, and gleans an idea of how their campaigns are progressing.

A delegation from Torchbears visits Chew, wondering how he feels about the Sons and Daughters, given his dismissal. Are you annoyed with them, he's asked?

"I ain't said I ain't." "Well," it's put to him again, "I ast you: Is you is or is you ain't?"

That phrase—it shows up more than once in the Birmingham canon—somehow caught hold, to the extent Louis Jordan wrote a song of that title in 1944, "Is You Is Or Is You Ain't My Baby?"

Moving along in the story, Chew is told Mashby is willing to loan the Torchbearers of Divinity $500 to take it over the top. Mashby will loan the money for 50 percent of the lodge's profit. Will he draw up a contract? He does. The contest ends. The Torchbearers come out on top, $1,500 to $1,400. But when the reckoning comes, it delights Chew no end to advise Mashby that, once his loan is repaid, they come out losers, having to turn over to the Sons and Daughters 40 percent of the borrowed $500.

At the same time, since the lodge has no profit, what Mashby has to divide is the loss. He owes $100. Mashby finally has to ask Dr. Brutus Herring whose bright idea it was to use the profit formula. "A slow grin decorated Doctor Herring's lips. 'That idea?' he retorted gently. 'Why, that suggestion come fum Lawyer Chew.'"

"I didn't start out to make Florian a leading man," Cohen told the *Des Moines Tribune*.[63] "The public did that. They started writing, referring to the 'Florian Slappey' stories, and of course I was no fool. I gave them more of what they liked."

How did he start the stories with African American characters?

"My first Negro story was called 'The Missing Clink.'[64] Instead of sending it to one of the pulp magazines, I sent it to the *Saturday Evening Post*," he told reporter Hazen.[65] "I said to myself: 'I'll try the *Post* first; if it comes back, then I'll mail it to one of the publications that take my stuff.'

"But the *Post* bought it. I can't tell you how pleased I was, you'll have to have such an experience to understand it. Well, then, for five years I wrote nothing else but Negro stories, and all for the *Post*. [He omits mention of the year of newspaper syndication.] And I still write for it. The *Post* has several of my Negro stories now.

"One of the secrets of the success of my Negro stories is that there are no white people in them.[66] I have never made what I think is a mistake by putting in a white man, because, if you do, you have to make one the inferior, so I let it alone.

"I received a great deal of mail from Negroes and I have never found any resentment from a one of them. And here's another thing that you may not have noticed about these stories. I have never had a criminal in them. I have had many sharp deals, that's true, but I have kept the criminal out."

The writer explained, "I was born and reared with Negroes—in Charleston, S.C. I didn't consciously acquire their dialect, but when I wrote it came to me without any effort. I was writing for the pulps when I wrote my first Negro story. I would have told it to anyone for $50."

A woman named Gladiola, Cohen revealed, triggered his interest in writing about blacks. It was 1916. His writing career was off to a good start. He was newly married. He had a newborn son. "My wife wasn't too strong," Cohen told a reporter in 1929,[67] "and we debated for many days whether we could afford a colored maid who would be obtained for $4 a week.

"We decided to get her. And Gladiola turned out to be a literal $1,000,000 investment. Because through her, I became acquainted with various characters in darktown Birmingham, and these in turn led to the series of negro stories which I have written for *The Saturday Evening Post* and other periodicals for more than eleven years. I call Gladiola my '$1,000,000 maid' because the story themes her employment inspired have since helped me earn $1,000,000."

Cohen at the time of the interview was in Hollywood, working on a story for Moran and Mack, the Two Black Crows,[68] who were shifting their blackface act from stage to screen. "Cohen was sought because of his facile gift of negro character delineations and dialogue." Cohen's first tenure in Hollywood followed the Broadway success of George Broadhurst's production of *The Crimson Alibi* (1919), when Goldwyn offered Cohen signed a five-year exclusive contract to write photoplays. Cohen apparently had enough after one year.[69]

Cohen was nothing if not empathetic with blacks. He appears to have come from an accepting home. His father when editor of the *Charleston World* spoke at the opening of the Southern Exposition at Raleigh, North Carolina, and supported black education: "The argument advanced in nearly every southern state against the school tax is that you will be helping to educate the negro's children. Of course you will; and why should no not, pray? The correct theory is that property should provide educational facilities, inasmuch as property finds its greatest protection in, and derives its principal value from, an enlightened populace."[70]

Cohen was an agile self-promoter. He sent a Birmingham anecdote to syndicated columnist Will Rogers, purportedly about a boy whose parents belonged to the Sons and Daughters of I Will Arise. The lad was sent to the butcher shop. He asked for raw, tough meat. Why? If the meat were tender, he said, his father would eat all before others had a chance. He then wagered the butcher, a dime against the meat. And won.[71]

Cohen nurtured a huge cast of players in his Birmingham stories, as already noted. While he was deep into his Midnight Picture Company phase, Cohen wrote what was announced would be six stories (it stretched to eight) for a periodical other than the *Post*, *Photoplay*. The *Photoplay* series ran from August 1926 to March 1927, this time without a noticeable break in the *Post* run.

Cohen had serious clout, if the *Post*'s powerful editor George Horace Lorimer let him get away with that.

Cohen put his regular cast of characters against an exotic setting. Typically, in "Safe and Seine,"[72] Slappey butts heads with lead actor Welford Potts. Slappey has written an embarrassing letter stating his true opinion of Midnight Picture's president, and Potts has gotten his hands on it:

Mr. Slappey was still disposed to be tactful. "You aint doin' me right, brother Potts."
"You is dawggone tootin' I aint. Not I don't aim to."
"I never meant fo' you to keep that letter I written. I craves to git it back."
"You better crave a diff'ent crave. 'Cause that letter is the most thing you aint gwine git. Unless—."
"Unless what?"
"—Unless you pay me one hund'ed dollars cash money. An' I don't mean no francs, neither."
"Blackmail!" withered Florian furiously.

Cohen regularly collected *Post* Birmingham stories for books, one a year from 1919 to 1932 (except 1924, with two, and 1929, with none), and a fifteenth book, *Florian Slappey*, in 1938. Dodd, Mead brought out the first six collections; D. Appleton published *Black to Nature*; Little, Brown issued three books; then D. Appleton published the last four. Longmans, Green published *Come Seven* the play. Cohen's dedication of *Carbon Copies* to Carl Brandt and *Black and Blue* to Zelma Corning Brandt is open acknowledgment that Brandt & Brandt was his literary agent.[73]

Some collections included stories that didn't first appear in the *Post*. Some of these extra stories may have been rejects. Some had been syndicated to newspapers, such as "Completely Done in Oils" in *Dark Days and Black Knights* (1923), which appeared in both the *Atlanta Constitution* for 9 April 1922 and the *Delmaria Sunday Star* (Wilmington, Delaware) for 8 July 1923. Some Cohen stories were distributed as "Blue Ribbon Fiction" by the Chicago Tribune Syndicate.

Cohen continued at the *Post* during the Wesley Winans Stout and Ben Hibbs editorial eras, though less frequently. Cohen became more playful with his characters; Florian professed to be a cowboy, in "Two-Gun Slappey Rides Again,"[74] to gain employment on Dormant Smith's Bar-Nothing Dude Ranch—and maybe woo sweet Nostalgia Jones. Some Slappey stories showed up in *This Week*. The last *Post* story was "Melody in F-4" for the 30 December 1944 issue. Cohen wrote four more (that have been located) stories after that, to end with "Florian Slappey—Private Eye" for an issue of *Elks Magazine* in 1950.

It was an amazing run.

By World War II, Cohen had channeled his energies elsewhere. "What few people realized," he said in the Des Moines *Tribune* interview in 1942,[75] "is that only about 15 percent of my writing has been about Negroes. For the past seven years I have largely concentrated on serial series—not about Negroes—for *Collier's*."

Cohen developed other running characters, such as the heavyweight private eye Jim Hanvey (*Jim Hanvey, Detective*), police detective David Carroll (*Midnight*) and investigator Lt. Max Gold (*Love Has No Alibi*).

One reader of the *Salt Lake Tribune* wondered, in 1921, if Cohen wrote both Birmingham and detective stories himself, or employed an assistant to write some of the stories. He wrote them all, Cohen assured the inquirer, and the shifts back and forth kept his ideas fresh.[76]

The author discussed the writing life with David W. Hazen: "There are cases where people just started off to be writers, and succeeded, but darn few of them. To be a successful writer, you not only have to have the urge to write, but you have to have something to write about.[77]

"First, I think it is best to knock around a lot to get some real experience. See life. Know life. My god, what use is it to be a good writer if you have nothing to write about. What use would it be to be a good reporter if you had nothing to report! There are thousands of persons who can write beautiful English but who will never be successful authors because they can't think of a thing that will interest anyone. So many people try to write who have nothing to say. It isn't just having a command of language that makes a successful writer."

Cohen once mentioned his favorite authors: "I rank Ring Lardner[78] as the greatest humorist ever produced in this country. I think that George Fitch[79] runs Lardner a close second and I grab for everything published under Stephen Leacock's[80] name," he said in *Our American Humorists*.[81]

Cohen noted of Katherine Brush's[82] stories: "She writes objectively and lightly. You can chuckle over her stuff, yet she is a truly great satirist. The humorist may tease us about our foibles, our eccentricities, our weaknesses, our human frailties; may refer to them gaily, mockingly, amusingly, but he has nevertheless turned them up to the light."[83]

One sees small communities at the heart of these writers—Cohen's métier. The same with these next writers. "I think the three best American novels I have read are Sinclair Lewis's *Main Street*,[84] Booth Tarkington's *The Turmoil* and Corra Harris's[85] *Happily Married*."

He explained how he tackled his fiction: "'I set myself a certain amount of work to do each day,' Mr. Cohen began, 'and I do it before I quit. I never know how long it will take, but I do the work I have set out to do that day if it takes two hours or eight hours or even longer. I am at my typewriter every morning at 8:15.'"

Cohen saw the world. In 1926, he toured Palestine and Rome in the company of Cortland Ryley Cooper.[86] In 1936 and again in 1940, Cohen and his wife traveled to Havana, Cuba.[87] He enjoyed ocean cruises—though he still wrote while relaxing in a deck chair.[88]

"'But when I take a vacation, I never touch a typewriter; I don't take work with me on a vacation. I have the old newspaper man's idea of writing on a typewriter[:] I use one finger on each hand and I write like hell. I go very fast!'"

Cohen admitted "his chief eccentricity is that he is a thoroughly normal man. He revels in a game of billiards—when he gets anyone to play with him—and plays horribly! He thoroughly enjoys flivvering over rough roads to keep his mental faculties in rapport with his earlier experiences, and he loves to eat chop suey," Wallace Munro wrote in the *Washington Post*.[89]

In the short story "Ham and Exit,"[90] from 1926, the Midnight Motion Picture Corp. has a twenty-three-member crew in Europe to film two-reelers. President Orifice R. Latimer and principal director Julius Caesar Clump are confident they can find a big audience back home for their pictures. They have Professor Aleck Champaign's Jazztown Orchestra along, as well as actresses Sicily Clump and Clorious Fizz and comedian Opus Randall.

Florian Slappey serves as translator for the company, though he only speaks English, and that only in his unique way. In Marseilles, Frenchman Marcel Chinard irritates Slappey. A toughie with a reputation, Chinard hires on as an extra in a scene that will contain dramatic violence. Forcep Swain agrees to rewrite his script to take advantage of Chinard's fighting talents. Chinard is even stronger than the huge actor Spokane G. Washington. Chinard shows off for child actor Excelsior Nix. Slappey thinks Chinard thinks too highly of himself, but finds himself sailing into harbor waters when he says a little too much to the Frenchman.

Slappey arranges that movie scenes be filmed at a particular location, recruits some Marseilles thugs, and, as cameraman Ethiope Hines cranks the camera, the fight begins. But to Slappey's dismay, Chinard bests everyone and is about to take on Florian, until Florian grabs a ham sandwich. Chinard is a Mohammedan and won't touch pork for any reason. Slappey is saved.

Florian Slappey conquered stage and movie theater.

Cohen's blackface play in three acts, *Come Seven* (1920), ran at the Broadhurst Theatre in New York City from July to September 1920, 72 performances. George Broadhurst was the producer. Earle Foxe appeared as Slappey. Others in the cast included Arthur Aylsworth, Harry A. Emerson, Thomas Gunn, Henry Hanlin, Gail Kane, Lucille La Verne, Carrie Lowe, Charles W. Meyer, Eleanor Montell and Susanne Willis.

Broadhurst (1866–1952), for whom the Broadhurst Theatre in Midtown Manhattan is named, co-wrote *Alibi* with Cohen. Cohen eventually crafted four more stage plays on his own.

"There isn't a white character in the play," the Duluth, Minnesota, *News-Tribune* said of *Come Seven*.[91] "Every character—as the program insists—is a 'colored character.' But each is played by a white player. The action takes place in the home of Mrs. Goins, a large old-fashioned house left her by her former mistress. Back from serving as a lady's maid to a social climber at Palm Beach, comes Vistar Goins. She is a lovely 'yellow girl' and has many social airs. She is horrified to find that her mother—a quiet old-fashioned negress—has rented 'the back drawing room' to Elzefir Nesbit and her no account husband Uria, whom Elzevir supports by taking in washing. Vying with Nesbit for Vistar's hand is Florian Slappey.

"Mr. Cohen writes much better of the every-day affairs of the American Negro than white actors play them," a *Christian Science Monitor* reviewer observed.[92]

A road version of *Come Seven* played the Hippodrome in Dallas in late 1922, also with a white cast in blackface. A flattering *Dallas Morning News* review strikes a sour note today: "Miss Claribel Fontaine as Vistar Goins, who has been a lady's maid at Palm Beach and profited by her experiences, is a 'high brown.' She plays the part as a nearly white octoroon but her aping of darky eccentricities is not only amusing but fascinating.

"Aside from Miss Fontaine, all the characters are almost coal black. Even the members of the orchestra, who are the jazz band for the party in the third act, have smeared on the burnt cork and their music for the intermissions consists almost entirely of negro melodies or blues."[93]

Learning that an NAACP branch in Newark, New Jersey, planned to stage *Come Seven*, national leader Roy Wilkins "strongly objected to Cohen's play, which featured 'caricatures of the race.' Exclaiming that it was not necessary that the cast perform a 'so-called Negro play,' Wilkins demanded the play's cancellation," according to historian Lauren Rebecca Skaroff.[94]

Al Christie's films, at least, had casts of African descent.

"The contracts with Cohen for the stories of the fancy doings of the dusky characters of Birmingham darktown will give the Christie Film company the exclusive rights to photograph these stories with dialogue in talking pictures," the *Spokane Daily Chronicle* reported.[95]

"The acquisition of the Cohen stories will make possible a striking novelty in screen entertainment and it is said that, with the advent of synchronized films, they will now find their logical use for pictures. The scenes will center around the famous Sons and Daughters of I Will Arise, Bud Peagler's Barbecue Lunch and Poolroom and Sallie Crouch's Cozy Home hotel, and will have such characters as Florian Slappey, Lawyer Evans Chew, Dr. Brutus Herring and Semore Mashby."

Christie[96] recruited cast members from Harlem's Lafayette Players Stock Company.

The Melancholy Dame, 21 minutes, was released 2 February 1929. Alfred A. Cohn (possibly an Octavus Roy Cohen pseudonym) wrote the screenplay based on Cohen's stories. Arvid E. Gillstrom directed Charles Olden as Slappey. Also in the cast were Edward Thompson, Evelyn Preer, Spencer Williams and Roberta Hyson. Al Christie produced the picture and others in the short series. Webster Dill (Williams) and his wife Sapho (Hyson) own a small jazz club in Birmingham and become entangled in a romantic melee.

Music Hath Harms, 21 minutes, was released 16 March 1929. Screenplay by Cohn, direction by Walter Graham. Harry Tracy performed as Slappey. Also featured were Spencer Williams (who had started with Christie as an audio technician and would later in *Amos & Andy* on television), Roberta Hyson, Nathan Curry, Leon Hereford, Curtis Mosby and Harry Porter. Musician Roscoe Griggins (Williams) has a crush on Zenia Sprowl (Hyson), who aspires to open her own beauty salon. Florian, though, has a grudge against Roscoe and interferes with the latter's scheme to make money.

The Framing of the Shrew, 20 minutes, was released 27 April 1929. Cohn wrote, Gillstrom directed. Charles Olden was Slappey with Edward Thompson as Privacy Robson and Evelyn Preer as Clarry Robson. Also appearing were Spencer Williams and Roberta Hyson. Slappey gives domestic advice to Privacy Robson (Thompson).

Oft in the Silly Night, 18 minutes, released 8 June 1929, was directed by Gillstrom, scripted by Cohn, starring Edward Tompson, Hyson, Arthur Ray, Williams and Laurence Criner, is about a chauffeur for an undertaker who falls in love with his boss's daughter.

The pictures were packaged as *Birmingham Black Bottom: The First All Black Cast Talkies* for DVD release in 2003.

Cohen had another stage nibble in 1942, when Harry A. Gourfain purchased rights to turn Florian Slappey's misadventures into a musical "which will be performed by an all-colored cast of 40 with the tentative title of 'Florian Slappey in Carbon Copies.'"[97]

The pilot for a *Florian Slappey—Private Detective* television program was filmed in 1951 but was not picked up by a network.

Slappey first takes up detecting in the story "Crash and Carry,"[98] when he and Spasm Johnson witness a bungled robbery of Jasper de Void's jewelry store. They end up with the stolen jewels, but Slappey is in no hurry to turn them in. He'd like to find an angle to collect a reward. So he and his oversized friend form The Sun and Moon We Never Sleep Detective Agency, "Only Colored Detective Agcy. In B'ham," as a cover for their scheme. They advertise, and end up doing some honest skip-trace work before resolving their store heist.

In "The Mystery of the Missing Wash,"[99] Slappey helps a woman solve a stolen laundry problem through an improbable solution, but in "Florian Slappey—Private Eye,"[100] the character has an office, a secretary named Miss Johnson and a new slogan: "All I Need Is One Clue & $24." This is an outright spoof of Sam Spade.

If you remove the ethnic bits, they're all very funny.

Epic Peters, a Pullman porter with the nickname "Hop Sure," works out of the Birmingham Terminal Station on the Atlanta or New York runs. In the story "The Berth of Hope,"[101] he is grousing about the poor tips. Maybe he'll put in for Chicago or Los Angeles instead. He assists two gentlemen, Garrison and Carson, in finding their drawing room. They entrust him with a valuable package. For the duration of the trip, one or another of the men asks Peters to bring the package, then secure it again. He pays little attention, appreciative of the $5 tips. As they near their destination, Peters is surprised, when the gentlemen are in the dining car, to be handed $2 to look the other way as their room is given the twice-over by a third man of authority. When the latter confronts the former, Garrison and Carson deny knowing anything about a package.

Peters, catching on, proffers the package in the presence of the third man. "Does you-all gemmun mean to stan' up there on yo' own two foots an' say you di'n't gimme this heah package to take care of fo' you until we arrove in New Yawk?" he asks. No, they insist. They flee when the train reaches Pennsylvania station. The third man, a detective, takes the package. He opens it. Diamonds and emeralds. He smiles and hands Peters a small reward, $50. Peters does the arithmetic; between all the tips and rewards, he's pocketed $85. His usual wages are $66 a month. Maybe he'll stay on the run after all.

Though Peters occasionally showed up in the other Birmingham stories, his Pullman tales were sufficient to fill one book. Porters had their issues with Pullman, but generally fared well on the economic ladder. Except, as in "The Berth of Hope," when Peters is going through a drought. He compares tips with his friend Joe:

> "Folks ain't so loose with their change as they once was. Seems like when they goes to New Yawk they don't make no 'lowance a'tall fo' tips. I has got two dimes, one two-bit piece and one half dollar, an' leavin' time ain't so long off." Epic proppied his elongated frame against the side of the Pullman. "Tell you the truff, Joe, Ise thinki' of applicatin' myself to another distric'— Chicago or maybe Los Angeles."

By story's end, Peters has helped police capture a crook, pocketed a $50 reward and is singing a different tune.

"Cohen's Pullman porter, Epic Peters, is one of the more sympathetically drawn black characters by a white author in his era," in the view of Mike Grust.[102]

Cohen's Birmingham stories—you liked them or you hated them.

Syndicated columnist O.O. McIntyre[103] loved them. "Twenty-three colored children in Birmingham have been named Octavus Roy for Octavus Roy Cohen," he gushed in 1936,[104] citing what has to be the most unusual (if true) tribute to a writer ever.

Hubert Harrison was generous in a 1921 review of Cohen's *Highly Colored* story collection[105]: "How negroes will take the brilliant short stories of Mr. Cohen will depend upon their sense of humor. We are still touchy about our tribe and tend to get huffy when the type that is amusing happens to be 'colored.' Yet we boast at the same time of the Negro's 'unfailing humor' as a godsend! But then there is the humor of malice and the humor of sympathy as well as the humor for sheer pleasure without any ulterior purpose. Mr. Cohen's humor in this book is of the latter sort. I think that the supreme dandy and man-about town, Mr. Florian Slappey, Lawyer Evans Chew and that close-fisted man of money, Mr. Semore Mashby, will live in the memory as outstanding types together with the stalwart society known as 'The Sons and Daughters of I Will Arise.' Of course they are drawn to the scale of humor, and on that scale they bulk large—even for Birmingham, Alabama."

Cohen's publisher tried to attract black readers to the books: "How come this man Cohen makes talk 'bouten us cullud genmen? Tells you, Florian Slappey, he's the man what if'n you cullud babies don' read his books you aint never gwine get interduced to yo'self," Dodd, Mead & Company said in an advertisement for *Assorted Chocolates* in the *New York Tribune* in 1922.[106]

In another case, the publisher assumed a white audience: "For one who likes nigger stuff Come Seven by Octavus Roy Cohen," headlined a distasteful ad in *Maclean's*.[107] A North Australian newspaper informed its readers in 1928, "The popular nigger stories of Octavus Roy Cohen, which have, for years, been a feature of the Saturday Evening Post, have been bought as material for future Paramount Christie comedies."[108]

Among the Cohen challengers was the editor of the National Association for the Advancement of Colored People's *Crisis* magazine, W.E.B. Du Bois,[109] who wrote George Horace Latimer in 1922 to complain about the treatment of Negroes in the *Saturday Evening Post*.[110]

"Especially have colored people objected to some of Irvin Cobb's stories, to nearly all of Roy Cohen's stories and lately to the story of 'Nick Pride' by Dingle.[111]

"I know that under the race conditions in the United States, colored people are apt to be supersensitive, and to want in art and fiction, only those things that paint them at their very bet. As a writer myself, I have the strongest belief in the freedom and truth of art and, therefore, while I sympathize with much of the criticism of the sort of thing you continually published in the *Post* about negroes, my chief criticism is not on what you *do* publish, but rather what you *do not* publish."

Du Bois allowed that some might see artistic merit in Cohen's work, but what about the rest of the Negro story? What about other, more upstanding Negroes as fictional characters?

"I am aware that you can expect comparatively little revenue from Negro readers or advertisers," Du Bois wrote reasonably, "and yet it seems to me that the larger duties and ideals of an editor in your influential place, ought to induce you to look for, or at least be willing to consider, other conceptions and portraits of Negroes, from those which you have in the past so persistently published."

The *Post* had once been in the hot seat—early in Lorimer's time, in 1905—when the periodical ran an article by Thomas Dixon, Jr.,[112] "Booker T. Washington and the Negro,"[113] in which he excused southern lynchings because black men lusted after white women and accused the federal legislature of "silently preparing us for the future of amalgamation," in other words, miscegenation, an increasing mix of the races. He further asserted—and was broadly challenged—"no amount of education of any kind, industrious, classical or religious, can make a Negro a white man or bridge the chasm of the centuries which separates him from the white man in the evolution of human history."

Critic Peter C. Rollins found Lorimer troubling both in his pro-business stance and in his negative attitude toward nonwhites. "It was also no matter of chance that Post regional stories abound with derogatory stereotypes of black Americans and immigrants. Irvin S. Cobb and Octavus Roy Cohen developed a specialty in the area of stories about the stupidity and dishonesty of the Negro race. For many regular readers of Lorimer's racist editorials, these stories must have provided an opportunity to look down the racial ladder at an irresponsible and immoral under-class."[114]

Rollin pointed out the contrast of Booth Tarkington's idyllic Indiana tales or Clarence Budington Kelland's "crackerbox philosophers in his stories of Vermont and New Hampshire," and Cohen's of city blacks, few with regular jobs, most working a deal.

Rollin pointed to the volume of Cobb and Hugh Wiley dialect stories in the *Post*. Cobb wrote 80 *Post* stories, Wiley 77.[115] Cohen wrote more Darktown stories over the years than the two of them together. Is it any wonder Du Bois chafed at the Cohen stories? They were ubiquitous.

Lorimer didn't reply directly. Du Bois received a letter from "the Editors" that said in part: "There is not the slightest intention or wish on our part to be unfair in our treatment of the colored people. When Paul Laurence Dunbar[116] was alive he was a regular contributor to our columns and we would welcome to our pages another colored writer with his ability. As a matter of fact we are inclined to think the critics to which you refer are just a little over sensitive. We do not remember ever having printed an ill-natured story about colored people and we print a great many more stories about white a la Cohen than we do about colored. We think that our critics really want not equality of treatment but preferential treatment."[117]

This of course did not satisfy Du Bois, who included a few barbs in editorials in *The Crisis* for April 1923 and October 1926.

Van Vechten was on the point in 1928 on the issue of literature and inner-city blacks: "The question is, Are Negro writers going to write about the exotic material [the urban setting] while it is still fresh or will they continue to make a free gift of it to white authors who will exploit it until not a drop of vitality remains?"[118]

Critic Richard A. Lupoff years later pointed out that this discussion reflected the emergence of a new literature that abandoned the slave stories and demeaning rural Mammy depictions for an urban setting. "These novels [and story collections] mirrored shifting social attitudes of the times. The growing, perhaps faddish interest in Black culture in the 1920s, assured their popularity. They also helped set the stage for the reading public to accept more accurate and disturbing depictions of Black life."[119]

The ripple in the 1920s grew to a rumble. Novelist Wallace Thurman[120] groused in November 1926: "Why Negroes imagine that any writer is going to write what negroes think he ought to write about them is too ridiculous to merit consideration. It would seem that they would shy away from being pigeon-holed, so long have they been the rather lamentable victims of such a typically American practice, yet Negroes would have all Negroes appearing in contemporary literature made as ridiculous and as false to type as the older school of pseudo-humorous, sentimental white writers made their Uncle toms, their Topsys, and their Mammies, or as the Octavus Roy Cohen school now make their more modern 'cullud' folk."[121]

In 1929 Benjamin Brawley[122] said the stories for a time "entertained the readers of the *Saturday Evening Post*, but the caricature soon became stereotyped and were never to be regarded as literature."[123]

"*The Saturday Evening Post*, possessing the largest circulation of any periodical in the world, regales its readers with the stories of Octavus Roy Cohen and Hugh Wiley," Nathan Van Patten[124] wrote in *American Speech* in 1931.[125] "Both of these men are competent craftsmen and their tales are very amusing. It is quite likely that they know something of Negro life in America but they publish only burlesque."

"His work is amusing at its best, but is pseudo–Negro," Sterling A. Brown wrote in *The Journal of Negro Education* in 1933. "Instead of being a handicap, however, that seems a recommendation to his audience. Trusting to most moth-eaten devices of farce, and interlarding a Negro dialect never heard on land or sea—compounded more of Dogberry and Mrs. Malaprop than of Birmingham Negroes, he has proved to whites that all along they have known the real Negro—'Isn't he funny, now!'—and has shown to negroes what whites wanted them to resemble."[126]

"It is the Florian Slappeys that I protest against most," novelist Richard Wright[127] said in 1945, by which time blacks had more than proven themselves during World War II. "Mr. Cohen is a widely read writer in the popular magazines and he sticks to the oldest and most dishonest tricks of the writing trade when he typecasts negroes—and does the most damage."[128]

The same year, columnist Mrs. Walter Ferguson[129] discussed popular literature in which "a certain type is labeled 'the American Negro.' It has been accepted by the public for so long that we can hardly see Negroes as they really are. Florian Slappey, the central figure of Octavus Roy Cohen's tales, may exist in rare cases, yet the colored race suffers because he is regarded as a national type.... In this way we have created vast misunderstandings between various groups and have contributed to vast misconceptions among the people of the world."[130]

Earl Conrad[131] derided the stories in *The Journal of Negro Education* in 1944: "When Octavus Roy Cohen uses his 'sezwhats,' 'whichalls' and 'howzats,' he reflects the Southern tradition of poking scorn at the Negro generally by showing a difference in word usages and word pronunciations—but showing them in unjustifiable situations, and with an unjustifiable prejudice and motive to begin with. But the very speech forms which he finds so intriguing, or profitable, will one day overwhelm him and all of his confederates [*sic*!], leave them behind as incorrect reporters and interpreters, and go on to something basic, acceptable, decent and inevitable."[132]

"The most ubiquitous purveyor of black stereotypes in American books was Octavus Roy Cohen," Caroline Goeser wrote in *Picturing the New Negro*,[133] "whose Florian Slippery [*sic*] series capitalized on the outmoded stereotype of black minstrelsy. Dressed in outlandish garb and constantly speaking in malapropisms, Slappery [*sic*] entertained many readers through the 1920s and 1930s. ... [These] stereotypes acted as specters of the worst aspects of American racism that, within the cacophonous diversity of American print culture, brushed with the pages of Harlem Renaissance production."

Cohen acknowledged the controversy in a 1929 interview with William Whitman.

"For the first two years that he wrote about negroes," Whitman said, "Cohen submitted every negro story to two readers, the janitor at the apartment house and his wife's maid. 'Negro fiction in this country has been divided into two classes, the very light side, that I have selected, and the very heavy side.

"'The people who read my stuff are also divided into two classes. One class, fortunately in the minority, thinks it is perfectly marvelous and a true picture of negroes. The other class thinks it is absolute nature faking and that my characters are not negroes at all. They are both wrong.'

"Octavius [*sic*] Roy Cohen knows the African negro, and they know and like him. He is a guest of honor at many of their functions, and it is from them that he gets many of the incidents that color his stories."[134]

Cohen had other defenders.

Robert Ruark[135] rued the impact racial sensitivity had on humor writers. "Octavus Roy Cohen used to write wonderful dialect stories about the wonderful Negroes of Birmingham, Ala., for the staid *Saturday Evening Post*," Ruark said. "Mr. Florian Slappey and the Sons and Daughters of I Will Arise were magnificently funny folks and completely free of offense. But Cohen gave them up. There was a growing pressure against presenting the Southern Negro in an undignified light."[136]

In its Cohen obituary notice in January 1959, the Ada (Okla.) *Evening News* observed, "thinking of him brings back happy memories of one of the high peaks in American light literature, both in magazine and book form and also in the theatre.

"That was before races got a crazy idea truthful and fanciful impersonations of members of a race reflect upon the intelligence of the entire race. There never has arisen in this country a more unintelligent thing than this, but it has just about stopped beautiful stories and songs of the Negroes in both slavery and after-war eras. We think publishers and producers of plays and TV shows are making a sad mistake in listening to a few misguided souls who are trying to eliminate all racial characteristics, past or present, truthful or fictional.

"Octavus Roy Cohen, of Jewish descent, wrote in the transition period from Negro slavery dialect to no dialect at all. So far as we recall he is the only writer who was able to catch accurately that transition dialect."[137]

Here one has to scoff. Transition dialect? Consider this exchange:

"'What I asks you straight an' plain: Is you gwine loant me them two dollars, or ain't you?' 'I ain't said I ain't.' 'You ain't said you is.' 'I ain't said nothing.' 'Well, I asks: Is you is or is you ain't?'"[138]

And Cohen admires the reverse sentence construction. In 1948 when British Prime Minister Winston Churchill made a statement, "This is nonsense up with which I will not put," the *Niagara Falls Gazette* couldn't resist commenting editorially, "As Florian Slappey, Octavus Roy Cohen's famous Negro character, might have said, "Emphatic language is one of the fondest things Mr. Churchill is of."[139]

Cohen is well aware of black society. He describes his characters by hues: Slappey has "chocolate-cream flesh" in "Net Profits."[140] The actress Evergreen Trapp in "The Bathing Booty"[141] is "a rather small and decidedly shapely woman whose creamy-brown complexion was suffused with the tint of cold fury." And Thesis Pratt in "Dark and Dreary"[142] found his way "blocked by a very large dark person." The street musicians Yodel Harris and Rancid Johnson in "Two for One": They were thoroughly insignificant; Mr. Johnson, small and skinny and excessively apologetic; Mr. Harris, several shades darker, two degrees thinner and infinitely more retiring."[143]

Cohen notes whenever his characters ride the Jim Crow car on the rail line, though they never say anything about it. Segregation is taken for granted.

An Ohio newspaper thought the Birmingham stories helped elevate the status of blacks. Calling Cohen a social historian, its editorial page writer said, "The stories for which he is best known dealt lightheartedly, but sympathetically, with the efforts of the urban Southern Negro to achieve status. His portraits of Lawyer Evans Chew, Florian Slappey and other memorable characters were gentle and free of malice.

"None of Mr. Cohen's 'Bummin'ham' folk were vicious or depraved or more than mildly knavish. They were whimsical and wise, generous and greedy, ambitious and shiftless, no different except in color and diction from those to be found in any close-knit community of any race or nationality.

"Growing sensitivity of the kind that has virtually suppressed Shakespeare's 'The Merchant of Venice' and 'Oliver Twist' is only partly responsible for the disappearance of fiction that seems disrespectful of minorities.

"Ours is a tense and jumpy world, far removed from the cheerful indifference of the 1920s, when Mr. Cohen's vogue was at its height. Not only are we touchier and readier to magnify affront, but we seem to have lost the capacity to view ourselves in anything but the gravest light.

"Now the mirthful glance has become ridicule, the genial thrust mortal insult. And what is regarded as politeness may be only a form of insecurity."[144]

So there's disagreement.

Let's look at another story, "Violent Ray."[145] The Birmingham Darktown baseball team of the Alabama Colored League recruits a ringer, pitcher Ray Mustard of Chattanooga, to pitch in a game. He feigns illness and recruits Ollie Napp to go in his stead. Nobody will recognize you, Mustard says. Napp, $75 in his pocket, shows up for the game only to discover that, while he's duping his team, Mustard is double-duping by coming on, under an alias, as pitcher for the rival Dorping team.

The rivals toy with him, swinging wide, striking out, stringing him along for several innings until the Birmingham club is ahead. Napp can think of only one solution to looming disgrace for himself and Birmingham. He orchestrates Mustard's removal from the game through his loud taunts, then he arranges his own ejection, confident the regular Birmingham pitcher is more than capable of completing the victory.

So what are we to make of Octavus Roy Cohen's Birmingham stories? His cast of dozens and dozens interacted in fascinating ways. They worked, they played, they schemed, they loved, they feared. The plot descriptions that weave through this essay omit the dialect. Presented that way, some of them could pass for Scattergood Baines plots, even Ephraim Tutt plots.

This in fact appears to be the only way to extract Cohen from hopeless literary oblivion: examine the universe he created devoid of its exaggeration. There's no other fiction series in the *Post*, if elsewhere, to compare with Cohen's Birmingham stories in duration, breadth and scope.

A Du Bois comment opens the door to looking at the Cohen stories in a different light. "I should not be surprised if Octavus Roy Cohen had approached *The Saturday Evening Post* to write about a different kind of colored folk than the monstrosities he has created"; Du Bois wrote, "but if he has, the *Post* has replied, 'No. You are getting paid to write about the kind of colored people you are writing about.'"[146]

Du Bois frames the above statement with a defense of some writers for exploring black worlds: "They cry for freedom in dealing with Negroes because they have so little freedom in dealing with whites. DuBose Heyward[147] writes 'Porgy' and writes beautifully of the black Charleston underworld. But why does he do this? Because he cannot do a similar thing for the white people of Charleston, or they would drum him out of town. The only chance he had to tell the truth of pitiful human degradation was to tell it of colored people."

And, Du Bois said, "In other words, the white public today demands from its artists, literary and pictorial, racial pre-judgment which deliberately distorts Truth and Justice, as far as colored races are concerned, and it will pay for no other."

The *Post*'s Lorimer had blinders when it came to racial tolerance. But if you take away race, Cohen's craft becomes more evident. Erase race, he was a pretty good writer. His characters frequently get into messes and have to extract themselves. Just like Botts. Just like Glencannon or Tish. No wonder Lorimer liked them. In that respect, they fit the *Post*.

There's no denying the Birmingham stories are demeaning, even if that wasn't Cohen's intention. Lower-class blacks are often (not always, but often) depicted as fools.

Cohen's exaggerated characters were in keeping with their time. But where Du Bois and others had concerns was, to many rural northern or western whites, even southern whites, this was their only information about blacks. The characters seemed real to those readers.

Poking fun as Wodehouse did with Bertie Wooster was to pick on a class that could take it. The same for Rinehart's Tish or Train's Tutt. Maybe not so much for Gilpatric's hard-drinking Scotsman Glencannon.

But each of these groups of whites—whether Edwardian elite or Midwestern business-people or New England townsmen—also had strong, favorable depictions in lots and lots of other stories and novels.

Blacks? Particularly with Cohen's ubiquitousness, not at all.

The *Post*'s editors said they couldn't find a capable black writer.

They ignored Langston Hughes.

It's wartime. On the piano at Sis Callie Fluker's boarding house, Florian Slappey has "decomposed" a tune he's sure will win a Sons and Daughters of I Will Arise contest. The story is "Slappey Days Are Here Again."[148]

The hero asks Fanfoot Johnson, conductor of the Toot Sweeters, to arrange the rousing "We're Gonna Go to Tokyo" and play it for him for the competition. Johnson not only agrees, he appropriates the tune as his own, despite Slappey's protestations. Nothing Slappey can do will discourage Johnson. So Slappey comes up with another, even better tune, "The Song of a Soldier Boy." When Johnson overhears that one, he decides to let Slappey have credit for his first piece and arrange and take credit for the second himself.

Come night of the contest, his friend Jasper de Void commiserates with Slappey. His song gets a good reception from the audience. But when Johnson plays "Soldier Boy," and de Void expects loud cheers, there's only silence. Lawyer Chew leaps to the stage and confirms Johnson claims to have written the song. Turning to the audience, Chew explains, "That number which Fanfoot Johnson just played, an' which he confesses he wrote himself, is the national hymn of Nazi Germany. Its real name is the Horst Wessel song." Slappey had pulled a fast one.

Florian Slappey has no fans today.

"Most of Cohen's dialect books have remained out of print for decades; and on balance, I suppose, that's a good thing—," summarized newspaper columnist Ben Windham in 2009, "even if Cohen could tell a good tale."[149]

Octavus Roy Cohen Notes

1. Carol Bird, "Away with Pessimism," *Youngstown Vindicator*, 15 December 1935, 27.
2. "Death Claims Octavus Cohen; Lawyer–Newspaper Man Dies at Residence," *News and Courier*, 7 October 1927, 8.
3. Backward Glances, *News and Courier*, 15 April 1910. Octavus Roy Cohen's sister, Dora Moise Cohen (1892–1987), married Lt. Col. John Knowles Gowen, USA (1894–1961), and raised a son, John Knowles Gowen, Jr. (1914–1997).
4. He addressed the graduating class there in 1934, after he'd achieved recognition as a writer.
5. Cohen was a sponsor when Clemson organized a Gamma Alpha Mu fraternity in 1933, and he donated a James Montgomery Flagg charcoal sketch of himself and a complete set of his books in 1938. "Clemson Fraternity Is Given Sketch of Cohen," *Herald-Journal*, 12 January 1938, 4.
6. "All About I" in Thomas L. Masson, *Our American Humorists*, 346–350.
7. "He'll Write of WAAC," *Des Moines Tribune*, 9 July 1942.
8. Ibid.
9. "A Theatrical Review," 26 May 1893, 3.
10. "A Theatrical Budget," 24 March 1902, 3.
11. "All About I," op cit.
12. "Below the Surface."
13. "Poorly-Paid Colored Maid Leads Cohen to $1,000,000," *Los Angeles Times*, 3 March 1929, C3.
14. "All About I" op cit., 346–350.
15. "Octavius [sic] Cohen, Jr., to wed Miss Tallman," *Tuscaloosa News*, 18 April 1944, 2. The bride was the daughter of Mr. and Mrs. Arthur Van Allen McHarg.
16. He refused to reveal the pen name to his parents, columnist O.O. McIntyre said in "New York By Day," 8 May 1936.
17. "Joins Waterbury Realty Agency," *Red Bank Register*, 13 April 1950, 1. The father left ORC Jr.

$1 in his will in 1959, saying "he had made a sincere effort during his lifetime to provide for his son," according to the *Trenton (N.J.) Evening Times*, 16 January 1959, 3. Most of ORC Sr.'s estate went to his friend Margaret M. Brigham of Los Angeles, with $200 a month going to an aunt, Nina Ottolingui of Asheville, North Carolina. ORC's wife Inez had died of a heart condition in 1953. "Death of Author's Wife Revealed," *Seattle Daily Times*, 17 February 1953, 15.

18. Ibid.
19. "Octavus Roy Cohen: Creator of Florian Slappey," *The Oregonian*, 9 January 1938.
20. "They Write Books," *Boston Daily Globe*, 22 April 1929, 14.
21. "False Alarm," 17 April 1915 issue.
22. "Story Writing a Cinch!," *Kansas City Times*, 15 September 1919.
23. "Author of Darky-Yarn Fame Turns Again to Love-Story Field with Fair Result," *Augusta Chronicle*, 8 August 1937, 5.
24. O.O. McIntyre in his "New York by Day" column, 12 February 1935, said the count for short stories then was 1,400, and Cohen would write for another two decades.
25. "Story Writing a Cinch!," op cit.
26. Whitman, op cit.
27. Cohen conveniently forgot that Harris Dickson was already submitting his Ole Reliable stories to the *Post*. The true distinction, as we will see, was that Cohen wrote urban, rather than rural, stories.
28. Dave Brinegar writing in the *Arizona Independent Republic*, 6 August 1939, 32, offered this likely apocryphal anecdote from songwriter Roy Marsh: "Marsh was stopping in a Phoenix hotel, and each evening called a cab. Though coincidence he was served several nights in a row by a young man whose name was Octavus Cohen. Cohen and Marsh became friendly and one night Cohen asked, 'How did you get started?' Marsh told him that to achieve a foothold in any line of creative endeavor one needed not only ability but sometimes a 'connection.' Cohen said he was interested in writing and asked Marsh if he would look at some of his work. Marsh said he would, and Cohen took some short stories to Marsh's hotel room. They were several of what later became known as the Birmingham stories—the ones about Florian Slappey and his friends. Marsh told Uncle Billy. I sat up until dawn reading them. A short time later Marsh was at the Grand Canyon and met a party of touring editors. Included was George Horace Lorimer and Marsh persuaded Lorimer to let him arrange a meeting with Cohen."
29. "They Write Books," op cit.
30. "Screen Life in Hollywood," *Alton Evening Telegraph*, 4 March 1929, 2.
31. *Saturday Evening Post*, 4 January 1919.
32. "Putting the Negro in Fiction," 99.
33. *My Father's People: A Family of Southern Jews*, 43.
34. "Man About Manhattan," *Free Lance-Star*, 10 October 1940, 5.
35. "Loafers' Club Belies Its Name," *Spokesman-Review*, 23 July 1927. Other members included Jack Bethea (1892–1928), author of *Bed Rock* and *Honor Bound*, and James Saxon Childers (1899–1965), author of *The Bookshop Mystery* and *A Novel About a White Man and a Black Man in the Deep South*.
36. Paul Warwick, "Florian's Dice Worried R. Cohen," *Atlanta Constitution*, 21 June 1922, 15.
37. Sophie W. Burkhim, "Royal Poinciana Hotel Closes Doors After Breakfast Today, Ending Brilliant 1930 Season," *Palm Beach Daily News*, 22 March 1930.
38. "Sidelights on Octavus Roy Cohen, Author of 'The May Day Mystery,'" 14 April 1933, 1.
39. "Mrs. J.I. Harrison Entertains Estes Embroidery Circle," *Tuscaloosa News*, 12 December 1929, 5.
40. Cooper (1886–1940) was a journalist and author of more than 30 books and 500 magazine articles. He was a friend of Buffalo Bill and J. Edgar Hoover.
41. Ross, Greg, "Dueling Chameleons," Futility Closet website.
42. "The Rambler," St. Petersburg, Fla., *Evening Independent*, 14 October 1930, 6.
43. *Saturday Evening Post*, 12 November 1921.
44. "More Otherwise Than Wise," *Macon Daily Telegraph*, 28 November 1921, 4.
45. Callway (1883–1948), a former *Ledger* reporter, later wrote for *Argosy*, *Cowboy Story Magazine* and other pulps.
46. "Opens Berkeley Office," *News and Courier*, 29 November 1935, 9.
47. "Harlem Girds Itself for Invasion from Alabama," 28 September 1935, 8.
48. Van Vechten (1880–1964) was a photographer, novelist, litterateur and advocate for the Harlem Renaissance. His controversial novel *Nigger Heaven* (1926) dwelt on gritty aspects of Harlem life, including racism.

49. Bontemps (1902–1973) was a poet, playwright and author of novels including *Black Thunder* (1936).
50. *Black Like You*, 191.
51. "Away with Pessimism," op cit.
52. *Saturday Evening Post*, 3 October 1936.
53. "Florian: He's Back in Octavus Roy Cohen Stories," *Pittsburgh Press*, 14 August 1938.
54. *Oregonian*, op cit.
55. "Sound Pictures to Succeed Silent Movies Very Soon," *Edwardsville Intelligencer*, 13 February 1929, 3.
56. "Octavus Roy Cohen, Prolific Writer, Dies," *Seattle Daily Times*, 7 January 1959, 47. He is buried in Forest Lawn Cemetery in Glendale, California.
57. "Author of 400 Negro Stories and Wife Sail for New York," 21 September 1940.
58. The reference is to the Irish saloon owner Martin J. Dooley of Chicago, broguish character in more than 700 humorous syndicated sketches by Finley Peter Dunne (1867–1936).
59. For example, in the *Fort Worth Star-Telegram* for 31 March 1920. The Charleston, S.C., *News and Courier* was at least one other paper to carry the columns.
60. "Octavus Roy Cohen's Famous Negro Stories to Appear Twice Each Week in Star-Telegram," *Fort Worth Star-Telegram*, 29 March 1920.
61. Ibid.
62. *Saturday Evening Post,* 28 April 1923.
63. Op cit.
64. Florian Slappey wasn't in that story, and he was absent from quite a few of the Birmingham series.
65. *Oregonian*, op cit.
66. He omits Jackson Ramsay, a "portly white man who operated the policy game" in "Pool and Genuine," and the bank president Willets in "Dark and Dreary," but they were secondary characters.
67. *Los Angeles Times*, 3 March 1929, op cit.
68. See Charles Mack later in this book.
69. "Other and abler writers have expressed themselves on this subject [of screenwriting] more aptly and profanely than I shall ever succeed in doing," he said in "All About I," op cit.
70. "The Negro in the South," *The Week* (New London, Conn.), 1 October 1891, 1.
71. "Will Rogers' Daily Story," *Boston Daily Globe*, 11 December 1925, 22.
72. *Photoplay*, February 1927.
73. Brandt and Brandt represented numerous authors in the 20th century, including Booth Tarkington, Joseph Conrad, Marjorie Kinnan Rawlings, Raymond Chandler and Judson Philips. Carl Brandt (1888–1957) formed the agency in 1912 with his brother Erdmann N. Brandt (1893–1968). Carl's first wife was the social activist Zelma Corning (1891–1990), who was active in the literary agency. The Brandts divorced in 1927. Carl married Carol Denny (1904–1984), chief story editor for MGM, in 1931. Erdmann left in 1934 to become an editor for the *Saturday Evening Post*. Carol joined the literary agency in 1955. Brandt & Brandt Contract Files, 1912–1995, are held by Princeton University Library Department of Rare Books and Special Collections; Octavus Roy Cohen 1924 papers are in Box 23, folder 3.
74. *Saturday Evening Post*, 14 October 1939. The next year, Jack Benny's Rochester (Eddie Anderson) as a pretend cowboy nearly walked away with the dude ranch motion picture *Buck Benny Rides Again*.
75. Op cit.
76. Question for Cohen, *Salt Lake Tribune*, 19 September 1921, 4. Same in *Appleton Post-Crescent*, same date, 4.
77. *Oregonian*, op cit.
78. Works by Lardner (1885–1933) include "Alibi Ike" and other sports short stories.
79. Fitch (1877–1915) wrote *Homeburg Memories* (1915) among other books.
80. Leacock (1869–1944) wrote *Sunshine Sketches of a Little Town* (1912) and other books.
81. Op cit.
82. Brush (1902–1952) wrote for *Cosmopolitan, Collier's, Harper's Weekly, College Humor* and various newspapers. Her story "Him and Her" won an O. Henry Award for best short story in 1929.
83. Carol Bird, "Away with Pessimism," op cit.
84. Lewis (1885–1951) also wrote *Babbitt* (1922), *Arrowsmith* (1925) and *Elmer Gantry* (1927).
85. Harris (1869–1935) wrote *A Circuit Rider's Wife* (1910) and other works.

86. Irvin S. Cobb, "Laughing Around the World," *Boston Daily Globe*, 4 June 1927.
87. "Havana Bound," *Miami News*, 13 November 1936.
88. O.O. McIntyre, "New York Day by Day," *Paris News*, 27 March 1925. Also, *Canadian Jewish Chronicle*, 19 April 1935, 4.
89. "Octavus Roy Cohen, Author," *Washington Post*, 11 May 1919.
90. *Saturday Evening Post*, 18 December 1926.
91. "New York Laughs at 'Come Sev'n,'" 1 August 1920.
92. "New Comedy by Octavus Roy Cohen," 27 July 1920.
93. "Negro Play Makes Hit at Hippodrome," *Dallas Morning News*, 18 December 1922.
94. *Black Culture and the New Deal*, 60.
95. "Christie to Make Cohen Stories," 31 August 1928.
96. Canadian-born Alfred Christie (1881–1951) honed his craft on *Mutt and Jeff* comedies and pictures for Nestor Studios in New Jersey.
97. "Gourfain Plans All-Colored Musical," *Afro-American*, 26 December 1942, 10.
98. *Black to Nature* (1935).
99. *Saturday Evening Post*, 22 January 1938.
100. *Elks Magazine*, 1950.
101. *Saturday Evening Post*, 12 January 1924.
102. Rogue Fiction Writers.
103. McIntyre (1884–1938) wrote with a mix of small-town integrity and big-city perspective. His "New York Day by Day" appeared in more than 500 newspapers at its peak.
104. "New York Day by Day," *Reading Eagle*, 9 January 1936.
105. "The Southern Black—As Seen by the Eye of Fiction," *Negro World*, 10 December 1921, reprinted in *A Hubert Harrison Reader*, Jeffrey B. Perry, ed., 336–337.
106. 10 September 1922 issue, 7.
107. 1 December 1920, as reproduced in "Florian Slappey," Thrilling Detective Web Site.
108. "Nigger Comedies," *Northern Territory Times*, 20 November 1928, 1.
109. See W.E.B. Du Bois, Appendix.
110. 22 December 1922, W.E.B. Du Bois Papers (MS 312). Special Collections and University Archives, University of Massachusetts Amherst Libraries, Amherst Mass. Reprinted in Herbert Aptheker, ed., *The Correspondence of W.E.B. Du Bois: Volume 1, Selections 1877–1934*, 259.
111. Reference is to Captain A.E. Dingle (1879–1947), author of sea stories, whose Nick Pride appeared in the *Post* for 9 December 1922.
112. Novelist Dixon (1864–1946) was a Baptist minister, playwright, lawyer and legislator who had a way of making his fiction appear to be fact. He was best known for his novel *The Clansman*, inspiration for D.W. Griffith's *The Birth of a Nation* (1915), both works derogatory of blacks.
113. 19 August 1905, 1–2.
114. *America Reflected: Language, Satire, Film, and the National Mind*.
115. Not all of these stories have been identified as featuring characters of African descent.
116. His *Post* stories were collected in *Old Plantation Days* (1903).
117. 29 December 1922, W.E.B. Du Bois Papers (MS 312). Special Collections and University Archives, University of Massachusetts Amherst Libraries, Amherst Mass. Reprinted in Herbert Aptheker, ed., *The Correspondence of W.E.B. Du Bois: Volume 1, Selections 1877–1934*, 259.
118. "The Crisis Symposium: The Negro in Art: How Shall He Be Portrayed," *Crisis*, May 1926, 219.
119. "Adventures in Exoticism: The 'Black Life' Novels of White Writers," *Western Journal of Black Studies*, 22 March 2002.
120. Active during the Harlem Renaissance, Thurman (1902–1934) wrote *The Blacker the Berry: A Novel of Negro Life* (1929).
121. "Fire Burns: A Department of Comment," *Fire!! A Quarterly Devoted to the Younger Negro Artists*.
122. Brawley (1882–1939) was an African American educator and author.
123. "The Negro in Contemporary Literature," *The English Journal*, March 1929, 194–202.
124. Van Patten (1887–1956) was chief librarian at Queen's University's library in Kingston, Ontario, then became director of Stanford University Libraries for two decades.
125. "The Vocabulary of the American Negro as Set Forth in Contemporary Literature," October 1931, 24–31.

126. "Negro Character As Seen by White Authors," Vol. 2, No. 2, April 1933, 191–192.
127. See Richard Wright, Appendix.
128. Coit Hendley, "Richard Wright Stresses Realism in Dealing with Fictional Negro Types," Washington *Sunday Star*, 11 November 1945.
129. Lucia Loomis (d. 1962), an early advocate for women's rights, wrote as Mrs. Walter Ferguson for her Scripps-Howard syndicated column "From a Woman's Viewpoint."
130. "Types," *Pittsburgh Press*, 26 February 1945.
131. Conrad (1912–1986) was a historian, critic and biographer.
132. "The Philology of Negro Dialect," 150–154.
133. Subtitle: *Harlem Renaissance Print Culture and Modern Black Identity*, 112.
134. "They Write Books," op cit.
135. Ruark (1915–1965) was an author and syndicated columnist. His work appeared in *Field & Stream*, among other periodicals.
136. "Touchiness Handcuffs Our Humor," *Berkshire County Eagle*, 31 March 1950, 3.
137. "A Great Loss in Art," 15 January 1959.
138. "Less Miserable," a Florian Slappey story in the *Chicago Tribune*, 25 September 1921, 1/3. The expression is also found in "Fifty-Fifty-Fifty," syndicated, *Washington Post*, 3 December 1922, 77, among others.
139. 29 March 1948.
140. *Saturday Evening Post*, 23 April 1932.
141. *Saturday Evening Post*, 4 October 1924.
142. *Saturday Evening Post*, 27 April 1929.
143. *Saturday Evening Post*, 13 December 1930.
144. "Octavus Roy Cohen," (Dover, Ohio) *Daily Reporter*, 21 January 1959, 6.
145. *Saturday Evening Post*, 15 December 1928.
146. "Criteria of Negro Art," reprinted in *Double-Take: A Revisionist Harlem Renaissance Anthology*, Venetria K. Patton and Maureen Honey, eds. Rutgers, 2001.
147. Heyward (1885–1940) and his wife Dorothy (1890–1961) adapted his 1925 novel about Charleston, South Carolina, into a play that later became the basis for the 1925 George Gershwin opera *Porgy and Bess*. The Heywards were white.
148. *Saturday Evening Post*, 11 March 1944.
149. Southern Lights, "Old Bachelors' Intrigue Hides Among Clutter," *Tuscaloosa News*, 26 April 2009.

Octavus Roy Cohen Selected Bibliography and Sources

BIRMINGHAM DARKTOWN STORIES OF FLORIAN SLAPPEY, LAWYER CHEW,
   EPIC PETERS AND MIDNIGHT MOTION PICTURE CORP.

"The Missing Clink" (*Saturday Evening Post*, 19 October 1918) illustrated by L.M. Gaitland
"Pool and Ginuwine" (*Saturday Evening Post*, 4 January 1919) (1) il. George Wright
"The Amateur Hero" (*Saturday Evening Post*, 18 January 1919) (1) il. H. Weston Taylor
"Tempus Fugits" (*Saturday Evening Post*, 1 February 1919) (1)
"Backfire" (*Saturday Evening Post*, 8 February 1919) (1) (8)
"Poppy Passes" (*Saturday Evening Post*, 15 February 1919) (1)
"Not Wisely but Too Well" (*Saturday Evening Post*, 22 February 1919) (1)
"A House Divided" (*Saturday Evening Post*, 1 March 1919) (1)
"All That Glitters" (*Saturday Evening Post*, 8 March 1919) (1)
"Painless Extraction" (*Saturday Evening Post*, 22 March 1919) (1) (2)
"Without Benefit of Virgie" (*Saturday Evening Post*, 26 April 1919) (3)
"The Fight That Failed" (*Saturday Evening Post*, 24 May 1919) (3)
"Alley Money" (*Saturday Evening Post*, 7 June 1919) (3)
"The Quicker the Dead" (*Saturday Evening Post*, 31 May 1919) (3)
"Twinkle, Twinkle, Movie Star" (*Saturday Evening Post*, 12 July 1919) (3)
"The Light Bombastic Toe" (*Saturday Evening Post*, 16 August 1919) (3)
"Cock-a-Doodle-Doo!" (*Saturday Evening Post*, 13 September 1919) (3)
"Auto-Intoxication" (*Saturday Evening Post*, 18 October 1919) (4)

"All's Swell That Ends Swell" (*Saturday Evening Post*, 8 November 1919) (4)
"The Survival of the Fattest" (*Saturday Evening Post*, 15 November 1919) (4)
"But the Worl' Gwine On" (United News, syndicated including in *Kansas City Times*, 18 December 1919)
"The Ultima Fool" (*Saturday Evening Post*, 24 January 1920) (4)
"Here Comes the Bribe" (*Saturday Evening Post*, 28 February 1920) (4)
"The Guvment Quits Controllin'" (United Features Syndicate, 31 March 1920) (feature tagged "Florian Slappey the Dooley Darkey" in *Fort Worth Star-Telegram*)
"Meddles for Everybody" (United Features Syndicate, 4 April 1920)
Title not identified (United Features Syndicate, 7 April 1920)
"Low Exchange Ain't No Robbery" (United Features Syndicate, 11 April 1920)
"It Rambles Right Along" (United Features Syndicate, 14 April 1920)
"Mistuh Macbeth" (*Saturday Evening Post*, 17 April 1920) (4)
"War at Any Price 1" (United Features Syndicate, 18 April 1920)
"War at Any Price 2" (United Features Syndicate, 21 April 1920)
"The Night-Blooming Serious" (*Saturday Evening Post*, 24 April 1920) (5)
"Free for All" (United Features Syndicate, 25 April 1920)
"Heavy Waits" (United Features Syndicate, 28 April 1920)
"Too Much Sociability" (United Features Syndicate, 2 May 1920)
"Sumthin for Sumthin" (United Features Syndicate, 5 May 1920)
"To Is or Not to Is" (United Features Syndicate, 9 May 1920)
"The Cat Done Come Back" (United Features Syndicate, 12 May 1920)
"Sweet Spirits" (United Features Syndicate, 16 May 1920)
"Too Bone Dry" (United Features Syndicate, 19 May 1920)
"Lo! The Poor German! 1" (United Features Syndicate, 23 May 1920)
"Lo! The Poor German! 2" (United Features Syndicate, 26 May 1920)
"Overalls All Over" (United Features Syndicate, 30 May 1920)
"The Republican Outlook" (United Features Syndicate, 2 June 1920) (tagged "by Florian Slappey as told to Octavus Roy Cohen" in *Syracuse Journal*)
"Turn About" (United Features Syndicate, 6 June 1920)
"Women's Rites" (United Features Syndicate, 9 June 1920)
"Movie Marriage" (United Features Syndicate, 13 June 1920)
"How High Is High?" (United Features Syndicate, 16 June 1920)
"Gravey" (*Saturday Evening Post*, 19 June 1920) (5)
"The Prohibitional Commandment" (United Features Syndicate, 20 June 1920)
"From Them Which Is Got" (United Features Syndicate, 23 June 1920)
"Too Much Is a Plenty" (United Features Syndicate, 27 June 1920)
Title not identified (United Features Syndicate, 30 June 1920)
"Noblesse Obliged" (*Saturday Evening Post*, 3 July 1920) (5) (18)
Title not identified (United Features Syndicate, 4 July 1920)
"The Fighting Spirit" (United Features Syndicate, 7 July 1920)
"Job Lots" (United Features Syndicate, 11 July 1920)
"Bevo La Mexico" (United Features Syndicate, 14 July 1920)
"Money Talks" (United Features Syndicate, 18 July 1920)
"Postal Deficiency" (United Features Syndicate, 21 July 1920)
"Mistuh Gompers Said It" (United Features Syndicate, 25 July 1920)
"When Pipe Dreams Come True" (United Features Syndicate, 28 July 1920)
"Luxury Taxes" (United Features Syndicate, 1 August 1920)
"The Truth Sho' Will Out" (United Features Syndicate, 4 August 1920)
"The Danger of Bridge" (United Features Syndicate, 8 August 1920)
"Ohio on the Job" (United Features Syndicate, 11 August 1920)
"Mistuh Wilson Plays Hands Off" (United Features Syndicate, 15 August 1920)
"Sausage for the Goose" (United Features Syndicate, 18 August 1920)
"Navies Is Navies" (United Features Syndicate, 22 August 1920
"A New Beginning 1" (United Features Syndicate, 25 August 1920)
"A New Beginning 2" (United Features Syndicate, 29 August 1920)

"The Fewer the Higher" (United Features Syndicate, 1 September 1920)
"The Ten-Year Plague" (United Features Syndicate, 5 September 1920)
"Mistuh Carpentier Done It" (United Features Syndicate, 8 September 1920)
"The Cup Stays Here" (United Features Syndicate, 12 September 1920)
"Ponzi Extracts" (United Features Syndicate, 15 September 1920)
"Treaty Treatment" (United Features Syndicate, 19 September 1920)
"Now That They've Got It" (United Features Syndicate, 22 September 1920)
"Weather Forecast: Wet or Dry?" (United Features Syndicate, 26 September 1920)
"Hot Stuff" (United Features Syndicate, 29 September 1920)
"Korea for Koreans" (United Features Syndicate, 3 October 1920)
"Three's a Crowd" (United Features Syndicate, 6 October 1920)
"Bucking Bolshevism" (United Features Syndicate, 10 October 1920)
"Something Else Rises" (United Features Syndicate, 13 October 1920)
"Rent by Strife" (United Features Syndicate 17 October 1920)
"Sleeping Dogs Don't Lie" (United Features Syndicate, 20 October 1920)
"A Fighter's Mite" (United Features Syndicate, 24 October 1920)
"Scandalous" (United Features Syndicate, 27 October 1920)
"The Next President" (United Features Syndicate, 31 October 1920)
"Real Red Blood" (United Features Syndicate, 3 November 1920)
"Strike Three" (United Features Syndicate, 7 November 1920)
"Yonder They Come" (United Features Syndicate, 10 November 1920)
"Bird of Pray" (*Saturday Evening Post*, 13 November 1920) (5)
"Home Pay and Less Work" (United Features Syndicate, 14 November 1920)
"Egypt Gets Hers" (United Features Syndicate, 17 November 1920)
"Fightin' Fools" (United Features Syndicate, 21 November 1920)
"Let Us Give Thanks" (United Features Syndicate, 24 November 1920)
"Weather or Not" (United Features Syndicate, 28 November 1920)
"Avoid the Rush" (United Features Syndicate, 1 December 1920)
"Gamaliel Gets a Chance" (United Features Syndicate, 5 December 1920)
"Hating Haiti" (United Features Syndicate, 8 December 1920)
"Presidential Election" (United Features Syndicate, 12 December 1920)
"Nothing for Something" (United Features Syndicate, 15 December 1920)
"Prohibition Prohibited" (United Features Syndicate, 19 December 1920)
"Heads I Win" (United Features Syndicate, 22 December 1920)
"Dancin' Fools" (United Features Syndicate, 26 December 1920, tagged "Florian Slappey and Lawyer Chew" in *Fort Worth Star-Telegram*)
"Tea for Two" (United Features Syndicate, 29 December 1920)
"Happy New Year" (United Features Syndicate, 2 January 1921)
"Coming Down" (United Features Syndicate, 5 January 1921)
"The Female of the Species" (United Features Syndicate, 9 January 1921)
"Peace for Any Prize" (United Features Syndicate, 12 January 1921)
"Red Tape" (United Features Syndicate, 15 January 1921)
"Nothing for Something" (United Features Syndicate, 19 January 1921)
"A Free Hand" (United Features Syndicate, 23 January 1921)
Title not identified (United Features Syndicate, 26 January 1921)
"From Them Which Has" (United Features Syndicate, 30 January 1921)
"Another Cup" (United Features Syndicate, 2 February 1921)
Title not identified (United Features Syndicate, 6 February 1921
"When Greek Meets Greek" (United Features Syndicate, 9 February 1921)
"Income Tax" (United Features Syndicate, 13 February 1921)
"Awful Blue" (United Features Syndicate, 16 February 1921)
"A Good Example" (United Features Syndicate, 20 February 1921)
Title not identified (United Features Syndicate, 23 February 1921)
Title not identified (United Features Syndicate, 27 February 1921)
"Foresight" (United Features Syndicate, 2 March 1921)
(Travel, title not identified) (United Features Syndicate, 6 March 1921)

"According to Schedule" (United Features Syndicate, 9 March 1921)
"Oft in the Silly Night" (*Saturday Evening Post*, 12 March 1921) (5)
"Peace on Earth" (United Features Syndicate, 13 March 1921)
"Bad for Health" (United Features Syndicate, 16 March 1921)
"Easy Come—Easy Go" (United Features Syndicate, 20 March 1921)
"Oils Well That Ends Well" (United Features Syndicate, 23 Mach 1921)
"Peace at Any Price" (United Features Syndicate, 27 March 1921)
"Batter Up!" (United Features Syndicate, 30 March 1921)
"H2O Boy!" (*Saturday Evening Post*, 4 June 1921) (5)
"The Evil Lie" (*Saturday Evening Post*, 10 September 1921) (5)
"Less Miserable" (syndicated, including in *Lexington (Ky.) Herald*, 24 September 1921, and *Chicago Tribune*, 25 September 1921)
"Chocolate Grudge" (*Saturday Evening Post*, 12 November 1921) (5)
"Music Hath Harms" (*Saturday Evening Post*, 26 November 1921) (6)
"The Widow's Bite" (*Saturday Evening Post*, 18 February 1922) (6)
"Presto Change!" (*Saturday Evening Post*, 18 March 1922) (6)
"Completely Done in Oils" (syndicated, including in *Rochester (N.Y.) Democrat Chronicle, Salt Lake Tribune* and *Morning Oregonian* 2 April 1922; *Atlanta Constitution* 9 April 1922; Wilmington, Del., *Delmaria Sunday Star* 8 July 1923) (6)
"Then There Were Nine" (*Saturday Evening Post*, 30 September 1922)
"One Half Dozen Raw" (*Saturday Evening Post*, 14 October 1922)
"Focus Pokus" (*Saturday Evening Post*, 21 October 1922) (6)
"To Have & Toe Hold" (*Hearst's International,* October 1922) il. Bud Peaglar
"Melancholy Dame" (*Hearst's International,* December 1922)
"Fifty-Fifty-Fifty" (syndicated, including in *Washington Post*, 3 December 1922)
"His Bitter Half" (*Saturday Evening Post*, 13 January 1923) (6)
"Far Better Than Worse" (*Saturday Evening Post*, 27 January 1923) (6)
"The Law and the Profits" (*Saturday Evening Post*, 28 April 1923) (7) (23)
"Protect at All Times" (Saturday Evening Post, 5 May 1923)
"The B.V. Demon" (1923) (6)
"The Wild Notes" (7)
"The Birth of a Notion" (*Saturday Evening Post*, 1 September 1923) il. J.J. Gould (7)
"Plain Black on White" (*Saturday Evening Post*, 13 October 1923)
"The Late Lamented" (*Saturday Evening Post*, 17 November 1923) (7)
"Wild and Wooly Vest" (*Saturday Evening Post*, 8 December 1923) (7)
"His Children's Father" (syndicated, including in *Springfield Republican* 23 December 1923, Cleveland *Plain Dealer* 30 December 1930, and *Baltimore Sun* 6 January 1924) (7)
"The Berth of Hope" (*Saturday Evening Post*, 12 January 1924) (14) (24)
"Ride 'Em and Weep" (*Saturday Evening Post*, 23 February 1924) (15)
"The Balm Before the Storm" (*Elks Magazine*, February 1924)
"The Battle of Sedan" (*Elks Magazine*, 1924) (*Famous Story Magazine*, August 1926) (7)
"Measure for Pleasure" (1924) (7)
"Bass Ingratitude" (*Saturday Evening Post*, 1 March 1924) (9) (11)
"Traveling Suspenses" (*Saturday Evening Post*, 22 March 1924) (15)
"Transportation Only" (*Saturday Evening Post*, 24 May 1924) EP
"Trunk and Disorderly" (*Saturday Evening Post*, 7 June 1924) (11)
"The Epic Cure" (*Saturday Evening Post,* 26 July 1924) (15)
"The Lady Fare" (*Saturday Evening Post*, 9 August 1924) (11)
"Every Little Movie" (*Saturday Evening Post*, 30 August 1924) (10)
"The Framing of the Shrew" (*Elks Magazine*, 1924) (syndicated, including in *Buffalo Sunday Express* and *Winnipeg Free Press* 13 June 1925) il. Burg Salg (*Best Stories of All Time*, January 1927) (11)
"Double Double" (*Saturday Evening Post*, 27 September 1924) (10)
"The Bathing Booty" (*Saturday Evening Post*, 4 October 1924) (10)
"A Little Child" (*Saturday Evening Post*, 18 October 1924) "A Little Child Shall Feed Them" (10)
"Inside Inflammation" (*Saturday Evening Post*, 1 November 1924) (10)
"White Lights and Amber" (*Saturday Evening Post*, 20 December 1924)

"Blackmale" (*Saturday Evening Post*, 17 January 1925) (11)
"The Lion and the Uniform" (*Saturday Evening Post*, 31 January 1925) (10)
"The Case Ace" (*Saturday Evening Post*, 28 February 1925)
"Write and Wrong" (*Saturday Evening Post*, 7 March 1925) (10)
"Barberous" (*Saturday Evening Post*, 14 March 1925) (11) Chew
"The Spider and the Lie" (syndicated, including in *Los Angeles Times* and *Trenton Sunday Times-Advertiser* 29 March 1925) (7)
"Miss Directed" (*Saturday Evening Post*, 11 April 1925) (9)
"On with the Lance" (*Saturday Evening Post*, 2 May 1925)
"The Union Suit" (syndicated, including in *Washington Post* 24 May 1925, *Atlanta Constitution* and *Los Angeles Times* 31 May 1925)
"Damaged Good" (*Saturday Evening Post*, 18 July 1925)
"Jazz You Like It" (*Saturday Evening Post*, 8 August 1925)
"A Bounce of Prevention" (*Saturday Evening Post*, 19 September 1925) (18)
"Plumes and Sable" (*Saturday Evening Post*, 10 October 1925) il J. Clinton Shepherd
"A Lass and a Lack" (*Saturday Evening Post*, 28 November 1925)
"Bear Facts" (syndicated, including in *St. Petersburg Times* 15 November 1925 and *Chicago Daily Tribune* 22 November 1925)
"Endurance Vile" (*Saturday Evening Post*, 5 December 1925)
"Skins and Groans" (*Saturday Evening Post*, 9 January 1926)
"The Claws in the Contract" (*Saturday Evening Post*, 6 February 1926)
"The Call of the Riled" (*Saturday Evening Post*, 6 March 1926)
"Cash and Carry" (*Saturday Evening Post*, 3 April 1926)
"Marcy, Monsieur!" (*Saturday Evening Post*, 8 May 1926)
"Battle Scared" (*Saturday Evening Post*, 12 June 1916)
"The Fly and the Ointment" (syndicated, including in *Washington Post* and *Chicago Tribune* 23 November 1924) (11)
"Grooms to Let" (syndicated, including in *Winnipeg Free Press* 9 July 1926, *San Antonio Express* and *Los Angeles Times* 11 July 1926)
"The Pay of Naples" (*Saturday Evening Post*, 17 July 1926) (13)
"Neapolitan Scream" (*Saturday Evening Post*, 14 August 1926)
"Ben Hurry" (*Photoplay*, August 1926) 1 of 6
"The Gotten Goat" (*Photoplay*, September 1926) il. J.J. Gould
"Horns Aplenty" (*Saturday Evening Post*, 4 September 1926) (13)
"Trés Sheik" (*Saturday Evening Post*, 16 October 1926) (13)
"Low but Sure" (*Saturday Evening Post*, 6 November 1926) (13)
"Love and Defection" (*Photoplay*, October 1926)
"On Account of Monte Cristo" (*Photoplay*, November 1926)
"Ham and Exit" (*Saturday Evening Post*, 18 December 1926) (13)
"Arabian Nights" (*Photoplay*, December 1926)
"The Roman Knows" (*Photoplay*, January 1927)
"Mate in America" (*Saturday Evening Post*, 8 January 1927) (13)
"Stew's Company" (*Saturday Evening Post*, 5 February 1927) (13)
"Safe and Seine" (*Photoplay*, February 1927) il. J.J. Gould
"French Leave" (*Photoplay*, March 1927)
"Between Halves" (*Saturday Evening Post*, 5 March 1927)
"Crude Interest" (*Saturday Evening Post*, 26 March 1927)
"The Pull by the Horns" (*Saturday Evening Post*, 7 May 1927)
"Sell Shock" (*Saturday Evening Post*, 21 May 1927)
"Insufficient Fun" (*Saturday Evening Post*, 4 June 1927)
"Blah Blah Black Sheep" (*Saturday Evening Post*, 2 July 1927)
"Idles of the King" (*Saturday Evening Post*, 6 August 1927) (17)
"The Porter Missing Man" (*Saturday Evening Post*, 20 August 1927) (15)
"The Trained Flee" (*Saturday Evening Post*, 17 September 1927) (15)
"Hearts and Glowers" (*Saturday Evening Post*, 8 October 1927)
"Seventh 'Leven" (*Saturday Evening Post*, 22 October 1927) (18)

"Double or Nothing" (*Saturday Evening Post*, 19 November 1927)
"Honestly It's the Best Policy" (*Saturday Evening Post*, 21 January 1928)
"Less Majesty" (syndicated, including in *Times-Picayune* 19 February 1928)
"The Sprinting Press" (*Saturday Evening Post*, 3 March 1928)
"Money for Sooth" (*Saturday Evening Post*, 24 March 1928) (17)
"Black Beauty" (*Saturday Evening Post*, 28 April 1928) (18)
"A Toot for a Toot" (*Saturday Evening Post*, 19 May 1928) (15) (22) (25)
"Brooch of Contract" (*Saturday Evening Post*, 14 July 1928)
"Bearly Possible" (*Saturday Evening Post*, 11 August 1928)
"Ball One, Strike One" (*Saturday Evening Post*, 15 September 1928)
"Meddle Play" (*Saturday Evening Post*, 13 October 1928)
"Violent Ray" (*Saturday Evening Post*, 15 December 1928) (17)
"Stranger Than Friction" (syndicated, including in Ottawa *Saturday Evening Citizen* 29 December 1928 and *Times-Picayune* 30 December 1928)
"Arabian Knights" (1928) (13) (14)
"French Leave" (1928) (13)
"After the Football Was Over" (*Saturday Evening Post*, 23 February 1929)
"Dark and Dreary" (*Saturday Evening Post*, 27 April 1929) (17)
"The Day of Daze" (*Saturday Evening Post*, 1 June 1929)
"Fast and Curious" (syndicated, including in *Seattle Sunday Morning Times*, *Atlanta Journal and Constitution* and *Hartford Courant* 19 May 1929 and *Los Angeles Times* 2 June 1929)
"Congealed Weapons" (syndicated, including in *Ottawa Citizen*, 14 June 1929, and *Miami News*, 16 June 1929)
"The Leased of These" (*Saturday Evening Post*, 13 July 1929) (17)
"The Permanent Waive" (*Saturday Evening Post*, 10 August 1929) (8)
"The Slappeyan Way" (*Saturday Evening Post*, 7 September 1929) (16)
"Cut and Dried" (*Saturday Evening Post*, 12 October 1929) (16)
"10,000 Pictures Can't Be Wrong" (*Saturday Evening Post*, 9 November 1929)
"Sizzling Sadie" (*Saturday Evening Post*, 14 December 1929) (16)
"5000 Feet Make One Smile" (*Saturday Evening Post*, 4 January 1930) (16)
"The Party of the Worst Part" (*Saturday Evening Post*, 15 February 1930) (16)
"The Loan Wolf" (*Saturday Evening Post*, 1 March 1930) (16)
"Comin' through the Sky" (*Saturday Evening Post*, 8 March 1930) (16)
"Supe & Fish" (*Saturday Evening Post*, 29 March 1930) (16)
"Vanity's Fare" (*Saturday Evening Post*, 19 April 1930)
"Nuts and Reasons" (*Saturday Evening Post*, 24 May 1930)
"Lemon Aid" (*Saturday Evening Post*, 7 June 1930) (17)
"Bout Face" (*Saturday Evening Post*, 28 June 1930)
"Once in a Wifetime" (syndicated, including in *Oregonian*, *Chicago Tribune*, *Hartford Courant*, *Seattle Sunday Times*, *Baltimore Sun* and *St. Petersburg Times* 17 August 1930)
"Ball and Jane" (*Saturday Evening Post*, 6 September 1930)
"Custard's Last Stand" (*Saturday Evening Post*, 18 October 1930) (8)
"Step Brothers" (*Saturday Evening Post*, 15 November 1930) (8)
"Two for One" (*Saturday Evening Post*, 13 December 1930) (17)
"Among Those Presents" (*Saturday Evening Post*, 7 March 7, 1931) (17)
"Fly Paper" (*Saturday Evening Post*, 11 April 1931) (8)
"Snakes Alive" (*Saturday Evening Post*, 16 May 1931) (17)
"Wedding Bills" (*Saturday Evening Post*, 27 June 1931) (8)
"Hoodoo and Who Don't" (*Saturday Evening Post*, 12 September 1931) (8)
"The Whites of Their Lies" (*Elks Magazine*, October 1932)
"A Stitch in Time" (*Elks Magazine*, November 1932)
"Concealed Weapons" (syndicated, including in *Boston Globe*, 1 November 1935)
"Crash and Carry" (8)
"Chukker Luck" (17)
"Silk and Satan" (*Saturday Evening Post*, 28 November 1931) (17)
"Rolling Bones" (*Saturday Evening Post*, 6 February 1932) (8)

"Black Booty" (syndicated, including in *St. Petersburg Times* 23 April 1932, *Washington Post, Times-Picayune* and *Hartford Courant* 24 April 1932 and *Los Angeles Times* 1 May 1932)
"Net Profits" (*Saturday Evening Post*, 23 April 1932) (8)
"Night Howls" (*Saturday Evening Post*, 9 July 1932) (8)
"Pronounced Hi-Li" (*Saturday Evening Post*, 13 August 1932)
"Picture Framed" (syndicated, including in *Daily Boston Globe* 4 September 1932) (16)
"Fast Black" (syndicated, including in *Hartford Courant* 23 October 1932)
"Mardi Gratis" (*Saturday Evening Post*, 24 December 1932) (18)
"Auto Motive" (*Saturday Evening Post*, 4 February 1933) (18)
"Deft and Dumb" (*Saturday Evening Post*, 7 May 1933) (18)
"Daylight Slaving" (*Saturday Evening Post*, 5 August 1933)
"Axe Me Another" (syndicated, including in *Spokesman-Review* (Spokane, Wash.) 25 August 1933, *Baltimore Sun* and *Hartford Courier* 27 August 1933 and *Roundup Record-Tribune and Winnett Times*, 9 November 1933)
"The Muchright Man" (*Saturday Evening Post*, 7 April 1934) il. George Brahm
"Alibi and the Forty Thieves" (*Saturday Evening Post*, 8 September 1934)
"Fast Blacks" (*Saturday Evening Post*, 10 November 1934)
"Sauce for the Dander" (*Saturday Evening Post*, 23 February 1935)
"Jungle Bells" (syndicated, including in *This Week* 19 April 1935 and *Milwaukee Journal*, 21 April 1935)
"Where the Wild Time Grows" (syndicated, including in *Spokesman-Review* 6 April 1935, *Hartford Courant, Youngstown Vindicator* and *San Antonio Express* 7 April 1935 and *Oregonian Fiction Weekly* 12 May 1935)
"Willie the Wisp" (syndicated, including in *This Week* and *Milwaukee Journal* 24 November 1935)
"A Lie for a Lie" (*Saturday Evening Post*, 31 December 1935) (18)
"Debt and Destruction" (syndicated, including in *Springfield Republican* and *Hartford Courant* 19 January 1936)
"Way Up Nawth in Dixie" (*Saturday Evening Post*, 29 February 1936) (18)
"Howdye Harlem" (syndicated, including in *Los Angeles Times* and *Hartford Courant* 23 August 1936)
"Personal Appearance" (*Saturday Evening Post*, 3 October 1936) (18)
"The Fatted Half" (*Saturday Evening Post*, February 20, 1937) (18) (26)
"Scars Fell on Alabama" (*Saturday Evening Post*, 15 May 1937)
"The Fist Shall Be Last" (*Saturday Evening Post*, 31 July 1937)
"The Mystery of the Missing Wash" (*Saturday Evening Post*, 22 January 1938) (18) (20)
"Stars and Tripes" (17)
"The Malady Lingers" (*Saturday Evening Post*, 12 November 1938)
"Altar Ego" (*Saturday Evening Post*, 18 March 1939)
"Two-Gun Slappey Rides Again" (*Saturday Evening Post*, October 14, 1939)
"We Maim to Please" (syndicated, including in *This Week* and *Milwaukee Journal* 24 December 1939)
"Slappy-Go-Lucky" (*Saturday Evening Post*, 20 July 1940)
"A Grapple a Day" (*Saturday Evening Post*, 22 February 1941)
"Information Flees" (*Saturday Evening Post*, 28 October 1941)
"Horse and Buggy Daze" (*Saturday Evening Post*, 29 August 1942)
"Black Booty" (*Saturday Evening Post*, 12 June 1943) *note 1932 story has similar title
"Slappey Days Are Here Again" (*Saturday Evening Post*, March 11, 1944)
"Melody in 4-F" (*Saturday Evening Post*, 30 December 1944)
"Ultra Violent" (*Argosy*, January 1945) (*Ellery Queen's Mystery Magazine*, January 1946)
"Profit Without Honor" (*Argosy*, April 1945)
"Slappey-Happy" (*Southern Fireside*, September 1949)
"Florian Slappey—Private Eye" (*Elks Magazine*, 1950) (*Ellery Queen's Mystery Magazine*, November 1953) (*Mystery Digest*, May 1958)
"Once Upon a Crime" (1952) (21)

SELECTED BOOKS
  (1) *Polished Ebony* (1919)
  (2) *One Issue: Just One 52nd of a Year* (1919)
  (3) *Come Seven* (1920)

(4) *Highly Colored* (1921)
(5) *Assorted Chocolates* (1922)
(6) *Dark Days and Black Knights* (1923)
(7) *Sunclouds* (1924)
(8) *Black to Nature* (1924)
(9) *Aces: A Collection of Short Stories* (1924) compiled by Community Workers of the New York Guild for the Jewish Blind
(10) *Bigger and Blacker* (1925)
(11) *Black and Blue* (1926)
(12) *Come Seven: A Negro Farce-Comedy in Three Acts* (1927)
(13) *Florian Slappey Goes Abroad* (1928)
(14) *The World's Fifty Best Short Novels (in Ten Volumes)* (1929) Grant Overton ed.
(15) *Epic Peters, Pullman Porter* (1930)
(16) *Lilies of the Alley* (1931)
(17) *Carbon Copies* (1932)
(18) *Florian Slappey* (1938)
(19) *Sixty Years of American Humor: The Best American Humor from Mark Twain to Benchley, a Prose Anthology* (1938) Joseph Lewis French, ed.
(20) *101 Years Entertainment* (1941) Ellery Queen, ed.
(21) *Best Detective Stories of the Year* (1952) David C. Cooke, ed.
(22) *Great Railroad Stories of the World* (1954) Samuel Moskowitz, ed.
(23) *Fiction Goes to Court* (1954) Albert P. Blaustein, ed.
(24) *Headlights and Markers* (1968) Frank P. Donovan Jr. and Robert Selph Henry eds.
(25) *Short Lines* (1996) Rob Johnson, ed.
(26) *Many Voices, Many Rooms: A New Anthology of Alabama Writers* (1998) Philip D. Beidler, ed.

PLAYS

Come Seven (1920) (12)
Antony and Cleopatra (Davidson, N.C., College *Davidsonian*, 12 March 1925) said to be "According to our friend Octavus Roy Cohen," but really a pastiche by C.F. Smith, managing editor of the college publication

FILMS

Music Hath Harms (1929)
The Melancholy Dame (1929)
The Framing of the Shrew (1929)
Oft in the Silly Night (1929)
Birmingham Black Bottom (1997) collects the four films

TELEVISION PILOT

Florian Slappey, Private Eye (1951)

SOURCES

Aptheker, Herbert. *The Correspondence of W.E.B. Du Bois: Volume 1, Selections 1877–1934*. Amherst: University of Massachusetts Press, 1997.
Assorted Chocolates review. *New York Times*, 24 September 1922.
"Author of 400 Negro Stories and Wife Sail for New York," *Los Angeles Times*, 21 September 1940.
"Backward Glances (Mrs. Octavus Cohen)," *News and Courier*, 15 April 1910.
Baggett, Jim. "Notes on Octavus Roy Cohen," *Birmingham Arts Journal*, Vol. 6 No. 3, 2009, 28–30.
Bailey, Frankie Y. *Out of the Woodpile: Black Characters in Crime*. Westport, CT: Greenwood, 1991.
Bird, Carol. "Away with Pessimism ... Octavus Roy Cohen; We All Need to Laugh at Ourselves as Well as at Others, Then the World Will Be More Delightful, Says Noted Delineator of Southern Characters," *Youngstown Vindicator*, 15 December 1935.
"Bobbacue What Am; Cohen Gives Recipes," *Los Angeles Times*, 21 April 1929.
Breen, Jon. "A Note on Octavus Roy Cohen," Mysteryfile. http://www.mysteryfile.com/cohen/Breen.html (viewed 18 January 2012).

Birmingham Black Bottom: The First All Black Cast Talkies. http://www.google.com/imgres?q=Octavus+Roy+Cohen&um=1&hl=en&sa=N&rlz=1G1GGLQ_ENUS293&biw=1372&bih=937&tbm=isch&tbnid=iCye1zR_LAkPjM:&imgrefurl=http://www.weirdwildrealm.com/f-birminghamblackbottom.html&docid=yJxQtUfPuxdl8M&imgurl=http://www.weirdwildrealm.com/filmimages/musichath.jpg&w=266&h=210&ei=LUkYT86DGOjZ0QGPp8jJCw&zoom=1&iact=rc&dur=718&sig=105603407090947320094&page=1&tbnh=139&tbnw=176&start=0&ndsp=46&ved=1t:429,r:2,s:0&tx=135&ty=65 (viewed 19 January 2012).

Brawley, Benjamin. "The Negro in Contemporary Literature," *The English Journal*, vol. 19 no. 3, March 1929, 194–202.

Brinegar, Dave. "Arizona: People, Places and Things," *Arizona Independent Republic*, 6 August 1939.

Brown, Sterling A. "Negro Characters as Seen by White Authors," *Journal of Negro Education*, Vol. 2, No. 2, April 1933.

Burkhim, Sophie W. "Royal Poinciana Hotel Closes Doors After Breakfast Today, Ending Brilliant 1930 Season," *Palm Beach Daily News*, 22 March 1930.

Calloway, Artemus. *The A.B.C.'s of Short-Story Writing*. Birmingham, AL: Birmingham Publishing, 1932.

"Christie to Make Cohen Stories; Negro Character Comedies to be Screened, with Dialogue," *Spokane Daily Chronicle*, 31 August 1928.

"Clemson Fraternity Is Given Sketch of Cohen," *Herald-Journal*, 12 January 1938.

Cobb, Irvin S. "Laughing Around the World: Coarse Comedy in the Catacombs," *Boston Daily Globe*, 4 June 1927.

Cohen, Octavus. "A Theatrical Budget," *Mansfield Daily Shield*, 24 March 1902.

_____. "A Theatrical Review," *Lewiston Evening Journal*, 26 May 1893.

Cohen, Octavus Roy. "All About I," in Thomas L. Masson, *Our American Humorists*. New York: Moffat, Yard, 1922.

_____. *Florian Slappey Says* (United Features Syndicate eight-page promotional booklet, 1920, Yale University Library)

_____. *Letters of Octavus Roy Cohen* (manuscript, University of Virginia Libraries, 1920).

Cohn, Jan. *Creating America: George Horace Lorimer and the Saturday Evening Post*. Pittsburgh: University of Pittsburgh Press, 1990.

Conrad, Earl. "The Philology of Negro Dialect," *The Journal of Negro Education*, Vol. 13, No. 2, spring 1944, 150–154.

Coons, Robin. "Screen Life in Hollywood," *Alton Evening Telegraph*, 4 March 1929.

"Dark Town Elite to Strut Their Stuff Tomorrow Night," *Torrance (Calif.) Herald*, 14 March 1929.

"Death Claims Octavus Cohen; Lawyer–Newspaper Man Dies at Residence," *News and Courier*, 7 October 1927.

"Death of Author's Wife Revealed," *Seattle Daily Times*, 17 February 1953.

"Death of the Post," *The Oregonian*, 13 January 1969.

Du Bois, W.E.B. "Criteria of Negro Art," reprinted in *Double-Take: A Revisionist Harlem Renaissance Anthology*, Venetria K. Patton and Maureen Honey, eds. New Brunswick, N.J.: Rutgers University Press, 2001.

_____. "Primary Source Criteria of Negro Art," *Crisis*, October 1926.

_____. Letter to George Horace Latimer, *Saturday Evening Post*, 22 December 1922. In Herbert Aptheker, ed. *The Correspondence of W.E.B. Du Bois: Vol. 1, Selections 1877–1934*. Amherst: University of Massachusetts Press, 1973.

Editorial comment. *Philadelphia Inquirer*, 6 October 1921.

Editorial comment. *Niagara Falls Gazette*, 29 March 1948.

Ferguson, Mrs. Walter. "Types," *Pittsburgh Press*, 26 February 1945.

"Florian: He's Back in Octavus Roy Cohen Stories," *Pittsburgh Press*, 14 August 1938.

"Florian Slappey," Thrilling Detective Web Site, http://www.thrillingdetective.com/slappey.html (viewed 18 January 2012).

Goeser, Caroline. *Picturing the New Negro: Harlem Renaissance Print Culture and Modern Black Identity*. Lawrence: University Press of Kansas, 2007.

"Gourfain Plans All-Colored Musical," *Afro-American*, 26 December 1942, 10.

Gowen, Dora Moise Cohen. Find a Grave. http://www.findagrave.com/cgi-bin/fg.cgi?page=gr&GRid=69717185 (viewed 7 February 2012).

"Great Loss in Art," *Ada (Okla.) Evening News*, 15 January 1959.

Grochowski, Mary Ann. Octavus Roy Cohen entry, *St. James Guide to Crime & Mystery Writers*, 4th edition, Jay P. Pederson, ed. Detroit: St. James Press, 1996.

Grost, Mike. "Rogue Fiction Writers," mikegrost.com/rogue.htm#cohen (viewed 12 March 2013).

Harper, Donna Akiba Sullivan. *Not So Simple: The 'Simple' Stories by Langston Hughes*. Columbia: University of Missouri Press, 1995.

"Havana Bound," *Miami News*, 13 November 1926.

Hazen, David W. *Interviewing Saints & Sinners*. Portland: Binford & Mort, 1942.

_____. "Octavus Roy Cohen: Creator of Florian Slappey," *The Oregonian*, 9 January 1938.

"He'll Write of WAAC: Octavus Roy Cohen, Florian Slappey's Creator," *Tribune* (Des Moines, IA), 9 July 1942.

Hendley, Coit. "Richard Wright Stresses Realism in Dealing with Fictional Negro Types," *Sunday Star* (Washington), 11 November 1945, C3.

Hornady, John R. *The Book of Birmingham*. New York: Dodd, Mead, 1921.

Hughes, Langston. *Simple States a Claim*. New York: Rinehart, 1957.

"Joins Waterbury Realty Agency: Octavus Roy Cohen, Jr., Writer, to be Salesman," *Red Bank (N.J.) Register*, 13 April 1950.

"June Speakers Chosen," *News and Courier*, 11 February 1934.

"Lawyer Evans Chew, Octavus Roy Cohen's Creation, Not Only Negro Legal Light in South—Nor the 'Sons and Daughters of I Will Arise' Only Benevolent Institution—Distinguished Negro Educator Tells a Story of Industrial Progress of His Race," Today's Feature by Sigma Chi, *St. Petersburg Times*, 30 March 1925.

Leeper, J.F. "Banking a la Octavus," *Saturday Evening Post*, 10 January 1925.

Liebenson, Donald. "Amos Shelved, but Not Andy," *Los Angeles Times*, 12 October 1997.

_____. "Folk Art or Racial Stereotypes?," *Chicago Tribune*, 18 September 1997.

Lemus, Rienzi E. "Harlem Girds Itself for Invasion from Alabama; Writer Who Held Southerners Up to Ridicule, Plans Same Thing in the North," *Afro-American*, 28 September 1935.

"'Loafers' Club' Belies Its Name; Membership Confined to Scribes Known to South as Hard Workers," *Spokesman-Review*, 23 July 1927.

Love, Edith Bell. "Author of Darky-Yarn Fame Turns Again to Love-Story Field with Fair Results," *Augusta Journal*, 8 August 1937.

Lupoff, Richard A. "Adventures in Exoticism: The 'Black Life' Novels of White Writers," *Western Journal of Black Studies*, 22 March 2002.

Masson, Thomas L. *Our American Humorists*. New York: Moffat, Yard, 1922.

McIntyre, O.O. "New York by Day," *Miami News*, 8 May 1936.

_____. "New York by Day," *Milwaukee Sentinel*, 12 February 1935.

_____. "New York by Day," *Milwaukee Sentinel*, 26 April 1937.

_____. "New York by Day," *Paris (Texas) News*, 27 March 1935.

_____. "New York by Day," *Reading Eagle*, 9 January 1936

"Meet Octavus Roy Cohen," *Miami Herald*, 13 September 1919.

"More Otherwise Than Wise," *Macon Daily Telegraph*, 28 November 1921.

"Mrs. J.I. Harrison Entertains Estes Embroidery Circle," *Tuscaloosa News*, 12 December 1929, 5.

Munro, Wallace. "Ocavus Roy Cohen, Author," *Washington Post*, 11 May 1919.

Nadell, Martha Jane. *Enter the New Negroes: Image of Race in America*. Cambridge: Harvard University Press, 2004.

"Negro in the South: He Is There to Stay, Editor Cohen Says His Children Must Be Educated," *The Week* (New London, Conn.) 1 October 1891, 1.

"Negro Play Makes Hit at Hippodrome," *Dallas Morning News*, 18 December 1922.

"New Comedy by Octavus Roy Cohen," *Christian Science Monitor*, 27 July 1920.

"New York Laughs at 'Come Sev'n': Cohen Play Offers 'Cullud Folks' in Comedy," *Duluth News-Tribune*, 1 August 1920.

"Nigger Comedies," *Northern Territory Times* (Darwin, North Australia), 30 November 1928.

"Noted Writer Cohen Dies," *Titusville Herald*, 7 January 1959.

"Octavus Cohen Dies," *Salt Lake Telegram*, 7 October 1927.

"Octavus Cohen Dies: Journalist, Lawyer, Father of Short-Story Writer," *New York Times*, 7 October 1927.

"Octavus Cohen Is Dead at 67," *Chicago Tribune*, 7 January 1959.
"Octavius [sic] Cohen, Jr., to Wed Miss Tallman," *Tuscaloosa News*, 18 April 1944.
"Octavus Cohen to Offer for Lieut. Governor," Charleston *Herald-Journal*, 25 November 1919.
"Octavus Cohen, Writer, Dies," *Milwaukee Sentinel*, 7 January 1959.
"Octavus Cohen, Writer's Father, Called by Death," *Atlanta Constitution*, 7 October 1927.
"Octavus R. Cohen, 'Florian Slappey' Author, 67, Dies," Springfield (Mass.) *Union*, 7 January 1959.
"Octavus Roy Cohen," Dover, Ohio *Daily Reporter*, 21 January 1959.
"Octavus Roy Cohen," *Dictionary of American Biography*. New York: Scribner's, 1980.
"Octavus Roy Cohen," *Encyclopedia Mysteriosa: A Comprehensive Guide to the Art of Detection in Print, Film, Radio, and Television* by William L. DeAndrea. New York: Prentice-Hall, 1994.
"Octavus Roy Cohen," OnRead.com. http://www.onread.com/writer/Cohen-Octavus-Roy-2525/ (viewed 2 February 2012).
"Octavus Roy Cohen Leaves $1 to Son," *Trenton Evening Times*, 16 January 1959.
Octavus Roy Cohen news item. *Canadian Jewish Chronicle*, 19 April 1935.
"Octavus Roy Cohen, Author, Dies at 67," *Washington Post and Times Herald*, 7 January 1959.
"Octavus Roy Cohen: Prolific Author, Creator of Florian Slappey," *Boston Globe*, 7 January 1959.
"Octavus Roy Cohen, Prolific Writer, Dies," *Seattle Daily Times*, 7 January 1959.
Octavus Roy Cohen, typescripts. Birmingham Public Library, Department of Archives & Manuscripts. http://www.birminghamarchives.org/LitandJournalism2.htm (viewed 25 January 2012).
"Octavus Roy Cohen: He'll Write of WAAC Florian Slappey's Creator," *Des Moines Tribune*, 9 July 1942.
"Octavus Roy Cohen's Famous Negro Stories to Appear Twice Each Week in Star-Telegram," *Fort Worth Star-Telegram*, 29 March 1920.
"Opens Berkeley Office," *News and Courier*, 29 November 1935.
Page, Brett. "New York Laughs at 'Come Sev'n," Duluth, Minn., *News-Tribune*, 1 August 1920.
Perry, Jeffrey B., ed. *A Hubert Harrison Reader*. Middletown, CT: Wesleyan University Press, 2001.
Piper, David L. "New Books in Critical Review," *Oregonian*, 1 July 1928.
"Plays and Playmakers," *Clinton Weekly Age*, 31 December 1897.
"Poorly-Paid Colored Maid Leads Cohen to $1,000,000," *Los Angeles Times*, 3 March 1929.
Portrait of author. *Saturday Evening Post*, 14 June 1919.
Question for Cohen. *Salt Lake Tribune*, 19 September 1921.
Rambler. St. Petersburg (Fla.) *Evening Independent*, 14 October 1930.
Reeman, James E.,"Octavus Roy Cohen," *Encyclopedia of the Harlem Renaissance*, vol. 1, ed. Cary D. Wintz and Paul Finkelman. New York: Routledge, 2004.
"Ring Lardner and Octavus R. Cohen: What a Pair!" *Fort Worth Star-Telegram*, 10 May 1920.
Roberson, Andrew. "Putting the Negro in Fiction," *The Editor*, Vol. 56, 1922.
Rogers, Will. "Will Rogers' Daily Story," *Boston Daily Globe*, 11 December 1925.
Rollins, Peter C. *America Reflected: Language, Satire, Film, and the National Mind*. Washington, D.C.: New Academia Publishing, 2011.
Ross, Greg. "Dueling Chameleons," Futility Closet. http://www.futilitycloset.com/category/hoaxes/page/6/ (viewed 16 February 2012).
Rubin, Louis Decimus. *My Father's People: A Family of Southern Jews*. Louisiana State University Press, 2002.
Ruark, Robert. "Touchiness Handcuffs Our Humor," *Berkshire County Eagle*, 31 March 1950.
"Sho, He Knows Bummingham," *Kansas City Star*, 16 February 1920.
"Sidelights on Octavus Roy Cohen, Author of 'The May Day Mystery,'" *Cass City (Mich.) Chronicle*, 14 April 1933.
Skaroff, Lauren Rebecca. *Black Culture and the New Deal*. Chapel Hill: University of North Carolina Press, 2009.
"Sound Pictures to Succeed Silent Movies Very Soon," *Edwardsville Intelligencer*, 13 February 1929, 3.
"Story Writing a Cinch!" *Kansas City Times*, 15 September 1919.
Strausbaugh, John. *Black Like You: Blackface, Whiteface, Insult & Imitation in American Popular Culture*. New York: Tarcher, 2007.
Van Patten, Nathan. "The Vocabulary of the American Negro as Set Forth in Contemporary Literature," *American Speech*, Vol. 8, No. 1 October 1931, 24–31.
Thurman, Wallace. "Fire Burns: A Department of Comment," in *Fire!! A Quarterly Devoted to the Younger Negro Artists*. November 1926.

Tucker, George. "Man About Manhattan," *Free Lance-Star*, 10 October 1940.
Van Vechten, Carl. "The Crisis Symposium: The Negro in Art: How Shall He Be Portrayed," *Crisis*, May 1926; reprinted in Henry Louis Gates, Jr. and Gene Andrew Jarrett, eds. *The New Negro: Readings on Race, Representation, and African American Culture, 1892–1938*. Princeton, N.J.: Princeton University Press, 2007.
Warwick, Paul. "Florian's Dice Worried R. Cohen: Four Sevens in Eighteen Throws," *Atlanta Constitution*, 21 June 1922.
Whitman, William. "They Write Books: Octavius [*sic*] Roy Cohen," *Boston Daily Globe*, 22 April 1929.
Windham, Ben. Southern Lights, "Old Bachelors' Intrigue Hides Among Clutter," *Tuscaloosa News*, 26 April 2009.

Harry Stillwell Edwards
(1855–1938)
Eneas Africanus

Is the story true? Everybody says it is.[1]—*Harry Stillwell Edwards*

Harry Stillwell Edwards wrote a very popular Lost Cause story of the "devoted southern darky" Eneas, who was enslaved to Major George E. Tommey.

Related through a sequence of advertisements and letters, the story begins with Marse's notice to the *Atlanta Constitution*: "I am writing to invoke your kind assistance in tracing an old family negro of mine who disappeared in 1864, between my stock farm in Floyd County and my home place, locally known as Tommeysville, in Jefferson County. The negro's name was Eneas, a small, grey-haired old fellow and very talkative. The unexpected movement of our army after the battle of Resaca,[2] placed my stock farm in line of the Federal advance and exposed my family to capture. My command, Tommey's legion, passing within five miles of the place, I was enabled to give them warning, and they hurriedly boarded the last southbound train. They reached Jefferson County safely but without any baggage, as they did not have time to move a trunk. An effort was made to save the family silver, much of it very old and highly prized, especially a silver cup known in the family as the 'Bride's Cup' for some six or eight generations...."

Trusted with the family treasure and told to take it to Jefferson County, Eneas had embarked on what turned out be an eight-year trek riding the old horse Lady Chain through seven states, all of which had a Jefferson County. Which Jefferson County was he supposed to find? Meanwhile, he had a series of adventures, as told by those he encountered. His Confederate money became unspendable. He wagered wisely, however, racing Marse's horse Lightning. He acquired a wife in Alabama and they started a family.

Master and (by now) former slave are eventually reunited after the war:

"Where is the trunk? repeated the Major, laughing [at the sight of Eneas's wagon full of children] and wiping his eyes. "Where did you leave it, Eneas?"
"I ain't lef' hit," said Eneas indignantly. "Git out o' dat wagon, niggers, fo' I bus' somer you wide open!" The little colony fell over the wheels like cooters from a log, and drawing aside the hay that had held them, Eneas brought forth a time and weather-defying hair trunk. He heaved a mighty sigh of relief as he dropped it to the ground:
"Dar 'tis, Marse George, an' I sho is glad to git shut o' dat ol' bunch o' hide an' har!"[3]

Eneas is said to have been based on a real person—at least that's what the author implies in his introduction.[4] It could have been. Decades later the phrase "Stockholm syndrome" was coined to explain how hostages can develop empathy for their captors. (Employees were held for six days in a bank vault in Sweden in 1973.) House servants during America's slavery era had the same experience. Blacks promoted from the fields to the house, where they avoided the hot sun and the whip, could come to feel a certain gratitude.

Paul Laurence Dunbar also wrote of doddery slave characters who loved their masters. "Maybe that's an old man's nostalgia for a poorly remembered youth. Maybe it's Stockholm syndrome. Still, the sentiment was neither ubiquitous norm nor unique," John Strausbaugh suggests in *Black Like You*.[5]

Born in Macon, Georgia, author Edwards attended local schools, then at age fifteen went to Washington, D.C., to clerk in the Treasury Department. He returned to Macon after three years. He graduated from Mercer University with a bachelor of laws degree in 1876.

He married Mary Roxie Lane of Sparta in 1881 and they had four children. She wrote children's stories[6] and encouraged her husband to try fiction. He sold his first story, "Elmer Brown's Backslide," to *Harper's Magazine*, and his second, "Two Runaways," to *Century*. These stories "showed, as few stories had ever done before, a genuine understanding of the Negro and of his dialect," according to John O.E. Eidson.[7]

After 1888, Edwards devoted all of his energies to creative writing. An early popular story was "Elmer Brown's Backslide" in *Harper's Magazine* in 1885. His work showed up in *Atlantic Monthly, Youth's Companion, Scribner's* and the *Saturday Evening Post*.

Collecting nine stories in *Two Runaways and Other Stories* for a Century Co. edition in 1889, Edwards said in an introduction, "The elements dealt with in these stories are the brighter and better parts of the older negro characters, and of some of the people whose lives touch or touched his. Naturally the humorous and pathetic features have been prominently brought forth, and this has necessitated at times glimpses at the religious side of his life. It should be state here that this negro is rarely ever irreverent; that, however his words appear in print, in reality they never suggest anything improper. Those who read them, however amused they may be by his odd and incongruous ideas, methods of expression, and the scenes in which he becomes involved, should bear this fact in mind."

Edwards became editor of the *Macon Telegraph and Messenger*. This was the newspaper that would publish Bridges Smith's Yamacraw yarns from 1909 to 1918. Edwards wrote poetry and he wrote about Eneas for the *Macon Evening News*,[8] of which he became co-owner and co-editor.

His "Tom's Strategy" was serialized in newspapers in 1892.[9] He introduced black characters and themes in 1896 with "De Valley an de Shadder," also syndicated.[10] That same year, he received the *Chicago Record*'s $10,000 prize for a short story, "Sons and Fathers."[11] The next year, newspapers serialized his "The Marbeau Cousins," and offered prizes to readers who could guess the outcome of the mystery.[12] Edwards put several of his black dialect poems to music.

Taking inspiration from a speech made by President William McKinley, Edwards in 1901 suggested "that a brass tablet be set into the pedestal of every Confederate monument in the south, inscribed with the sentiment expressed by Mr. McKinley in his Atlanta speech, when he advocated the care of the Confederate dead by the national congress," the Columbus *Daily Enquirer* reported.[13] Edwards, after all, was godson of Jefferson Davis.[14]

Edwards couldn't resist voicing his positive opinion when President Theodore Roosevelt made some political appointments of black prospects over whites.[15]

He was a delegate-at-large to the 1904 Republican National convention in Chicago and seconded the nomination of his friend Roosevelt. He stuck with Roosevelt even as the latter was obliged to form his Bull Moose Party in 1912. Edwards was postmaster in Macon from 1900 to 1913. Also in 1913, he was elected to the American Academy of Arts and Letters—"the Only Georgian to Be So Honored."[16]

In 1914, Edwards opened his Holly Bluff Country Club, "the home of the famous White Elk mineral water, the purest, with one exception in the world," according to the *Macon Telegraph*.[17] Georgia elite attended the opening barbecue. The clubhouse overlooked a lake. Members already numbered more than 100.

He helped establish the Georgia School of Technology. He ran as a Bull Moose Progressive for the U.S. Senate in 1920. He advocated that a Stone Mountain Memorial fifty-cent piece be minted.[18] He lectured widely, usually reading *Eneas*. As examples, the author gave readings in Augusta, Georgia,[19] and in Lexington, Kentucky, the latter to benefit the Blue Grass Tuberculosis Sanitarium.[20] The story came out in a 40-page chapbook, *Eneas Africanus*, published by J.W. Burke Printers of Macon in 1919. At 25 cents paper, 50 cents (board), $1.25 (illustrated) and $2.50 (autographed), it sold some 2 million copies.[21]

"The book has never gone out of print," according to John Lowe. "Read today, the story seems cloyingly sentimental, overtly patriarchal and stereotypical, and hardly worth our attention. It has, however, some rather deep roots in mythic literature—particularly that of the Bible—and constitutes a heretofore unnoticed but important literary resource for one of William Faulkner's masterworks, *Go Down, Moses* (1942), a book heavily indebted to the plantation traditions of Page."[22]

The story, subtitled "Who Has This Cup?,"[23] was syndicated to the *Milwaukee Journal*[24] (taking up nearly three pages, with line art), the Columbia *State*[25] (jammed on one page, with no art) and presumably other newspapers in 1921.

A sequel, *Eneas Africanus, Defendant*, came from the same book publisher in 1921. Eneas this time was before a church board on charges of immorality. Church elder Brer Manuel points his finger:

> "He is scused o' breakin de law o' dish yah chutch! I seen es wife Yallerhama Sue er plowin' er mule one Sunday mornin'! She was er plowin, er patch er taters, an' hit was de patch Enus claims as his'n. I asked 'er,—'Nigger'—des so,—'nigger, what for you plowin' dish yah patch, an' hit Sunday?' An' she up na' flung back dat she was er plowin' hit because Enus made 'er plow hit."[26]

Edwards "has written several novels," according to Alexander Jessup, "but he is essentially a writer of human-nature sketches. 'He is humorous and picturesque,' says Fred Lewis Pattee, 'and often he is for a moment the master of pathos, but he has added nothing new and nothing commandingly distinctive.'"[27]

A reviewer in *Woman's Enterprise* praised *Eneas*, calling it "a delicious blend of humor and pathos," and "replete with the atmosphere and charm of those vanished days towards which the true Southerner, regardless of his environment, finds 'his heart is turning ever.'"[28]

After his wife died in 1922, Edwards lived at Holly Bluff plantation. He built Kingfisher

Cabin, a writing retreat, with his son, Jackson Lane Edwards, in 1928 and 1929. It was here he wrote a weekly column, "Coming Down My Creek," for the *Atlanta Journal*.[29] The cabin was moved to Wesleyan College in 1941, and moved again to the grounds of the Museum of Arts and Sciences in 1964. The cabin was restored in 2006.

His friends honored Edwards at a banquet at the Hotel Dempsey in Macon in 1935.[30] Two years later, the 155,000-word novel he wrote in twenty-three days, *Sons and Fathers*, was scheduled for a sixth printing, in a limited edition. Interviewed at Kingfisher Cabin, he said, "I am chiefly concerned in preserving the original story, which has been repeatedly cut in its five printings, as reflecting a phase of Southern life long gone."[31]

Edwards died in 1938 in Macon. They played "Oh Sweet Mystery of Life" at his funeral.[32] Grosset & Dunlap brought out a new edition of *Eneas Africanus* in 1941, with illustrations by Ernest Townsend.[33]

Eneas Africanus still has fans. The *Augusta Chronicle* in 1986 reported collector Jane Rowland had gathered copies of all of the book's editions. "She was intrigued when she found some paperback editions of the story at an estate sale. One bore the author's autograph."[34]

Harry Stillwell Edwards Notes

1. Introduction, *Eneas Africanus*, 2. "The lore and literature of plantations show time and again that people held in slavery formed profound attachments to the families who owned them," according to Henry Wiencek in *Master of the Mountain*, 38.

2. On the Oostanaula River in Georgia.

3. *Eneas Africanus*, 36.

4. John O.E. Eidson accepts the fact in his Harry Stillwell Edwards entry, *Southern Writers: A Biographical Dictionary*, 140.

5. Page 183.

6. "Woman Writer Dead," Columbia, S.C., *State*, 6 August 1922, 1.

7. *Southern Writers*, op cit., 140.

8. Inventory of the Papers and Books of the Harry Stillwell Edwards Collection, held in the Valdosta State University Archives.

9. Including the San Jose, Calif., *Evening News*, beginning 22 November 1.

10. Including in the *San Jose Evening News*, 3 March 3.

11. "Receiving Congratulations," *Macon Telegraph*, 10 March 1896, 6, and "Georgian Wins $10,000," Columbus (Ga.) *Daily Enquirer*, 22 March 1896, 8.

12. "The Marbeau Cousins: Harry Stillwell Edwards Latest Story to be Published in the Capital," *Kansas Semi-Weekly Capital*, 15 June 1897, 6.

13. "Harry Stillwell Edwards' Suggestion," 22 September 1901, 2.

14. "Prize Dixie Novel to Be Republished," *Times-Picayune*, 11 July 1937, 29.

15. "The president in his own defense pointed out he had appointed a white man to replace a black as postmaster in Athens and another to replace a surveyor in Atlanta. On the other hand, he had appointed blacks to postmaster and collector posts in South Carolina and Georgia. "Why the appointment of one should cause any more excitement than the appointment of the other I am wholly at a loss to imagine." "A Letter to an Editor," Cleveland (Ohio) *Gazette*, 7 March 1903, 2. See also "The President's Policy," Indianapolis, Indiana, *Freeman*, 31 January 1903, 4.

16. "High Honor Conferred on Harry Stillwell Edwards," *Macon Telegraph*, 21 December 1912, 7.

17. "Holly Bluff Club Opens; Barbecue and Dance at Harry Stillwell Edwards' Country Club Largely Attended," 11 June 1914, 6.

18. "Conceived Idea of New Memorial Coin," Augusta (Ga.) *Chronicle*, 13 April 1924, 3.

19. "Harry Stillwell Edwards to Render 'Aeneas Africanus' at Partridge Inn March 19," Augusta (Ga.) *Chronicle*, 7 March 1928, 5.

20. "Georgia Author Pleases Crowd," *Lexington Herald*, 15 November 1921, 5.

21. "Re-creating a Public for the Plantation: Reconstruction Myths of the Biracial Southern 'Family,'" *Bridging Southern Cultures: An Interdisciplinary Approach*, 226.
22. Ibid., 228.
23. A lost silver cup figures in the biblical story of Joseph and his brothers.
24. 2 October 1921, 4–6.
25. 4 September 1921, 15.
26. *Eneas Africanus Defendant*, 19.
27. *Best American Humorous Short Stories*.
28. Robin Coons, "A Tale of the Old South," review of *Eneas Africanus, Woman's Enterprise*, 10 March 1922, 14.
29. Some information from Gary Kerley's Harry Stillwell Edwards entry, *Southern Writers: A New Biographical Dictionary*, 121–122. The column's title was the same as one Edwards wrote for the *Macon Evening News*.
30. "Edward Stillwell Edwards at Eighty," Augusta (Ga.) *Chronicle*, 23 April 1935, 4.
31. "Prize Dixie Novel to Be Republished," op cit., 29.
32. "Georgia Author Taken by Death," Augusta *Chronicle*, 23 October 1938, 1.
33. "New Edition of Southern Minor Classic," Springfield (Mass.) *Republican*, 9 February 1941, 49.
34. "Private Libraries—Rare Books, Cookbook, Romances Fill Shelves," 12 January 1986, 1.

Harry Stillwell Edwards Selected Bibliography and Sources

ENEAS STORIES

"Eneas Africanus" originally appeared in 1918 in the Macon *Evening News*. It was later syndicated to at least the *Milwaukee Journal* (2 October 1921) and the *Columbia State* (4 September 1921).

BOOKS

Eneas Africanus (1919)
Eneas Africanus, Defendant (1921)

SOURCES

"Conceived Idea of New Memorial Coin," Augusta (Ga.) *Chronicle*, 13 April 1924.
Coons, Robin. "A Tale of the Old South," review of *Eneas Africanus, Woman's Enterprise*, 10 March 1922.
Eidson, John O.E. "Harry Stillwell Edwards," *Southern Writers: A Biographical Dictionary*, Joseph M. Flora, Louis Decimus Rubin, Jr., eds.
Guide to the Harry Stillwell Edwards Collection. Clifton Waller Barrett Library of American Literature, University of Virginia, Charlottesville. http://ead.lib.virginia.edu/vivaxtf/view?docId=uva-sc/viu00217.xml (viewed 2 November 2012).
"Georgia Author Pleases Crowd," *Lexington Herald*, 15 November 1921.
"Georgia Author Taken by Death," Augusta (Ga.) *Chronicle*, 23 October 1938.
"Georgian Wins $10,000," Columbus (Ga.) *Daily Enquirer*, 22 March 1896.
"Harry Stillwell Edwards at Eighty," Augusta (Ga.) *Chronicle*, 23 April 1935.
Harry Stillwell Edwards Collection, 1897–1967. Valdosta State University Archives. http://ww2.valdosta.edu/library/find/arch/archon/index.php?p=collections/findingaid&id=458&q= (viewed 2 November 2012).
Harry Stillwell Edwards entry. "Lawyers and Poetry," Strangers to Us All. http://myweb.wvnet.edu/~jelkins/lp-2001/edwards.html (viewed 2 November 2012).
"Harry Stillwell Edwards' Suggestion," Columbus (Ga.) *Daily Enquirer*, 22 September 1901.
"Harry Stillwell Edwards to Render 'Aeneas Africanus' at Partridge Inn March 19," Augusta (Ga.) *Chronicle*, 7 March 1928.
"High Honor Conferred on Harry Stillwell Edwards," *Macon Telegraph*, 21 December 1912.
"Holly Bluff Club Opens; Barbecue and Dance at Harry Stillwell Edwards' Country Club Largely Attended," *Macon Telegraph*, 11 June 1914.
Inventory of the Papers and Books of the Harry Stillwell Edwards Collection, held in the Valdosta State University Archives. http://ww2.valdosta.edu/library/find/arch/findingaids/MS-51.htm (viewed 24 November 2012).

Jessup, Alexander, ed. *Best American Humorous Short Stories*. E-book, 2004.
Kerley, Gary. "Harry Stillwell Edwards," *Southern Writers: A New Biographical Dictionary*, Joseph M. Flora and Amber Vogel, eds. Baton Rouge: Louisiana State University Press, 2006. Louisiana State University Press, 2005.
Kingfisher Cabin. Museum of Arts and Sciences, http://www.masmacon.org/kingfisher-cabin (viewed 2 November 2012).
Lowe, John, ed. *Bridging Southern Cultures: An Interdisciplinary Approach*. Baton Rouge: Louisiana State University Press, 2011.
"Marbeau Cousins: Harry Stillwell Edwards Latest Story to Be Published in the Capital," Topeka (Kan.) *Kansas Semi-Weekly Capital*, 15 June 1897.
"New Edition of Southern Minor Classic," Springfield (Mass.) *Republican*, 9 February 1941.
"President's Policy," Indianapolis (Ind.) *Freeman*, 31 January 1903.
"Private Libraries—Rare Books, Cookbook, Romances Fill Shelves," Augusta (Ga.) *Chronicle*, 12 January 1986.
"Prize Dixie Novel to Be Republished," *Times-Picayune*, 11 July 1937.
"Receiving Congratulations," *Macon Telegraph*, 10 March 1896.
Roosevelt, Theodore. "A Letter to an Editor," Cleveland (Ohio) *Gazette*, 7 March 1903.
"Woman Writer Dead," Columbia (S.C.) *State*, 6 August 1922.
Smith, Nelle Edwards. *Harry Stillwell Edwards: A Man Not Without Honor*. Macon, GA: Eneas Africanus Press, 1969.
Strausbaugh, John. *Black Like You: Blackface, Whiteface, Insult & Imitation in American Popular Culture*. New York: Jeremy P. Tarcher/Penguin, 2006.
Wiencek, Henry. *Master of the Mountain*. New York: Farrar, Straus & Giroux, 2012.

Arthur LeRoy Kaser
(1890–1956)
Mush and Poke

> Remus. Jes' staht somethin' an' we joins in.
> Sam. No, sah, not me. Yestaday I stahted sumpin' an' de cops joined in.
> —from *Merry Men's Minstrels*

"Fort Johnson Minstrels to Fill Bookings," the Amsterdam *Evening Recorder* headlined a story on 29 March 1938. The annual firemen's minstrel and variety show promised, "Mush and Poke, the sun-burned ash haulers in the persons of George Connelly and Clark Carr, will open the show with a laugh-provoking skit."

The *Antioch News* for 1 September 1949 said, "W.S.G.S. Will Sponsor Black Face Fun Night at High School, sponsored by the Woman's Society of Christian Service." "Mush and Poke, Detectives," the Dixie Belles, "Two Coons in a Wreck" and Bob Wilton and Bill Dow in "Black Vamp." "The slow, good humor of the 'darkies,' the negro who uses the long words in the wrong places."

Arthur L. Kaser's snappy blackface skits thrived in the decades between the wars, a last gasp of a genre long overdue to retire.

"One of the most prolific writers of amateur minstrel materials, Arthur LeRoy Kaser, wrote that amateur minstrel shows had become 'so very popular' that 'if one is not given occasionally in a community everybody wonders why,'[1] according to historian Susan Smulyan.

According to Kaser, in "a well-performed minstrel show there are no dull moments—it is all meat."[2]

Kaser was born in Michigan City, Indiana, in 1890, the son of carpenter David Kaser and his wife, Nettie Walker. The family moved to La Porte, Indiana, where young Arthur was enthralled by the vaudeville performers who came through town. He sold snacks at Hall's Opera House and watched the jugglers and dancers and jokesters who pranced and mugged on the stage.

After the family moved to South Bend in 1905, Arthur worked as a carpenter, a factory laborer and a bank teller. He became active in amateur performance, and could mimic a variety of immigrant nationalities. He covered his face in burnt cork for his own blackface routines.

He served for a year and a half with the U.S. Army Infantry during World War I.

Back home, he was still interested in minstrelsy and submitted a script for his own routine to T.S. Denison & Co. in Chicago. It was published in 1920. He wrote another, and it was published the next year. He wrote some more, and three titles came out in 1922. He sold material to another printer, Walter H. Baker Co. of Boston. He found other welcoming publishing houses. This was fun. And profitable.

Arthur LeRoy Kaser excelled at making fun of people. His only series—appearing briefly on radio, and in a series of scripts from Dennison 1930 to 1934—featured Mush and Poke.

He married Leah Ione Steele (1894–1980) of South Bend in 1922 and they settled in Philadelphia. They eventually raised three children, the first born after they returned to South Bend in 1924. He decided to become a full-time writer, entering a modest but long-standing tradition. Charles Townsend, as an example, published scripts and stage directions for amateurs; his *Negro Minstrels with End Men's Jokes, Gags, Speeches, etc.: Full Instructions for Getting Up Darky Entertainments* appeared in 1891. Robert McIntyre's *Darktown Jokes ... Coon Jokes and Stories* came out in 1910, Irv Ott's *New Black Face Joke Book* in 1915, Edward B. Warren's *Meeting of the Darktown Literary Society* in 1922.

"By the late 1920s [Kaser] published 1,500 pages of stage material each year," according to Smulyan. "He was prolific and fast, and publishers found it easy to work with him. One story recounted his visit to the Walter H. Baker publishing company in Boston. Baker described a book he needed and asked Kaser if he would like to write it. Kaser replied, 'I believe I would.... Where's a typewriter.'"[3]

The Kasers relocated to St. Joseph, Indiana, then, in 1931, to Niles, Michigan.

One of Kaser's early Negro works was *The Filming of "Uncle Tom's Cabin,"* published by Denison in 1922. In his version, Uncle Tom is "very dignified and pompous" and wears a "large imitation diamond stud, and jewelry galore." Little Eva is chubby and has curly blonde hair and wears shell-rim glasses. Simon Legree is "very sissified in manner and costume," while Topsy is "dressed in man's golf suit." An addition character is Levi Shootzum, "typical stage Hebrew, scraggly beard, tight frock coat, oversized derby hat." He's the director trying to make a motion picture.

His publishers promoted Kaser's scripts. One advertising page describes the skit "No Sense, Nohow": "Negro talking act, by Arthur Leroy Kaser; 2 males. Time, 15 minutes. A merry skit for two blackface comedians, with laughter well apportioned, neither character being a feeder. The ragtime dispute in the 'Fizzle-Fuzzle language' is a scream. Chance for song or dance specialty."

And "They're In Again": "Taking skit, by Arthur LeRoy Kaser; 2 females. Time, 15 minutes. Two 'cullud ladies' meet on the street and have a heated argument over the cause of their husbands being in jail. Can be played by women, or by men in feminine attire. A hilarious negress comedy."[4]

Kaser was so prolific that he used at least 60 pen names, according to David Kaser. He was Rose Campion, Vance Clifford, Katherine Connelsby, Hanford Conswell, Gumption Cute, Richard Drummond, Bob Ellinger, Robert Ellinger, Jeff Gannett, Harry S. Grant, Gordon Griffith, H.I. Larity, Harlan Hayford, Mark Kent, Arthur Landis, Roy Lee, Lucille Longman, Doris N. Malcom, Bob Mannion, Catherine Marshall, Forbes Milliken, Bob Mills, Ward Morley, Franklin Phelps, Bob Royce, Reynolds Ryan, Don Sheridan, Nina Stafner, Loah Steele, Sidney Steele, Hiram L. Walker, Kent Walker, Phil Wayne and Jane Wheeler.

Arthur LeRoy Kaser was a byline used by Kaser himself and also by Jean Lee Latham and Ruth Perry.

Kaser mentored novice performers. He wrote in 1929 that his books "will provide a salvation for the many amateur minstrel troupes which lack the personal counsel and guidance of an experienced director. Thoroughly professional in style, yet entirely practical for amateurs and give big opportunity for localized jokes."[5]

Much of Kaser's stage material was tame. But Kaser could be an equal opportunity bigot. Besides blackface gibberish he wrote rube, Irish, Jewish, German, Italian, Dutch, wedding, court and other burlesques, something to offend everyone.

This is taken from a typical blackface monologue, "I'se Sentenced for Life"[6]:

Monologist. Well, heah I is, folks. An' gals, I got a surprise foh you-all. An' if I tells you wot it am I hopes you doan go sob yoh hearts out. I's married. Boy, oh boy! Been married two days, an' we isn't had a fight yet. Now I's on may honeymoon. Gwine all by mahself account I wants to hab a good time an' save money. Mebbe I'll go to Niag'ra Falls if dat place am still runnin'. Cose it am gwine be a long walk, bu I reckon I kin make it. Travelin' might be good foh de mind, but it sho' isn't good foh flat feet, an' mah feet am flatter'n mah pocketbook. When I used to hab a car I used to travel on flats most o' de time, so I reckon I kin stand it. Dem tires was allus flat on de bottom an' dass jes' whar I is flat now.

Here's another example of Kaser's humor, with the black character Rufus:

King. You're quite some philosopher, aren't you?
Rufus. No, sah. I's Meth'dist on mah mammy's side, Dem'-crat on mah pappy's side, black on de outside...[7]

And another:

King. [*laughs*]. Say, what is your name?
Rufus. Dey call me Rufus foh short, an' Rufusufus foh extra short.

Kaser's patrons by the early 1930s were experiencing change. It was getting harder to make fun of ethnics when they were making up a larger share of the audience.

"Yet, although Art read of the Depression," according to David Kaser, "and saw the changes taking place in the professional stage, his markets remained quite strong."[8]

The biographer went on, "For a time in 1929 he wrote a continuing blackface series for radio—a show somewhat like 'Amos and Andy' called 'Mush and Poke'—but he soon gave it up. Five of those skits were later published."[9]

Denison brought out the scripts in its blackface plays series.

Mush and Poke are what Amos 'n' Andy might have been, had their creators not steered in a non-mistral direction. All yucks, no heart.

Mush and Poke, typically, take over a funeral parlor as payment of a debt in *Mush and Poke, Undertakers*. They have big ideas. Poke wants to name the business "De Black-Bury Corp'ration." They make their first visit to the morgue:

Mush (*shivers*). Br-r-r! An' dis am de—de—de Mawg?
Poke. Dis am de mawg. Doan' look like a race track. Do it?
Mush. Br-r-r! Golly! Poke, if anyfing stahts to happen, I's gwine to make a race-track out'n it. Poke, I nevah wa in a undertakin' mawg befo.'
Poke. Well, den you isn't got nuffin' to brag about no mo,' cause you is in one now. Boy, set down befo' you falls to pieces. (*Mush sits and shivers with fright.*) Wotsa mattah? You got chills?[10]

When one venture fails, the Chicago pair tries something else. They open a private investigation agency, in *Mush and Poke, Detectives*. But when Mush checks out a firearm:

Mush. Wot you skeered ob? Can't you see I got mah thumb ovah de end?
Poke. Humph! I s'pose dat bullet hit your thumb it'll jes' bounce right back in de shell, huh?[11]

They are little better as meat cutters, in *Mush and Poke, Butchers*:

Mush. Poke, how does you cut dis heah beefsteak to make poke chops?
Poke. Don' be so dumb. You don' use beefsteak to make poke chops. You uses veal. Now hush up.[12]

And they fail as teamsters in *Mush and Poke, Ash Haulers*:

(*The phone rings.*)
Poke. Push me dat phone. You messed it all up de las' time. (*Mush hands him the phone and Poke removes receiver and talks into mouthpiece.*) Commence! (*Pauses.*) Yea, sah. Us totes ashes an' evahfing. (*Pauses.*) How's dat? (*Pauses.*) Oh, sho' 'nough, de park boa'd am speakin'. An' wot does you crave, Mistah Park Boa'd? (*Pauses.*) Uh-huh. (*Pauses.*) Uh-huh. (*Pauses.*) I see. Yes, sah; I'll hab a man down dere mmejiate. Yes, sah. (*Hangs up receiver.*) Dat's de way to it orders, Mush. Ten dollah ordah right offn' de bat.
Mush. Mebbe it's de same man what called awhile 'go.
Poke. No,m 'tain't. Dis am de park boa'd.
Mush. Dat a brothah to de divin' boa'd?
Poke. 'Co'se not. De park boa'd b'longs to de city. Dey is got some haulin' to do at one ob de parks.
Mush. Wot dey wants hauled?
Poke. A lion.

Mush (*nearly faints*). Huh?
Poke. Dey craves to hab one ob de lions moved from one park to anothah park.
Mush. Wot us got to do wif dat?
Poke. Dona' you comperhen'? Dey wants us to move de lion.[13]

Mush and Poke, you see, aren't very good at anything, including being idle. They can't even thumb a ride to Poke's uncle's succotash farm in Missouri. This is from *Mush and Poke, Hitch-Hikers*:

Mush. Poke, is you posilute dat us am headed in de right die-rection?
Poke: If mah dogs keep on hurtin', I isn't gwine in no die-rection.
Mush. Wot dat las' town us ankle froo?
Poke. Joliet.
Mush. Dat's where Romeo live?
Poke. Wot you talkin' 'bout?
Mush. Romeo an' Joliet.
Poke. Mush, if brains was money you'd shuah be in debt to yoh parents.[14]

The plays, inane as they are, appealed to amateur performers. When the Arcadia High School senior class in Iowa staged a minstrel show in 1941, skits included *Mush and Poke, Undertakers*, featuring Alvin Jentzen and Melvin Noethe.[15] Edward Conley and John Mullen took the leads in *Mush and Poke, Undertakers* at a Portsmouth Players program in New Hampshire in 1955.[16]

Kaser gradually faded from the scene. By 1935, his health issues forced him, on doctor's advice, to take up carpentering. He still wrote and sold his skits, just not as many.

Kaser died in 1956, of a heart condition.

"During the thirty-six years that he wrote," according to his biographer, "his bibliography of separately-issued publications grew to 463 items, totaling almost 16,000 pages, to say nothing of his many contributions to collections of works. He would be considered an impressive monument to the memory of any man."[17]

The Brown University John Hay Library's Harris Collection of American Poetry and Plays has a large holding of Kaser's blackface skits and other humor—ideal for research, dubious for performance.

Arthur Leroy Kaser Notes

1. *Popular Ideologies: Mass Culture at Mid-Century*, 16.
2. Ibid.
3. Smulyan, op cit., 27, quoted a publisher's blurb from one of Kaser's booklets.
4. *Dixie Minstrel First Part* by John E. Lawrence, advertisement, 39.
5. Quoted in Smulyan, op cit., 30.
6. *Kaser's Complete Minstrel Guide* (1934).
7. *Kaser's Complete Minstrel Guide*, 105.
8. Op cit., 98.
9. "Arthur L. Kaser; Gag Man for the Amateur," *Friends of the Library of Brown University*, 97.
10. *Mush and Poke, Undertakers*, 6.
11. *Mush and Poke, Detectives*, 6.
12. *Mush and Poke, Butchers*, 6.
13. *Mush and Poke, Ash Haulers*, 7.
14. *Mush and Poke, Hitch-Hikers*, 7.
15. "Senior Class Play," Carroll (Iowa) *Daily Herald*, 26 April 1941, 6.

16. "Local Players Plan Presentation," Portsmouth (N.H.) *Herald*, 22 April 1955, 7.
17. "Arthur L. Kaser; Gag Man for the Amateur," 99.

Arthur Leroy Kaser Selected Bibliography and Sources

Mush and Poke Minstrel Show Scripts

"Mush and Poke, Detectives" (1930)
"Mush and Poke, Hitch-hikers" (1930)
"Mush and Poke, Undertakers" (1930)
"Mush and Poke, Ash Haulers" (1931)
"Mush and Poke, Butchers" (1934)

Selected Other Minstrel Show Scripts

The following, culled from some 414 entries Brown University's Harris Collection of American Poetry and Plays, identifies only those minstrel scripts that are for blackface or "darky" shows.

"The Black Vamp" (1921)
"Two Scared Coons" (1921)
"Filming of 'Uncle Tom's Cabin'" (1922)
"No Sense, Nohow" (1922)
"Awful Appetite" (1923)
"Black Recruit: A Darky Skit" (1923)
"A Henpecked Coon: A Darky Monologue" (1923)
"Lend Me Fo' Bigs" (1923)
"Rickety Rackety Radio" (1924)
"Safety Razors First" (1924)
"They're In Again" (1924)
"Burnt Cork Entertainer" (1925)
"My Old Man's Sick: A Darky Monologue" (1925)
"One Hambone for Two" (1925)
"Doctor Cut-up: A Blackface Talking Act" (1926)
"Eat 'em Up: Street Chatter for Two Colored Ladies" (1926)
"Enough's Enough" (1926)
"Socks and Soapsuds: A Talking Act for Two Colored Ladies" (1926)
"Ashes and Coal Dust: A Blackface Talking Act" (1927) as by Vance Clifford
"Black Clouds: A Disputation for Two Cullud Ladies" (1927) as by Vance Clifford
"Hush Money" (1927) as by Vance Clifford
"Slowin' Up the World" (1927) as by Vance Clifford
"Brung in de Pris'ner: A Blackface Musical Mock Trial" (1928)
"Come 'long Henry" (1928)
"Comp'ny 'tention! A Blackface Army Travesty" (1928)
"De Low-Down on Scientifics" (1928) as by Vance Clifford
"De Lowdown on Scientifics" (1928)
"In Doctor Rimcut's Office" (1928)
"O, You Sinnahs!" (1928)
"Laffalot Minstrel Book" (1928)
"Rastus Comes to the Point" 1928)
"Scrambled Courtship" (1928) as by Vance Clifford
"Spooks an' Hootin' Owls" (1928)
"Whar's Mah Pants?" (1928) as by Vance Clifford
"Black Clouds in China: A Blackface Talking Act" (1929)
"Colored Commotion" (1929) as by Kent Walker
"Giggle Gravy: A Blackface Sketch" (1929) as by Frank Phelps
"High-Hattin' Coon" (1929) as by Vance Clifford
"Much-Married Coon" (1929) as by Vance Clifford
"Whar's de Groom?" (1929) as by Forbes Milliken

"On Yo' Way, Niggah!" (1929) as by Franklin Phelps
"Winnin' Dat Gal: A Blackface Sketch" (1929) as by Forbes Milliken
"Birmingham Button Busters" (1930)
"Burnt Corkers' Jamboree" (1930)
"Chocolate Cream Wedding" (1930)
"Pilvered Pants" (1930)
"Down on the Levee: A Blackface Act for a Singing Quartet" (1930) as by Vance Clifford
"Two Coons in a Wreck" (1930) as by Franklin Phelps
"You Doggone Sinnahs! A Blackface Sermon" (1930) as by Don Sheridan
"Can't Lib Wifout You! A Hectic Coon Proposal" (1931) as by Don Sheridan
"Pinky White's Black Lawn Party" (1931)
"Two Scared Coons" (1931)
"Blood and Thunder Health Sanitorium" (1932)
"Election Night in Slumpdump: A Riotous Time for Blackface Comedians" (1932)
"Gridiron Sells His Movie Studio" (1932)
"High Speed Courtship" (1932) as by Forbes Milliken
"Monday Morning in Short Circuit Court" (1933)
"On the Inside Out Inn" (1933)
"I'se Sentenced for Life, in *Kaser's Complete Minstrel Guide*" (1934)
"Burnt Cork Cut-ups" (1934) "Coon Valley Minstrel" (1935) as by Jeff Gannett
"Darkies' Jamboree" (1935)
"Order of the Boiled Owl: Blackface Travesty in Three Spasmodic Scenes" (1935)
"Jungle Bungle" (1936)
"Romance and Razors" (1936) as by Forbes Milliken
"Jolly Pickaninnies Minstrels: A Complete Minstrel Program for the Grades" (1937)
"Men About Town Minstrels" (1938)

SOURCES

"Class to Present Six One-Act Plays," Charleston (W.Va.) *Daily Mail*, 15 May 1929.
"Drama Club," Iola (Kan.) *Register*, 19 September 1973.
"Fort Johnson Minstrels to Fill Bookings," Amsterdam, N.Y., *Evening Recorder*, 29 March 1938.
Kaser, David. "Arthur L. Kaser; Gag Man for the Amateur," *Friends of the Library of Brown University*, Vol. 18, No. 3, March 1958.
Lawrence, John E. *Dixie Minstrel First Part*. Chicago: T.S. Denison, 1924.
"Local Players Plan Presentation," Portsmouth (N.H.) *Herald*, 22 April 1955.
"Minstrel a Hit; Finale Tonight," *Greenville Record Argus*, 4 October 1947.
"Senior Class Play," Carroll (Iowa) *Daily Herald*, 26 April 1941.
Smulyan, Susan. *Popular Ideologies: Mass Culture at Mid-Century*. Philadelphia: University of Pennsylvania Press, 2007.
Source for the Study of 19th and 20th Century Blackface Minstrelsy, Brown University. http://library.brown.edu/collections/harris/minstr.php (viewed 24 October 2012).
"W.S.G.S. Will Sponsor Black Face Fun Night at High School, sponsored by the Woman's Society of Christian Service," *Antioch News*, 1 September 1949.

Hugh Wiley
(1884–1968)
Wildcat

"Shoots two bits. Fade me, does you crave action."
"You's faded. Roll 'em, Wilecat."
"Wham! An' I reads ... six-ace. Shoots de package. De big nugget keeps de pikers out. Gallopers, see kin you clatter home to yo' box-stall, Bam! And I reads ... six-five. Shoots de dollar. Little cubes show yo' fo'th dimension. I rolls a fo' and a trey, or de

Hugh Wiley's Wildcat Marsden traveled the country in company of his goat. *Fo' Meals a Day* came out in 1927. The stories originally appeared in *The Saturday Evening Post* from 1919 to 1934.

winnin' number. I got two dollars. Shoots fifty cents ... and I read six. I's a sixie f'm Dixie. Six is mah objective. Football dice, sco' yo' touchdown ... an' I reads fo'-deuce. Shower down."

And so Wildcat Vitus Marsden, for it was he, with his fortune of two dollars and fifty cents, went forth to the nearest bookstore to buy Hugh Wiley's well and elegant book, published yesterday, and entitled "Lady Luck."

—Book notice, *New York Tribune*[1]

Hugh Wiley wrote forty short stories that ran in the *Saturday Evening Post* from 1919 to 1934. They were about a young black man who is yanked by Lady Luck and pushed by Old Man Trouble. He sometimes toils as a field hand, sometimes plays as a musician, sometimes caters to rail passengers as a Pullman waiter.

Wildcat (real name Vitus) Marsden has one true companion, his mascot goat Lily. He has other occasional mates such as the reliable Demmy, and for a brief time a parrot, as he travels from Chicago to California to Florida in pursuit of a square meal and clean bed and a little spending money.

When we first meet Wildcat, he has passed up a job trimming hedges and mowing lawns in order to sit in on a craps game. He'll take work when he has to, but Lady Luck, he feels, is in his corner.

We read in the first story, "Four-Leaved Wildcat":

"In the back room of Willie Webster's barber shop the Wildcat knelt in a circle of his kind, getting action on the three-fifty. A pair of mercury dice introduced by a lodge brother, failed to respond. The Wildcat shot a dollar and let it lay for three passes. He picked up the accumulated wealth and warmed the dice with the breath of victory.

"'I'se a fo'leaf wile-cat an' I'se on my prowl! Shoots five dollahs!'"[2]

Barely into the book's second chapter, and we have the stereotype of black man as gambler.

Wildcat returns to his boarding house only to be served his draft papers. He's going into the First Service Battalion. He has to report to the provost marshal in Memphis. Now he knows where his mess will come from, where his cot will be. If he survives basic training. You see, he has a few issues. For one thing, he calls every white soldier "Gen'ral." For another, he still has his straight razor in his hip pocket. He stands as straight as he can, so it won't be seen—and is duly elected corporal of Company C for his good posture.

Wiley adds two elements to the modest subgenre of "humorous" Negro stories of the 1920s and 1930s. One is that blacks served in the U.S. military and proved themselves capable soldiers. The other is that, after the war, many of these same blacks were unrooted, and of necessity traveled the country.

Otherwise the writer incorporates the same vernacular and superstitions and in Wildcat's case blind reliance on Lady Luck. Sometimes Wildcat has as much as $5,000 in his possession. Sometimes his pockets are bereft of anything but a razor, a pair of dice and lint.

Wiley was born in 1884 in Zanesville, Ohio, the son of Eliphalet Wiley and Rose McDonald. When the family moved to Cascade Locks, Oregon, the father supervised construction of a canal around rapids on the Columbia River.

Wiley attended schools in Oregon and in St. Louis and Illinois. As a young man he adventured in Mexico and in Canada. He worked mostly as a construction laborer. He wrote

The popularity of Pullman porters inspired the cover art of *Lady Luck*, a Wildcat Marsden adventure from 1921.

a Mississippi River yarn, "On the Altar of Hunger," and successfully submitted it to *Scribner's* for the October 1916 issue. He wrote and sold four more stories before World War I intervened. He served as a captain in the 18th Engineers. From France he sent a story to the *Saturday Evening Post,* which accepted it for the 8 March 1919 number.[3]

"On the ship returning to the United States," Wiley told Thomas L. Masson for *Our American Humorists,* "the second Wildcat series was written."

Returning to civilian life, Wiley continued to write fiction.

Wildcat Marsden's story echoed that of the author at first. Drafted into the American Expeditionary Force, he's just returned stateside to find no work, no prospects. Wildcat, in a reflection of a mushrooming defection of Southern blacks, moved on. Returning to civilian life with a smelly mascot goat in tow, he signs on as a Pullman waiter on the Chicago route. The country is his to conquer.

Wiley's stories caught on with *Post* readers, though his way of writing them didn't immediately appeal to the periodical's editor, George Horace Lorimer. "'I asked him one day,' laughed Mr. Wiley, 'if many of the contributors to the *Saturday Evening Post* dictated their stuff.' 'I should say not!' replied Mr. Lorimer. 'I never have seen a dictated story that was worth a hang. They're all impossible.'"[4]

Prior to becoming a writer, said the *Oregonian* in 1920, "Hugh Wiley was civil engineering hither and yon, with sirloin steaks few and far between. He supervised the laying of a pipe line across the Willamette river, to bring Bull Run water to the city. He built bridges and surveyed rights-of-way, and the thought most remote was that his true forte lay in the narration of life through the keys of a typewriter. When fate overtook him and set him to his appointed task he was in Seattle, more than a little weary and somewhat convinced that the future was as drab as a cold buckwheat."[5]

"At first I bought some books on how to write short stories. They served to convince me that the fellows who wrote them didn't know any more about it than I did. One of them, boiled down, gave me the only thought in the bunch. It was this—start your yarn and keep it moving, galloping right through to the finish. And when you're through, quit. Sometimes in my work I pencil three words on a sheet of cardboard, big letters and easy to see: 'Tell the story.' I hang that card up where I can't fail to see it, and it serves to keep me on this track."

Where did Wildcat come from? "The Wildcat stories are 99 percent hop.... I have no particular colored character, from real life, in mind as I write them, though I did observe many of the type while in France. Four more stories, I think, will finish the Wildcat. Most of the letters commendatory of my work concern these stories, but I'm as firm a believer in Lady Luck as he is. So I want to quit while the going is good. Stories of that sort will travel only so far, and then the public will begin to tire of them," he said in the *Oregonian.*[6]

The author took a break, but kept writing about Wildcat for another fourteen years. The break was necessitated by a bout of appendicitis. "The sick spell has been forgotten and in a new story that will appear in the *Post* some time in October the nimble-minded negro character will take leave of San Francisco and make his way to New Orleans, according to Mr. Wiley. The story takes The Wildcat through his next series of adventures in Louisiana and leaves him heading straight for Memphis, Tenn., in the land where at the age of 9 he first learned the thumb crook for loaded dice from his grandfather."[7]

As he recuperated, Wiley, who lived near San Francisco, put together another Wildcat book, *Lady Luck*, and also a book of his Oriental stories, *Jade*.

"I am flitting about between my San Francisco shack, the Los Angeles studios and a five-acre 'rest cure' on which the apricots and other insects are racing for supremacy...," he wrote columnist Roy H. Moulton. "My Wildcat has begun to act a little uppity here on the coast, and so I am giving him a ride back to the south, via the Panama canal."[8]

Wiley set one of the Wildcat stories in the Portland, Oregon, area—he was a frequent visitor (staying at the Multnomah Hotel) because his parents then lived there.

A local newspaper was thrilled at the modest notoriety. "In the current number of the *Saturday Evening Post*," it told readers in 1920, "the Wildcat jumps a train somewhere above The Dalles during a holdup, makes his way to the river's brink, scoops out with his hands enough smelt to satiate his appetite for a while, later falls in the river, is carried into a fish wheel and does battle with fleets of steelheads and 100-pound Chinooks.

"As we say, we are grateful to the author for having the Wildcat try his Lady Luck with the fish of the Columbia river, but it is only fair that those unfamiliar with this section should not gain their ideas of Columbia river fishing wholly from fiction, as they have gained their misconception of western ranch life, cowboys, sheriffs, mining camps and the like.... To catch smelt with the hands is pretty difficult, if not impossible."[9]

In another issue, the *Oregonian* said: "Concerning The Wildcat's fishing experience, Wiley said that he lived for a time at Cascade Locks, and that while there he used to dip his hands into the Columbia and bring out scoopsful of smelt."[10] The reporter said Wiley was "one of the highest-paid short-story writers in the country."

Wiley gave a nod to Octavus Roy Cohen, who also reaped a crop of black fictional characters. "'He's a darb,' said Mr. Wiley. 'I've never met him, but I surely want to. That boy is the Belgian hare of American short-story writers. Persistent and productive, and a wizard with words.'"[11]

Cohen was familiar with Wiley. "I think Hugh Wiley's negro stories are wonderful, but his Chinese yarns are even better. Wiley I regard as the master of the staccato style of story-telling. I'd write in the same style but I can t get away with it," Cohen said.[12]

One reviewer of African descent by far preferred Cohen's stories to Wiley's. Andrew Roberson wrote in the *Editor* in 1922: "The difference that makes the negro reader like Cohen best [over E.K. Means or Wiley] is that they never feel insulted or put upon after reading tale by him, for he never uses the three or four words that are the pet aversions of negroes. The words are 'nigger,' 'darky,' 'shine,' 'coon' and 'boy.'...[13]

"Hugh Wiley's characters resemble true-to-type negroes just about as a blackface comedian does a person of the race he is impersonating. He looks like a black but you know he isn't."

Presumably white, reviewer J.E. Binford Jr. said of *Lily*, "This ebony hero of Hugh Wiley's is hardly done with one escapade before he is on with another. His travels carry him from San Francisco back to Cap'n Jack in Memphis. There is some good humour in Lily with many a sly dig at human nature. It is utterly free from any form of pretentiousness. Hugh Wiley has done what he set out to do: depicted a negro clown whose purpose is to entertain and be entertaining. Wiley is not concerned with the negro story written with an artistic point of view, but he is concerned with these traits of negro character which make for the ridiculous. There is many a laugh in this story."[14]

A *Morning Oregonian* reviewer gushed about the same book: "Short of a masterpiece, few characters in contemporary American fiction stand out as does Hugh Wiley's 'Wildcat,'" with his mascot goat, "Lady Luck."[15] Publication of *Lily* introduces neither this humorously philosophic coon nor his comprehending goat; it carries them on to new adventures for the delight of friends and followers."[16]

Wildcat, the reviewer continued, "is something very close to unique. This combination of negro laziness and philosophy and happiness dependent upon food, sleep and fortune, is a reversal of the 'land, labor and capital' idea in that food and sleep are the derived factors from fortune, while capital is derived from land and labor. All of which has nothing much to do with the Wildcat in actual thought.

"His dependence upon luck, personified by his mascot, Lady Luck, continues in the same vein as it always has. The Wildcat starts back for Memphis and Captain Joe's [*sic*] kitchen, accompanied by Lady Luck. His inside vest pocket is well lined with currency until, as he sleeps away the hours until his boat is to sail, the currency is extracted by a nimble-fingered gentleman. The Wildcat awakes to find his fortune diminished to $5, and this he spends immediately for a plain white mule."[17]

Editor and author Charles S. Johnson wasn't taken with Wiley's black fiction, deploring "time-saving generalizations, stereotypes, myths, conventions, dogma" appearing in popular literature, "the Octavus Roy Cohen, Hugh Wiley and Irvin S. Cobb type of humorous fiction repeated with unvarying outline, having helped to build up and crystallize a fictitious being unlike any Negro."[18]

Wildcat is remarkably gullible. In "Pop," from *Fo' Meals a Day*, he and his friend Demmy, with Lily in tow, venture from Chicago, where ends are dead, to California, where there must be promise somewhere. They encounter Perdue Grandy, a con man who once sold them a worthless shoeshine business. Grandy wants to stage a minstrel show, and persuades the duo to become his orchestra, Wildcat on drums, Demmy on sliphorn.

"'Hot dam, Perdue! I neveh knowed dey was so much money in de show business,'" Wildcat tells the hustler, who anticipates by several years Correll and Gosden's Kingfisher. (While it may be a dubious contribution to the English language, Wiley is credited with coining the expression "hot dam.")

The conversation continued: "'I told you dey was! Kain't you see it wid yo'own eyes? How come ev'y place you looks dey is buildin' millium-dollah theaters? Now is de time, an' befo' us quits strikin' whilst de iron is hot you learns a lot mo' 'bout de show business dan whut you knows at present.'"

The scheme goes awry, as you might expect.

Did Wildcat learn anything? No. A few chapters later, in "Hot House," Wildcat signs on to a money-making fantasy woven by his old nemesis, Honeytree Boone, that culminates in a Prohibition raid.

Wiley deserves credit for the story "Barefoot," which, if cleansed of its stereotypes, would be an entertaining enough tale of Wildcat harvesting four bales of cotton for the Cunnel, only to learn the Cunnel has announced he cannot pay for cotton this year. Wildcat takes a mule and strikes off for town, where through a series of misadventures he comes into possession of a satchel that contains bank robbery loot. He spends a day in jail, the mule is returned to its owner and Wildcat, somehow, ends up with a reward for capturing the robber. So there, Cunnel.

Wiley in 1920 had hopes of taking Wildcat to Broadway, but nothing came of it. He provided a Wildcat storyline for the 1929 motion picture *Fowl Play*, starring two black Kentuckians, piano player Ford Washington Lee (Buck) and rhythm tap dancer John William Sublett (Bubbles). Wiley storylines did get used in other Buck and Bubbles movies, *Black Narcissus* (1929) and *Laugh Jubilee* (1946).

As noted, Wiley wasn't satisfied to annoy just one ethnic group; he also annoyed a second, Chinese-Americans, with his series of stories about James Lee, also known as Mr. Wong, though the writer managed to do it without resorting to the pidgin English of Earl Derr Biggers' Charlie Chan. Wong was Yale-educated, after all. Seventeen Wong stories appeared in *Collier's* from 1934 to 1940. A dozen were collected in *Murder by the Dozen*[19] and Boris Karloff played the character in six movies from Monogram.

As an example of this fiction, the detective[20] in "The Heart of Kwan Yin,"[21] from *Collier's* for 17 February 1940, helps police solve the of the murder of a collector of Oriental art, Frank Clayton, a killing for which a young man named Sung Mock is blamed.

Examining the crime scene, Lee sees an artifact of Kwan Yin.

"This writing is very interesting, Sergeant. The last four characters are not easy to translate."
"All that Chink writin' is Greek to me," growled Roper. "What has that got to do with the crime?"

Chink. Charming.

Wiley had broad interests, and also wrote on engineering and early Chinese jade and bronze, topics in which racial matters didn't arise.

He died of influenza in 1968.

Hugh Wiley Notes

1. 26 November 1921.
2. *Saturday Evening Post*, 8 March 1919.
3. "Four-Leaved Wildcat" became the first chapter of *The Wildcat* (1920).
4. "Hugh Wiley Visits Portland for a Day," *Oregonian*, 27 September 1920.
5. Ibid.
6. Ibid.
7. "Writer Double-Tracks," *Oregonian*, 14 September 1921.
8. "On the Spur of the Moment," *Aberdeen Daily News*, 30 December 1921, 4.
9. "Fish as They Are," *Oregonian*, 27 December 1920, 6.
10. "Author Visitor in City," 3 January 1921.
11. "Hugh Wiley Visits Portland for a Day," op cit. Some readers, apparently, couldn't tell Wiley from Cohen. C.C.S., the "Through the Smoke Screen" columnist for the *Philadelphia Inquirer*, in the 20 November 1921 number gave a nod to Wiley: "Patiently have we waited for Hugh Wiley et al to come across with a story, entitled, 'The Wildcat Gets His Bonus Berries,' or something of the sort, the concluding paragraph of which, we imagine, should be something as follows: 'How come?' inquired Deacon Jones, resting on his rations. 'How come de President doan gib us dis adjusted conversation.' 'Adjusted conversation?' replied the Wildcat, scornfully. 'Adjusted conversation is sumpin' of which dat gemmun ain't got nothing' else but.'" That last grammatical construction is absolutely a Cohen trademark.
12. "All About I" in Thomas L. Masson, *Our American Humorists*, 346–350.
13. "Putting the Negro in Fiction," vol. 56, 99.
14. *Columbus Enquirer Sun*, 17 December 1922.
15. The goat is named Lily. Lady Luck is an unseen character.
16. Richard V. Haller, "Books," *Morning Oregonian*, 26 November 1922, 3.
17. "White mule" was gin.

18. "Public Opinion and the Negro," *Opportunity*, July 1923. Quoted in Martha Jane Nadell, *Enter the New Negroes; Images of Race in American Culture*, 33, and Abby Arthur Johnson and Ronald Maberry Johnson, *Propaganda and Aesthetics: The Literary Politics of African American Magazines in the Twentieth Century*, 51.

19. Other books included *The Room of Death, Cold Blood, No Witnesses, Scorned Woman, The Bell from China, The Feast of Kali* and *Seven of Spades*.

20. An agent for the U.S. State Department.

21. *Collier's*, 17 February 1940.

Hugh Wiley Selected Bibliography and Sources

WILDCAT STORIES

"The Four-Leaved Wildcat" (*Saturday Evening Post*, 8 March 1919)
"The Boom-a-Loom Boom" (*Saturday Evening Post*, 19 July 1919)
"The Prowling Prodigal" (*Saturday Evening Post*, 22 November 1919)
"Ramble Gamble" (*Saturday Evening Post*, 10 January 1920)
"Mister Lady Luck" (*Saturday Evening Post*, 17 January 1920)
"Memphis Bound" (*Saturday Evening Post*, 13 March 1920)
"The Konkrin Hero" (*Saturday Evening Post*, 26 June 1920)
"Excess Baggage" (*Saturday Evening Post*, 25 September 1920)
"Fresh Fish" (*Saturday Evening Post*, 25 September 1920)
"C.O.D." (*Saturday Evening Post*, 8 January 1920)
"Wildcat Luck" (*Saturday Evening Post*, 19 February 1921)
"The Temple of Luck" (*Saturday Evening Post*, 9 July 1921)
"Wildcat Thirteen" (*Saturday Evening Post*, 15 October 1922)
"The Tide of Fortune" (*Saturday Evening Post*, 7 January 1922)
"The Black Angel" (*Saturday Evening Post*, 28 January 1922)
"Single, Double, Trouble" (*Saturday Evening Post*, 27 May 1922)
"Wishbone Luck" (*Sunset*, July 1922)
"Wildcat Joss" (*Sunset*, August 1922)
"Three and Out" (*Sunset*, September 1922)
"The Red Tape Cutter" (*Saturday Evening Post*, 2 September 1922)
"Pay-Day Dice" (*Sunset*, October 1922)
"The Self-Started" (*Saturday Evening Post*, 6 January 1923)
"The Rain Maker" (*Saturday Evening Post*, 10 March 1923)
"The Jonah Fish" (*Saturday Evening Post*, 14 April 1923)
"Turkey Talk" (*Saturday Evening Post*, 5 May 1923)
"Money Mud" (*Saturday Evening Post*, 5 April 1923)
"Held for Rancid" (*Saturday Evening Post*, 15 November 1924)
"The Darker Horse" (*Saturday Evening Post*, 27 June 1924)
"Pop" (*Saturday Evening Post*, 7 November 1925) (5)
"Sick Per Cent" (*Saturday Evening Post*, 21 November 1925) (5)
"Flim-Flamingo" (*Saturday Evening Post*, 1 May 1926) (5)
"The Pluvitor" (*Saturday Evening Post*, 5 June 1926) (5)
"Barefoot" (5)
"Hot House" (5)
"Plated Goldfish" (5)
"Below the Belt" (5)
"Microphony" (*Saturday Evening Post*, 31 January 1931)
"The Quack That Ducked" (*Saturday Evening Post*, 27 June 1931)
"Wildcat" (*Cosmopolitan*, January 1932)
"Run, Sheep, Run" (*Saturday Evening Post*, 12 May 1934)

BOOKS
 (1) *The Wildcat* (1920)
 (2) *Lady Luck* (1921)

(3) *Lily* (1923)
(4) *The Prowler* (1925)
(5) *Fo' Meals a Day* (1927)

Films

Honest Crooks (announced 1929)
Fowl Play (1929)
Laugh Jubilee (1946)

Sources

"Author Visitor in City," *Oregonian*, 3 January 1921.
Binford, J.R. *Lily* review, *Columbus Enquirer Sun*, 17 December 1922.
C.C.S. "Through the Smoke Screen," *Philadelphia Inquirer*, 20 November 1921.
Chung, Sue Fawn. "From Fu Manchu, Evil Genius, to James Lee Wong, Popular Hero: A Study of the Chinese-American in Popular Periodical Fiction from 1920 to 1940," *Journal of Popular Culture*, winter 1976, 534–547.
Cohen, Octavus Roy. "All About I" in Thomas L. Masson, ed., *Our American Humorists*. New York: Moffat, Yard, 1922.
"Fish as They Are," *Oregonian*, 27 December 1920.
Haller, Richard V. "Books," *Morning Oregonian*, 26 November 1922.
"Hugh Wiley Tells of 'Wildcat' Boy," *San Jose Mercury News*, 24 August 1921.
"Hugh Wiley Visits Portland for Day," *Oregonian*, 27 September 1920.
Johnson, Abby Arthur, and Ronald Maberry Johnson. *Propaganda and Aesthetics: The Literary Politics of African American Magazines in the Twentieth Century*. Amherst: University of Massachusetts Press, 1991.
Johnson, Charles S. "Public Opinion and the Negro," *Opportunity*, July 1923.
Lady Luck review, *New York Tribune*, 26 November 1921.
Masson, Thomas L. *Our American Humorists*. New York: Moffat, Yard, 1922.
Moulton, Roy W. "On the Spur of the Moment," syndicated column, *Aberdeen (S.D.) Daily News*, 30 December 1921.
Nadel, Martha Jane. *Enter the New Negroes; Images of Race in American Culture*. Cambridge: Harvard University Press, 2004.
"Pathe Productions," *Dallas Morning News*, 18 August 1929.
Roberson, Andrew. "Putting the Negro in Fiction," *The Editor*, vol. 56, 1922.
Rothel, David. *The Case Files of the Oriental Sleuths: Charlie Chan, Mr. Moto and Mr. Wong*. Albany, GA: Bear Manor Media, 2011.
"Writer Double-Tracks," *Oregonian*, 14 September 1921.

Arthur K. Akers
(1886–1980)
Bugwine Breck

"I'se a detective," gurgled the disembarking Mr. Breck wildly.—"Jail-House Jeopardy"[1]

Bugwine Breck the Human Bloodhound, who sniffed out crime in fifty stories in the McCall Company's *Red Book* and *Blue Book* magazines from 1925 to 1934, was an out-and-out caricature made all the more so by Everett Lowry's exaggerated illustrations that accompanied the prose.

Arthur Kellogg Akers provided stories to *McClure's Magazine* as early as 1909 and the *Saturday Evening Post* starting in 1910. He wrote for *Railroad Stories, Argosy Weekly, War Stories, Battle Stories* and *Pearson's Magazine*. Some of his stories were syndicated to newspapers.[2]

Illustrated by Everett Lowry

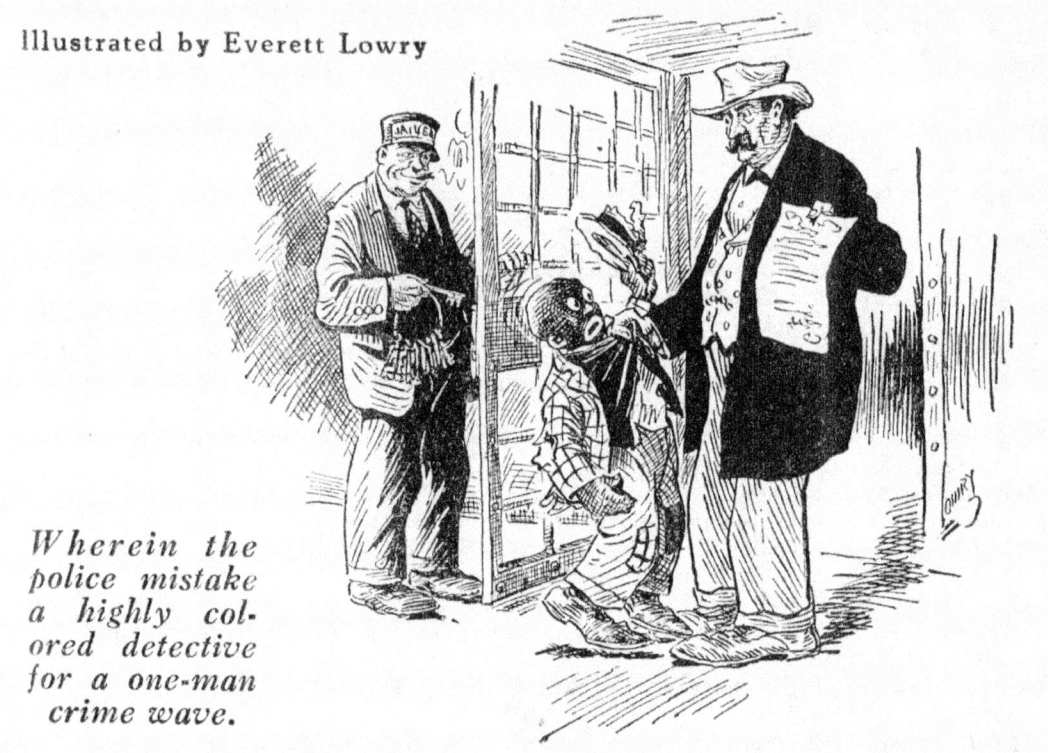

Wherein the police mistake a highly colored detective for a one-man crime wave.

Jail-house Jeopardy

By Arthur K. Akers

WITH siren screaming and loudspeaker blaring, the full staff of the Columbus Collins Detective Agency, for Colored, shot uproariously through startled streets, *en route* to a crime.

Clinging madly to their radio-equipped implications. Beyond any doubt, murder was being done!

"Hold eve'ything! Bugwine Breck, de human bloodhound, ridin' to de rescue!" yelped the agency's junior partner excited'y to an evident victim of foulest play as he opened yet wider th

Arthur K. Akers's bumbling private eye, Bugwine Breck, ended up behind bars in "Jail-house Jeopardy," from the July 1933 issue of *Blue Book*.

"Fast-finishin' Frogface" Reeves was a rare black Prohibition-era character, a "fixer," who appeared in the story "Liquid Assets" in *Argosy Weekly* for 30 May 1931. The story, which had all the makings of a series, begins: "'Tells you all time I's somep'n! Look here whut de mail-man done bring me,' the corpulent 'Frogface' Reeves, gentleman of color, interrupted his undersized satellite, Marmaduke Brown, in his task of sweeping out their place of business over a pool room. 'Ain't nobody never write you nothin' like dis! Got be somebody befo' you gits dis kind of letter.'"

Akers wrote two series for *Blue Book* featuring black characters, Darktown stories and Bugwine Breck misadventures.

Breck was "assistant sleuth" for the Columbus Collins Detective Agency for Colored in the burg of Demopolis. In the typical story "Jail-house Jeopardy," from *Blue Book* for July 1933, agency detectives race to a crime scene in a motorcycle and sidecar, and run smack into a parked automobile. It belongs to their client, a "weazened, boat-footed little darky with blood in his eye," whose name is "Half-portion Williams."

Breck, not a large man himself, is laden by the suspicion that his employer, who is also his roommate, may take and pawn his silverware. "'So carries 'em in my pants between meals, alongside de bear-trap handcuffs and de burglar-tools for evidence gittin,'" he explains.

Bugwine attempts to sort out a parking-in-front-of-a-fire-hydrant ticket issued to Williams, suggesting the car had been stolen. The police challenge his credentials:

"'Detective? Show me!'" demands the officer.
"Bugwine leaped for the loophole. His badge! Pinned inside his overalls, it would save him. Frantically he fumbled at his buttons—and his regular brand of luck resumed business at the old stand! For as he flipped back his garment there cascaded and clattered damningly to the sidewalk about his feet six forks, two spoons, and a silver knife!
"Instantly and justifiably the Law jumped to fresh conclusions. 'What th—Hold everything!' Heavy hands clamped down on the shrinking and horrified Mr. Breck. 'Where'd you get all this table-stuff, huh?'
"H-hit's mine!' wailed a Bugwine who no longer believed himself, in the face of this."

And that's enough of Bugwine's outrageous minstrelsy and hijinks.

Akers' fiction writings apparently never made it between book covers; his stories are to be found today only in aging and increasingly rare pulp and slick magazines, mostly in private collections.

Akers teamed with Dudley Williams to create a Bugwine daily newspaper comic strip for Allied Features for a very brief run in 1935.

Akers was born in Kentucky in 1886, the son of a Richmond Central University modern languages professor, James Tazewell Akers,[3] and his wife, Clara Elizabeth Harris. The father graduated from Washington and Lee University, the mother from Mount Holyoke College. There were two daughters and three sons in the family. The father died in 1901.

Arthur K. Akers worked for Western Union Telegraph Co. and was promoted to manager of the Jackson, Mississippi, office in 1906.[4] He and his wife, Nancy, eventually relocated to Gulfport, Mississippi. They had one son, Arthur K. Akers Jr., born in 1917 in Virginia. The older Arthur K. Akers became an advertising executive. He was a longtime member of the Rotary Club. He lived in Homewood, Alabama, in 1930. He was a Rotary conference secretary in Birmingham, Alabama, in May 1935. He was identified as "formerly, printing and publishing" living in Gulfport, Mississippi, in a letter to *The Rotarian* in October 1969. Akers was still writing in 1971—he contributed a nonfiction profile to the *Rotarian*. An author blurb said he was "a retired magazine writer and advertising man" and "he was at one time executive secretary of the Rotary Club of Birmingham. He now lives on the Mississippi Gulf Coast and is a senior active member in the Gulfport Rotary Club."[5]

Then living in Madison, N.J., Akers died in 1980.

Arthur K. Akers Notes

1. *Blue Book Magazine*, July 1933.
2. An example is "Crazy River Bridge," found in the Burlington (Vt.) *Weekly Free Press*, 6 June 1912.
3. Fred A. Engle, "Remembering Central University," with reference to a 1963 "I Remember Richmond, 1886–1901" manuscript by Akers. Also other sources, including Eastern Kentucky University Milestone Yearbook, Class of 1898, 22. The elder Akers was also a professor of Latin and a librarian.
4. "Changes in Western Union Office Force," *Lexington Herald*, 21 September 1906, 5.
5. "Meet Roy Hickman: Work Made the Man," *Rotarian*, June 1972.

Arthur K. Akers Selected Bibliography and Sources

BUGWINE BRECK STORIES

"Old Man Debbow" (*Red Book*, April 1925)
"The Execution of Bugwine" (*Red Book*, May 1925)
"Meet the Manager" (*Red Book*, September 1925)
"Hound Bait" (*Red Book*, July 1926)
"The Investor" (*Red Book*, October 1926)
"Muddyfoots" (*Red Book*, March 1927)
"High John, Conqueror" (*Red Book*, May 1927)
"Canned Goods" (*Red Book*, August 1927)
"Women Can't Ax No Mo'" (*Red Book*, September 1927)
"Accident's the Best Policy" (*Red Book*, November 1927)
"Clothes Make the Man" (*Red Book*, December 1927)
"Dark and Double Dealings" (*Red Book*, January 1928)
"Big Money an' Frequent" (*Red Book*, February 1928)
"It Takes Brains to Worry" (*Red Book*, March 1928)
"You's Holdin' Up de Weddin'" (*Red Book*, April 1928)
"Women Sure Worry a Boy" (*Red Book*, June 1928)
"Mr. Tuxedo Junction" (*Red Book*, July 1928)
"You've Lied Yo'r Last Lie!" (*Red Book*, August 1928)
"He Knows Women" (*Red Book*, September 1928)
"It's Hard to Explain to Ladies" (*Red Book*, November 1928)
"Where You Loafs and Fishes" (*Red Book*, January 1929)
"Don't Mess Wid No Lions!" (*Red Book*, March 1929)
"Step on Dem Eggs!" (*Red Book*, April 1929)
"Powder Costs Money" (*Red Book*, July 1929)
"Tiger Tonic" (*Red Book*, August 1929)
"Domestic and Business Entanglements" (*Red Book*, September 1929)
"Gas an' Matches" (*Red Book*, October 1929)
"The Crash of His Career" (*Red Book*, November 1929)
"Accidents a la Carte" (*Red Book*, December 1929)
"No Luck Lyin' to Ladies" (*Red Book*, January 1930)
"Wolf! Wolf!" (*Red Book*, February 1930)
"Bloodhound for a Night" (*Red Book*, March 1930)
"Lumbago on the Left" (*Red Book*, April 1930)
"Detecting" (*Red Book*, May 1930)
"Adam and Eve" (*Red Book*, June 1930)
"Fair Means or Foul" (*Red Book*, July 1930)
"No School for Scandal" (*Red Book*, September 1930)
"Double Entry" (*Red Book*, November 1932)
"Cash Money for Casualties" (*Red Book*, December 1932)
"Bugwine Sells Short" (*Blue Book*, October 1932)
"Breeches Burned Behind" (*Blue Book*, February 1933)
"Wild Owl Milk" (*Blue Book*, March 1933)
"Settled Out of Court" (*Blue Book*, April 1933)

"Black Beauties" (*Blue Book*, May 1933)
"Framed Like a Picture" (*Blue Book*, June 1933)
"Jail-House Jeopardy" (*Blue Book*, July 1933)
"Recovery, Here We Come" (*Redbook,* March 1934)
"Keep Out of Banks" (*Blue Book* (June 1934)
"Bugwine Goes to the Dogs" (*Blue Book*, July 1934)
"Bugwine in the Lion's Den" (*Blue Book*, August 1934)

Note: Some of the Red Book stories may be Gladstone Smith or Darktown stories.

DARKTOWN STORIES
"Baptist Hill's Dog Derby" (*Blue Book*, December 1930)
"Five Rounds to Live" (*Blue Book*, February 1931)
"Rumble Seat Evidence" (*Blue Book*, March 1931)
"The Sorrows of Skilletface" (*Blue Book*, October 1931)
"One Bear—As Is!" (*Blue Book*, November 1931)
"A Black Hand Boomerang" (*Blue Book*, December 1931)
"Bloodhounds Beats Brains" (*Blue Book*, April 1932)
"Board and Dodging" (*Blue Book*, November 1934)

COMIC STRIP
"Bugwine" (1935, Allied Features) with artist Dudley Williams

SOURCES
Akers, Arthur K. Letter, *The Rotarian*, October 1969.
_____. "Meet Roy Hickman: Work Made the Man," *Rotarian*, June 1972.
Arthur K. Akers transcript. Birmingham Public Library. http://www.bplonline.org/resources/archives/collections.aspx (viewed 28 September 2012).
Arthur Kellogg Akers listing. Rootsweb. http://wc.rootsweb.ancestry.com/cgi-bin/igm.cgi?op=GET&db=jewelfamily&id=I1703 (viewed 28 September 2012).
"Changes in Western Union Office Force," *Lexington Herald*, 21 September 1906.
Engle, Fred A. "Remembering Central University," *Richmond Register*, 5 May 2009. http://richmondregister.com/lifestylescommunity/x155223827/Remembering-Central-University/print (viewed 28 September 2012).
"James Tazewell Akers," Eastern Kentucky University Milestone Yearbook, Class of 1898. http://www.e-yearbook.com/yearbooks/Eastern_Kentucky_University_Milestone_Yearbook/1898/Page_22.html (viewed 28 September 2012).
James Tazewell Akers listing. Rootsweb. http://wc.rootsweb.ancestry.com/cgi-bin/igm.cgi?op=GET&db=jewelfamily&id=I482 (viewed 28 September 2012).

Roark Bradford
(1896–1948)
Bugaboo Jones
Little Bee Bend Plantation

"I wants," Giles said bluntly, "fo' hund'ed and fifty pound er cotton outn you, befo' sundown tomorrow. And tell Cooter he better pick me fo' hund'ed. Or you and him bofe is gonter be huntin' dat long highway y'all singin' 'bout."
—Giles Arnold, Little Bee Bend Plantation foreman, "The Cows in the Corn"[1]

Roark Bradford was second only to Octavus Roy Cohen in his outpouring of African American-populated, "humorous" short stories. Where Cohen gravitated to Birmingham's inner city, Bradford set his Bugaboo Jones tales along the Mississippi River and his Little Bee Bend Plantation stories in rural Louisiana.

"Roark Bradford, once a copyreader for *The Times-Picayune* ... is credited by critics with having done more than any other living writer to interpret the religious spirit of the negro," Gwen Bristoe wrote.[2]

Roark Whitney Wickliffe Bradford was born in 1896, one of eleven children of Richard C. and Patricia Adelaide Tillman Bradford. Both of Roark's grandfathers fought for the Confederate Army.

The author's son, Richard Bradford,[3] gave this succinct bio of his parent: "My father was born in Tennessee, on a farm. He didn't go to college. In fact, he didn't finish high school.[4] When he was in tenth grade, he ran away from home and joined the army, spent World War I in the army, though not in France, was commissioned, somehow, got out of the army, married his first wife,[5] his high-school English teacher (I think I've got the order straight here), became a newspaper man in New Orleans, and at some point in the late '20s began to write free-lance. He and my mother met, I think at what is known as a 'literary tea,' in New York. And he got divorced[6]; they got married; I was born in 1932 in Chicago."[7]

Let's flesh that out.

Serving in the U.S. Army Artillery Reserve during World War I, Roark Bradford was a second lieutenant initially assigned to the Puget Sound with the Coast and Geodetic survey to make maps and surveys, then to the Panama Canal Zone. He was in New York City, awaiting a ship to go to France, when the war ended. For a time, he instructed military science and tactics at Mississippi Agricultural and Mechanical College (now Mississippi State University).

Bradford was a boxer (known as "Nig" Bradford, a lightweight who sparred in Galveston, Texas, and New Orleans) and a baseball player (he turned down an offer to join the Seattle club of the Pacific Coast League as a third baseman). He played football for the University of California and, according to playwright Marc Connelly, was inadvertently involved in the hazing of a black teammate that left him forever an advocate of equal treatment of blacks.

"He looks at the Negro with a steady eye and considers him with an alert and honest brain," Connelly wrote. "His negro talk has the rhythm and actuality of life and his fun making is such that his [football] team mate could share with him."[8]

He might have pursued a career in law,[9] but Bradford instead became a reporter for the Atlanta *Georgian,* the Lafayette *Daily*

Roark Bradford wrote dozens of short stories with characters of African descent.

Harry Burne's menacing depiction of Bugaboo Jones, for Roark Bradford's short story "Monkey Man" in *Collier's* for May 5, 1928, would seem to turn away, rather than attract, readers (author's collection).

Advertiser and the Macon *Telegraph* from 1920 to 1922. He was night editor and later Sunday editor for the *Times-Picayune* in New Orleans in 1924 and 1925. He lived in the French Quarter, and later owned Little Bee Bend Plantation in Benton, Louisiana.[10]

His earliest, failed attempts at writing fiction had been South Seas tales and whaling yarns. Eventually he got the hang of prose wrangling, and specialized in folklore—even if, at times, he made it up.[11]

"One day he happened to see a negro fishing in the Mississippi, a bell tied at the end of his pole to jingle and awaken him, when a fish bit," according to the *Times-Picayune*.[12] "He did a story about it and sold it to the New York *World*. From then on Bradford drew on his background—his boyhood on the family plantation in Lauderdale County, Tenn., for more and more Negro tales—stories that brought him fame and some fortune." These stories had titles such as "The Adulteration of Old King David" and "Nigger Deemus." De Lawd was a venerable cotton planter.

By 1925, Bradford left newspapering to write for periodicals.

His second short story, "Child of God," appeared in *Harper's* and won the 1927 O. Henry Award. The story dealt "with the elemental psychology of the negro of the South."[13]

His stories for the *World* were collected in 1928 in *Ol' Man Adam an' His Chillun*. The whimsical Negro interpretation of Bible stories took on a new life when Marc Connelly used them as the basis of the play *Green Pastures*, which was performed 640 times in New York City, was the basis of a 1926 motion picture and was later restaged several times. The play was both lauded and panned, lauded for embracing Negro folk religion, panned for the same. The play won a Pulitzer Prize for Drama in 1930, and a National Association for the Advancement of Colored People Spingarn Medal in 1931 for actor Richard B. Harrison.

Bradford was fond of his humorous depiction of black life: "There is nothing really funnier than a funny 'nigger,'" he wrote in the foreword to *Ol' Man Adam an' His Chillun*.

To Bradford, this account of God creating the earth, freely adapted from a black preacher's orations he'd heard as a child, was funny:

> Well, de firmament runned on de yearth, and hit runned in de rivers and creeks and ditches—'cause firmament wa'n't nothin but a fancy name for water—and dar was de yearth wid de firmament dreened off and a heap of dry land left.
>
> "Now looky what you done done, Lawd," say Gabriel. "Cou'se hit ain't none of my business, 'cause I got to practice on my hawn all the time. But somebody got to go work dat land, 'cause you know good as me dat de land ain't gonter work hitself."
>
> Well, de Lawd looked round to see who he gonter send to work his land, and all de angels was mighty busy. "Well," he say, "I guess I got to pass one more miracle to git somebody to work dat land. And I bet de next time I pass a miracle for some firmament I bet I won't git so brash about hit."
>
> So de Lawd got a handful of dirt and made hit in a ball and passed a miracle over hit and say, "Let dis dirt be mankind." And de dirt turn to a man.
>
> De Lawd looked at de man and say, "What's yo' name, man?"
>
> "Adam," say de man.
>
> "Adam—which? " say de Lawd.
>
> "Jest plain Adam," say de man.
>
> "What's yo' family name? " say de Lawd.
>
> "Ain't got no family," say Adam.
>
> "Well," say de Lawd, "I got to change dat. I ain't gonter have none of deseyar single mens workin' on my farm. They runs around wid de women all night and come de next day they's too sleepy to work."[14]

Bradford once "admitted he was more interested in 'the nigger' than in 'the Negro,'" meaning less educated, less sophisticated, rustic.[15]

Years later, Bradford as a consultant to the English Department would tell freshmen at Tulane University "that real humor is never cruel and that another's mistakes are not to be considered funny."[16]

Bradford garnered considerable acclaim for his novel *John Henry* (1931), a retelling of the legendary life of a railroad laborer who bested a steam drill in a dramatic one-on-one confrontation. Bradford used what the *Dallas Morning News* labeled a peculiar literary style, from time to time making use of a "darkey chorus" to sing the deeds of the black Paul Bunyan.[17] This was appropriate as "John Henry" was the "granddaddy of the Negro ballads," according to musicologist Alain Locke,[18] and was "recorded over forty times by Black singers in the 1920s," according to music historian Paul Oliver.[19]

Bradford's novel aired as a CBS radio show in 1933[20] and became a Broadway play in 1939,[21] with Paul Robeson in the lead part in 1940.

Bradford was aware of controversy over his black characters. Hamilton Basso, for one, pointed out that *John Henry* showed Negroes as bawdy, amusing, picturesque, whereas the truth was closer to poverty, hardship, illiteracy and humiliation.[22]

Bradford's second wife, and Richard's mother, Mary Rose Sciarra Himler, a former editor at Bobbs-Merrill, became his literary agent. Bradford did his writing mostly in New Orleans, some at his brother Richard's plantation near Bossier City, and at the last in Santa Fe.

Bradford continued to write biblically themed fiction about blacks, collected in such books as *Ol' King David an' the Philistine Boys* (1930), *Kingdom Coming* (1933) and *The Three-Headed Angel* (1937).

Wilson Jefferson was among readers who complained of Bradford's fictions. Writing in the *Plain Dealer* in 1931, he said: "Roark Bradford and Julia Peterkin[23] and Carl van Vechten,[24] in the stories which they have written about Negroes, have invariably tried to fit Negro life to a pattern that take in all of the white man's prejudice and all his misinformation.

"This false approach towards the wealth of material in negro life is made intentionally by these writers and by other of the kind. These writers know that a majority of their readers have never come into intimate contact with the race. They also are aware of the fact that their prospective readers do know a stage-bred traditional Negro. These authors the conclude that it is easier and more remunerative to cater to this empty half knowledge than to attempt to relate the black man artistically to that humanity which is the world."[25]

Jefferson expanded on his gripe: "In books written by authors of this type a funny Negro, or a scheming negro or a bad Negro is never true to himself in the sense that a white character in a book is true to himself. The poor Negro travesty always has his audience, the white folks, in mind. And you can put it down that never once will this black character in a white man's book go back on his raising."

David Russell in the *Dallas Morning News*, on the other hand, thought Bradford improved with each book. Writing about *Kingdom Coming* in 1933, the reviewer noted: "In this volume Mr. Bradfield [sic] has achieved a unity of character which he has never succeeded in catching before. Always a master of the negro idiom, being able to set down the rich flavor and the native humor of their speech, he has never before been able to sketch his darkies into full and believable characters. He came nearest to doing this in *This Side of Jordan*, but even here his Young Jack, Didge and Aunt Crip never came really to life. They were but shadows that embodied the urges and the superstitions of their race."[26]

Russell said further of this novel about a six-year-old slave boy, Grammy: "His admirable 'Ol' Man Adam an' His Children,' upon which the now famous play, 'Green Pastures' was based, and his equally meritorious 'Ol' King David an' the Philistine Boys' were admittedly centered chiefly on the folklore, and while they were convincing as far as idiom as concerned they yielded nothing in the way of a sustained character.

"It is this that marks the chief achievement in 'Kingdom Coming.' Until this time Mr. Bradford has written objectively and there has been something of a conflict between his characters and the writer's interpretation of them. Here he lets the characters interpret their own story, and a new subjective power is achieved which makes the reader feel there is an authenticity here not found in this writer's earlier books."

Bradford in the introduction to *Ol' Man Adam and His Chillun* distinguishes what he perceives to be three types of African Americans: the Negro, who is a leader, concerned with economic success more than equal rights; "the colored person," of lighter skin, who "frequently of mixed blood, loathes the blacks and despises the white.... He has the black man's emotions and the white man's inhibitions," prone to protest. And "the nigger," irresponsible, ill-educated, crude—and hilarious.

"I believe I know them pretty well. I was born on a plantation that was worked by them; I was nursed by one as an infant and I played with one when I was growing up. I have watched them at work in the fields, in the levee camps, and on the river. I have watched them at home, in church, at their picnics and their funerals."[27]

Sterling A. Brown, among others, disputed Bradford's justification: "All of this, he believes, gives him license to step forth as their interpreter and repeat stereotypes time-hallowed in the South. It doesn't. Mr. Bradford's stories remain highly amusing; his generalizations about *the* Negro remain a far better analysis of a white man than of *the* Negro. We see that, even in pontifical moments, one white Southerner cannot escape being influenced by current folk-beliefs."[28]

Bradford took his success in stride. "Bradford is a stocky young fellow in his early thirties," the *Augusta Chronicle* in Georgia wrote in 1933, "broad-shouldered, swarthy, blue-eyed and bashful, whose name appears on almost a shelf of books in the Public Library as the author of their naïve and humorous comics, who in one year shared in $130,000 royalties from a drama suggested by one of these and who has created for himself a modest home in Arizona to work in more and escape an army of publishers' agents, admirers and curiosity seekers who, if permitted, would lionize him to the point of distraction."[29]

The author apparently did not enjoy the task of writing. "It is [his wife] Mary Rose's job to see that he puts in a certain number of hours in the workshop," a writer in the *Trenton Evening News* said in 1936. "Brad admits that he would rather do anything else than write, but as long as Mary Rose is around he has to do what he dislikes. And it happens to be what he does best.

"Brad and Mary Rose could retire and take it easy on their share of the royalties on 'The Green Pasture.' So could the author of the play, Marc Connelly. But Brad has a commitment—that of interpreting the life of the southern bayous and the Gulf cities—which will keep him busy the rest of his life."[30]

Bradford's fiction, he once said, derived from stories he heard from three childhood playmates—children of sharecroppers on his father's cotton plantation near Nankipoo, Tenn., named Algy, Ed and Sweet[31]—and from old "Uncle Wes." "He also studied (after a fashion) black life in Louisiana, spending many hours standing on Rampart Street, just watching, and going to services at a Baptist church across the river in Algiers where the preacher was an evangelist widely known as 'the Black Billy Sunday.'"[32]

Of particular interest here are Bradford's stories for *Collier's*, the series of twenty stories about roustabout Bugaboo Jones, who handles freight on Captain Cooley's steamboat *John D. Grace*, a Mississippi River packet boat, and another 65 stories about Little Bee Bend Plantation where Giles Arnold was the foreman, the Widow Duck arranged romances and kept church matters in hand, the Rev. Sin-Splitter Samuel over-praised the Lord and Zeno Yates and Po-Chile Albright and the one-legged blacksmith B'r Charlie and other characters led contented if occasionally fractured lives.[33] They were shown as naïve but surviving under white guidance.

The first Bugaboo story, "The Tricker,"[34] relates how Jones persuaded the black foreman on the *John D. Grace*, Old Folks, to give him a job. Old Folks had seen Bugaboo on the riverbank, his line in the water, attached to a bell. Your muscles are too soft, Old Folks said.

"'I get harded up in no time,' Bugaboo declared.

"Old Folks considered for a minute. 'I been seein' you settin' out yonder fishin' wid a bell,' he said. 'So don't think you gonter come none er dat stuff on me. Does I ever ketch you rattin', I's gonter beat you ha'f to death wid dis stick.'"

Once on the job, Bugaboo finds it great sport to carry great weights down the plank to shore, with some of the pretty young women of the port looking on.

He finds it equal sport to sneak Old Folks' gin jug away from him one night, just before they're scheduled for a midnight landing to unload a shipment of rolled barbed wire. Bugaboo gets his drink of gin, and not a few whacks of the hickory from Old Folks, before he has to lug the wire down the plank, one roll under each arm, singing this outrageous song:

> Got a brown-skin gal at Natches;
> Got a black at Baton Rouge.
> Maybe my brown she don't love me,
> But my black sweet mamma do's.

Bugaboo in "Monkey Man"[35] thinks he's outsmarted money-lender Elder. He's squirreled fifty cents into a pocket and, come payday, when he usually squanders all his earnings on liquor, women and gambling, he'll have enough to attend the fish fry. He was too clever, however; he didn't allow for needing more funds so he could escort May Liza to the meal. He tries to get the money from a card game with Elder, only to be sharked out of his modest ante. May Liza reluctantly agrees to advance Bugaboo the money, but at the fish fry, she shows up on the arm of Elder.

Bugaboo seethes as he listens to Elder tell the gathering a far-fetched story in order to solicit funds. He can't stand any more, and runs at Elder wielding an open razor. Elder leaves, May Liza smiles—and how many stereotypes did you see in that description? Drinking. Gambling. Violence.

Widow Duck of Little Bee Bend Plantation goes on the warpath with a different weapon, in "Too Much Sin."[36] B'r Charlie has stirred up trouble in the Old Ship of Zion Church, a church that dates to slavery time, before she was born. B'r Charlie is a preacher as well as a shoer of horses and hammerer of hinges, has raised her ire.

"'You was in a big hurry last night to name dat Ringgold strumpet de haid deaconess, soon as you kotched me outa de church,'" she challenges Charlie. "'Now, you come hyar, I got certain words to speak wid you!'

"B'r Charlie knew if he got into an argument with the Widow Duck he was bound to lose, In spite of that he crutched over to her porch.

"'Now, Mis' Duckie,' he begun defensively, 'you hadn't out to fly off'n de handle so quick. Sissie Ringgold is a good woman, and young.'

"'Yeah,' sniffed the Widow Duck, 'and a fool about preachers.'"

Told she doesn't know her Bible, the 200-pound widow fumes and plots her return to status. As she walks past her neighbors' cabins, she can tell who voted for her, who against, while she was away on an errand for the foreman Giles. Everyone shows up at church that night for Sissie's installation. Still head deaconess until the ceremony, Widow Duck begins to sing a song, saying she will then march out the door and Sissie can go to amen corner and take over duties. Widow Duck sings, not a hymn, but the "Old John Song." "*Shoot de liquor to me, John!*" A brouhaha erupts, and the singing continues. Mamie T starts a counter song, when Sissie doesn't know one. Sissie assaults Mamie T. "I'm de song leader hyar," she says. When the dust clears, B'r Charlie is sitting on the floor, Widow Duck is back in charge, and Sissie has disappeared.

Magazine illustrations went a long way to draw readers into a story. Or not. Harry Burne's[37] black-and-white, two-page artwork for "Monkey Man" shows Bugaboo Jones, the purported hero of the story, racing toward the elder in the pulpit, an open razor in hand, the congregation staring aghast. The picture realized all the fears whites had of blacks. All of the characters were at least modest exaggerations, a few with stereotypical sausage lips.

Slightly tamer, William Mead Prince's[38] toned-paper technique yielded remarkably interesting depictions of, say, Bugaboo Jones and Iron Man in "Kansas Brown"[39] or Bee Bend Plantation denizens in "The Stepbaby."[40] The art is so exceptionally rendered as to suggest it was drawn from life. Still, there are stereotypical toothy grins and wide, white eyes. But the illustrations suggest a higher level of story is there. The most curious of the Bradford-Prince collaborations was "The Projeckin' Son,"[41] a short short story in verse, with six illustrations.

Two Bugaboo and one Bee Bend stories made it into the collection *Let the Band Play Dixie* in 1934, more appeared in the obscure *Short Stories from Collier's* in 1943. Of the former, a *Times-Picayune* reviewer said in 1934: "In this collection is 'Child of God,' winner of the O. Henry short-story award, and unquestionably a polished piece of work. Devotees of Mr. Bradford will remember the striking negro character in this tale—the man who was hanged and went to heaven and who was allowed to return to earth and speak the few words that had been denied him on the scaffold.

"The episodes in the lives of Bugaboo Jones, Blue Steel or Hopper Joe are less impressive. Yet these characters are, as types, unforgettable. It is always obvious that Mr. Bradford has no end of sympathetic understanding of his characters."[42]

Some plantation stories have complex plots. In "Old Average Lightning,"[43] for example, the boss man has a large mule named Lightning, who weighs 1,600 pounds and outpulls, outworks any other beast, despite attempts to pair him with another mule. A newcomer, Newman Dyke, lasts longer than any other hand with Lightning's reins. But as the season goes on, and it gets dryer and dryer, the superstitious blacks wonder if Lightning isn't the devil, and Newman his agent. One evening there's a terrific storm, a funnel cloud sets down, the skies burst. After it's all over, the mule and man are gone. Gone back to where they came from, is the belief of the Satan theorists. The belief persists, "Even when the story was circulated a year or two later that a strange man, woman and mule were rent-farming up in the hills, no one tried to connect the rumor with Newman, Lightning and the cotton-chopper. No one doubts his own version of the affair enough to trouble."

The Rev. Sin-Splitter Samuel takes center stage in several Plantation stories, including

"The Wages of Sin-Splitter."[44] Foreman Giles has rounded up some 200 black laborers to work on the road, as part of a Works Progress Administration project. Sin-Splitter rides up on his sorrel mule Balaam, curious about what's going on. Giles, who has no use for the preacher, shoos him away, begrudgingly explaining they are working because they have to work, with no expectation of remuneration. Sin-Splitter is curious, checks into the WPA and signs on to be at the front of the labor gang, singing spirituals and encouraging the men, while Giles prods them from the rear.

To the surprise of all but Sin-Splitter, there is an actual payday. The men receive $1 a day for their eleven days of work. Sin-Splitter situates himself right outside the bank, hat in hand, seeking contributions for his cause. When Giles finds out Sin-Splitter was paid by the WPA and is now taking money from the WPA-paid laborers, well, the preacher makes a hasty departure from town.

Bradford made three attempts to write novels. Two manuscripts had black characters. None found a publisher.

When he wasn't writing, Bradford "liked to fish and he liked to travel," according to an obituary notice.[45] "But he was always anxious to come back to New Orleans. He became a sailing enthusiast after he had the *Widow Duck*, a gaff-rigged 36-foot sloop, built. He named it after the character in the Little Bee Bend Plantation the fictional counterpart of a plantation Bradford owned near Vanceville, La.,[46] until last year [1927].

"He was a golfer who played solely for fun and the companionship of the links. He painted when the mood struck. He liked to make red wine on a small wine press. He tried to make white wine but gave it up in disgust because it turned out so badly.

"His life was built around good talk and good friends," the newspaper said of the chunky, balding writer.

"'Brad' was a good horseman, but hadn't ridden in years. He played the guitar well and knew hundreds of hillbilly, Negro and cowboy songs. Far off radio stations frequently played requests for him in the early morning hours, and 'Brad' had a huge collection of cheap phonograph records."

Bradford "thought it great sport to find a wandering Negro musician and take him home for a song-fest," the *Times-Picayune* said.[47]

It was good research.

The story "Music Got to Moan"[48] finds Captain Cooley doing something for the first time in his sixty-three years on the river: Stopping to pick up a saxophone player. Summer business was slack, and Cooley in a lax moment agreed to take customers out on the river in an evening and let some of his roustabouts play music. The customers loved it, and danced for hours. To upgrade his band—which consisted of squat, muscular Iron Man on harmonica, Jesse Dunbar on trap drum, Egbert, the second cook, on guitar and Henry Lane on bass viol—the giant Bugaboo Jones, when he could get his hands on a washboard, provided further percussion, percussion so enthusiastic that he wore out one or more instrument each session. The new saxophone artist will replace Jones.

The *John D. Grace* musicians don't like the saxophone player, Georgia Pain. He's too good. And he's above working during daylight hours, shouldering cordwood onto the ship:

"'Wawks like he got a poker in he pants,' observed a short, sturdy, bow-legged rouster known as Iron Man. 'He too stiff in de laigs.'

"'No mind, de stiff laigs,' grinned Bugaboo Jones, a black giant. 'Wait to us hits a wood pile. Hit ain't nothin' will grease a man's knees like totin' wood down a steep plank. And de old man's hickory. Dat hickory and dat woodpile learn anybody to coonjine.'

"'Man, man,' agreed the short rouster, sadly. I wisht I'd never learnt dat thing. I might be out yonder benhind the levee right now, plowin' me a mjule , ef'n I hadn't learn dat coonjine step.'"

The "coonjine step," to interrupt briefly, is a term Bradford first brought into print in *John Henry*, to describe a rolling gait workers developed as they carried heavy cord wood or baled cotton along springy planks from dockside to decktop. "And so John Henry got a spring in his knees and weave in his hips, and a buck in his back ... 'Jine it, you coon, jine it' said the mate. 'Grab your cotton and jine that step!'"[49]

The roustabouts in "Music Got to Moan" make the saxophone player feel unwelcome, and he takes off before an evening event billed as featuring a five-piece band. Have to cancel the show, Cooley says. But if you let me play, Bugaboo pleads, you'll have five musicians. What was the captain to do?

With the outbreak of World War II, Bradford in the period 1942–1946 was a lieutenant in the U.S. Naval Reserve, assigned to the Bureau of Aeronautics Training, training literature division, in the African Theatre. He belonged to the Reserve Officers Association and the National Institute of Arts and Letters. In 1946, he was a visiting lecturer at Tulane University.

He took a break from writing fiction to provide *Collier's* with "Make Mine the Human Race,"[50] his appraisal of race relations.

"Social dislocations caused by the war have brought to the surface of American life a great many submerged and half-forgotten evils. Large among these are the uncorrected abuses suffered by Negroes during the past three hundred years. It now appears that unless sound common sense replaces emotion in dealing with this situation, our land is in line for some ugly postwar race trouble," he wrote.

"The only actual difference between members of the Negro race and members of any other human race is the degree of pigmentation under the skin. The other so-called 'racial characteristics' one hears so much about—bone structure of the head, their 'carefree shiftless spirit,' and other similar claims—are pure hogwash. It should be borne in mind by leaders of both races who are interested in stopping interracial evils that all of a negro's troubles are not due to his color. Many of his troubles are due to the fact that he is a human being; negroes have no monopoly on trouble, although they do have more than a lot of people. As with some other 'social groups,' Negroes suffer from three main evils: prejudice, discrimination and exploitation." And so on.

He goes on to tell of the time his oldest sister, with a year of "liberal" Yankee education under her belt, to modernize relations with the blacks on their father's farm. She gathered some black children and began a discussion of the Creation:

"'Was de Lawd a white man or a black man?' Sweet asked.

"'White man, fool!' Algie answered. 'Cause de fust thing de Lawd command when he stepped out was, 'Let hit be de sun.' But ef'n he'd 'a' been a black man when he step out, his fust command would 'a' been, 'Let me be white!'"

"My sister adjourned the class sine die, passed out the gingerbread and boiled custard and gave up home missionary work then and there, forever.

"Admittedly, the answer to Sweet's question about the Lord's complexion left much unsaid but, to date, no one has come forward with a more complete answer."

And that explains some of Bradford's home-grown theology.

The Widow Duck, in "The Pearl-Handled Humbug,"[51] confronts a religious issue. B'r Charlie, the Old Ship of Zion Church pastor, wants the congregation to donate for the purchase of a new, gilded, illustrated Bible—a "pearl-handled Bible"—for the pulpit. It costs $200. Widow Duck thinks that's outrageous, and Uncle Henry, senior deacon, agrees. The congregation is enjoying an influx of young men back from the service, and young women back from jobs in the city. They have a little extra cash, and would be willing to give their expected due. But maybe they have more important things to spend their money on.

The widow and the deacon have each set aside $100 for emergencies. They take the money and go in plantation superintendent Giles' "Gee Buggy" (an Army-surplus Jeep, replacing mules and horses) to Shreveport to buy the Bible.

"'I and you gonter buy dat Bible. Not for de Lawd, cause He don't need it. And not for B'r Charlie, cause he don't deserve hit. But for de young members which is savin' they money to buy farms and stuff wid,'" she tells Henry.

At the Atomic Novelty Company, the two find themselves talking with a hustler. He only paid $50 for the Bible, he tells them. He'll sell it for $100, and passing the plate for the congregation will bring them $100 profit.

Quite a hustle, Uncle Henry observes, and challenges the salesman to a wager: the winner of a simple cut of a deck of cards will take the salesman's $50 and the Bible. Henry, of course, no slouch at a sleight of hand, draws an ace of spades to the salesman Tony's ten of clubs. Back at the church, B'r Charlie is given his comeuppance, and Widow Duck and Uncle Henry are given their spiritual satisfaction.

The story was Bradford's 107th for *Collier's*, the editor noted. "As he himself puts it: 'If I hadn't spent all of the money you-all paid for these yarns, I'd probably be so rich I could afford to be doing what I'm doing now: sitting at my typewriter working on a new yarn.'"

Though he didn't realize it, Bradford wouldn't see out the year. He reminisced, "I've ... lived through two panics, a depression, five Republican administrations, and a voter's insurrection when the Populists carried the Hoop Pole Ridge settlement about 1900. At present I'm getting rid of some *amoebae Histolyticae* (Latin, 1st declension, plural, for amoebic dysentery) picked up three years ago while in the Navy. I don't mind their eating what I ate, but I hate like Harry having to chew for them.

"Mr. Bradford traces The Pearl-Handled Humbug to the fact that every sharpshooter in the country is stirring about with a phony deal these days to mulct a fast dollar from the negro farm hands.

"'For once, they are well heeled,' reveals Brad. 'Last fall, B'r Charlie, who is exactly as described in the story, approached me for a gift of $200 to purchase a pearl-handled pulpit Bible for his church, Old Ship of Zion. I looked into the deal, found it a promotion cutback scheme, about as I tell it. I didn't buy the Bible but did contribute a Daisy Burner stove, which seemed to please everyone as well. Just now we are living in N'Orleans, a delightful city simply lousy with charm. Soon we expect to move over to Santa Fe for a piece.'"[52]

Over time, Bradford's short stories have been reappraised, and, while they made strong use of black folk traditions, they have lost their luster due to patronizing attitudes, demeaning dialects and stereotypical images.

Bradford's decline, according to Contemporary Authors online, "reflects at least some change in American society, even as the earliest success indicates the pervasiveness of racism during the first five decades of the twentieth century." In the view of critic Wade Hall, "Despite the fact that [Bradford] lived among blacks most of his life and observed them closely, he was still an outsider who was seldom able—or willing—to penetrate black consciousness."[53]

Critic Lewis P. Simpson observed that Bradford's stories "are clearly now significant only in the historical sociology of American literature."[54]

While in the navy in 1943, Bradford had spent time in French West Africa and, as he said earlier, he contracted amebiasis, a disease that claimed his life in New Orleans in November 1948. He disdained funerals and asked that his ashes be spread over the Mississippi River.

Roark Bradford Notes

1. *Collier's*, 15 October 1938.
2. Bristow, Gwen, "Vieux Carré Inspires Authors," *Times-Picayune*, 23 February 1933, 26.
3. Richard Roark (1932–2002) wrote *Red Sky at Morning* (1968), which was made into a film, and *So Far from Heaven* 1973). Both books were set in racially divided desert towns in New Mexico. He grew up in New Orleans, New York and Santa Fe.
4. Other sources suggest Roark Bradford attended a college in Louisiana and received an LL.B. degree from the University of California.
5. Her name was Lydia, according to John Shelton Reed, *Dixie Bohemia*, 58.
6. *Time* magazine, 14 March 1932, said Lydia Sehorn Bradford sued for separation, charging abandonment, and added: "Mrs. Bradford lies abed with tuberculosis in Arizona." On 31 July 1933, *Time* said Bradford divorced his first wife in Mexico, then, in El Paso, Texas, married Mary Rose Sciarra Himler of Indianapolis, who had the year before given birth to their son.
7. Roark Bradford, Ancestry.com.
8. "Story about Roark Bradford," *Wings*, 11–13.
9. According to "Noted Author Is Taken by Death," 14 November 1948, 1, his father was also a judge.
10. He sold the plantation in 1947, according to "Roark Bradford, 52, Author of Negro Folk Tales, Dies," *Long Beach Press Telegram*, 14 November 1948.
11. Bradford and Lyle Saxon, a fellow *Times-Picayune* employee, concocted and published stories about the giant river woman Annie Christmas, according to John Shelton Reed, *Dixie Bohemia*, 159.
12. "Noted Author Is Taken by Death," op cit.
13. "Colleagues Honor Roark Bradford," *Times-Picayune*, 30 January 1928, 4.
14. "Eve and That Snake," *Ol' Man Adam an' His Chillun*, 4–5.
15. Michael North, *The Dialect of Modernism: Race, Language, and Twentieth Century Literature*, 118.
16. "Real Humor Not Cruel, Says Roark Bradford," *Pittsburgh Press*, 9 January 1948, 15. He held up Mark Twain as an outstanding American humorist, and William Faulkner (whom he had gotten to know in New Orleans) as a top contemporary novelist.
17. "In His New Book Roark Bradford Tells Some Tall Tales of Black Paul Bunyan," 6 September 1931, 8.
18. "The Negro and His Music," as quoted in Paul Oliver, *Barrelhouse Blues*, 42.
19. *Barrelhouse Blues*, 42.
20. "John Henry," *Cleveland Plain Dealer*, 22 January 1933, 30.
21. Libretto by Bradford, music by Jacques Wolfe (1896–1973).
22. "Black Beowulf," *New Republic*, 30 September 1931, 196–187, as summarized in Inez Hollander Lake's *The Road from Pompey's Head*, 81.
23. See Appendix.
24. Van Vechten (1880–19640) was an essayist and photographer, friend to many Harlem Renaissance writers and author of the controversial novel *Nigger Heaven* (1926).
25. "White Writers Mirror Their Prejudice in Books," 16 October 1931, 2.

26. "In Portraying Negro Character Roark Bradford Sets New Mark," 24 September 1933, 4. The article gives a history of how Bradford's book became the play *Green Pastures*.
27. Introduction, *Ol' Man Adam and His Chillun*, ix.
28. "Negro Characters As Seen by White Authors," 150.
29. "Newspaper Man Is Responsible for 'Green Pastures,'" 15 October 1933, 4.
30. "Lucky Author," 18 March 1936, 11.
31. Austin Doyle, "'Green Pastures' Author Throws Away His Clock," *Milwaukee Journal*, 4 November 1941.
32. John Shelton Reed, *Dixie Bohemia*, 159.
33. Bradford let Iron Man take the lead in some of the Bugaboo Jones stories, and tried two Bubber and two Little Blue Steel stories, neither character catching on.
34. *Collier's*, 31 December 1927.
35. *Collier's*, 5 May 1928.
36. *Collier's*, 14 July 1936.
37. The Australia-born artist also did artwork for *Boys' Life*, *McClure's*, *Adventure* and *St. Nicholas*.
38. A Virginia-born artist, Prince (1893–1951) was in charge of the University of North Carolina's art department during World War II. He later worked in advertising in Chicago, and eventually settled in Westport, Connecticut, to do magazine work. His clients included *The Country Gentleman*.
39. *Collier's*, 17 December 1938.
40. *Collier's*, 9 July 1938.
41. *Collier's*, 4 June 1938.
42. *Times-Picayune*, 14 October 1934, 42.
43. *Collier's*, 1 October 1932.
44. *Collier's*, 11 March 1939.
45. Ibid.
46. On Palmetto Road in Benton.
47. Ibid.
48. *Collier's*, 16 March 1929.
49. The term shows up in folk songs and dance music.
50. 4 August 1945.
51. *Collier's*, 1 May 1948.
52. "The Week's Work," *Collier's*, 1 May 1948.
53. *Dictionary of Literary Biography, Vol. 86: American Short-Story Writers*, 43–48.
54. *Southern Writers: A Biographical Dictionary*, 45.

Roark Bradford Selected Bibliography and Sources

BUGABOO JONES STORIES

"The Tricker: Here Is Fresh Humor—a Breeze Off the Mississippi" (*Collier's*, 31 December 1927) (*Milwaukee Journal Magazine*, 17 July 1931)
"The Old He-Coon of the John D. Grace: A New Humorist Contributes Another of His Delightful Mississippi River Comedies" (*Collier's*, 17 March 1928)
"Monkey Man: Arriving, After Many Difficulties, at Pop, Catfish and B'iled Custard" (*Collier's*, 5 May 1928)
"Poor May Liza: Bugaboo Jones Has Some Trouble with His 'Women fo'ks'" (*Collier's* 22 September 1928)
"Other Men's Poison: A Fresh and Funny Story of a Mississippi Black Boy Who Talks That Way" (*Collier's*, 15 December 1928)
"Music Got to Moan: Melody Making on the Mississippi" (*Collier's*, 16 March 1929)
"The Indian Summer of Bugaboo Jones: Too Many Bad Men Make an Elegant Story of Good Times on the Mississippi" (*Collier's*, 14 September 1929) (1)
"The Rambling Rouster: Bugaboo Jones Helps a Friend" (*Collier's*, 9 November 1929)
"Come Day, Go Day" (*Harper's Magazine*, May 1930) (1)
"True Love Tracks: Bugaboo Jones and a Girl from Arkansas" (*Collier's*, 4 April 1931)
"The Dirty Dozens: Another Bugaboo Jones Story" (*Collier's*, 8 August 1931) (2)
"The All-and-All Woman: Bugaboo Sings a Weary Song" (*Collier's*, 21 May 1932) (2)

"Lady, Don't You Grieve: Sudden Matrimony on the John D. Grace" (*Collier's*, 19 August 1933) (2)
"Three for a Nickel: Bermuda Onions Are Out of Place on the Father of Waters" (*Collier's*, 23 September 1933) (1)
"Bugaboo Jones Affiliates: Ethiopian Strive in New Orleans" (*Collier's*, 2 November 1935)
"Easy Pickings: Greenville Gals Are Very Handy with Ice Picks" (*Collier's*, 23 November 1935) (2)
"The Gimme Woman: Two Women Too Many for Bugaboo Jones" (*Collier's*, 3 May 1936) (2)
"The Hoodoo Bonus" (*Collier's*, 31 October 1936) (2)
"Gentleman from Barbados: Quick Razor Work" (*Collier's*, 23 April 1938) (2)
"Kansas Brown: Iron Man and Bugaboo Jones in Search of a Lady" (*Collier's*, 17 December 1938) (2)
"Hot Shot from Texas" (*Collier's*, 5 August 1939) (2)
"Manuscript Dice: The Law of Probabilities Is Repealed by Iron Man" (*Collier's*, 9 November 1940) (2)

LITTLE BEE BEND PLANTATION STORIES

"The Mule Man: Zeno Gets a Job of Work" (*Collier's*, 30 November 1929)
"The Money Maze: Explored by a Dusky Financier" (*Collier's*, 28 February 1932) (2)
"Love and Laughter: Drama in the Cotton Fields" (*Collier's*, 11 June 1932) (2)
"Old Average Lightning: A Miracle at Little Bee Bend" (*Collier's*, 1 October 1932) (1) (2)
"You've Got to Rule 'Em: Mules and Women—It Applies to Both" (*Collier's*, 22 October 1932)
"War Baby's Mama: Skullduggery and Hilarity on Little Bee Bend Plantation" (*Collier's*, 18 February 1933
"Cotton Need Pickin': Poetic Justice on Little Bee Bend Plantation" (*Collier's*, 15 July 1933) (2)
"The Grass in the Cotton: An Excess of Holiness That Led to Trouble" (*Collier's*, 18 November 1933) (2)
"The Witch of Willow Chute: Black Magic on Little Bee Bend" (*Collier's*, 7 April 1933)
"The Sin-Splitter: A Battle of the Prophets on Little Bee Bend" (*Collier's*, 10 February 1934)
"The Lotman's True Love: Science Invades Little Bee Bend, Harmlessly" (*Collier's*, 19 May 1934)
"Fortune's Toy: The Story of a Cautious Man—and a Couple of Women" [Zeno Yates] (*Collier's*, 7 July 1934) (2)
"The Boll Weevil Gentleman: Comedy in Black and White" (*Collier's*, 22 September 1934) (2)
"The Helpin' Fool: The Dangers of Excessive Holiness" (*Collier's*, 10 November 1934) (2)
"Juju Powder: Black Magic on Little Bee Bend" (*Collier's*, 16 March 1935) (2)
"The Widow Man: Penalties of a Hero on Little Bee Bend" (*Collier's*, 18 January 1936)
"Too Much Sin: Adjustments for Widow Duck" (*Collier's*, 4 July 1936)
"Medicine Man: Black Magic" (*Collier's*, 8 August 1936) (2)
"The Hoodoo Bonus: Painful Popularity on Little Bee Bend" (*Collier's*, 31 October 1936) (2)
"Prosperity Blues: Little Bee Bend 'Hits Dat Lick'" (*Collier's*, 20 February 1937) (2)
"Bible-Talking Mule: A Miracle, Passed by the Reverend Sin-Splitting Samuel" (*Collier's*, 28 August 1937) (2)
"Swing Low the Chariot: Church Trouble on Little Bee Bend" (*Collier's*, 28 August 1937)
"Too Much Texas: Horses and Marriages on Little Bee Bend" (*Collier's*, 25 September 1937)
"The Stepbaby: One Extra Child on Little Bee Bend" (*Collier's*, 9 July 1938)
"Promised Land: High-Ballin' on Down to Texas!" (*Collier's*, 20 August 1938)
"The Cows in the Corn: Little Bee Bend vs. Uncle Sam" (*Collier's*, 15 October 1938)
"East Wind Blows in the Valley: Mister Mack's Domestic Crisis" (*Collier's*, 11 March 1939)
"The Wages of Sin-Splitter: Too Many and Too Fancy" (*Collier's*, 11 March 1939)
"Seven Pins in a Candle: A Little Hoodoo Goes a Long Way" (Collier's, 29 April 1939) (2)
"The Guvmer's Green Shirt: Sartorial Splurge on Little Bee Bend" (*Collier's*, 10 June 1939)
"Hot Shot from Texas: Small Package of Bad News for Little Bee Bend" (*Collier's*, 5 August 1939) (2)
"Guv'mer Blues: The All-overs on Little Bee Bend" (*Collier's*, 30 September 1939) (2)
"Two-Tongue Truth: Scandal on Little Bee Plantation" (*Collier's*, 6 January 1940)
"The Manner of Heaven: Sin-Splittin' Samuel, Salvation for Cash" (*Collier's*, 20 January 1940) (2)
"One-legged Backsliding: B'r Charlie Finds the Way to Grace" (*Collier's*, 20 April 1940)
"Call Your Sheep: There Are Saints as Well as Sinners on Little Bee" (*Collier's*, 18 May 1940) (2)
"The Mule-Angel: People Are Easy to Handle If You Know Mules" (*Collier's*, 6 July 1940) (2)
"The Bible Boys' Cotton: A Victory for Scriptures, the Widow Duck Assisting" (*Collier's*, 2 November 1940) (2)

"City Sin: With Sin-Splitting Sam Cashing In on It" (*Collier's*, 22 February 1941) (2)
"Red Pants Ain't No Sin: But They Can Start a Lot of Trouble" (*Collier's*, 29 March 1941) (2)
"One-Legged Backsliding" (Collier's, 20 April 1940) (2)
"Money in the Sack: Sin-Splitting Samuel Turns a Nice Profit in Salvation" (*Collier's*, 24 May 1941) (2)
"Po-Chile No More: A Lucky Two Bits Raises Cain in Shreveport" (*Collier's*, 5 July 1941) (2)
"The Lonesome Gigolo: Little Bee Bend Raises Cotton and Scandal" (*Collier's*, 13 September 1941) (2)
"Satan's Blacksmith Shop: B'r Charlie Learns of the Evils of Idleness" (*Collier's*, 25 October 1941) (2)
"One of We's Own: Little Bee Bend Is No Place for a Loose-footed Man" (*Collier's*, 29 November 1941) (2)
"Hypocrite Bait: Big Doings on Little Bee Bend" (*Collier's*, 3 January 1942) (2)
"Sin for Your Supper: Sin-Splitting Sam Does an Evangelistic Hand-Spring" (*Collier's*, 28 February 1942) (2)
"The Cooter Blues: Music Hath Charms Down in Little Bee Bend" (*Collier's*, 8 August 1942) (2)
"Double-Yolk Hoodoo: Black Magic in Little Bee Bend" (*Collier's*, 12 September 1942) (2)
"The Pirate-in-Law: Charlie Does a Little Privateering for the Coast Guard" (*Collier's*, 19 December 1942)
"Old Sergeant Somebody: More Doings Down at Little Bee Bend" (*Collier's*, 26 December 1942) (2)
"Miracle Come to Pass: Uncle Henry and Widow Duck Are on the Side of the Angels" (*Collier's*, 9 January 1943) (2)
"1-A Johnson Grass: As It Sows, Old Ship of Zion Church Reaps" (*Collier's*, 20 February 1943) (2)
"The Sin-Splitter's Split: Preaching the Gospel Brings Its Rewards" (*Collier's*, 3 April 1943) (2)
"Some Changes Made: The O.C.&D. Catches Up with Little Bee Bend" (*Collier's*, 8 May 1943) (2)
"One-Legged Angels Can't Fly: Or Can They? The Question Throws Little Bee Bend Plantation into an Uproar" (*Collier's*, 19 June 1943)
"Cupid Up the Bayou: The Widow Duck's Hands Were Full—of Other People's Business" (*Collier's*, 28 February 1948)
"The Pearl-Handled Humbug: The Widow Duck Knew It All Along; All Is Not Gold That Glitters" (*Collier's*, 1 May 1948) (2)
"The High Hip Rider: Another Hilarious Little Bee Bend Plantation Story" (*Collier's*, 31 July 1948) (2)
"Low-Down Cotton" (*Collier's*, 26 February 1948)
"Rich Man, Rich Man" (*Collier's*, 13 November 1938) (2)
"Slow Down de Chariot" (*Collier's*, 25 June 1949)

BUBBER STORIES

"The Somebody Man: Just Because He Was a Somebody, Bubber Got into a Mighty Lot of Trouble" (*Collier's*, 27 April 1929)
"Fast Company: Life Speeds Up for Bubber and Things Happen Long Before the Appointed Cotton-Pickin'" (*Collier's*, 6 July 1929)

LITTLE BLUE STEEL STORIES

"Blue Steel's Eva" (*The Dial*, September 1927) (1)
"The Razor Man" (*Collier's*, 17 December 1932) (1) (2)

BOOKS

(1) *Let the Band Play Dixie and Other Stories* (1934)
(2) *Short Stories from Collier's* (1943)

SOURCES

Adams, Marjorie. "Roark Bradford's Negro Characters," master's thesis, University of Texas at Austin, 1948.
Basso, Hamilton. "Black Beowulf," *New Republic*, 30 September 1931.
Bowman, Marnie Inez. "The Negro in the Works of Three Contemporary Louisiana Writers," master's thesis, George Peabody College for Teachers, 1931.
Bradford, Roark. "Funny Nigger," foreword to *Ol' Man Adam an' His Chillun* (New York: Harper & Brothers, 1928).
_____. "Make Mine the Human Race," *Collier's*, 4 August 1945.

Bristow, Gwen. "Vieux Carré Inspires Authors," *Times-Picayune*, 23 February 1933.
Brown, Sterling A. "Negro Characters as Seen by White Authors," in *A Son's Return: Selected Essays of Sterling A. Brown*. Boston: Northeastern University Press, 1996.
"Colleagues Honor Roark Bradford," *Times-Picayune*, 30 January 1928.
Connelly, Marc. *Green Pastures*. New York: Farrar and Rinehart, 1929.
_____. "Story About Roark Bradford," *Wings*, Vol. 5, No. 9, September 1931.
Denny, Diane. "The Delightful Art of William Meade Prince," *The Saturday Evening Post,* http://www.saturdayeveningpost.com/2010/11/13/art-entertainment/delightful-art-william-meade-prince.html
Doyle, Austin. "'Green Pastures' Author Throws Away His Clock," *Milwaukee Journal*, 4 November 1941.
Folsom, Sarah Blanton. "Roark Bradford: His Life and Work," master's thesis, collection of Auburn University, no date.
Gleeson, Tony. "William Meade Prince and Writer Roark Bradford," *Today's Inspiration*, 15 May 2012, http://todaysinspiration.blogspot.com/2012/05/william-meade-prince-and-writer-roark.html (viewed 28 September 2012).
_____. "William Meade Prince—Some Biographical Info," *Today's Inspiration*, 16 May 2012, http://todaysinspiration.blogspot.com/2012/05/william-meade-prince-some-biographical.html (viewed 28 September 2012).
_____. "William Meade Prince (1893–1951)," *Today's Inspiration*, 14 May 2012, http://todaysinspiration.blogspot.com/2012/05/william-meade-prince-1893-1951.html (viewed 28 September 2012).
Gormin, Ken. "Noted Author Is Taken by Death," *Times-Picayune*, 14 November 1948.
Hall, Wade. "Roark Bradford," *Dictionary of Literary Biography, Vol. 86: American Short-Story Writers*. Detroit: Gale, 1989.
"In His New Book Roark Bradford Tells Some Tall Tales of Black Paul Bunyan," *Dallas Morning News*, 6 September 1931.
"In Portraying Negro Character Roark Bradford Sets New Mark," *Dallas Morning News*, 24 September 1933.
Jefferson, Wilson. "White Writers Mirror Their Prejudice in Books," *Plain Dealer*, 16 October 1931.
"John Henry," *Cleveland Plain Dealer*, 22 January 1933.
Lake, Inez Hollander. *The Road from Pompey's Head: The Life and Work of Hamilton Basso*. Baton Rouge: Louisiana State University Press, 1999.
"Let the Band Play Dixie" review, *Times-Picayune*, 14 October 1934.
"Lucky Author—His Wife Makes Him Work," *Trenton Evening Times*, 18 March 1936.
Milestones. *Time*, 14 March 1932.
Milestones. *Time*, 31 July 1933.
"Newspaperman Chronicles Simple Bible Stories in Style of Negro Sermons," *Dallas Morning News*, 3 May 1928.
"Newspaper Man Is Responsible for 'Green Pastures,'" *Augusta Chronicle*, 15 October 1933.
North, Michael. *The Dialect of Modernism: Race, Language, and Twentieth Century Literature*. New York: Oxford University Press, 1994.
"Real Humor Not Cruel, Says Roark Bradford," *Pittsburgh Press*, 9 January 1948.
Reed, John Shelton. *Dixie Bohemia: A French Quarter Circle in the 1920s*. Baton Rouge: Louisiana State University Press, 2012.
"Richard Bradford, Novelist of the Southwest, Dies at 69," *New York Times*, 30 March 2002.
"Roark Bradford—Author on Black Lauderdale County Experiences?," Black Ripley, http://blackripley.wordpress.com/2012/05/22/roark-bradford/ (viewed 28 September 2012).
"Roark Bradford, 52, Author of Negro Folk Tales, Dies," *Long Beach Press-Telegram*, 14 November 1948.
"Roark Bradford," Ancestry.com. http://boards.ancestry.com/surnames.bradford/1464.1.1.1/mb.ashx (viewed 10 October 2012).
"Roark Bradford," Books and Writers, http://www.kirjasto.sci.fi/rbradf.htm (viewed 28 September 2012).
"Roark Bradford," Contemporary Authors online. http://gdc.gale.com/gale-literature-collections/contemporary-authors/. Detroit: Gale, 2003.
"Roark Bradford," *Encyclopedia of Arkansas History & Culture*. http://www.encyclopediaofarkansas.net/encyclopedia/entry-detail.aspx?entryID=3412 (viewed 28 September 2012).
"Roark Bradford, Famed Author, Former State Resident Dies," *Arkansas Democrat*, 14 November 1948.

Roark Bradford Papers. Howard-Tilton Memorial Library Special Collections, Tulane University. http://specialcollections.tulane.edu/archon/?p=collections/controlcard&id=19 (28 September 2012).
Simpson, Lewis P. "Roark Bradford," *Southern Writers: A Biographical Dictionary*, Robert Bain, Joseph M. Flora, Louis D. Rubin Jr., eds. Baton Rouge: Louisiana State University Press, 1979.
"Southern Park of Heaven," Preservation Society of Chapel Hill, http://chapelhillpreservation.com/2012/southern-part-of-heaven/ (viewed 28 September 2012).
Thomas, James W. "Roark Bradford," *Encyclopedia of Louisiana History, Culture and Community*. http://www.knowla.org/entry.php?rec=653 (viewed 28 September 2012).
Tracy, Steven C., ed. *John Henry: Roark Bradford's Novel and Play*. New York: Oxford University Press, 2011.
"Week's Work," *Collier's*, 1 May 1948.
"William Meade Prince," *Saturday Evening Post*, http://www.curtispublishing.com/bios/Prince.shtml (viewed 28 September 2012).
William Meade Prince and Lillian Hughes Prince papers. Southern Historical Collection, Louis Round Wilson Special Collections Library, UNC University Libraries, http://www.lib.unc.edu/mss/inv/p/Prince,William_Meade_and_Lillian_Hughes.html (viewed 28 September 2012).
Yarbrough, Robert. "The Life and Works of Roark Bradford," master's thesis, University of Mississippi, 1981.

Charles Correll
(1890–1972)

Freeman F. Gosden
(1899–1982)

Sam 'n' Henry
Amos 'n' Andy

> In its way, Amos 'n' Andy was sympathetic toward a part of America that was unrepresented—not *under*represented, but totally *non*represented—on network radio at the time when that medium was the only broadcast game in town. The show almost always portrayed its characters in a loving manner.
>
> —Jerrold M. Packard[1]

It's 1927 and two hard-on-their-luck Birmingham chawbacons, Sam Smith and Henry Johnson, take a bumpy ride to the station in a mule-drawn wagon, purchase tickets with their dwindling dimes and nickels and board a train to Chicago to seek improved fortune. Not long after they arrive, they hire on at a construction site, and in their off-time explore the city:

> Sam. Henry, I didn't know dis heah place is as big as it is.
> Henry. Dis heah is a big place, ain't it?
> Sam. An' de wuk ain't hahd eithah. Dey done had us doin' a lot o' crazy things ovah heah though.
> Henry. It's a good thing dey keeps us wukkin' togetah 'case I kin tell you whut to do—you do mos' ig'nant boy I done evah seed.[2]

The exchange isn't riotously funny; in fact, the radio program *Sam 'n' Henry* was conceived as a six-day-a-week drama, its amusement deriving from the Deep South dialogue and the bewildered reactions of the two men to the metropolis. The exotic naifs, a theme Mark Twain employed in *A Connecticut Yankee in King Arthur's Court* and *The Beverly*

Charles A. Correll and Freeman Gosden rubbed burnt cork on their faces for this photograph of Amos and Andy contemplating a baseball, date unknown (author's collection).

Hillbillies adopted on television, in this case had legitimacy in the steady black migration of the 1910s and '20s.

"The early broadcasts, which portrayed the innocent characters' troubles in Chicago, mirrored the difficulties Southern blacks had in adjusting to life in the Northern cities,"[3] according to historian Arthur Frank Wertheim.

On the other hand, Wertheim continued, "It perpetuated clichés about Negroes and reassured white listeners that their new neighbors from the South were less intelligent and less diligent than themselves."[4]

Charles Correll and Freeman F. Gosden created *Sam 'n' Henry*.

Charles James Correll's folks lived at 711 Hancock Street in Peoria, Illinois, when he was born in 1890. Freeman Fisher Gosden's parents resided at 711 East Marshall Street in Richmond, Virginia, when he made his first appearance in 1899.

"They were lucky, 7 come 11 or not!" quipped reporter Larry Wolters in 1952.[5]

Correll as a youth performed skits with his friends, ushered at a playhouse, clog danced in minstrel shows, played piano at a silent movie theater, worked as a stenographer and learned to be a bricklayer.

SAM 'N' HENRY

"Brothers, as officers of de Jewels of de Crown, de problem dat now refronts us is dis."

Scripts from Correll and Gosden's first show in 1927, *Sam 'n' Henry*, appeared in the *Chicago Tribune*—the newspaper that owned the radio station that broadcast the series.

Gosden as a kid performed magic, was a skilled impersonator and worked in a drugstore. He was a wireless operator in the U.S. Navy during World War I and later sold tobacco products.

Correll's first marriage, to Marie Janes, after ten years ended in divorce in 1927. Correll that same year married Alyce McLaughlin and they had six children.

Gosden had also married in 1927. Leta Marie Schreiber divorced him in 1940. In 1944 he married Jane Stoneham. He had two children with each marriage.

Showbiz flowed in their veins. Correll and Gosden both took part in minstrel shows in their hometowns. They met in 1921 in Durham, North Carolina, and became coworkers with the Joe Bren Producing Co. Correll was a rehearsal coach. Gosden was a director.

They were keenly interested in radio's potential to offer a steady income. Their *Correll and Gosden, the Life of the Party* aired over WEBH in 1925. Correll played piano. Gosden strummed ukulele. They both told jokes. The next year, their *Sam and Henry* went on the air in broadcasts from the Drake Hotel in Chicago and started to attract listeners to WGN.[6]

WGN was searching for a hit, according to reporter Wolters. "Henry Selinger, W-G-N program director, turned to Balaban and Katz[7] for help. Will Harris, a talent scout, mentioned Correll and Gosden, a little known minstrel team appearing at McVicker's theater. They were not playing (or eating) regularly and were happy to try radio. They started out singing and making jokes.[8] Quin Ryan recalled yesterday that he went to the public library

Amos 'n' Andy enjoyed a short run in a newspaper comic strip in 1928 and 1929.

to study Octavus Roy Cohen's stories about Negroes to get atmosphere for their show. (Years later they hired Cohen at a fabulous price to write for them.)"[9]

Minstrelsy didn't appeal to WGN listeners. Maybe an adaptation of the popular *Gumps* comic strip would. "So Ben McCanna, manager of the station, directed Selinger to develop a nightly 'comic strip of the air,' for them. The idea, of course, was inspired by the success of the *Tribune*'s comics.

"Gosden and Correll bucked like steers at this idea, Selinger recalled. He pleaded with them to give the idea a try. They were ashamed of it, since they regarded themselves primarily as singers. Then the fan letters began coming in, first in driblets, soon in waves. And Gosden and Correll were on their way to fame and fortune."[10]

In a variant telling by Wertheim, Correll and Gosden were keen on their Sam 'n' Henry concept as they had strong southern backgrounds. Correll's grandparents were from the Deep South and his grandfather had been imprisoned in a Union camp during the Civil War. Only later did the family move to Illinois. In Gosden's family, his father had been a member of Mosby's Raiders. Gosden was raised by a mammy and his parents raised Garrett "Snowball" Brown, a young black, until he was sixteen. Correll and Gosden felt they knew the people and the dialect sufficiently to do a creditable show.[11]

As Gosden said in a years-later interview, "We chose black characters because blackface comics could tell funnier stories than whiteface comics."[12]

Amos 'n' Andy were featured in the Tracey's Radio float in a small-town parade in Great Barrington, Massachusetts, in 1930—proof, if any was needed, of the wide appeal of the characters in the Depression era (Great Barrington Historical Society).

In other words, as historian Elizabeth MacLeod explained, the performers, as others before them, found a certain liberation in masquerade, in hiding behind the burnt cork. It's interesting that whites thrived behind the mask of choice, while blacks lived behind a mask of necessity—a veil, as W.E.B. Du Bois called it—for survival.

With radio, Correll and Gosden didn't need the makeup. Gosden had a knack with impersonations, and the duo played not only their main characters, but any others they wrote into the scripts. Through a change in voice, an alteration of dialect, a change in distance and angle from the microphone, they created the illusion of multiple cast members in the studio.

Sam 'n' Henry, considered radio's first situation comedy, debuted on 12 January 1926. Correll and Gosden performed their own sketches for ten minutes a night, six nights a week.[13] The episodes had continuity—an element new to radio.

"Early *Sam 'n' Henry* scripts were rough and soon reverted to typical minstrel show material," according to Peter H. Johnson Jr. "However, the characters gradually took on very human personalities, and surprisingly the show was a success. Sam and Henry found work as meat packers and later worked at Montgomery Wards and even went into business as teamsters with a beat-up, broken down wagon and an old horse named 'Gram-pa.'"[14]

"Neither performer had ever entertained literary aspirations," according to MacLeod, "and the only real writing experience they had had was in creating broad comedy material for the Bren Company's stage shows. With Correll and Gosden having had no experience in the creation of even semirealistic characters, it was inevitable that the earliest episodes of *Sam 'n' Henry* would lean heavily on overt stereotypes."[15]

Airing at 10 p.m. the program caught listeners' attention. "'Sam 'n' Henry' are proving a popular feature at station WGN, Chicago," the *Kokomo Tribune* said within a month of the debut. "This pair of humorists translate low comedy into radio entertainment."[16]

The characters joined the Jewels of the Crown lodge and were taken under the wing of (and often taken monetarily by) the Most Precious Diamond, the presiding officer. Sam kept in touch as best he could with his Birmingham sweetie, Liza. Sam participated in a prize fight with Dangerous Dan. Henry's trousers were stolen by a mysterious man from their boardinghouse. Sam nervously gave a speech before the Jewels of the Crown. And the two were arrested for shooting craps.

One day, the men listened to a pitch from an Investment Insurance Company of Cincinnati, Ohio, salesman. Sam bites. Henry doesn't:

> Sam. Well, Mistah, dat certainly is cheap 'nuf, ain't it?
> Agent. It's the greatest buy in America today.
> Sam. Henry, what you think 'bout dis heah thing?
> Henry. You got money. Go on—buy de thing.
> Sam. Well, Mistah, I take one of 'em. Put my name down on it.
> Agent. Ah—that's fine. Sam Smith.—Now, how old are you?
> Sam. I'se thirty-two.
> Agent. (filling in policy)—Thirty-two. And what is your address?
> Sam. General delivery.
> Agent. All right, here you are—here's your certificate. The first premium is two dollars and after that it's ten cents a week.
> Sam. *Two dollahs?*
> Agent. That's the first premium. You understand that, of course?
> Sam. Henry—do you know what dat means?
> Henry. Sho' give de man de two dollahs—give de man de money.
> Sam. Pays you two dollahs now—is dat it, Mistah?
> Agent. That's the idea. You give me two dollars now and then only ten cents a week after that.
> Henry. Give de gent'man de two dollahs.
> Sam. (handing him his money)—Heah you are. Mistah—heah's de two dollahs.
> Agent. (turning to Henry)—What's your name?
> Henry. My name's Henry Johnson.
> Agent. Now, I'll fix you up with one of these policies, too, Henry.
> Henry. Nossah, Mistah, don' bothah 'bout me. I'se protected.[17]

The *Tribune* promoted the radio show heavily. "Every Sunday during much of 1927, the newspaper published the script of a current Sam 'n' Henry episode, written in a 'dialect' and accompanied by caricatures of the principal characters in action. The paper used the feature as one of the main selling points for its new Metropolitan Section—a weekly collection of humor columns, adventure narratives, and other attractions—and it syndicated the Sam 'n' Henry column to other newspapers," according to historian Melvin Ely.[18]

Samuel Jay Smith illustrated the first of the script reprints in the *Tribune*, drawing big, boisterous Henry and small, gullible Sam with exaggerated minstrel characteristics. Smith provided drawings for a *Tribune* book collecting the first twenty-five radio scripts. Thirty-five scripts[19] were published in the newspaper from 6 February to 2 October 1927.

Correll and Gosden participated in broadcasts, as their black characters, live from the Kentucky Derby and the Indianapolis 500. Sam 'n' Henry candy bars showed up in corner markets and newsstands. Correll and Gosden recorded Victor phonograph records, which were released in 1926 and 1927. They gave live performances in Port Arthur, Texas,[20] and East Chicago.

Dialect acts popped up on the airwaves. R.R. Thompson, for example, offered Negro stories to listeners on the Fort Worth, Texas, *Star-Telegram's* radio station WBAP in late 1927. Thompson also gave his fractured 20-minute orations over KSD in St. Louis.[21]

But *Sam 'n' Henry* took hold. "More than 10,000 letters have come to 'Sam 'n' Henry' in their year of entertainment," the *Tribune* reported on the show's first anniversary, "and Correll and Gosden, who play the parts of Henry and Sam, respectively, were the only artists selected from the Midwest to entertain at the great radio trades dinner in New York last September. This week, as a special feature of their birthday celebration, the boys will appear at the Chicago theater, offering songs and Sam 'n' Henry dialogue."[22]

Sam 'n' Henry started their own freight hauling company. In "The Boys Move Their First Trunk,"[23] they wrestle a large trunk onto their fragile wagon and deliver it as requested. The recipient thinks someone else has already paid for the service:

> Mr. Allen. Well boys, I heard you open the door and I was talking on the telephone so I just excused myself for a minute to see that everything was all right. You tell my friend Pete that I appreciate this very much and maybe some day I'll be able to do something for him. (Starting back into the house.) Glad you boys came over and don't forget to tell Pete how much I thank him. Now you boys excuse me because I must get back to the telephone. Much obliged to both of you. (Mr. Allen closes door and disappears.)
> Henry. (dumfounded)—Oh—oh
> Sam. (speechless)—Awa—awa—awa.

"Awa—awa—awa"[24] became the first phrase by Correll and Gosden to enter pop culture. Later on radio, Amos said "Aw-wah" and "Hold de phone" and "Ain't dat sumpin'?" and Andy said "I'se regusted," and "Holy mack'rel" and Kingfish said "Buzz me, Miss Blue" and other phrases that also became part of the lexicon of the day.

WGN owned the rights to *Sam 'n' Henry*. With the success of the Victor recordings, Correll and Gosden, after their initial contract ended, had ideas about syndicating the program in what they called a "chainless chain." They wanted to distributed prerecorded shows to a network of radio stations. WGN balked.[25] The creators took their idea to the *Chicago Daily News* and WMAQ. They couldn't take the name with them.

They still hadn't settled on a new name, according to reporter John Crosby in *Collier's*. They'd considered Jim and Charlie, Tom and Harry. They were riding an elevator to the studio for the first broadcast 19 March 1928.

"The elevator man, they found, was a friendly soul who welcomed each of his regular patrons with a wisecrack. On the way up he took on a passenger with the remark: 'Well, well. Famous Amos.' Then, when a carpenter got on, he said, 'Hello, Handy Andy.'

"A few minutes later, Correll and Goden were on the air under the names that have been with them ever since. One year and five months later they were on the full NBC network earning $100,000 a year, the highest price in radio."[26]

The last part is true, at any rate. The elevator ride story is apocryphal, according to

Bart Andrews and Ahrgus Juilliard. The writers say Correll and Gosden came up with the alliterative names Amos, which sounded biblical, and Andy, which sounded lazy.[27] Elizabeth MacLeod offers a third alternate story, that Gosden found the names in the back of a dictionary.[28]

Correll and Gosden weren't too worried about the changeover. "Although the boys had spent two years building up the characters of Sam and Henry, they cheerfully gave them up and started anew under new names, with a new story, and with an extended radio audience. The success which immediately followed the introduction of 'Amos 'n' Andy' to the radio public justified their confidence in their project," the creators wrote in *All About Amos 'n' Andy*.[29]

Amos Jones and Andrew Brown were farm hands from Atlanta, rather than Birmingham, but otherwise little changed from Sam 'n' Henry. Arriving in Chicago, they briefly take laborer jobs until Andy is inspired to buy a dilapidated automobile for $75, and starts a cab service:

> Andy. Amos, we is now in de taxicab bizness. De Fresh Air Taxicab Company. I don't know if we ought to git incorpulated today or wait a few days.
> Amos. Will it help us any if we git dat done to us?
> Andy. Well, if we incor-pulates, we is always got de corpulation back of us.
> Amos. Whut you mean, we got de corpulation back of us?
> Andy. Well, yere's de automobile.
> Amos. Yeah, here's de automobile—I 'grees wid you dere—we got dat a'right.
> Andy. Now, de nex' thing we is goin' in de taxicab business. 'Spose we has a accident. If we is incorpulated we don't have to worry—let de corpulation worry. Dat's de 'vantage o' doin' dat.
> Amos. Dat's a good idea a'right. I gues we ought to git incor-pulated.[30]

Correll and Gosden expanded the shows's cast. They introduced the Kingfish on 25 May 1928, just as he has lost $800 on a bad investment tip, and in fractured fashion, advises Amos and Andy on the machinations of the stock exchange:

> Kingfish. Well, if you buy a stock fo' so much money, de fust thing you know it gits cheaper, den you lose.
> Andy. Well, whut makes de stock go up?
> Kingfish. Well, some o' dese big mens down on Wall Street git in a pool, an' when dey git behind de stocks, dey say dat's whut make it go up.

As the country slid into the Great Depression, the show reverberated with radio listeners, according to Andrews and Juilliard: "The nation could empathize with the jobless, scheming, money-hungry, victimized Harlem blacks that the show satirized.... For fifteen minutes every evening, down-and-out America forgot its own troubles by identifying with the adventures and the troubles of Amos and Andy and Kingfish and lawyer Calhoun and Lightnin' and Madam Queen, many of whom were, like their listeners, member of the vast unemployed or underemployed."[31]

Amos 'n' Andy was syndicated coast to coast through WMAQ, a CBS affiliate, but the national network was not interested in picking up the show. NBC Blue Network was, with Pepsodent as sponsor, and the transition took place on 19 August 1929. Correll and Gosden and announcer Bill Hay moved to NBC, and *Amos 'n' Andy* moved to Harlem. They had a new theme song, "The Perfect Song."

Listeners liked it.

Amos 'n' Andy hadn't been heard in New York City before, and the performers' perfunctory back story for a new audience—they concentrated in establishing their characters, rather than their purpose—brought a withering criticism from a reviewer in the New York *Sun*. The actor/writers quickly made up for the deficit the second night. The show broadcast at 11 p.m. (still 10 p.m. Chicago time, for that audience). New York listeners regardless soon began to pay attention. The show soon moved to 7 p.m. in New York, Correll and Gosden handling the time zone issue by making two nightly broadcasts, a policy that lasted until 1943, when the 15-minute shows ended.

The program's ratings rocketed.

Correll and Gosden reinforced their program's appeal with books (*All About Amos 'n' Andy and Their Creators Correll & Gosden* in 1929 and *Here They Are, Amos 'n' Andy* in 1931) and merchandising material. Charles Mueller drew an *Amos 'n' Andy* newspaper comic strip that was syndicated by the *Chicago Daily News* from 19 March 1928 to 30 September 1929.[32]

"Correll and Gosden proved to be the first great radio actors, perfecting a subdued, naturalistic approach to microphone acting that differed sharply from the broad manner that stage actors brought to the air—and their continued insistence on complete privacy while creating their scripts and broadcasting their episodes contributed to this manner of performance," according to *The Original Amos 'n' Andy*.[33]

A larger cast of characters provided new plot opportunities. Ruby Taylor became Amos's love interest, and Madam Queen became Andy's dilemma. The annual Christmas program in which Amos relates the Bible story to his daughter Arbadella became a classic and was rebroadcast each year.

Some new players on the show found it a challenge to master the dialect. As radio historians J. Fred MacDonald in *Don't Touch That Dial* and Andrews and Juilliard describe in *Holy Mackerel*, the lingo owed as much to minstrel tradition as it did to southern. Lillian Randolph had to study with a vocal coach before she could handle the role of Madame Queen to suit the director. "Johnny Lee said that he 'had to learn to talk as white people believed Negroes talked.'"[34]

The two men joined the Mystic Knights of the Sea lodge, over which George Stevens, the manipulative Kingfish, presided, often bilking money from Andy, but at the same time getting his comeuppance form his shrill wife Sapphire. The blustering Kingfish, in fact, nearly nudged Amos out of the stories, his personality was so strong.

Here's a 1934 exchange between Kingfish and Lightnin'. The former is trying to collect dues from the latter:

> Lightnin'. Well I just ain't got it. If yo' would lend me some money, I would pay the lodge.
> Kingfish. Whut yo' mean, *me* lend yo' some money? I is flat as a pancake. I got about fifteen cents, an' I gotta git a dollar by tonight somewhere. We goin' have comp'ny fo' supper. De butcher done tighten up on me. I gotta git a couple o' po'k chops in dat house some way. Yo' can't ast de people comin' to supper to eat gravy *all* de time.
> Lightnin'. Yessah.
> Kingfish. Money is bad wid me. Just talked to my wife—she's puttin' de pressure on *me*.
> Lightnin'. Yesah, it sho is a mess all right. I wonder where all de money is now?
> Kingfish. I seed a banker de other day. He had a funny look on his face.
> Lightnin'. It done gone somewhere.[35]

"It has been estimated that at its peak the program had more than forty million listeners," according to Jack Gaver and Dave Stanley. Other programs since have had fanatical fans, but none has had such rabid listeners as 'Amos 'n' Andy.' People just had to be at their radios when 7 p.m. arrived, come hell or high water."[36]

The Oregonian, among other newspapers, published plot summaries to keep listener interest alive. For example, this is "Brother Crawford Objects to Kinfolk's Mooching; Andy Sidesteps Talking 'Cold Turkey' to Uncle Hastings":

> Andy was thinking seriously of cutting more slits in his shoes during last night's broadcast of Amos 'n' Andy over KGW, radio service of *The Oregonian*. While he was thus engaged Brother Crawford came in to complain to Andy about the kinfolk eating at the lunch room and then charging the bill, which was $4.50, to Andy. Brother Crawford claimed that there was a "disconnection" in Andy's head.
>
> When the telephone rang, Andy "resguised" his voice, but it was Uncle Hastings calling to complain about the treatment that he received at the lunchroom. Brother Crawford was unable to get Andy to talk "cold turkey" to Uncle Hastings, so he took the telephone from Andy and told Uncle Hastings himself. Uncle Hastings immediately insulted him and his wife. This made Brother Crawford very mad.
>
> Andy finally consented to go and see Uncle Hastings, but asked for the key to the taxi. He told Amos that he would see Uncle Hastings next week and that he was going down to Central Park to look at the tigers, as any thing would look pleasant after seeing brother Crawford's face when he was mad.[37]

The history of the radio program, the ill-fated motion picture that brought Correll and Gosden's blackface appearance to an end and the popular television show that had an all-black cast, are well told elsewhere. It's time to look at the controversy.

The dialect used on the radio broadcasts was an issue. G.F. Guthrie, manager of Radio Corporation of America, with a voice of authority in 1929 said, "Amos 'n' Andy have got this dialect down fine. A common mistake is for white comedians imitating the colored people to use the expression 'you-all' when referring to only one person. When a colored person says 'yo-all,' he means the whole family. I was on a street in Atlanta when a beggar said to me, 'Won't you-all give me a nickel?' I was all alone at the time and knew instantly that the man was a northerner. When a colored person says 'you' he pronounces it exactly as we do, but when he uses 'your' he says 'yo.'"[38]

"Episodes flow from natural situations and are lived rather than acted," the *Dallas Morning News* asserted. "They are not dialogue or jokes in the vaudeville sense, for the humor is derived largely from the logical circumstance and reactions in character."[39]

None of these writers has a clue that if the show were written by blacks, its humor would be much different, biting in a different way, reflecting an internalized repression.

Bishop W.J. Walls of the African Methodist Episcopal Zion Church in 1930, on the other hand, charged Amos and Andy were strictly lower-class characterizations and the program riddled with "crude, repetitious, and moronic dialog."[40]

Robert Lee Vann, publisher of the black newspaper the *Pittsburgh Courier*, mounted a major anti–A 'n' A crusade the next year and claimed 675,000 signatures on a petition to have the show taken off the air.

At the same time, another black newspaper, the *Detroit Defender*, ran stories about Correll and Gosden attending a picnic arranged by the publication, introducing them to the crowd with "Perfect Song."[41]

Little remembered today are the NBC broadcasts featuring native Georgians Pick Malone and Pat Padgett, white vaudeville comics in blackface (figuratively, since it was radio) on the minstrel-style variety show *Pick and Pat* from 1934 to 1935, with the characters finding new homes on different network variety shows, indicative of its dying audience.

Decades later, Michele Hilmes objected that the characters in *Amos 'n' Andy* were depicted living in a separate, nonwhite universe. "Usually, supporting characters do not speak in dialect; their race is rarely identified, leaving open the possibility that blacks and whites could interact far more freely and equally than in fact was the case at the time. Certainly the black characters never seem to encounter any injustice or even unfriendliness; indeed, reference to whites or to the system of racial segregation is almost never made," she wrote.[42]

The NAACP didn't take part in Vann's protest, but in 1951, with the advent of the television show, it listed reasons the show should be removed from broadcast lineups: "It tends to strengthen the conclusion among uninformed and prejudiced people that Negroes are inferior, lazy, dumb and dishonest; every character in this one and only TV show with an all Negro cast is either a clown or a crook; Negro doctors are shown as quacks and thieves; Negro lawyers are shown as slippery cowards, ignorant of their profession and without ethics. Negro women are shown as cackling, screaming shrews, in big-mouthed close-ups, using street slang, just short of vulgarity; all Negroes are shown as dodging work of any kind; millions of white Americans see this Amos 'n' Andy picture of Negroes and think the entire race is the same."[43]

CBS ended the series in 1953 after 78 episodes.[44]

Historian MacLeod acknowledged Gosden made considerable use of malapropism and hypercorrection in his characters' dialog, not just to make fun, but to delineate character. She asserted that the later years of the radio show, when writing was out of Correll and Gosden's hands, and the years of the television show removed any psychological depth of character and played the broadest of humorous strokes.

Correll and Gosden didn't like the controversy over their creation. Correll said in 1961, "As Amos and Andy, Freeman and I never did anything to demean Negroes—we never typed them. But a national sponsor would be a fool to risk putting it on a network today. Things have changed too much."[45]

CBS continued to circulate the show in repeats.[46] Black audiences watched the programs, even as they went into their thirteenth year of repeats in Chicago and elsewhere. The Rev. Jesse Jackson said, "I remember growing up as a kid watching Stepin Fetchit, and watching 'Amos 'n' Andy' with Tim Moore.[47] You know, black people had enough sense to appreciate them as funny people playing out roles. Their [opportunities] were so limited we laughed at them and laughed at their roles."[48]

In 1966, however, under continued fire, CBS withdrew the television shows permanently.

Henry Lewis Gates, Jr. recalled, "Everybody loved 'Amos and Andy.' The day they took 'Amos and Andy' off the air was one of the saddest days in Piedmont. As far as we were concerned, the foibles of Kingfish or Calhoun were the foibles of individuals who happened to be funny."[49]

Correll and Gosden were inducted into the National Association of Broadcasters Hall of Fame in 1962. They were given a star on the Hollywood Walk of Fame in 1969.

Correll, a California resident, died in Chicago in 1972, following a heart attack.

Gosden, also a California resident, died in Los Angeles in 1982 of congestive heart failure.

Efforts of a New York producer, Stephen M. Silverman, to bring Amos 'n' Andy back as a Broadway musical ended up in court, with CBS showing it had purchased all rights to the property from Correll and Gosden in 1948. Copyrights of the original radio scripts had never been renewed, however, and were in public domain. But any copies of the television series were considered bootleg. Judge Gerard L. Goettel, District Court for the Southern District of New York, in 1989 ruled that post–1948 radio scripts and the television shows were properly renewed and belonged to CBS and a stage show potentially could infringe on CBS's rights. By then, Silverman had exhausted his financial resources.

Carl Clay and his Black Spectrum Theater Company in New York City in 2006 framed an off–Broadway play, *Kingfish, Amos and Andy*, around a young researcher probing a television archive. The show drew rave reviews and ran for nearly six months.

One of the actors, Gil T., told *New York Daily News* columnist Denis Hamill, "The TV show was excellent. But it got a bum rap because the radio show and vaudeville was done by whites. Sometimes in blackface. But when it was cast as a TV sitcom with an all-black cast and set in Harlem, it was brilliant. It wasn't about welfare families, dope pushers or gangbangers. It was about working- and middle-class black people in New York. One character was a lawyer, another owned a cab company, a teacher, a cop. Everybody worked, and everybody struggled."[50]

The debate continues.

Charles Correll and Freeman F. Gosden Notes

1. *American Nightmare: The History of Jim Crow*, 204.
2. *Sam 'n Henry*, Chapter 13.
3. *Radio Comedy*, 33.
4. Ibid., 32.
5. "Fame of Radio's Durable Pair Born at W-G-N," B1.
6. WGN stood for World's Greatest Newspaper, aka *The Chicago Tribune*.
7. A theatrical agency run by A.J. and Barney Balaban and Sam and Morris Katz, organized in 1925 in Chicago.
8. According to Arthur Frank Wertheim, *Radio Comedy*, 23, they received $250 a week.
9. "Fame of Radio's Durable Pair Born at W-G-N," B1.
10. Ibid.
11. *Radio Comedy*, 18–32.
12. Interview with Jerry Lazarus, *Richmond Times-Dispatch*, 20 August 1981, quoted in Elizabeth McLeod, *The Original Amos 'n' Andy*, 26.
13. "Strand Books Sam and Henry," *Port Arthur News*, 24 February 1928, 12, and other sources.
14. *Brother Gos and Brother Charlie: The Story of Amos 'n' Andy*, 3.
15. *The Original Amos 'n' Andy*, 30.
16. "What Broadcasters Are Doing," *Kokomo (Ind.) Tribune*, 13 February 1926, 7, also *Bluefield (W.Va.) Daily Telegraph*, 14 February 1926, 4.
17. "Sam Almost Eats," *Chicago Tribune*, 6 February 1927, F1. This is from the radio show that aired 27 May 1926. In the Victor recording, the exchange was shortened and Henry says, "Not me, Mistah. See me some other time."
18. *The Adventures of Amos 'n' Andy*, 56.
19. The newspaper "stories" merged more than one script.
20. "Strand Books Sam and Henry," *Port Arthur (Texas) News*, 24 February 1928, 12.

21. "Negro dialect stories, jokes and finally a typical negro sermon was given form by the Arkansas visitor in an inimitable fashion that proved to be exceedingly entertaining and a large number of acknowledgments resulted from the concert," according to "Negro Dialect Stories Please Radio Listeners," *Fort Worth Star-Telegram*, 28 December 1927, 4. Thompson was president of Crescent College for Girls at Eureka Springs, Arkansas.
22. "Sam 'n' Henry to Celebrate First Anniversary," 9 January 1927, D8.
23. *Chicago Tribune*, 29 May 1927, F3.
24. Amos Jones later used the same phrase of exasperation.
25. WGN employed other performers to continue *Sam 'n' Henry* as a musical variety show until 14 July 1928. Elizabeth McLeod identified them as Henry Moeller and Hal Gilles, "Some History of Amos 'n' Andy," Part 2.
26. "Amos 'n' Andy—Ain't Dat Sumpin'," 32.
27. *Holy Mackerel*, 15–16.
28. *The Original Amos 'n' Andy*, 38.
29. Page 40.
30. *Here They Are: Amos 'n' Andy*, 154–155.
31. *Holy Mackerel*, 23.
32. Allan Holtz, *American Newspaper Comics*, 54.
33. Page 57.
34. *Holy Mackerel*, 35. Gosden, according to Edward T. Clayton writing in *Ebony*, October 1961, 70, was "asked not to come on the [television] set after a run-in with Spencer Williams and his characterization of Andy. 'We couldn't get together on this use of dialect,' Williams explained. 'He wanted me to say "dis here and dat dere" and I just wasn't going to do it.'"
35. Reprinted in *Liberty*, 3 May 1941, 29–31, and *There's Laughter in the Air*, 143.
36. *There's Laughter in the Air*, 141.
37. *The Orgonian*, 21 August 1931, 13.
38. "Poor Negro Dialects on Air," *Springfield Republican*, 24 November 1929, 38.
39. "Much Humor and Human Nature in Way Amos 'n' Andy Develop their Celebrated Radio Broadcast Act," 29 September 1929, 7.
40. "What About Amos 'n' Andy? *Abbott's Monthly*, December 1930, 38–40.
41. "35,000 Cheer Amos 'n' Andy at Bud's Picnic," 22 August 1931, 16.
42. "Invisible Men: Amos 'n' Andy and the Roots of Broadcast Discourse," *Studies in Critical Mass Communication*, December 1993.
43. "Why the Amos 'n' Andy TV Show Should Be Taken Off the Air," *NAACP Bulletin*, 15 August 1951.
44. Clayton in an *Ebony* article in 1961 (page 66) made a lot of the fact the leading actors in the television series had a hard time finding new roles while the series was running, and after it ended. For "Spencer Williams, who played Andy, and Alvin Childress, who played Amos, it brought mostly grief. Neither has received a dime from the series in the seven years since the last film was shot in November 1954, and work has been hard to come by."
45. Charles Denton, "Experience Talks," *Los Angeles Herald Examiner TV Weekly*, 15 October 1961.
46. "Amos 'n' Andy Kept Despite Protest," *Dallas Morning News*, 15 December 1962, 16.
47. Moore played Kingfish on the television series.
48. As quoted in Andrews and Juilliard, *Holy Mackerel*, 113–114.
49. From his memoir *Colored People*, as quoted in *Black, White, and in Color* by Sasha Torres.
50. "'Amos 'n' Andy' Show for Laughs," 19 February 2006.

Charles Correll and Freeman F. Gosden Selected Bibliography and Sources

SAM 'N' HENRY SCRIPTS

"Sam Almost Eats" (*Chicago Tribune*, 6 February 1927)
"A Toothache" (*Chicago Tribune*, 13 February 1927)
"[Dentist]" (*Chicago Tribune*, 20 February 1927)
"[Pay Day]" (*Chicago Tribune*, 27 February 1927)

"A Letter to Liza" (*Chicago Tribune*, 6 March 1927)
"A Long Distance Call" (*Chicago Tribune*, 13 March 1927)
"[Trouble Starting]" (*Chicago Tribune*, 20 March 1927)
"The Boys Face a Mean Judge" (*Chicago Tribune*, 27 March 1927)
"[Sam's Hand Hurts]" (*Chicago Tribune*, 3 April 1927)
"Poolroom Pete Fixes to Sell 'Em a Hoss" (*Chicago Tribune*, 10 April 1927)
"President Henry Is Sho a Hard Working Man!" (*Chicago Tribune*, 17 April 1927)
"It Seems to Be a Horse on the Two Boys" (*Chicago Tribune*, 24 April 1927)
"Henry Makes Sam Head of de Advertisin' Department" (*Chicago Tribune*, 1 May 1927)
"[Lost Key]" (*Chicago Tribune*, 8 May 1927)
"The Sad Morning After the Glad Night Before!" (*Chicago Tribune*, 15 May 1927)
"The Wagon They Bought Just Lies Down and Dies" (*Chicago Tribune*, 22 May 1927)
"The Boys Move Their First Trunk and Sam Says 'Awa—Awa'" (*Chicago Tribune*, 29 May 1927)
"[No Pay]" (*Chicago Tribune*, 5 June 1927)
"The Boys Are Broke and Things Look Mighty, Mighty Dark" (*Chicago Tribune*, 12 June 1927)
"There's Money in the Treasury, the Treasurer Eats!" (*Chicago Tribune*, 19 June 1927)
"President Henry Sells Sam Fifteen Thousand Shares of Stock!" (*Chicago Tribune*, 26 June 1927)
"Sam Prepares for His Debut as an Orator" (*Chicago Tribune*, 3 July 1927)
"Sam Delivers His Oration with Henry's Help" (*Chicago Tribune*, 10 July 1927)
"Sam Writes His Honey Bunny—With Love from Her Rival" (*Chicago Tribune*, 17 July 1927)
"The Boys Indulge in Frenzied Finance; Henry on Short End" (*Chicago Tribune*, 24 July 1927)
"Hoodwinked? They Know It After One Look Under Hood" (*Chicago Tribune*, 31 July 1927)
"The Boys Find Plenty of Attractions on the Beach" (*Chicago Tribune*, 7 August 1927)
"Sam Phones His Sweetie, Liza, in Birmingham" (*Chicago Tribune*, 14 August 1927)
"The Secketary's Trick Money Box" (*Chicago Tribune*, 21 August 1927)
"Henry Dictates; Sam Draws the Pictures" (*Chicago Tribune*, 28 August 1927)
"The Boys Try to Divide the Day's Profits" (*Chicago Tribune*, 4 September 1927)
"Sam May Get into the Race for Cal's Job" (*Chicago Tribune*, 11 September 1927)
"Sam Buys a Silk Hat for Inauguration" (*Chicago Tribune*, 18 September 1927)
"Our Heroes Wise Themselves Up on the Lodge Secrets" (*Chicago Tribune*, 25 September 1927)
"Gram'pa and Henry Get into the Pictures" (*Chicago Tribune*, 2 October 1927)

Amos 'n' Andy Stories

"[Amos 'n' Andy free a murder suspect]" (*Startling Detective Adventure*, May 1931)
"Shake Well Before Using" (*Liberty*, 3 May 1941) script

Sam 'n' Henry Radio

Sam 'n' Henry, 12 January 1926 to 18 December 1927 (WGN, 10-minute show, six nights a week, 586 episodes) (Continued after a two-week hiatus as a musical variety program with other performers until 14 July 1928, 30-minute show)

Amos 'n' Andy Radio

Amos 'n' Andy, 19 March 1928 to 16 August 1929 (WMAQ, 15-minute show, five nights)
Amos 'n' Andy, 19 August 1929 to 13 July 1934; 17 September 1934 to 31 December 1937 (NBC Blue, 15-minute show, six nights until 1932, then five nights)
Amos 'n' Andy, 3 January 1938 to 31 March 1939 (NBC Red, 15-minute, five nights)
Amos 'n' Andy, 3 April 1939 to 19 February 1943 (CBS, 15-minute, five nights)
Amos 'n' Andy, 8 October 1943 to 16 June 1944; 22 September 1944 to 1 June 1945 (CBS, 15-minute, Friday) (4,091 15-minute shows since 1928)
Amos 'n' Andy, 2 October 1945 to 28 May 1946; 1 October 1946 to 27 May 1947; 30 September 1947 to 25 May 1948 (NBC, 30-minute, Tuesday)
The Amos 'n' Andy Show, 10 October 1948 to 8 May 1949 (CBS, 30-minute, Sunday)
The Amos 'n' Andy Show, 9 October 1949 to 21 May 1950; 24 September 1950–10 June 1951; 30 September 1951 to 24 May 1952; 29 September 1952 to 24 May 1953; 27 September 1953 to 23 May 1954 (CBS, 30-minute, Sunday)

The Amos 'n' Andy Show, 26 September 1954 to 22 May 1955 (CBS, 30-minute, Sunday, 426 shows)
Amos 'n' Andy Music Hall, 13 September 1955 to 25 November 1960 (CBS, 30-minute, five nights)

PUBLICATIONS (REPRINTING SCRIPTS)

Sam and Henry (1926) retitled *Sam and Henry: Original Story of Amos 'n' Andy* (1930) illustrated by Samuel Jay Smith
All About Amos 'n' Andy and Their Creators Correll & Gosden (1929) illustrated with photographs
Here They Are, Amos 'n' Andy (1931) illustrated by Margery Stocking
An Amos 'n' Andy Radio Episode: Amos' Wedding (NBC, 1935) Pepsodent promotion
Amos and Andy 'Eagle's-Eye View of Weber City' Map delineated by Andrew H. Brown and Amos Jones Assistant Map Maker (1935) Pepsodent promotion
There's Laughter in the Air! Radio's Top Comedians and Their Best Shows (1945) Jack Gaver and Dave Stanley, eds., script

AMOS 'N' ANDY NEWSPAPER COMIC STRIP

Amos 'n' Andy (Chicago Daily News Syndicate, 19 March 1928 to 30 September 1929) Charley Mueller artist
Amos and Andy, four-page, promotional four-color comic book (ca. 1949)

SAM 'N' HENRY VICTOR TALKING RECORDS

Sam Phoning His Sweetheart Liza
Sam & Henry at the Dentist
Sam's Speech at the Colored Lodge
Sam & Henry at the Fortune Teller's
Sam & Henry: Rolling the Bones
Sam & Henry Buying Insurance
Sam's Big Night
The Morning After

AMOS 'N' ANDY SHEET MUSIC

The Perfect Song, Musical Theme of The Pepsodent Hour featuring Amos 'n' Andy (1929)
Three Little Words Featured in Check and Double Check with Amos 'n' Andy (1930)
Amos 'n' Andy with Ukulele Arrangement (1930)

AMOS 'N' ANDY FILMS

Check and Double Check (1930)
The Rasslin' Match (1934) animated short
The Lion Tamer (1934) animated short (issued as a Melton Mascot 8mm film strip)
Big Broadcast of 1936 (1936)

AMOS 'N' ANDY TELEVISION

The Amos 'n' Andy Show (1951 to 1953) 78 episodes, withdrawn from syndication in 1966

AMOS 'N' ANDY PLAY

Kingfish, Amos and Andy (2006) written by Carl Clay

SOURCES

"America Mimics Amos and Andy," Augusta (Ga.) *Chronicle*, 26 October 1930.
Amos 'n' Andy: Anatomy of a Controversy, television documentary (M.R. Avery Productions, 1983) with George Kirby, Stanley Sheff, dir.
"Amos 'n' Andy and Their Friends," *Radio Digest*, May 1930.
"Amos 'n' Andy Display Speed in Rich Dialect,' *Seattle Daily Times*, 4 November 1930.
"Amos 'n' Andy Explained," *Popular Science Monthly*, June 1930.
"Amos 'n' Andy in Harlem," *Radio Digest*, June 1930.
"Amos 'n' Andy Kept Despite Protest," *Dallas Morning News*, 15 December 1962.
"Amos 'n' Andy Recording Negro Dialect," *Los Angeles Tribune*, 27 December 1943.

"Amos 'n' Andy: Past as Prologue," Jim Crow Museum of Racist Memorabilia. file:///Users/bernard drew/Desktop/Question%20of%20the%20Month.webarchive (viewed 17 October 2012).
"Amos 'n' Andy Renew Contract with NBC Net," *Dallas Morning News*, 31 July 1930.
"Amos 'n' Andy Strut Stuff on Talkie Screen," *Chicago Daily Tribune*, 27 October 1930.
"Amos 'n' Andy: The Air's First Comic Strip," *Literary Digest*, 19 April 1930.
"Amos 'n' Andy Will Be Heard on NBC System," *Dallas Morning News*, 26 July 1929.
"Amos, Otherwise Gosden, Come by Accent Naturally for Popular Black-Face Series Now on NBC," *Dallas Morning News*, 13 October 1929.
Andrews, Bart, and Ahrgus Juilliard. *Holy Mackerel: The Amos 'n' Andy Story*. New York: E.P. Dutton, 1996.
"Brother Crawford Objects to Kinfolk's Mooching," *Oregonian*, 21 August 1931.
Clarke, A. Wellington. "If Amos and Andy Were Negroes: What Numerous Negroes in Various Walks of Life Think of the Boys," *Radio Digest*, August 1930.
Clayton, Edward T. "The Tragedy of Amos 'n' Andy," *Ebony*, October 1961.
Crowby, John. "Amos 'n' Andy—Ain't Dat Sumpin,'" *Collier's*, 16 October 1948.
Denton, Charles. "Experience Talks," *Los Angeles Herald Examiner TV Weekly*, 15 October 1961.
Ellett, Ryan. "Amos 'n' Andy: The Chicago Defender's Response." http://otrr.org/FILES/Articles/Ryan_Ellett_Articles/Amos%20And%20Andy%20-%20The%20Chicago%20Defender's%20Final%20Response.pdf (viewed 12 October 2012).
Ely, Melvin Patrick. *The Adventures of Amos 'n' Andy: A Social History of an American Phenomenon*. New York: Free Press, 1991.
Eskew, Garnett L. "Judith Waller—Manager, Station WMAQ, Chicago, and Former Boss of Amos and Andy—Tells of Pioneering Days in the Broadcast Game," *Radio Digest*, August 1930.
Frazier, George. "Amos & Andy: Two Angels in Blackface," *Coronet*, March 1948.
Hamill, Denis. "'Amos & Andy' Show for Laughs," New York Daily News, 19 February 2006. http://articles.nydailynews.com/2006-02-19/local/18330660_1_amos-cosby-show-gil (viewed 19 October 2012).
Hampton, Wilborn. "Amos, Andy and Company Are Seen Through Time's Lens," *New York Times*, 15 March 2006.
"Here Are Your Old Time Favorites," advertisement (Victor Records), Grimes Music Co., *Charleston (W.Va.) Gazette*, 19 January 1928, 17.
Holtz, Allan. *American Newspaper Comics: An Encyclopedic Reference Guide*. Ann Arbor: University of Michigan Press, 2012.
"Invisible Men: Amos 'n' Andy and the Roots of Broadcast Discourse," *Studies in Critical Mass Communication*, December 1993.
Johnson, Peter H., Jr. "Brother Gos and Brother Charlie: The Story of Amos 'n' Andy." www.knightstemplar.org/articles/0607/amosandy.pdf (viewed 12 October 2012).
"Kingfish Loses His Money; Also His Watch," *Oregonian*, 16 October 1930.
Lazarus, Jerry. Freeman Gosden interview, *Richmond Times-Dispatch*, 20 August 1981.
Margolick, David. "Rights Tiff Stalls Amos 'n' Andy Musical Revival," *New York Times*, 10 September 1985.
McLeod, Elizabeth. "Amos 'n' Andy—In Person," http://www.midcoast.com/~lizmcl/aa.html (viewed 18 October 2012).
_____. *The Original Amos 'n' Andy: Freeman Gosden, Charles Correll and the 1928–1943 Radio Serial*. Jefferson, N.C.: McFarland, 2005.
_____. Some History of Amos 'n' Andy, part 1, http://jeff560.tripod.com/amos.html, and Part 2, http://jeff560.tripod.com/amos2.html (viewed 17 September 2012).
"Much Humor and Human Nature in Way Amos 'n' Andy Develop Their Celebrated Radio Broadcast Act," *Dallas Morning News*, 29 September 1929.
"Must Caricature Go?" *Dallas Morning News*, 25 March 1932.
"Negro Dialect Stories Please Radio Listeners," *Fort Worth Star-Telegram*, 28 December 1927.
Nisbet, Fairfax. "Arbitrator, Spare Those Dialecticians," *Dallas Morning News*, 6 April 1947.
Packard, Jerrold M. *American Nightmare: The History of Jim Crow*. New York: St. Martin's Griffin, 2002.
"Poor Negro Dialects on Air," *Springfield Republican*, 24 November 1929.
Sam 'n' Henry radio show, eight segments. http://archive.org/details/SamnHenryakaAmosAndy (heard 17 October 2012).

"Sam 'n' Henry to Celebrate First Anniversary; Comical Colored Boys W-G-N Feature," *Chicago Tribune*, 9 January 1927.
Silverman v. CBS Inc. 870 F.2d 40, United States Court of Appeals, Second Circuit, 6 February 1989.
"Story of Creation in Negro Folk Lore," *Springfield Republican*, 12 June 1930.
"Strand Books Sam and Henry," Port Arthur (Texas) *News*, 24 February 1928.
"35,000 Cheer Amos 'n' Andy at Bud's Picnic," *Detroit Defender*, 22 August 1931.
Torres, Sasha. *Black, White, and in Color: Television and Black Civil Rights*. Princeton, N.J.: Princeton University Press, 2003.
"Twelve Thousand and Some Nights," *TV Radio Mirror*, May 1958.
Victor Discography for Sam 'n' Henry. Good Old Days Ol' Time Radio http://home.hiwaay.net/~ajohns/retro/Sam&Henry.htm (viewed 17 October 2012).
Walls, W.J. "What About Amos 'n' Andy?" *Abbott's Monthly*, December 1930.
Watkins, Mel. "What Was It About 'Amos 'n' Andy'?" *New York Times*, 7 July 1991.
Wertheim, Arthur Frank. *Radio Comedy*. New York: Oxford University Press, 1979.
"What Broadcasters Are Doing," *Bluefield (W.Va.) Daily Telegraph*, 14 February 1926.
"What Broadcasters Are Doing," *Kokomo (Ind.) Tribune*, 13 February 1926.
"Why the Amos 'n' Andy TV Show Should Be Taken Off the Air," *NAACP Bulletin*, 15 August 1951.
Wolters, Larry. "Fame of Radio's Durable Pair Born at W-G-N," *Chicago Tribune*, 15 November 1952.

Paul F. Ernst
(1899–1985)
Joshua and Rosabel Newton

"Josh and Rosabel Newton are articulate, intelligent and brave—but use the fact that they are black to play off the racism of the time and get the bad guys to consistently underestimate them."

—Tim DeForest[1]

Pulp fiction writers generally shied from depicting individuals of any ethnicity other than white, exceptions being sinister "Orientals" or war-whooping Native Americans. It was a rarity, then, that in the posse of crime-fighting hero Richard Benson, alias the Avenger, there appeared two positively depicted, educated and married blacks.

Author Paul Frederick Ernst (1899–1985), known for his quirky heroes, wrote confession stories for the *Los Angeles Times* and *Young's Realistic Stories Magazine* in the late 1920s. He distinguished himself as a science fiction writer. Editor Farnsworth Wright at *Weird Tales* took his stories including the 1930 serial "The Black Monarch" and the 1935 serial "Rulers of the Future."

He wrote several Dr. Satan stories for *Weird Tales*, incorporating elements of black magic and the supernatural. He wrote for *Ghost Stories* and *Oriental Stories, Thrilling Detective and Popular Detective* and *Dime Mystery Magazine, Amazing Stories* and *Astounding Stories, Strange Tales of Mystery and Terror* and more.

"When *Strange Detective Mysteries* was launched in the fall of 1937...," wrote pulp historian Will Murray, "it was made to order for Paul Ernst. His bizarre hero Seekay appeared in the first two issues, and promised to be a regular or semi-regular feature."[2]

Seekay had a disfigured face and wore a celluloid mask prosthetic. He may have been a veteran of World War I; the author never specified. Nor are we sure Seekay was his name. Ernst came up with the character for Popular Publications as a way to distinguish himself in a crowded field. *Strange Detective Mysteries* lasted only two issues. The publishing house had trouble securing writers who could turn out adequate weird menace prose. After a short run of *Captain Satan*, Popular put on the schedule a new magazine called *Detective Tales*, and ran three inventoried Ernst stories. By then Ernst was under contract to write a new series for Street & Smith.

Ernst brought characteristics of his earlier broken hero to Richard Benson.

The pulps filled a niche below the slick magazines, just above the comic books, in the 1920s to 1940s. Publishers churned out the cheap-paper periodicals by the dozens. Writers came and went. The best writers found regular work at Street & Smith, Popular, Munsey's or one of the other larger houses. Some, such as Ray Bradbury and Max Brand, broke out to broader fame. Some writers were busy for a while, then disappeared.

"I wrote four days a week, 5,000 words a day, for fifty-two weeks a year—a million words a year, from 1934 to 1940," Ernst told historian Robert Kenneth Jones. "I worked from nine in the morning until one thirty. I learned to do it right the first draft. It was letter perfect. I got an idea, sat down at the typewriter, numbered page one, and proceeded from there. I sold ninety percent of my material."[3]

Living in Bucks County, Pennsylvania, Ernst traveled one day a week to Street & Smith's offices in New York City to consult with editor John Nanovic. Nanovic asked Ernst to take on a new heroic character series. The Avenger, a character brainstormed by Lester Dent (who as Kenneth Robeson wrote Doc Savage adventures) and Walter Gibson (who as Maxwell Grant was responsible for the Shadow's Tales). Ernst was reluctant—until Nanovic mentioned a dollar amount.

"Justice Inc." appeared in the September 1939 issue of the *Avenger* magazine. The hero is Richard Benson. A villain kills his wife and daughter. Benson suffers an enormous shock. His facial muscles are paralyzed, to the extent that he can mold his face as if it were clay. That is handy for disguise. Benson recruits two assistants, Mac and Smitty, and puts together the crime-fighting organization he calls Justice Inc. Nellie Gray joins the team in the second story, "The Yellow Hoard." And in the third, the Avenger recruits the Newtons, Joshua and Rosabel—a black couple.[4]

The Newtons have been working undercover as servants to inventors Max and Robert Gant. When the Gants are ruthlessly murdered, the Avenger investigates, and interviews Newton, nicknamed "Sleepy" for his lazy demeanor, and Newton's wife, Rosabel, "the pretty Negress." He soon sees beyond their façade. Both are college educated—honor graduates of Tuskeegee Institute—intelligent and quick-thinking:

"'They-all busted up the lab'tory somethin' terrible,' said Josh to the man with the awesome eyes.
"The eyes turned on him in all their clarity, and the colored man had the swift feeling that they were going clear through him.
"'You don't have to talk that way,' the man said to Josh. 'You're very well educated.'
"I'se talkin' nachral—'
"The little gold key I see between the third and fourth buttons of your jacket tells a different story.'
"Josh hurriedly shoved the mentioned article back under his house coat. Then he relaxed.
"'Very well, sir. These murderers, I'm afraid, have completely wrecked the laboratory.'"

The Newtons would appear off and on in the next twenty-one books Ernst wrote for the series. Time did not come to a standstill with progressive Ernst's black characters. But maybe a few minutes were gained for parity.

Ernst gradually backed off writing for the pulps,[5] shifting to the slick-paper *Redbook*,[6] *Saturday Evening Post*[7] and *Good Housekeeping*.[8]

He died in Florida in 1985.

Paul F. Ernst Notes

1. "Devil's Horns," Comics, old time radio and other cool stuff.
2. *The Casebook of Seekay and Other Prototypes of the Avenger*.
3. *The Shudder Pulps*, 221.
4. Black action heroes are scarce. British penny dreadful author S. Clarke Hook wrote stories about Jim, Buck and Rastus ("The Eagle of Death" in the *Ranger*, 23 January 1932, the first of nine stories), also Dan, Bob and Darkey stories and Pete, Jack and Sam stories. Pete, from the latter sequence, was a tall, outgoing black, a one-time sailor and circus strongman. He was leader of the trio. He also spoke in a black patois.
5. See Don Hutchinson, "The Great Pulp Heroes No. 3: The Avenger."
6. Such as "Flight from Scandal," June 1951.
7. Such as "The Old Gang," 11 July 1942, which was turned in to the 1943 motion picture *Kid Dynamite*.
8. Such as "The Blackout," July 1971.

A rare black character in the pulp magazines, Josh Newton in Paul Ernst's Avenger adventures often pretended to be uneducated and humble ("The Frosted Death," *The Avenger*, January 1940).

Paul F. Ernst Selected Bibliography and Sources

Avenger Pulp Magazine Novels Written as by Kenneth Robeson

Josh and Rosabel Newton first appeared in the third novel. They did not appear in every one of the later Avenger stories. When *The Avenger* ended its run, *Operator #5* and *The Spider* writer Emile Tepperman under the Kenneth Robeson house name wrote six short stories, five of which ran in *Clues Detective* (September 1942 to May 1943), one in *The Shadow* (August 1944). The original twenty-four novels were issued in paperback in the 1970s, and proved sufficiently popular that Warner Books engaged Ron Goulart to write a dozen more novels in 1974 and 1975. *The Avenger Chronicles*, an anthology of new stories about the characters, edited by Joe Gentile and Howard Hopkins, came out in 2008.

"Justice Inc." (*The Avenger*, Street & Smith, September 1939)
"The Yellow Hoard" (*The Avenger*, Street & Smith, October 1939)
"The Sky Walker" (*The Avenger*, Street & Smith, November 1939)
"The Devil's Horns" (*The Avenger*, Street & Smith, December 1939)
"The Frosted Death" (*The Avenger*, Street & Smith, January 1940)
"The Glass Mountain" (*The Avenger*, Street & Smith, February 1940)
"The Blood Ring" (*The Avenger*, Street & Smith, March 1940)
"Stockholders in Death" (*The Avenger*, Street & Smith, April 1940)
"Tuned for Murder" (*The Avenger*, Street & Smith, May 1940)
"The Smiling Dogs" (*The Avenger*, Street & Smith, June 1940)
"The River of Ice" (*The Avenger*, Street & Smith, July 1940)
"The Flame Breathers" (*The Avenger*, Street & Smith, September 1940)
"Murder on Wheels" (*The Avenger*, Street & Smith, November 1940)
"Three Gold Crowns" (*The Avenger*, Street & Smith, January 1941)
"House of Death" (*The Avenger*, Street & Smith, March 1941)

"The Hate Master" (*The Avenger*, Street & Smith, May 1941)
"Nevlo" (*The Avenger*, Street & Smith, July 1941)
"Death in Slow Motion" (*The Avenger*, Street & Smith, September 1941)
"Pictures of Death" (*The Avenger*, Street & Smith, November 1941)
"The Green Killer" (Street & Smith, January 1942)
"The Happy Killers" (*The Avenger*, Street & Smith, March 1942)
"The Black Death" (*The Avenger*, Street & Smith, May 1942)
"The Wilder Curse" (*The Avenger*, Street & Smith, July 1942)
"Midnight Murder" (*The Avenger*, Street & Smith, September 1942)

COMIC BOOKS

The Shadow Comics (Street & Smith, 1940s) The Avenger was a backup feature
Justice Inc. (DC, 1975) four issues
The Shadow (DC, 1975) issue No. 11, guest appearance
Justice Inc. (DC, 1980s) two issues

RADIO

"The Avenger" (1941) 26 episodes, scripted by Walter B. Gibson

SOURCES

Bleiler, Richard. "Paul Ernst," *The Encyclopedia of Science Fiction*, John Clute and Peter Nicholls, eds. New York: St. Martin's Press, 1993.
DeForest, Tim. "Devil's Horns," Comics, Old Time Radio and Other Cool Stuff, 27 September 2012. http://sd2cx1.webring.org/l/rd?ring=otr;id=94;url=http%3A%2F%2Fcomicsradio%2Eblogspot%2Ecom%2F2012%2F09%2Fthe%2Ddevils%2Dhorns%2Ehtml (viewed 18 November 2012).
Hopkins, Howard. *The Gray Nemesis*. Golden Perils Press, 1992.
Hoppenstand, Gary, and Ray B. Browne. *The Defective Detective in the Pulps*. Bowling Green, OH: Bowling Green State University Popular Press, 1983.
Hutchinson, Don. "The Great Pulp Heroes No. 3: The Avenger," *New Captain George's Whizbang* No. 12, 1971.
Jones, Robert Kenneth. *The Shudder Pulps*. West Linn, OR: FAX Collector's Editions, 1975.
"Justice Inc.," Dr. Hermes Journal. http://dr-hermes.insanejournal.com/2009/09/23/ (viewed 27 September 2012).
Lai, Rick. "A Chronology of the Avenger." Pjfarmer.com/woldnewton/Avenger-Chron.pdf (viewed 27 September 2012).
Murray, Will, introduction. *The Casebook of Seekay and Other Prototypes of the Avenger*. CreateSpace, 2010.
Paul Ernst entry, Science Fiction Data Base. http://www.isfdb.org/cgi-bin/ea.cgi?1205 (viewed 27 September 2012).
Weinberg, Robert, ed. *Dr. Satan*. Oak Lawn, Ill.: Weinberg, 1984.

Will Eisner
(1917–2005)
Ebony White

Ebony White, the ridiculously offensive racial caricature..., was the Spirit's sidekick for the better part of a decade.... This kind of thoughtless racism needs to be laid at comics' doorstep at least as much as it does at [Will] Eisner's. Comics is a language, a system of abstract visual signs with an agreed-upon meaning, and like how in Twain's day "nigger" was a relatively commonplace part of English, in Eisner's this kind of racial caricature was a part of the comics lexicon.

—Matt Seneca[1]

Will Eisner was "an innovative comic-book artist who created The Spirit, a hero without superpowers, and the first graphic novel, 'A Contract with God,'" *The New York Times* said in an obituary in 2005.[2] The artist was recipient of one of the most prestigious awards in the world of graphic art, the Eisner, which was, in fact, named for him.

Yet for all the deserved praise, the influential Eisner from the beginning of his best-known creation in 1940 gave his crime-fighting comic hero a big-lipped, bug-eyed, slang-talking sidekick named Ebony White. Eisner mostly defended his depiction of Ebony. He sometimes apologized for Ebony. He eventually replaced Ebony with Blubber Wales the Eskimo boy for seven stories in 1946,[3] then with the white boy Sammy[4] from July 1949 until the series ended in 1952.

Ebony White could be a hero, could solve crimes, could ride to the rescue. He could get beyond his blackness, if that was in fact a negative. And he could get past his goombah dialect and exaggerated image for most of Eisner's readers in his day. Decades later, it's more difficult.

Born in 1917 in Brooklyn, New York, William Erwin Eisner was the first of three children born to Shmuel (Samuel) Eisner, of Albanian ancestry, and Fannie Ingber, of Romanian background. Father Eisner was an artist who found little work during the depression, other than painting scenery for Yiddish theater or painting houses for his neighbors. Mother Eisner, who worked in a factory, could not read or write. Young Will experienced anti–Semitism in his Bronx neighborhood, and decades later examined the issue in his graphic novels.

Selling newspapers to Wall Street businessmen during the depression, Eisner became entranced with E.C. Segar's *Thimble Theatre* and Lyman Young's *Tim Tyler's Luck*, then-popular newspaper comic strips. He read Horatio Alger's dime novels and was inspired by the writer's up-from-poverty plots. He read pulp fiction magazines. He and a classmate produced an illustrated school literary magazine while at DeWitt Clinton High School. He attended the Art Students League for a summer. He went to work for the *New York American's* advertising department at age 19, eventually leaving to become a freelancer. He provided comic pages for *Wow! What a Magazine* and other publications.

He partnered with Jerry Iger to form Eisner-Iger Studio, which hired artists including Bob Kane (creator of Batman), Jack Kirby (creator of the Fantastic Four), Lou Fine (who later ghosted some Spirit episodes) and others to work in a bullpen to produce art for Eisner-created series Sheena, Queen of the Jungle, and Hawks of the Seas, Dollman and Blackhawk.

Eisner went into partnership with Everett M. "Busy" Arnold, publisher of Quality Comics, to supply the Register and Tribune Syndicate with a sixteen-page comic book section that would appear with leading newspapers. The insert would have a seven-page crime story featuring the Spirit, and backup stories about Klaus Nordling's Lady Luck and Bob Powell's Mr. Mystic.

The section began publication in June 1940 with a million and a half readers in the *Detroit News, Baltimore Sun, Newark Star Ledger, Philadelphia Beacon, Wichita Sunday Beacon*, Washington, D.C., *Sunday Star* and others. "At its height *The Spirit* insert appeared in twenty major market newspapers with a combined circulation of 5 million readers each Sunday, quintupling the circulation of America's best-selling monthly comic book," according

Will Eisner was an innovative cartoonist and graphic artist who, as may be seen from this 1941 photograph, worked any time, anywhere (copyright © Will Eisner Studios, Inc., used with permission; image courtesy Denis Kitchen Art Agency).

to Denis Kitchen, who became one of Eisner's later publishers and his agent.[5] The insert comic ended after 634 issues, in July 1952. A daily newspaper comic strip, *The Spirit*, was syndicated from October 1941 to March 1944.

Eisner had a small regular cast to go with his main character, Denny Colt, a Central City criminologist whom everyone thought was dead but who was really hiding out in Wildwood Cemetery and solving crimes. The Spirit wore a blue suit and fedora, and a blue domino mask (much to Eisner's chagrin, as he never wanted a costumed hero). Police Commissioner

Eustace Dolan knew Colt's secret. Dolan's pretty daughter, Ellen, thought The Spirit was simply dreamy. And versatile young Ebony White was often on the scene when The Spirit needed a quick rescue.

The artist took risks and learned in those first Spirit years. "Eisner was undergoing a striking artistic metamorphosis as well, experimenting wildly with different techniques. Almost every issue would feature some new way to ink backgrounds—featuring, cross-hatching, stippling, silhouettes, crazy little patterns—a regular encyclopedia of shading. As time went by the heavy solid blacks which were to become his virtual post-war trademark slowly began to displace these ingenious, pulp-type mannerisms," according to Cat Yronwode.[6]

"In some stories, he [The Spirit] was just a walk-on," Eisner said of his flexible story style. "It was always written for an adult audience, not a comic book audience."[7]

"Adults were drawn to *The Spirit* because of Eisner's ability to produce and tell a noir 'B' movie every week in just seven pages," according to historian Bob Andelman. "And his opening splash pages were amazing and consistently innovative. Unlike other artists, Eisner didn't rely on a set logo every time, a practice that was unheard of in comic books, newspapers or magazines."[8]

Eisner was adept at rendering rain and water with his artist's pen. He was a master of high perspectives. His stories could be moody, they could be funny, they could be fantastic, they could be gripping.

"I was very concerned with reading rhythm," Eisner said, "but by the mid-'30s, cinema became dominant. So I began using many of the techniques of film—photographing from under a chair or from the ceiling, bird's-eye view, worm's eye view, deep black shadows, perspective."[9]

Eisner told interviewer Pete Hamill, "I was an avid short story fan, but more importantly, I suppose, I was a frustrated serious painter and a frustrated serious writer. I could do both reasonably well but not well enough to make a name for myself in either media by itself. But with the euphoria you bring to something when you know it's the big time, I attacked it as if I were a young Dostoevsky. I also equated myself with Ben Hecht and some of the pulp writers, who were my heroes at the time. Short stories are sort of dead now but they were very big in the '30s."[10]

Eisner admitted to working in isolation. "It was a true ghetto, the field of comics, trapping those artist-writers in a world of limited outlook," he wrote in the *New York Times Book Review*.[11] "When a cartoonist left the old neighborhood and went 'uptown' to show his work to mainstream publishers, the work baffled prospective editors. It wasn't anything like the style and technique required, say, by *The Saturday Evening Post*."

Eisner in 1942 left for World War II military service and eventually turned writing and art chores over to others. He returned from the war three years later to take back the comic and for the next several years turned out what most consider to be his best Spirit work. While in the service, Eisner produced educational material for *Army Motors*.

In peacetime, the artist continued his education art and established a studio called American Visual Corp. to produce more *PS* material for the military. Eisner was creative director from 1951 to 1972. That's why, after *The Spirit*'s run ended, Eisner disappeared from mainstream comic books for two decades. By then Eisner was married to Ann Weingarten and they had two children.

Will Eisner was aware that his Ebony White character was controversial. This one-page "interview" was his response for the 1971 *Underground Spirit* comic book (copyright © Will Eisner Studios, Inc., used with permission; image courtesy Denis Kitchen Art Agency).

According to biographer Michael Schumacher, Eisner's "perceptions began to change during World War II, when he witnessed troop segregation, and his views continued to change over the following two decades, when national consciousness turned to the civil rights movement. By then, the Spirit and Ebony had been retired and Eisner had moved on."[12]

Ebony wasn't the only instance of Eisner relying on cliché. In fact, his experience with characters he drew for *PS Magazine* to explain basic mechanical, electrical and other routine matters—Sgt. Half-Mast McCanick, Pvt. Joe Dope (something of a ditz) and ace mechanic Connie Rodd (a pinup gal)—shows, as the artist once told the *New York Times*, how the need for haste in completing assignments made natural his use of stereotype to quickly establish character. It was what comic book artists did. Eisner used Dope and Rodd to get his readers' attention. They served the purpose in getting across subtleties of inventory and weapon cleaning and the like. Eisner's army supervisors eventually obliged him to smarten up the dumb mechanic Joe and ease off on Connie's sex appeal (in one illustrated story, for example, she struggled with buttons popping off her shirt while talking about vehicle maintenance to a bug-eyed private).[13]

When in the 1970s comic book convention organizers invited Eisner to come to speak, and underground and small-press comics publishers asked to bring out Spirit reprints, Eisner reentered the world of mainstream comics. He again took up the pen. He is credited with developing the graphic novel format for *A Contract with God* in 1978. DC Comics in 2000 and for the next several years collected all of the Spirit art in a series of twenty-six hardcover volumes. Eisner wrote instructional books for artists, including *Comics and Sequential Art* (1985).

Eisner was rightly honored.

But let's look at the character Ebony White. He shows up in the very first Spirit section, 2 June 1940, driving a cab. Ebony doesn't have much to say until the second issue, when, still at the wheel, he takes his passengers across lonely Wildwood Cemetery Road:

Man. I say, driver, must you go so fast along here?
Ebony. Sorry, boss, dis car jes' nachelly speeds up when ah drive past Wildwood Cemetery.

And his grammar and pronunciation never get any better.

Ebony has two strikes as a stereotype: His vernacular speech and his appearance. Sometimes he appears to be a boy. Other times, he is old enough to pilot an airplane. On a third point, his actions, we can be more forgiving. He's totally attached to The Spirit. And he's a capable sidekick. In no time, he's learned how to operate The Spirit's ridiculous (Eisner would agree) auto-airplane. What he doesn't get a lot of is respect. This exchange is from the 25 August 1940 issue:

The Spirit (talking to a boy named Billy). This is my assistant, Ebony White ... get me the file on "Ripper Regan."
Ebony. Yassum, Mis' Spirit Boss!

Ebony has the splash page to himself for the 15 September 1940 issue. Ebony has bug eyes, puffy lips, bulbous forehead and buck teeth. The Spirit is trying to figure out a crime-fighting invention and goes to the hardware store. Ebony has some ideas of his own, but ends up causing an explosion in The Spirit's underground laboratory. He can now see through walls. Fortunately, at adventure's end, Ebony's affliction is nothing that can't be remedied by a bop to the forehead from his employer.

"It was one of my first attempts at all-out comedy," Eisner told interviewer Tom Heintjes in 1992.[14] Does he regret his depiction of Ebony? Yes. "This is humor that was part of its time. I'm not going to defend it in today's terms. But I know that all humor is a reflection of its time in which it appears. Later on, Ebony became more educated and intelligent, because that's the way the years progressed. At no time was he ever a buffoon based on his racial characteristics."

Eisner posited that the medium depended on stereotypes to quickly communicate with the reader. Accepting the criticism, the artist said he had no regrets in making the sidekick character black.

Eisner's wartime experiences did nothing to change his Ebony White drawings. The caricature particularly stands out on the cover of the 13 October 1946 issue. Ebony, obviously smitten, his irises heart-shaped, is shown looking adoringly at a pretty black girl, Rosie Lee. Rosie Lee has crinkly hair but otherwise no exaggerated black features. Ebony still has mush-mouf lips. Oh, and their language is different:

Ebony. Miss Rosie Lee, Mastuh Ebony White callin'....
Rosie. Now look here Ebony.... Four times this week you were told I'm not at home.... Can't you take a hint??
Ebony. But golly Rosie ... an am just flatfooted ovum you.... Gosh, yo so sweet an' purty ah gits rocks in mah throat when ah looks at yo.'
At story's end, Rosie agrees to go to the Thanksgiving dance with the lad.

"Ebony, with his Amos & Andy-style dialect and clownish appearance, is certainly offensive to modern sensibilities, as is Blubber, with his monkeyish demeanor," in Arie Kaplan's view. "But it's also worth noting that during the strip's run, Eisner introduced the character of detective Grey, one of the first black private eyes seen in mainstream newspaper strip, who was as signified and well-spoken as any of the other characters. In 1946, perhaps due to changing attitudes toward minorities in the postwar era, Eisner realized that Ebony's dialect humor was insulting, and the Spirit's sidekick was quickly sent to the all-black Carter School for Boys to rid himself of his 'minstrel accent.'"[15]

Ebony's romantic rival, army captain Fraternization H. Shack, is black and speaks with a fine British intonation. School does Ebony no good, by the way. When he returns, Ebony still has his dialect. This is from the issue of 12 May 1946. Now that Ebony's returned, Blubber wants to go home to Alaska:

Blubber. Thanks for helpin' me pack, Ebony, ol' pal.... Guess I'd better get going now, before the Spirit gets back!
Ebony. Golly, ah'm sorry yo're goin', Blubber! ... ere.... Here's fifty cents.... All ah have lef' ovah fum mah school spendin' money!

"Ebony never drew criticism from Negro groups, (in fact, Eisner was commended by some for using him), perhaps because, although his speech pattern was early Minstrel Show, he himself derived from another literary tradition: He was a combination of Tom Sawyer and Penrod, with a touch of Horatio Alger hero, and color didn't really come into it," according to Marilyn Mercer.[16]

Eisner offered a different take in a one-page story for the first issue of *Underground*

Spirit, in which a reporter asks Ebony about his apparent Uncle Tomism. Ebony is about to answer when the Spirit comes into the room to ask if anything had come of his tailing a drug pusher.

> Ebony (pointing to a criminal, tied up). Well, Spirit ... I took about 15 photos of this rat makin' a big buy ... then I took 98 shots of him selling the stuff in a school yard!! Then he spotted me! So I hadda ack fast.... He chased me up an alley ... I rolled a trash can at him.... He tripped, knocked hisself out on a fire escape ladder, then I jes' dragged him in.... You can book him with all the evidence!
> Spirit. Great!
> Ebony (to reporter). Sorry, now would you mind repeating the question?

We have to accept Eisner's sincerity on one point: "My stories are all centered around the human being," he said, "the business of survival, of struggling against the forces of life itself."[17]

Eisner died in 2005 of complications from quadruple bypass surgery.

Will Eisner Notes

1. "Your Monday Panel 49," Death to the Universe, 14 February 2011.
2. "Will Eisner, a Pioneer of Comic Books, Is Dead at 87," 5 January, C14.
3. 17 February 1946 to 12 May 1946.
4. 31 July 1949 to 14 September 1952.
5. "Will Eisner," http://deniskitchen.com/docs/bios/bio_will_eisner.html (viewed 27 March 2013).
6. "The Spirit of the Spirit," *Comic Reader*, No. 172, October 1979, 11.
7. "Spirit Moves DC to Reprint Colorful Comic Book Noir," *USA Today*, 12 July 2000, 6D.
8. *Will Eisner: A Spirited Life*, 57.
9. Ibid.
10. "The Spirit Strikes Back," *Village Voice*, 21 April 1975, 12–13.
11. "Getting the Last Laugh: My Life in Comics," 14 January 1990, 26.
12. *Will Eisner: A Dreamer's Life in Comics*, 180.
13. Eddie Campbell, ed., *Will Eisner PS Magazine*, 17.
14. "Writing the Rules," *The Spirit: The Origin Years*, No. 4, November 1992, 32.
15. *Masters of the Comic Book Universe Revealed!*, 8.
16. "The Only Real Middle-Class Crimefighter," *New York Herald Tribune*, 9 January 1966.
17. Alan Woollcombe, Will Eisner obituary, London *Independent*, 6 January 2005, 43.

Will Eisner Selected Bibliography and Sources

THE SPIRIT NEWSPAPER COMIC STRIP AND SECTION

The Spirit syndicated comic section, 2 June 1940 to 5 October 1952 (645 issues). Ebony White did not appear in every episode.

The weekly sections for the most part were untitled. Archivist Catherine Yronwode gave tentative titles in her checklist that first appeared in seven parts in *The Spirit Magazine* Nos. 22 to 28 (Kitchen Sink Press) and is now available online. The sixteen-page sections featured seven-page Spirit stories in Nos. 1 to 32, stories 219 to 638, eight-page stories in Nos. 33 to 218, four-page stories 635 to 645. Will Eisner handled writing and artwork until he was drafted; in Nos. 101 to 290, he gradually ceded art chores to Lou Fine and others, scripts to Many Wade Wellman and others; with No. 291, Eisner returned to drawing and writing *The Spirit*. Eisner did one last story, "The Spirit Returns," for *New York, the Sunday Herald Tribune Magazine*, in 1966.

In later years he provided covers and other art for the reprint series.

Ebony White first appeared in the second issue of *The Spirit Section,* as a taxi driver. He was first spotlighted on the cover of the sixteenth issue. He later had a black friend, Pierpont. He was replaced by Blubber Wales the Eskimo boy for seven stories, No. 299, 17 February 1946, to No. 311, 12 May 1946.

The white boy Sammy became the sidekick, No. 479, 31 July 1949, to No. 642, 14 September 1952, a month before the series ended.

The Daily Spirit, newspaper comic strip, syndicated 13 October 1941 to 11 March 1944. Jack Cole took on art and writing duties when Eisner went into the army, and when Cole left to work on *Plastic Man*, Lou Fine finished the run.

Comic Books (Reprints)

Police (Quality, Nos. 11 to 92, 94 to 99, 101 to 102, 1942 to 1944, when the Spirit came out in his own title)
The Spirit (Quality, Nos. 1 to 22, 1944 to 1950)
Spiritman (bootleg, Nos. 1 to 2, 1944)
3 Comics Magazine (bootleg, No. 1, 1944)
Modern Comics (Quality, No. 102, 1944)
The Spirit (Fiction House, Nos. 1 to 5, 1952 to 1954)
Spirit (IW/Super, Nos. 11 and 12, 1963 and 1964)
Plastic Man (IW/Super, No. 18, 1964)
The Spirit (Harvey, Nos. 1–2, 1966–1967)
The Spirit Bag (Gibson/Eisner, Nos. 1 to 4 [five to a bag], 1972 and 1973) (for some reason, omitted was a reprint of fourth issue, 23 June 1940)
The Spirit (Kitchen Sink, underground, Nos. 1 and 2, 1973)
Eerie (Warren, Nos. 54 and 55, 1972)
The Spirit Magazine (Warren, Nos. 1 to 16, 1974 to 1976)
The Spirit Special (Warren, No. 1, 1975)
Underground Spirit (Kitchen Sink, 1973)
The Daily Spirit (Real Free Press, Nos. 1 to 4, 1974 to 1975)
The Spirit Dailies (Ken Pierce Books, Nos. 1 to 4, 1975 and 1976)
The Spirit Magazine (Krupp Comic Works, Nos. 17 to 41, and No. 1 Special, 1976 to 1983)
Comix International (Warren, No. 5, 1977)
Will Eisner Quarterly (Kitchen Sink Press, Nos. 1 to 8, 1983 to 1985)
The Outer Space Spirit: 1952 (Kitchen Sink Press, 1983)
The Spirit (Kitchen Sink Press, Nos. 1 to 87, 1982 to 1992)
Heavy Metal Magazine (1983)
Will Eisner's 3-D Classics Featuring The Spirit (Eclipse, 1985)
The Spirit Casebook (Kitchen Sink Press, Nos. 1 and 2, 1990 to 1998)
The Spirit: The Origin Years (Kitchen Sink, Nos. 1 to 10, 1992 and 1993, reprinting first forty issues)
Spirit Jam (Kitchen Sink Press, 1998)
The Spirit: The New Adventures (Kitchen Sink Press, Nos. 1 to 8, 1997 and 1998)
DC Comics Millennium Edition: The Spirit (DC, 2000)

Comic Books (New Stories and Art) Non-Eisner

Batman/The Spirit (DC, No. 1, 2005)
Will Eisner's The Spirit (DC, Nos. 1 to 32, 2006 to 2009)
The Spirit (DC First Wave, Nos. 1 to 10, 2010 and 2011)
The Rocketeer/Spirit: Pulp Friction (IDW Publishing/DC Entertainment, Nos. 1 to 4, 2013)

Books

Will Eisner Color Treasury (Kitchen Sink Press, 1981)
The Spirit Color Album (Kitchen Sink Press, Nos. 1 to 3, 1981 to 1983)
Will Eisner's The Spirit Archives (DC, 2000 to 2005)
   (1) June to December, 1940
   (2) January to June, 1941
   (3) July to December, 1941
   (4) January to June, 1942
   (5) July to December, 1942
   (6) January to June, 1943
   (7) July to December 1943

(8) January to June, 1944
(9) July to December, 1944
(10) January to June, 1945
(11) July to December, 1945
(12) January to June, 1946
(13) July to December, 1947
(14) January to June, 1947
(15) July to December, 1947
(16) January to June, 1948
(17) July to December, 1948
(18) January to June, 1949
(19) July to December, 1949
(20) January to June, 1950
(21) July to December, 1950
(22) January to June, 1951
(23) July to December, 1951
(24) January to October, 1952
(25) The Complete Dailies, 1941–1944
(26) After the Section: 1952–2005

Best of The Spirit (DC, 2005)
Will Eisner's The Spirit Archives (Dark Horse Comics, 2009)
(27) The New Adventures
Will Eisner's The Spirit: Artist's Edition (IDW Publishing, 2013)
The character Ebony White did not appear in every story.

FILMS (NONE WITH EBONY WHITE)

Cartoons (date unknown)
The Spirit (1987)
The Spirit (2008)

SOURCES

Andelman, Bob. *Will Eisner: A Spirited Life*. Milwaukie, Ore.: M. Press, 2005.
Beritasky, Noah. "Will Eisner Is No Mark Twain," The Hooded Utilitarian, 15 February 2011. http://hoodedutilitarian.com/2011/02/will-eisner-is-no-mark-twain/ (viewed 7 October 2012).
Boxer, Sarah. "Will Eisner, a Pioneer of Comic Books, Is Dead at 87," *New York Times*, 5 January 2005.
Brick, Scott. "Will Eisner: The Spirit of Comics," *Comics Buyer's Guide* No. 1308, 11 December 1998.
Campbell, Eddie, ed. *Will Eisner PS Magazine: The Best of The Preventive Maintenance Monthly*. New York: Abrams ComicArt, 2011.
Colton, David. "Spirit Moves DC to Reprint Colorful Comic Book Noir," *USA Today*, 12 July 2000.
Drew, Bernard. "Spenser: Hardboiled Roots," *Xenophile*, Vol. 2 No. 8, February 1976.
Eisner, Will. "Getting the Last Laugh: My Life in Comics," *New York Times Book Review*, 14 January 1990.
Hamill, Pete. "The Spirit Strikes Back," *The Village Voice*, 21 April 1975.
Heintjes, Tom. "Writing the Rules," *The Spirit: The Origin Years*, No. 4, November 1992.
Holtz, Allan. *American Newspaper Comics: An Encyclopedic Reference Guide*. Ann Arbor: University of Michigan Press, 2012.
Kaplan, Arie. *Masters of the Comic Book Universe Revealed!* Chicago: Chicago Review Press, 2006.
Kitchen, Denis. "Will Eisner," http://deniskitchen.com/docs/bios/bio_will_eisner.html (viewed 27 March 2013).
Mercer, Marilyn. "The Only Real Middle-Class Crimefighter," *New York Herald Tribune*, 9 January 1966.
Schumacher, Michael. *Will Eisner: A Dreamer's Life in Comics*. New York: Bloomsbury, 2010.
Seneca, Mike. "Your Monday Panel 49," Death to the Universe, 14 February 2011. http://deathtotheuniverse.blogspot.com/2011/02/your-monday-panel-49.html (viewed 18 November 2012).
Woollcombe, Alan. Will Eisner obituary, London *Independent*, 6 January 2005.
Yronwode, Cat. "The Spirit of the Spirit," *Comic Reader*, Nos. 172 to 174, October to December 1979.
Yronwode, Catherine. "The Spirit Checklist," http://www.luckymojo.com/spiritchecklist.html (viewed 7 October 2012).

Langston Hughes
(1902–1967)

Jesse B. Semple

> Like a welcome summer rain, humor may suddenly cleanse and cool the earth, the air and you.—Langston Hughes

Langston Hughes was a poet, social activist, novelist, playwright, short story writer and columnist active during the Harlem Renaissance and after.

If anyone demonstrated how a black writer could craft entertaining pieces about blacks, it was Langston Hughes. His stories about Jesse B. Semple (most often called "My Simple Minded Friend," or "Simple," by the nameless narrator of the stories) appeared in Hughes's "Here to Yonder" columns in the *Chicago Defender* and, later, the *New York Post*. They are about an everyday Harlem man—a working-class transplant from the South—who muses on everyday subjects with his better-educated friend at the neighborhood tavern. They're often serious, sometimes amusing, never riotously funny, never demeaning, always thought-provoking.

Born in Joplin, Missouri, in 1902, Langston Hughes was the son of Carrie Mercer Langston and James Nathaniel Hughes. After his parents divorced, young Langston was raised by his grandmother, Mary Patterson Langston, in Lawrence, Kansas. His father moved to Cuba and Mexico. His mother moved to Lincoln, Illinois, and Langston joined her and her new husband there in 1915. Langston began to write verse. He was elected high school class poet, though forever believed it was because of the teacher's beliefs: "I was a victim of a stereotype. There were only two of us Negro kids in the whole class and our English teacher was always stressing the importance of rhythm in poetry. Well, everyone knows, except us, that all Negroes have rhythm, so they elected me as class poet," he said.[1]

Hughes developed a lifelong pride in his racial heritage. Hughes wrote from the additional perspective of having paternal great-grandfathers who were white slave owners in Kentucky. His paternal great-grandmothers were of African descent.

The family moved to Cleveland. After he graduated from high school, Hughes spent a year in Mexico, and persuaded his father to pay for a year at Columbia University, where he studied engineering. He worked variously as an assistant cook, busboy and laundryman. He became a seaman long enough to travel to Africa and Europe. He continued to write. One of his best-known poems is "The Negro Speaks of Rivers," published in *The Crisis* in 1921.

He moved to Washington, D.C., in 1924, and two years later his first book of poetry, *The Weary Blues*, came out. He completed degree requirements at Lincoln University in Pennsylvania in 1929. The next year, he won the Harmon Gold Medal for Literature for his first novel, *Not Without Laughter*. He went to Europe to report on the Spanish Civil War for the Baltimore *Afro-American*. When he returned to New York, he helped establish a black theater in Harlem. In 1939, he co-wrote the *Way Down South* screenplay. He wrote an autobiography, *The Big Sea*, in 1940. He was seldom idle.

Hughes spent most of his creative life in Harlem. He never married. Some believe he was quietly homosexual.

Hughes's alter ego Simple came to life in the waning years of Octavus Roy Cohen's Birmingham characters—in a 13 February 1942 *Defender* column that, until then, had carried Hughes's nonfiction and opinion.[2] Simple went on to appear in five books and a Broadway play. Florian Slappey by the time of Simple's debut would have only four more *Post* appearances, and five stories elsewhere after that. The Birmingham folks had run their course.

This is from Simple's first appearance:

Langston Hughes brought realism, as well as light humor, to his Simple stories for the *Chicago Defender* (Carl Van Vechten image, Library of Congress).

> "It hurts my soul," said my Simple Minded Friend. "To be Jim Crowed hurts my soul. To have on my uniform and have to be Jim Crowed."
>
> "If you beat Hitler, though, you'll be helping to beat Jim Crow."
>
> "I want to beat Jim Crow first," said my Simple Minded Friend. "Hitler's over yonder, and Jim Crow is here."
>
> "But if the Nazis ever got over here, and Hitler and Jim Crow ever got together, you would have an awful time beating the two of them. In fact, you would be hog-tied. They would have curfew laws for Negroes—just like they have curfew laws for Jews in Germany. And you couldn't stay up after nine."[3]

When Simple began, Hughes's biographer Arnold Rampersad said, "For three consecutive weeks, Langston's column in the *Defender* featured conversations between the educated, somewhat stuffy narrator, whom the readers could only take to be Langston Hughes himself, and his racially defensive but curiously wise and amusing 'Simple Minded Friend.' The basic topic remained the war and blacks. Then the man disappeared from the column for six weeks. In mid–April, without warning, he returned to 'Here to Yonder,' and thereafter appeared on an unpredictable but enduring basis."[4]

The format was a logical one, in the view of critic Phyllis R. Klotman: "The skit technique, adapted to the demands of the newspaper column, is a natural form for the tales. The oral tradition of the Afro-American was carried on in the vaudeville and burlesque routines which were so popular in the twenties and thirties. Those routines had elements that we also see in the Simple stories: two stand-up comics playing against and to each other, fast-paced dialogue and a quick cut."[5]

Semple (his name became known only when Hughes adapted some of the columns for a book) and the unidentified companion at the tavern (who was only given a name, Ananias Boyd, when Hughes wrote the play) evinced greater depth, more dignity and milder intentions than Cohen's Birminghamers. Hughes didn't go for belly laughs. He went for poignancy.

But he liked humor. And he often incorporated plot twists or irony at the end of his short pieces. Simple liked to dress well; so did Slappey. Other characters, including Joyce Lane, who eventually became Simple's wife, joined the storylines.

"Space limitations in my paper prevent me from giving Simple's friends and associates a greater play," Hughes explained. "The space limits for 'Here to Yonder' in the *Chicago Defender* are one column of print—or three typewritten pages double-spaced. If I run over three pages, the editor is forced to cut something out. The *Chicago Defender* does not censor its columnists, but they cannot stretch their space, so when something is too long it must be cut."[6]

Critic Arthur P. Davis remarked on the value of Hughes's literary setup: "He has made Simple the very highly articulate spokesman of the untrained-worker group and himself the voice of the educated Negro liberal. The merit of this arrangement is that the two attitudes tend to complement each other. Simple generally exemplifies the directness and single-mindedness of the untrained Negro and Hughes the sophisticated tolerance and broad-mindedness of the black intellectual. The clash and interplay of these attitudes furnish much of the humor in Simple, but they also serve a deeper purpose; they point up and accentuate the two-level type of thinking which segregation tends to produce in all Negroes."[7]

Hughes began to write about Simple two decades after Cohen had taken his Slappey and Lawyer Chew vignettes to newspaper syndication—another interesting parallel. The year's worth of Slappey/Chew newspaper pieces were structurally the same as the Simples: 400- or 500-word dialogues between two characters. Cohen's readership was much wider than Hughes's.

Simple, Hughes said in *The Best of Simple*, "talks about the wife he used to have, the woman he loves today, and his one-time play-girl, Zarita. Usually over a glass of beer, he tells me his tales, mostly in high humor, but sometimes with a pain in his soul as sharp as the occasional hurt of that bunion on his right foot. Sometimes, as the old blues says, Simple might be 'laughing to keep from crying.' But even then he keeps you laughing, too."[8]

Hughes never ventured into true short story form with Simple, never found a slick-paper magazine market, but he did hone his character, giving him greater depth of personality, so he could appear in books. The process was a rigorous one, as Hughes was juggling several projects at the time.

Hughes took on current topics such as the Nazis, lynchings, military service, Southern brotherhoods and Uncle Tomism in his discussions. Cohen was content to keep his characters relatively cardboard, and they appeared in books that way. Hughes's character was a race man; he was cognizant of and discussed blackness and whiteness. Cohen's characters were often, though not always, shallow, often hustling to get by, always bustling. Hughes had a poetic, literary bent. Cohen never denied his pulp roots.

Could a black poke fun at blacks? Bio-bibliographer Donna Akiba Sullivan Harper noted many critics "place humor in the Simple stories firmly into a context of black folk tradition, including both oral and written precedents."[9]

Some readers and critics didn't like the humor.

Hughes offered a defense of humor on his own behalf. Referring to critical pieces appearing in *Crisis* and *Phylon*, Hughes wrote: "These magazines evidently think the race problem is too deep for comic relief. Such earnestness is contrary to mass Negro thinking.

Colored people are always laughing at some wry Jim Crow incident or absurd nuance of the color line. If Negroes took all the white world's daily boorishness to heart and wept over it as profoundly as our serious writers do, we would have been dead long ago."[10]

Some readers and critics didn't like the dialect or the emphasis on race.

"There are many touching moments in this book and many amusing ones, too," a Charleston *Gazette* reviewer said of *Simple Speaks His Mind*. "The first half of the book, when Hughes keeps the racial question subordinate, is excellent. The second half, in which it becomes predominate, serve almost to defeat his purpose. Everything he has to say is no doubt true, much to America's shame, but he wearies the reader by over-emphasis."[11]

Hughes would have scoffed. As he wrote in "To Negro Writers" in 1935, "Negro writers can seek to unite blacks and whites in our country, not on the nebulous basis of an interracial meeting, or the shifting sands of religious brotherhood, but on the solid ground of the daily working-class struggle to wipe out, now and forever, all the old inequities of the past."[12]

Critic Sam G. Riley argues that Hughes was writing literary journalism. "Literary writing tends to be of lasting value and interest," he said. "It withstands the test of time, and Simple has done that.... One reason for the enduring interest in Simple, of course, is the continuing nature of the race issue in American life."[13]

An example is Simple's gripe about authority:

"I definitely do not like the Law," said Simple, using the word with a capital letter to mean *police* and *courts* combined.
"Why?" I asked.
"Because the Law beats my head. Also because the Law will give a white man one year and give me ten."
"But if it wasn't for the Law," I said, "you would not have any protection."
"Protection?" yelled Simple. "The Law always protect a white man. But if *I* holler for the Law, the Law says, 'what do you want, Negro?' Only most white polices do not say 'Negro.'"[14]

Simple wasn't only a race man. He was also a man caught in a gender whirlwind, as Melvin G. Williams points out: "All women are 'sweet worriations' ... to Simple, but four of them in particular cause him problems. Isabel, his first wife, taunts him about the divorce they both want but do not want to pay for. Zarita is his playgirl of parties and the bars. Joyce, eventually his second wife, is always devoted to the high culture of church and concert and teas. And his landlady complicate his life with her signs in the bathroom, her pet dog Trixie, and her insistence on being paid."[15]

One might add a fifth woman, Cousin Minnie, who shows up unexpectedly demanding the expected: money. As Simple relates in "Cousin Minnie Wins," "Them that lives to the hilt and wears their worries like a loose garment lives the longest. I do believe my Cousin Minnie is going to live to be one hundred and ten. She worries about nothing, except sometimes wondering can she borrow Five Dollars from Me. When I say no, she frowns up."[16]

"Simple speaks with a poetic and easy logic ('It is better to be wore out from living than to be worn out from worry') in a voice that comes straight out of the African American folk tradition," *Kirkus Reviews* said, "but Hughes' slices of urban black life belong also to the larger continuum of great American humor, from Mark Twain to Armistead Maupin. Quite simply, an indispensable part of our cultural heritage."[17]

Hughes through Simple asks that blacks be given their due: "All these plays, dramas, skits, sketches, and soap operas all day long and practically nothing about negroes. You would think no Negroes lived in America except Amos and Andy [and they are white]. White folks have all kinds of plays on the radio about themselves, also on TV. But what have we got about us?"[18]

Critic Julian C. Carey points out, "Simple, however, is not entirely antagonistic to white people. He would just like for them to experience and endure his life; he wants to 'share and share alike.'"[19]

Too bad the *Saturday Evening Post* wasn't prepared to do that. But by World War II's end, the editors no doubt felt they had exhausted the genre with Cohen, and had no interest in breaking new ground.

Hughes died in 1967 in New York of complications from prostate cancer.

Langston Hughes Notes

1. "Langston Hughes, Writer, 65, Dead," *The New York Times*, 23 May 1967.
2. His last appearance was in the *New York Post* for 31 December 1965, *Chicago Defender* 6 January 1966.
3. "Conversation at Midnight," *Chicago Defender*, 13 February 1943.
4. *The Life of Langston Hughes: Volume 2: 1914–1967*, 64.
5. "Jesse B. Semple and the Narrative Art of Langston Hughes," *The Journal of Narrative Technique*, Vol. 3, No. 1, 66.
6. Langston Hughes, "Simple and Me," *Phylon*, Vol. 6, No. 4, 349.
7. "Jesse B. Semple: Negro American," *Phylon*, Vol. 15, No. 1, 23.
8. Foreword, viii.
9. Donna Akiba Sullivan Harper, *Not So Simple*, 63.
10. Foreword, "Let's Laugh a Little," *Simple Stakes a Claim*, 11–12.
11. 16 April 1950, 11.
12. As reprinted in *American Writer's Congress*, Henry Hart, ed.
13. "Langston Hughes's Jesse B. Semple Columns as Literary Journalism," *American Periodicals,* Vol. 10, 69.
14. "The Law," in *The Return of Simple*," adaptation of the column "Simple and the Law," *Chicago Defender*, 13 January 1945.
15. "Langston Hughes's Jesse B. Semple; A Black Walter Mitty," *Negro American Literature Forum*, Vol. 10 No. 2, 66.
16. "Cousin Minnie Wins," reprinted in *The Later Semple Stories*, 290.
17. Review of *The Return of Simple*, 20 May 2010. The column quoted is "Cousin Minnie Wins," *The Later Semple Stories*, 290.
18. Simple speaking, unidentified column, excerpted in Julian C. Carey, "Jesse B. Semple Revisited and Revised," *Phylon*, Vol. 32, No. 2, 159.
19. Ibid., 160.
20. Donna Akiba Sullivan Harper in *Not So Simple* shows a column for 30 October 1948: "Simple Says Some Folks Don't Have a Moral Right for a Day," but a search of the *Chicago Defender* electronic archive shows a column titled "U.S. Likes Nazis and Franco Better Than Its Own Negroes," a non–Simple column.
21. Harper in *Not So Simple* shows a column titled "Simple Talks at Random About Some Mean People in the South" for 22 January 1949, but the archive shows this title.

Langston Hughes Selected Bibliography and Sources

Jesse B. Semple Stories

Langston Hughes began his "Here to Yonder" column 21 November 1942 in the *Chicago Defender* and continued it until 8 January 1966. The "Here to Yonder" column name was dropped 16 October

1948. The column beginning with the issue of 6 April 1957 was titled "Week by Week" for a time. The *New York Post* carried the column from 1962 to 1965. This listing covers only the *Chicago Defender*, which had some lapses in carrying the Hughes column. The listing is for Simple essays only.

"Conversation at Midnight" (*Chicago Defender*, 13 February 1943)
"Wives, War and Money" (*Chicago Defender*, 20 February 1943)
"My Friend Wants to Argue" (*Chicago Defender*, 27 February 1943)
"Jews, Negroes and Hollywood" (*Chicago Defender*, 17 April 1943)
"Mugging" (*Chicago Defender*, 1 May 1943)
"God, War, and Swing" (5 June 1943)
"Let the South Secede" (*Chicago Defender*, 26 June 1943)
"Simple Looks for Justice" (*Chicago Defender*, 28 August 1943)
"Simple and the Landladies" (*Chicago Defender*, 9 October 1943)
"Simple and the Darak [sic] Nuance" (*Chicago Defender*, 13 November 1943)
"Simple and the Late Date" (*Chicago Defender*, 27 November 1943)
"Equality and Dogs" (*Chicago Defender*, 11 December 1943)
"Happy New Year" (*Chicago Defender*, 1 January 1944)
"Share—and Share Alike" (*Chicago Defender*, 29 April 1944)
"Simple Sees 'Othello'" (*Chicago Defender*, 3 June 1944)
"On Women Who Drink You Up" (*Chicago Defender*, 24 June 1944)
"On Being Black" (*Chicago Defender*, 8 July 1944)
"Dark Glasses at Night" (*Chicago Defender*, 29 July 1944)
"Simple and the Elections" (*Chicago Defender*, 12 August 1944)
"Too Good a Time" (*Chicago Defender*, 2 September 1944)
"Not So Simple" (*Chicago Defender*, 16 September 1944)
"The Disadvantages of Race" (*Chicago Defender*, 28 October 1944)
"Simple's Rainy Day" (*Chicago Defender*, 25 November 1944)
"Simple in the Hospital" (*Chicago Defender*, 9 December 1944)
"Simple's Merry Christmas" (*Chicago Defender*, 23 December 1944)
"Simple and the Second Coming" (*Chicago Defender*, 30 December 1944)
"Simple and the Law" (*Chicago Defender*, 13 January 1945)
"Simple Pins on Medals" (*Chicago Defender*, 17 February 1945)
"Simple on Race Relations" (*Chicago Defender*, 3 March 1945)
"Simple Wants to Be Genius" (*Chicago Defender*, 14 April 1945)
"Simple's Last Whipping" (*Chicago Defender*, 19 May 1945)
"Simple in the Dark" (*Chicago Defender*, 9 June 1945)
"Simple and the NAACP" (*Chicago Defender*, 16 June 1945)
"Here Comes Old Me" (*Chicago Defender*, 14 July 1945)
"Simple Starts at Rock Bottom" (*Chicago Defender*, 21 July 1945)
"This Snaggle-Tooth World" (*Chicago Defender*, 28 July 1945)
"Simple and the Atom Bomb" (*Chicago Defender*, 18 August 1945)
"Simple's Selfish Peace" (*Chicago Defender*, 15 September 1945)
"Simple's Final Fear" (*Chicago Defender*, 13 October 1945)
"Simple Speaks of Shouting" (*Chicago Defender*, 10 November 1945)
"Simple's Indian Blood" (*Chicago Defender*, 3 November 1945)
"Black Is Fine" (*Chicago Defender*, 24 November 1945)
"Simple and Cosmic Time" (*Chicago Defender*, 1 December 1945)
"Simple's Christmas Wish" (*Chicago Defender*, 8 December 1945)
"Simple Views the News" (*Chicago Defender*, 5 January 1946)
"Simple and the Fur Coats" (*Chicago Defender*, 19 January 1946)
"Simple and the GI's" (*Chicago Defender*, 9 February 1946)
"Simple and the Secret" (*Chicago Defender*, 23 March 1946)
"Resolving Ain't Solving" (*Chicago Defender*, 13 April 1946)
"Simple and the Heads" (*Chicago Defender*, 27 April 1946)
"Simple's Psychosis" (*Chicago Defender*, 18 May 1946)
"Simple Sees Double" (*Chicago Defender*, 6 July 1946)

"Summer Ain't Simple" (*Chicago Defender*, 13 July 1946)
"Simple and the Country" (*Chicago Defender*, 27 July 1946)
"Simple on Commentators" (*Chicago Defender*, 17 August 1946)
"Simple's Vacation" (*Chicago Defender*, 28 September 1946)
"Simple and Harlem" (*Chicago Defender*, 5 October 1946)
"Simple's Landlady's Dog" (*Chicago Defender*, 26 October 1946)
"Simple Late at Night" (*Chicago Defender*, 2 November 1946)
"Simple Shivers" (*Chicago Defender*, 23 November 1946)
"Simple and the Dance" (*Chicago Defender*, 14 December 1946)
"Simple After the Holidays" (*Chicago Defender*, 11 January 1947)
"Simple and the Year Gone By" (*Chicago Defender*, 25 January 1947)
"Simple Lets Off Steam" (*Chicago Defender*, 1 March 1947)
"Simple, Soaring, and Sleeping" (*Chicago Defender*, 8 March 1947)
"Simple's Income Tax" (*Chicago Defender*, 15 March 1947)
"Simple and the High Prices" (*Chicago Defender*, 19 April 1947)
"Simple Sees Red" (*Chicago Defender*, 26 April 1947)
"Simple and the Seasons" (*Chicago Defender*, 7 June 1947)
"Simple's Un-Americanism" (*Chicago Defender*, 21 June 1947)
"Simple's Donation Problem" (*Chicago Defender*, 5 July 1947)
"Simple Woos the Muse" (*Chicago Defender*, 16 August 1947)
"Simple Dines Out" (*Chicago Defender*, 23 August 1947)
"Simple and Jackie" (*Chicago Defender*, 6 September 1947)
"Simple Writes a Book" (*Chicago Defender*, 27 September 1947)
"Simple Begs to Differ" (*Chicago Defender*, 11 October 1947)
"Simple and Temptation" (*Chicago Defender*, 25 October 1947)
"Simple at the Bar" (*Chicago Defender*, 22 November 1947)
"Simple Rocks a Rocket" (*Chicago Defender*, 24 January 1948)
"Simple and the License" (*Chicago Defender*, 7 February 1948)
"Simple at the Party" (*Chicago Defender*, 14 February 1948)
"Simple Plays with Fire" (*Chicago Defender*, 21 February 1948)
"Simple Down Under" (*Chicago Defender*, 28 February 1948)
"Simple Gets Confused" (*Chicago Defender*, 17 April 1948)
"Game Preserves for Negroes" (*Chicago Defender*, 24 April 1948)
"Simple and the Rosenwald Fund" (*Chicago Defender*, 12 June 1948)
"Simple and the Lingerie" (*Chicago Defender*, 3 July 1948)
"Simple Spins a Yarn" (*Chicago Defender*, 10 July 1948)
"Simple Goes on Record" (*Chicago Defender*, 17 July 1948)
"Simple's If" (*Chicago Defender*, 7 August 1948)
"Simple Betrayed" (*Chicago Defender*, 14 August 1948)
"Dumb, Dumber, Dumbest" (*Chicago Defender*, 21 August 1948)
"Simple and His Sins" (*Chicago Defender*, 28 August 1948)
"Simple After Hours" (*Chicago Defender*, 4 September 1948)
"Simple Thinks He's Simple" (*Chicago Defender*, 18 September 1948)
"Simple Brings Condemnation on Himself for a Simple Remark" (*Chicago Defender*, 23 October 1948)[20]
"Being No Vegetarian, Simple Wants, Gets Meat, But How!" (*Chicago Defender*, 13 November 1948)
"Simple's Cousin Slick Gets the Cure from Sister Clarina-Ray" (*Chicago Defender*, 27 November 1948)
"Simple Is No Patron of the Arts; Loves Music He Can Understand" (*Chicago Defender*, 11 December 1948)
"Brownskin Cards, Sepia Dolls, All Mean a Merrier Christmas" (*Chicago Defender*, 25 December 1948)
"Simple and the Clerk" (*Chicago Defender*, 1 January 1949)
"Simple on Recession" (*Chicago Defender*, 15 January 1949)
"Without a Word of Warning Simple Discloses His Creative Self" (*Chicago Defender*, 22 January 1949)[21]
"Simple Listens to a Bar-side Speech on Contrary Democracy" (*Chicago Defender*, 19 February 1949)
"Friend Simple Makes Startling Discovery About Other People" (*Chicago Defender*, 19 March 1949)
"Friend Simple's Philosophy: Let Other Fellow Do the Figuring" (*Chicago Defender*, 9 April 1949)
"Joyce Says, 'It's Just Matter of Taste'; Simple Gets Jealous" (*Chicago Defender*, 16 April 1949)

"Simple Contemplates Crossing the Ocean and Coming Back a Foreigner" (*Chicago Defender*, 30 April 1949)
"Simple Swears Off Pyramids; Finds Them Hard Work and Very Dangerous" (*Chicago Defender*, 14 May 1949)
"Simple Thinks Liberals Need a Mascot Like the Demos and GOP" (*Chicago Defender*, 21 May 1949)
"With Money, Love Is a Sweet Orange, Without, It's a Lemon" (*Chicago Defender*, 28 May 1949)
"Simple Says with Four Feet He Could Have Stood in More Places" (*Chicago Defender*, 9 July 1949)
"Words He Shouldn't Use Get Simple into the Dog House" (*Chicago Defender*, 23 July 1949)
"Don't Spring a Surprise, Simple Advises, Unless You Can Take One" (*Chicago Defender*, 13 August 1949)
"Simple Does Some Talking About Dogs, Cars, Houses and Lots" (*Chicago Defender*, 3 September 1949)
"Simple Gets a Letter That Brings Him Freedom and Changes His Life" (*Chicago Defender*, 10 September 1949)
"Simple Tells a Tall Tale That Might or Not Be True" (*Chicago Defender*, 17 September 1949)
"Simple Supposes What Would Happen if Our People Were Immune to Atom Bomb" (*Chicago Defender*, 29 October 1949)
"Simple Declares Be-Bop Music Comes from Bop! Bop! Bop! Mop!" (*Chicago Defender*, 19 November 1949)
"Simple Says for Thanksgiving There Are Some Things Better Than Turkey" (*Chicago Defender*, 26 November 1949)
"Simple Wants to Be Santa Claus Just for One Day" (*Chicago Defender*, 17 December 1949)
"Simple Makes Up a Xmas Song About the Black Wise Man" (*Chicago Defender*, 24 December 1949)
"Simple Resolves to Keep His 1950 Resolutions This Year" (*Chicago Defender*, 7 January 1950)
"If Simple Had $1,000,000, He'd Get His Wife a Job First Thing" (*Chicago Defender*, 21 January 1950)
"Simple Does Not Believe Climate Bears a Relation to Achievement" (*Chicago Defender*, 28 January 1950)
"According to Joyce, White Women Are Out to Ruin the Negro" (*Chicago Defender*, 25 February 1950)
"Joyce Says If a King Give Up His Throne, Shame on Him" (*Chicago Defender*, 11 March 1950)
"Jess Simple Is Charged, but It's Not with What You Think It Is" (*Chicago Defender*, 18 March 1950)
"Simple Says Joyce Is Just Like a Small Mule When Her Mind Gets Set" (*Chicago Defender*, 1 April 1950)
"Joyce Prepares for the Easter Parade While Simple Speaks His Mind" (*Chicago Defender*, 8 April 1950)
"Simple Becomes a Book and So Looks Forward to a New and Better Life" (*Chicago Defender*, 15 April 1950)
"Simple Wants to Change the Calendar All Around Just to Suit Himself" (*Chicago Defender*, 22 April 1950)
"Simple Makes Talk About FEPC but Joyce Has Bigamy on Her Mind" (*Chicago Defender*, 6 May 1950)
"Simple Declares That It Is True, but Science Would Say It Is a Lie" (*Chicago Defender*, 27 May 1950)
"Simple Makes a Graduation Speech for Black Children in a White World" (*Chicago Defender*, 10 June 1950)
"Simple Would Like to Be a Bird, but Not Pretty Enough for a Cage" (*Chicago Defender*, 24 June 1950)
"Simple Goes from Coast to Coast and Is Now Heading for London" (*Chicago Defender*, 1 July 1950)
"When Your End Come, You Will Go, But Simple Wonders How He Can Live Till Then" (*Chicago Defender*, 8 July 1950)
"For Once, Jess Simple Has Money Due ... in Fact ... Overdue" (*Chicago Defender*, 22 July 1950)
"Joyce Informs Simple of a Certain Technicality Relative to Marriage" (*Chicago Defender*, 29 July 1950)
"Simple Has His Picture Taken to Decorate Joyce's Dresser" (*Chicago Defender*, 19 August 1950)
"Simple Makes Up Proverbs Right Out of His Own Head" (*Chicago Defender*, 26 August 1950)
"Simple Knows It Ain't Good to Say 'Ain't,' He Care Not" (*Chicago Defender*, 2 September 1950)
"Mail Me Some More Kinds of Greens if I Missed Any, Says Simple" (*Chicago Defender*, 16 September 1950)
"Simple Says if He Is Not Wanted Where He Would Like to Go, Woe!" (*Chicago Defender*, 23 September 1950)
"Simple Says If He Was a Landlord All Tenants Would Have Their Own Bells" (*Chicago Defender*, 7 October 1950)
"Simple Speaks of War and Peace and Comes Out in a Circle" (*Chicago Defender*, 28 October 1950)

"Under One Condition Only Will Simple Become a Philatelist" (*Chicago Defender*, 4 November 1950)
"Simple Is Glad That Christmas Cheer Does Not Come but Once Each Year" (*Chicago Defender*, 23 December 1950)
"So Many Are the Clothes We Wear, I'd Just as Leave My Back Was Bare" (*Chicago Defender*, 6 January 1951)
"Jess Simple's Mind Wanders from Things to 'The Thing'" (*Chicago Defender*, 13 January 1951)
"When It Comes to Selling Tickets for a Tea, Simple Had Rather Die" (*Chicago Defender*, 27 January 1951)
"Simple Speaks of Winter, Wings, and Being Washed Whiter than Snow" (*Chicago Defender*, 10 February 1951)
"Simple Says He Has Lost His Boundaries and Can't Find No Way Out" (*Chicago Defender*, 17 February 1951)
"Simple Remembers an Empty Room When the Roomer Went Away" (*Chicago Defender*, 24 February 1951)
"Simple Says One Drop Makes All Who Have It the Same" (*Chicago Defender*, 3 March 1951)
"Chinches, Says Simple, Can Really Bug a Man, but So Can a Woman" (*Chicago Defender*, 17 March 1951)
"Simple Says Women Bring Everything Down to Their Own Level—Which Is Personal" (*Chicago Defender*, 24 March 1951)
"Simple Says a Formal Costs Almost as Much as a Funeral—and Only One Flower" (*Chicago Defender*, 14 April 1951)
"Simple, in His Simple Way, Visualizes a Great Day" (*Chicago Defender*, 5 May 1951)
"Simple Meets Zarita at a Five O'Clock Cocktail Sip" (*Chicago Defender*, 12 May 1951)
"Silence, Simple Declares Simply, Is All of the Cold He Possesses" (*Chicago Defender*, 19 May 1951)
"Simple Defines Love ... but Doesn't Want an Angel" (*Chicago Defender*, 9 June 1951)
"Simple Says the Question May Be Foolish, but the Answer Is Criminal" (*Chicago Defender*, 23 June 1951)
"Simple Bases His Version of Democracy on What Sugar Ray Did in France" (*Chicago Defender*, 30 June 1951)
"Simple Has Problems and They Begin in the Morning" (*Chicago Defender*, 28 July 1951)
"It's OK to Be Reserved, Says Simple, but Not at My Expense" (*Chicago Defender*, 8 September 1951)
"A Man Is as Young as a Woman Inspires Him to Be, Says Simple" (*Chicago Defender*, 15 September 1951)
"Simple Woos the Muse Again, but the Results Are Clear Only to Himself" (*Chicago Defender*, 22 September 1951)
"If Wishes Were Real, Then Simple Would Chance Reality" (*Chicago Defender*, 20 October 1951)
"Simple Says a White Sheep Is Worse Than a Black Sheep Anyday" (*Chicago Defender*, 3 November 1951)
"Simple Argues About Thanksgiving and Wishes a Happy One to You" (*Chicago Defender*, 24 November 1951)
"Simple Writes Letter to Leader He Did Not Know Was Leading" (*Chicago Defender*, 1 December 1951)
"Politics, Says Simple, Is Like a See-Saw, Republicans on One End and Democrats on the Other" (*Chicago Defender*, 5 January 1952)
"To Simple, Second-Hand Clothes Bring Some Second-Hand Woes" (*Chicago Defender*, 19 January 1952)
"Once in a Wife-Time, Says Simple, Women Will Give In on an Argument" (*Chicago Defender*, 26 January 1952)
"Simple Has Butts on the Brain, So He Writes to Him Again" (*Chicago Defender*, 2 February 1952)
"The High Cost of Love, Says Simple, Simply Brigs a Poor Man Down Low" (*Chicago Defender*, 23 February 1952)
"Simple Says the Road Is Longer in Front Than It Is Behind" (*Chicago Defender*, 1 March 1952)
"Simple Would Put His White Friends to the Final Test ... Their Vote" (*Chicago Defender*, 15 March 1952)
"If Wishes Were Horses, Simple Would Give Zarita One Today" (*Chicago Defender*, 22 March 1952)
"To Backslide Is Bad, Says Simple, but Worse When You Are Left on Your Back" (*Chicago Defender*, 19 April 1952)

"Far from Living Up to Its Name, Dixie Has Neither Manners Nor Shame" (*Chicago Defender*, 26 April 1952)

"Simple Says Lots of Folks Migrate North but Almost Nobody Migrates South" (*Chicago Defender*, 17 May 1952)

"Simple Works Like a Negro All Day to Live Like White Folks at Night" (*Chicago Defender*, 7 June 1952)

"What Makes Society, Asks Simple, Manners, or Morals, or Money?" (*Chicago Defender*, 14 June 1952)

"Simple's Next Door Neighbor Asks a Question That Gives Him Pause" (*Chicago Defender*, 28 June 1952)

"Dinner Was All Right, but the Conversation Got Simple Down" (*Chicago Defender*, 12 July 1952)

"There Is as Much Difference Between Day and Night as There Is Between Races" (*Chicago Defender*, 19 July 1952)

"Simple Discusses the News and Gets It All Confused" (*Chicago Defender*, 2 August 1952)

"No Man Broke Up Simple's Marriage but the Word Still Begins with 'M'" (*Chicago Defender*, 23 August 1952)

"What Can a Man Say to a Woman That Is Not Wrong?" (*Chicago Defender*, 30 August 1952)

"Joyce Is Going Away but Simple Doesn't Know How Far" (*Chicago Defender*, 6 September 1952)

"Simple Is Always Bringing up 'Race' Because He's Always Coming Face to Face with 'Race'" (*Chicago Defender*, 27 September 1952)

"A Vacation Keeps You Broke, Busted, Disgusted and Rest-Broken, Says Simple" (*Chicago Defender*, 4 October 1952)

"Simple Wants to Know How Complex Can a Complex Be" (*Chicago Defender*, 25 October 1952)

"Crowded, Colored, and Crowded Simple Says First Clown Down, Then Unclown" (*Chicago Defender*, 29 November 1952)

"Christmas Is a Merry Time—Therefore, I Will Make a Rhyme" (*Chicago Defender*, 3 January 1953)

"There's No Jim Crow, Says Simple, for a Dog-Gone Dog" (*Chicago Defender*, 24 January 1953)

"Simple Would Lend Ike His Book on the Vicarious Experiences of Jim Crow" (*Chicago Defender*, 7 February 1953)

"Simple's Imagination Runs Riot Again—And It Is Truly Wonderful" (*Chicago Defender*, 21 February 1953)

"Simple Declares Joyce Said Some Magazines Make Her Face Red" (*Chicago Defender*, 7 March 1953)

"Simple Preaches Jim Crow's Funeral and Actually Lays His Soul to Rest" (*Chicago Defender*, 21 March 1953)

"Some Things a Man Should Not Think of Before Marriage, Says Simple" (*Chicago Defender*, 4 April 1953)

"There's Nothing Amiss About Wedded Bliss, Says Simple" (*Chicago Defender*, 30 May 1953)

"'Simple Takes a Wife' and Thus Two Become as One" (*Chicago Defender*, 6 June 1953)

"Simple Says Sometimes He Feels Lost in the Backyard of the World" (*Chicago Defender*, 13 June 1953)

"Simple and Einstein Both Tackle the Riddle of the Universe" (*Chicago Defender*, 27 June 1953)

"Simple Says a Balled-Up Fist Beats a Stretched-Forth Hand" (*Chicago Defender*, 11 July 1953)

"Simple Says It Is Hard to Remember to Forget" (*Chicago Defender*, 12 September 1953)

"No Regrets and No Fears Says Simple, Bring No Fears" (*Chicago Defender*, 17 October 1953)

"Gospel Singers and Gospel Swingers Are Gone, Says Simple, Gone!" (*Chicago Defender*, 12 December 1953)

"Simple Says Uncle Sam Should Worry About Harlem Not Trieste" (*Chicago Defender*, 19 December 1953)

"Simple Enjoys Silent Night, Holy Night When the Big Kitchenette Fight Is Over" (*Chicago Defender*, 26 December 1953)

"Simple Says If He Were Puerto Rican, He Would Not Understand Either" (*Chicago Defender*, 2 January 1954)

"Simple Says It Is Nobody's Business but His Very Own" (*Chicago Defender*, 23 January 1954)

"Simple Says Emily Post in His Home Was the Most" (*Chicago Defender*, 30 January 1954)

"Simple Wants to Start Himself Another Magazine" (*Chicago Defender*, 8 February 1954)

"When the Atom Comes, Negroes Goes Out, Says Simple" (*Chicago Defender*, 27 February 1954)

"Simple Speaks His Mind Concerning High-Tone Dogs" (*Chicago Defender*, 6 March 1954)

"In His Case, Says Simple, Two Sides Are Not Enough" (*Chicago Defender*, 13 March 1954)

"How Jim Crow Will Jim Crow Air Raid Shelters Be, Asks Simple" (*Chicago Defender*, 20 March 1954)
"House-Rent Parties Returning; Simple Sees Depression Coming" (*Chicago Defender*, 27 March 1954)
"Simple Confuses Golfing and Goofing in Georgia" (*Chicago Defender*, 3 April 1954)
"Simple Says, 'What's So Wonderful About Doing Right?'" (*Chicago Defender*, 29 May 1954)
"Charged with Atoms, Simple Takes Charge" (*Chicago Defender*, 10 July 1954)
"Joyce Discusses Hats and Bombs with Jesse B. Simple" (*Chicago Defender*, 17 July 1954)
"Simple Had Rather Die Than Diet—Without Pork" (*Chicago Defender*, 7 August 1954)
"Simple Casts a Dark Eye on That First Day in School" (*Chicago Defender*, 14 August 1954)
"When It Comes to Housing, Says Simple, Things Move in Circles" (*Chicago Defender*, 28 August 1954)
"Situations Cause Triggeration, According to Simple" (*Chicago Defender*, 11 September 1954)
"Joyce Brings Simple Down to Earth by Handing Him a Broom and Dust Rag" (*Chicago Defender*, 18 September 1954)
"Simple's Bank Is Held Up and His Pride Let Down" (*Chicago Defender*, 25 September 1954)
"Simple Says Jazz, Jive and Jam Could Help Integration Along" (*Chicago Defender*, 16 October 1954)
"Joyce Brings Simple Down to Earth with Dust Rag" (*Chicago Defender*, 30 October 1954)
"Simple Says It's Hard to Be Above What You're Underneath" (*Chicago Defender*, 6 November 1954)
"Two Chapters in the Bible Read the Same, Says Simple" (*Chicago Defender*, 20 November 1954)
"A Simple Tale About a Dog Named Trilby" (*Chicago Defender*, 27 November 1954)
"Simple Commits a Faux Pas in Harlem English" (*Chicago Defender*, 29 January 1955)
"Simple Has New Idea for a Public Dance" (*Chicago Defender*, 5 February 1955)
"Wigs, Women and Falsies Flabbergast Simple" (*Chicago Defender*, 26 February 1955)
"Simple Wonders if Eartha Kitt Owns the Colored Magazines" (*Chicago Defender*, 12 March 1955)
"Simple Says Certain Hidden Bandits Outdo Real Ones" (*Chicago Defender*, 19 March 1955)
"Well, All Right, Says Simple, Here's to Saturday Night" (*Chicago Defender*, 26 March 1955)
"Easter Comes but Once a Year, Husbands, Be of Good Cheer" (*Chicago Defender*, 9 April 1955)
"Simple Says White Folks Should Be Born Old, Not Young" (*Chicago Defender*, 23 April 1955)
"Simple Says Nobody Names Girls After February or August—Why?" (*Chicago Defender*, 30 April 1955)
"No Civil War Without an Atom Bomb, Says Simple" (*Chicago Defender*, 28 May 1955)
"Simple Points Out How to Count as a Count" (*Chicago Defender*, 4 June 1955)
"Simple Wonders Why Some Folks Are Just Born Evil" (*Chicago Defender*, 11 June 1955)
"Barber Shops and Women Are Both Problems, Says Simple" (*Chicago Defender*, 18 June 1955)
"Simple Wonders Why There Are No Lady Pallbearers" (*Chicago Defender*, 16 July 1955)
"Simple Says You Take Reason and He'll Take Right" (*Chicago Defender*, 27 August 1955)
"Whit Folks Are Playing a New Kind of Dozens, Says Simple" (*Chicago Defender*, 3 September 1955)
"Peace for World—If No Husbands Lies at Home, Says Simple" (*Chicago Defender*, 24 September 1955)
"Simple Evaluates the Tone of a Community" (*Chicago Defender*, 8 October 1955)
"I Feel Mississippi's Fist in My Own Face, Says Simple" (*Chicago Defender*, 15 October 1955)
"Big Money and Big Cigars, Says Simple, Naturally Go Together" (*Chicago Defender*, 29 October 1955)
"Three Balls, Says Simple, Often Kept Him from Behind the 8-Ball" (*Chicago Defender*, 5 November 1955)
"To Bypass Laws That Castigate, Simple Will Not Premeditate" (*Chicago Defender*, 12 November 1955)
"Simple's Plan for Worship in Peace: Make Church Fort" (*Chicago Defender*, 19 November 1955)
"Simple Outlines Platform for His Own Election Race" (*Chicago Defender*, 3 December 1955)
"Simple Speaks of Rivers and Seeking a Dry Land" (*Chicago Defender*, 18 February 1956)
"Joyce Proves Herself Hip to Cousin Minnie's Live" (*Chicago Defender*, 25 February 1956)
"Simple: Home-Grown Colored Folks Have Less Weight Than Foreign" (*Chicago Defender*, 3 March 1956)
"Speak-Easy Freedom Even Is No Hype, Says Simple" (*Chicago Defender*, 7 April 1956)
"It's All According to Whose Ox Is Gored, Says Simple" (*Chicago Defender*, 17 March 1956)
"When Push Comes to Shove, Says Minnie, 'Don't Worry About Me'" (*Chicago Defender*, 21 April 1956)
"Simple: "Does King Cole Still Sing, 'Straighten Up and Fly Right'?" (*Chicago Defender*, 28 April 1956)
"Simple Says It Isn't Funny When Relatives Borrow Money" (*Chicago Defender*, 5 May 1956)
"Simple Claims Harlem as Perry Claimed the Pole" (*Chicago Defender*, 12 May 1956)
"Since Minnie Found Friends Simple No Longer Lends and Lends" (*Chicago Defender*, 19 May 1956)
"Simple Produces a Film on an Afro-American Theme" (*Chicago Defender*, 2 June 1956)
"Simple Speaks His Mind Concerning the Vogue for Cellophane" (*Chicago Defender*, 9 June 1956)

"Simple on the Merits and Demerits of a Neighbor" (*Chicago Defender*, 16 June 1956)
"'Death, Where Is Thy Sting?' Bert Williams Used to Sing" (*Chicago Defender*, 14 July 1956)
"Simple: Egypt on the Brain Can Cause a Man Much Pain" (*Chicago Defender*, 11 August 1956)
"Between the Cup and the Lip There's a Slop and a Slip" (*Chicago Defender*, 25 August 1956)
"Simple Speaks His Mind on Woes of House Cleaning" (*Chicago Defender*, 8 September 1956)
"Summer All Too Short and Schools Opening Too Soon" (*Chicago Defender*, 22 September 1956)
"Simple Wants to Know What Is Extreme About Negroes" (*Chicago Defender*, 29 September 1956)
"Simple Dreams Up a Nightmare for the Deep South" (*Chicago Defender*, 6 October 1956)
"Like Nothing Human, Is the Way Simple Describes New Hair-Do's" (*Chicago Defender*, 17 November 1956)
"Simple Says, Left or Right, Both Are White" (*Chicago Defender*, 19 January 1957)
"Goodbye, Yesterday, Says Simple, Let's See What Tomorrow Brings" (*Chicago Defender*, 26 January 1957)
"Simple Goes Through Mississippi, Letter by Letter" (*Chicago Defender*, 2 February 1947)
"Simple Wants to Celebrate Another History Week Each Year" (*Chicago Defender*, 9 February 1957)
"In History All's Well That Ends Well, Says Simple" (*Chicago Defender*, 16 February 1957)
"Simple and the Hungarians: Be Broadminded, Please!" (*Chicago Defender*, 23 February 1957)
"Simple Says Acting Right Is Better Than Writing Right" (*Chicago Defender*, 23 March 1957)
"Chips on the Shoulder Pay for No Beers at the Bar" (*Chicago Defender*, 6 April 1957)
"Simple: Hands Versus Head Leaves Hand in Lurch" (*Chicago Defender*, 1 June 1957)
"Let's Organize as Well as Mobilize, Says Simple" (*Chicago Defender*, 8 June 1957)
"Life Is Too Short for Simple" (*Chicago Defender*, 29 June 1957)
"Simple's Cousinship with Minnie is Adrift" (*Chicago Defender*, 6 July 1957)
"A Native Enemy, Says Simple, Is No Good Either" (*Chicago Defender*, 20 July 1957)
"Simple on Manners and Morals, Past and Present" (*Chicago Defender*, 27 July 1957)
"Simple Wants to be a Turnkey at Tuskegee" (*Chicago Defender*, 10 August 1957)
"Simple Speaks His Mind on Juvenile Delinquency" (*Chicago Defender*, 17 August 1957)
"Juke Box Melodies on Simple's Song Sheet" (*Chicago Defender*, 24 August 1957)
"Society's Not What It Is Cracked Up to Be" (*Chicago Defender*, 21 September 1957)
"The Mice Will Play When the Cat's Away" (*Chicago Defender*, 28 September 1957)
"Beauty Is as Beauty Looks" (*Chicago Defender*, 12 October 1957)
"Simple Ruminates on Bird in the Hand" (*Chicago Defender*, 2 November 1957)
"Simple's Same Old Seven-and-Six" (*Chicago Defender*, 9 November 1957)
"Simple Says an Egg Is Laid in Democracy's Nest" (*Chicago Defender*, 16 November 1957)
"[Conversation]" (*Chicago Defender*, 30 November 1957)
"Why Not Fool Our White Folks?" (*Chicago Defender*, 4 January 1958)
"Simple's World of Black and White" (*Chicago Defender*, 25 January 1958)
"Simple, Indians, and the K.K.K." (*Chicago Defender*, 1 February 1958)
"Simple on Sermons" (*Chicago Defender*, 8 March 1958)
"Simple on Women in the Past" (*Chicago Defender*, 15 March 1958)
"I See in the News, Says Simple" (*Chicago Defender*, 22 March 1958)
"Simple on the Other Side of God" (*Chicago Defender*, 29 March 1958)
"[Conversation]" (*Chicago Defender*, 5 April 1958)
"Simple on Tasteless Integration" (*Chicago Defender*, 12 April 1958)
"'Vengeance Is Mine,' Sayeth the Children" (*Chicago Defender*, 26 April 1958)
"Simple's Vicissitudes" (*Chicago Defender*, 10 May 1958)
"Work, Wives, Weariness, and Simple" (*Chicago Defender*, 24 May 1958)
"Nixon, Simple, Little Rock and Why" (*Chicago Defender*, 31 May 1958)
"Simple Says, 'Black Is Basic'" (*Chicago Defender*, 5 July 1958)
"Simple Simplifies Matters" (*Chicago Defender*, 12 July 1958)
"Simple Discourses on Summer Reading" (*Chicago Defender*, 19 July 1958)
"Simple's United Front" (*Chicago Defender*, 26 July 1958)
"Simple Remembers Rumble Seats" (*Chicago Defender*, 2 August 1958)
"Simple on Dogs, Dog Days, and Dogwood" (*Chicago Defender*, 23 August 1958)
"Simple on the Color of the Law" (*Chicago Defender*, 6 September 1958)
"Simple on Men and Mice" (*Chicago Defender*, 20 September 1958)

"These Children Nowadays" (*Chicago Defender*, 27 September 1958)
"How Simple Can You Get?" (*Chicago Defender*, 4 October 1958)
"Simple's Shadow, the Blues" (*Chicago Defender*, 11 October 1958)
"Simple Discusses Rocks" (*Chicago Defender*, 18 October 1958)
"Simple on Juvenile Delinquents" (*Chicago Defender*, 25 October 1958)
"How Many Words for 'Drunk?'" (*Chicago Defender*, 1 November 1958)
"Simple on Cats and Dogs" (*Chicago Defender*, 8 November 1958)
"Simple's Certain Time of Day" (*Chicago Defender*, 22 November 1958)
"The Last Shall Be First, Says Simple" (*Chicago Defender*, 29 November 1958)
"Simple on Fighting Souls" (*Chicago Defender*, 6 December 1958)
"'Stop Reaching for Moons,' Says Simple" (*Chicago Defender*, 13 December 1958)
"Simple on Feet, Feet and Feet" (*Chicago Defender*, 3 January 1959)
"Simple Recollects Too Much" (*Chicago Defender*, 17 January 1959)
"Simple Discusses Ladyhood" (*Chicago Defender*, 31 January 1959)
"Let's Take Back Our African Names" (*Chicago Defender*, 7 February 1959)
"Simple on Negro History Week" (*Chicago Defender*, 21 February 1959)
"Corked and Crowned All at Once" (*Chicago Defender*, 28 February 1959)
"Simple Contemplates a Change" (*Chicago Defender*, 7 March 1959)
"'If I Was President,' Says Simple" (*Chicago Defender*, 21 March 1959)
"[Youth]" (*Chicago Defender*, 25 April 1959)
"[Great-grandmother an Indian]" (*Chicago Defender*, 2 May 1959)
"Simple Dreams Some Dreams" (*Chicago Defender*, 9 May 1959)
"Uncle Talmadge Cuts Hog" (*Chicago Defender*, 16 May 1959)
"Simple Pays His Respects" (*Chicago Defender*, 6 June 1959)
"Simple Is a Dreaming Fool" (*Chicago Defender*, 13 June 1959)
"A Cracker Prays a Prayer" (*Chicago Defender*, 20 June 1959)
"Chicken Is Just a Bird" (*Chicago Defender*, 27 June 1959)
"Simple Contemplate His Crimes" (*Chicago Defender*, 4 July 1959)
"Simple Speculates on Peace" (*Chicago Defender*, 11 July 1959)
"Bull Session at the Bar" (*Chicago Defender*, 26 September 1959)
"Cousin Minnie Lays a Hype" (*Chicago Defender*, 10 October 1959)
"Cousin Minnie Borrows Again" (*Chicago Defender*, 31 October 1959)
"Footholds and Toeholds" (*Chicago Defender*, 7 November 1959)
"Gone to the Dogs" (*Chicago Defender*, 14 November 1959)
"Reflections at the Bar" (*Chicago Defender*, 30 January 1959)
"Simple Rings a Bell" (*Chicago Defender*, 6 February 1960)
"Simple on Negro History Week" (*Chicago Defender*, 13 February 1960)
"Simple's Political Platform" (*Chicago Defender*, 12 March 1960)
"Letter to the President" (*Chicago Defender*, 26 March 1960)
"In the Name of Douglass" (*Chicago Defender*, 2 April 1960)
"Simple's Extra Minutes" (*Chicago Defender*, 9 April 1960)
"Women and Problems" (*Chicago Defender*, 23 April 1960)
"Simple's Million Dollars" (*Chicago Defender*, 30 April 1960)
"Simple's of Courses" (*Chicago Defender*, 7 May 1960)
"Simple Dreams Up a Breeze" (*Chicago Defender*, 21 May 1960)
"White Folks, Watch Out" (*Chicago Defender*, 28 May 1960)
"Dreams on a Wide Veranda" (*Chicago Defender*, 4 June 1960)
"Simple at the Summit" (*Chicago Defender*, 11 June 1960)
"Simple's Top and Bottom" (*Chicago Defender*, 18 June 1960)
"Simple and Sex" (*Chicago Defender*, 25 June 1960)
"Simple and the Sounds" (*Chicago Defender*, 2 July 1960)
"Simple's Connections" (*Chicago Defender*, 9 July 1960)
"Simple, Sammy Davis and Joyce" (*Chicago Defender*, 30 July 1960)
"[Conversation]" (*Chicago Defender*, 13 August 1960)
"[Opera]" (*Chicago Defender*, 27 August 1960)
"[Bad Hair]" (*Chicago Defender*, 10 September 1960)

"Simple and 'The New York Times'" (*Chicago Defender*, 15 October 1960)
"Simple and the Ads" (*Chicago Defender*, 22 October 1960)
"Simple at the U.N." (*Chicago Defender*, 29 October 1960)
"Democrats and Republicans" (*Chicago Defender*, 5 November 1960)
"Simple a la Carte" (*Chicago Defender*, 3 December 1960)
"Cousin Minnie's Candle" (*Chicago Defender*, 10 December 1960)
"Minnie's Way with Men" (*Chicago Defender*, 17 December 1960)
"Simple's Happy New Year" (*Chicago Defender*, 31 December 1960)
"Simple Sits in Judgment" (*Chicago Defender*, 7 January 1961)
"Love, Work and Money" (*Chicago Defender*, 14 January 1961)
"Heads, Hair and Dreams" (*Chicago Defender*, 21 January 1961)
"Simple's Sermon on Speed" (*Chicago Defender*, 28 January 1961)
"One Word Leads to Another" (*Chicago Defender*, 4 February 1961)
"Hipsters, Hypes and Hustling" (*Chicago Defender*, 25 February 1961)
"Imagination Stretches Only So Far" (*Chicago Defender*, 4 March 1961)
"Meat, Mecca, and Beer" (*Chicago Defender*, 11 March 1961)
"Western, White, and Wicked" (*Chicago Defender*, 18 March 1961)
"Simple's Lively Ghost" (*Chicago Defender*, 1 April 1961)
"Simple's Promulgations" (*Chicago Defender*, 8 April 1961)
"Simple as a Missionary" (*Chicago Defender*, 22 April 1961)
"Cousin Minnie's Candle" (*Chicago Defender*, 28 April 1961)
"Simple on Sex" (*Chicago Defender*, 13 May 1961)
"Simple's Complex" (*Chicago Defender*, 20 May 1961)
"[Conversation]" (*Chicago Defender*, 27 May 1961)
"Simple's Questionnaire" (*Chicago Defender*, 3 June 1961)
"'Adventure Guaranteed'—Simple" (*Chicago Defender*, 24 June 1961)
"Simple for President" (*Chicago Defender*, 1 July 1961)
"Even Presidents Is Simple, Says Simple" (*Chicago Defender*, 8 July 1961)
"Simple at the Golden Gate" (*Chicago Defender*, 22 July 1961)
"Hamlet in Mississippi" (*Chicago Defender*, 29 July 1961)
"Simple: Jail-ins" (*Chicago Defender*, 5 August 1961)
"Beer, Berlin and Simple" (*Chicago Defender*, 12 August 1961)
"Simple at the U.N." (*Chicago Defender*, 23 September 1961)
"[African Americans]" (*Chicago Defender*, 7 October 1961)
"Nothing but a Dog" (*Chicago Defender*, 4 November 1961)
"Simple's Atomic Dream" (*Chicago Defender*, 11 November 1961)
"Data for Simple's Census" (*Chicago Defender*, 18 November 1961)
"Simple Lives Again" (*Chicago Defender*, 25 November 1961)
"Simple Writes a Letter" (*Chicago Defender*, 2 December 1961)
"Christmas Gifts for Satan" (*Chicago Defender*, 16 December 1961)
"Simple's Ups and Downs" (*Chicago Defender*, 22 September 1962)
"Flay or Pray?" (*Chicago Defender*, 6 October 1962)
"Oh, Careless Love..." (*Chicago Defender*, 13 October 1962)
"Second Civil War" (*Chicago Defender*, 20 October 1962)
"A Toast to 'Ole Miss'" (*Chicago Defender*, 27 October 1962)
"Simple's Nobel Prize" (*Chicago Defender*, 3 November 1962)
"Violent or Non" (*Chicago Defender*, 17 November 1962)
"Negroes and Missiles" (*Chicago Defender*, 24 November 1962)
"Jim Crow's Epitaph" (*Chicago Defender*, 1 December 1962)
"Face and Race" (*Chicago Defender*, 8 December 1962)
"Two Ends of a Bar" (*Chicago Defender*, 22 December 1962)
"Haircuts and U.S.A." (*Chicago Defender*, 29 December 1962)
"Something Real and Personal" (*Chicago Defender*, 5 January 1963)
"A Swinging New Year" (*Chicago Defender*, 19 January 1963)
"Disgrace and Race" (*Chicago Defender*, 26 January 1963)
"Simply Doggy" (*Chicago Defender*, 2 February 1963)

"Simple's Hard Luck" (*Chicago Defender*, 16 February 1963)
"Simple on Women and Work" (*Chicago Defender*, 2 March 1963)
"Simple, Mona Lisa and Joyce" (*Chicago Defender*, 16 March 1963)
"Simple's Kin Left No Will" (*Chicago Defender*, 23 March 1963)
"Thorns in White Man's Side" (*Chicago Defender*, 27 April 1963)
"Home Is an Open Door" (*Chicago Defender*, 4 May 1963)
"Simple as President of All People" (*Chicago Defender*, 25 May 1963)
"Harlem Rough for Little Child" (*Chicago Defender*, 1 June 1963)
"Racism, America's Dilemma" (*Chicago Defender*, 8 June 1963)
"Memories of a Picture" (*Chicago Defender*, 15 June 1963)
"Just to Keep from Going Crazy" (*Chicago Defender*, 22 June 1963)
"Simple Talks on Kneel-Ins" (*Chicago Defender*, 13 July 1963)
"Racists Bugged by Protests" (*Chicago Defender*, 27 July 1963)
"Old Folks with Nobody" (*Chicago Defender*, 10 August 1963)
"Simple—Pro and Con" (*Chicago Defender*, 17 August 1963)
"Old, Old, How Old Is Old?" (*Chicago Defender*, 24 August 1963)
"By and Large" (*Chicago Defender*, 13 February 1965)
"[Conversation]" (*Chicago Defender*, 27 February 1965)
"Miss Boss" (*Chicago Defender*, 20 March 1965)
"Drinks, Deacons, Dollars" (*Chicago Defender*, 27 March 1965)
"Simple's Cousin Lynn" (*Chicago Defender*, 10 April 1965)
"New Plan" (*Chicago Defender*, 17 April 1965)
"If Simple Went to Selma" (*Chicago Defender*, 24 April 1965)
"Uncle Sam" (*Chicago Defender*, 1 May 1965)
"The Hypocrite" (*Chicago Defender*, 22 May 1965)
"Not Enough" (*Chicago Defender*, 29 May 1965)
"It's a Gasser" (*Chicago Defender*, 5 June 1965)
"Not Far Enough" (*Chicago Defender*, 19 June 1965)
"Birth Control" (*Chicago Defender*, 3 July 1965)
"Ruminations" (*Chicago Defender*, 7 August 1965)
"Misplaced Race?" (*Chicago Defender*, 21 August 1965)
"[Watts]" (*Chicago Defender*, 4 September 1965)
"Beards and Beer" (*Chicago Defender*, 25 September 1965)
"On Angel Equity" (*Chicago Defender*, 16 October 1965)
"Simple Is Heard All Over the World" (*Chicago Defender*, 20 November 1965)
"Black-White Unite to Write" (*Chicago Defender*, 27 November 1965)
"Send King to Rhodesia" (*Chicago Defender*, 11 December 1965)
"Yule Gift List for Simple" (*Chicago Defender*, 25 December 1965)
"'The Beginning...' '...And the End'" (*Chicago Defender*, 8 January 1966)

BOOKS
   (1) *Simple Speaks His Mind* (1950)
   (2) *Simple Takes a Wife* (1953)
   (3) *Simple Stakes a Claim* (1957)
   (4) *The Best of Simple* (1961)
   (5) *Simple's Uncle Sam* (1965)
   (6) *The Simple Omnibus* (1978) (15 stories from [3])
   (7) *Laughing to Keep from Crying: 25 Jesse Semple Stories* (1981)
   (8) *The Return of Simple* (1994) ed. Donna Akiba Sullivan Harper
   (9) *The Early Semple Stories* (Collected Works of Langston Hughes, Vol. 7) ed. Donna Akiba Sullivan Harper (2002) (1) (2) (and other stories)
   (10) *The Later Semple Stories* (Collected Works of Langston Hughes, Vol. 8) (2002) ed. Donna Akiba Sullivan Harper (3) (5) (and other stories)

PLAY
Simply Heavenly (1957) (musical folk comedy in two acts, book and lyrics by Langston Hughes, music by David Martin)

SOURCES

Carey, Julian C. "Jesse B. Semple Revisited and Revised," *Phylon*, Vol. 32, No. 2 (second quarter 1971), 158–163.
Davis, Arthur P. "Jesse B. Semple: Negro American," *Phylon*, Vol. 15, No. 1, first quarter, 1954), 21–28.
De Santis, Christopher C. *Langston Hughes and the Chicago Defender: Essays on Race, Politics, and Culture, 1942–1962*. Urbana: University of Illinois Press, 1995.
Dickinson, Donald C. *A Bio-bibliography of Langston Hughes 1902–1967*. Second edition, revised. Hamden, CT: Archon Books, 1972.
Gibson, Donald B. *Not So Simple* review, *African American Review*, Vol. 31, No. 3 (1997).
Harper, Donna Akiba Sullivan. *Not So Simple: The "Simple" Stories of Langston Hughes*. University of Missouri, 1996.
Hughes, Langston. "Simple and Me," *Phylon*, Vol. 6 No. 4, fourth quarter, 1945.
_____. "To Negro Writers," reprinted in *American Writer's Congress*, Henry Hart, ed. New York: International Publishers, 1935.
Klotman, Phyllis R. "Jesse B. Semple and the Narrative Art of Langston Hughes," *Journal of Narrative Technique*, Vol. 3, No. 1 (January 1973), 66–75.
"Langston Hughes, Writer, 65, Dead," *The New York Times*, 23 May 1967.
O'Daniel, Therman B. "Langston Hughes: An Updated Bibliography," *Black American Literature Forum*, Vol. 15, No. 3 (autumn 1981), 104–107.
Rampersad, Arnold. *The Life of Langston Hughes: Volume 2: 1941–1967, I Dream a World*. New York: Oxford University Press, 2002.
Return of Semple, review, *Kirkus Reviews*, 1 May 1994.
Riley, Sam G. "Langston Hughes's Jesse B. Semple Columns as Literary Journalism," *American Periodicals*, Vol. 10 (2000), 63–78.
Simple Speaks His Mind, review, Charleston (W.Va.) *Gazette*, 16 April 1950, 11.
Simple Speaks His Mind, review, *Kirkus Reviews*, 14 April 1950.
Simple Stakes a Claim, review, *Kirkus Reviews*, 16 September 1957.
Williams, Melvin G. "Langston Hughes's Jesse B. Semple: A Black Walter Mitty," *Negro American Literature Forum*, Vol. 10, No. 2 (summer 1976), 66–69.

III

Additional Writers of Interest

Writers white and black delineated the black experience before the Civil War, during Reconstruction and throughout the Jim Crow era into the 1960s. Some authors nostalgically recreated the plantation days. Others were strong abolitionists who railed against slavery. Several writers attempted lightness or humor. Some were dead earnest. Petroleum V. Nasby excelled at satire. Women writers were less amused and were less apt to write humor, or for newspapers. On the other hand, they were more drawn to write for children and juveniles and they were often more overtly political.

Simultaneously, black writers of both genders struggled to find their voices, to find audiences, to submit more authentic portrayals of past and present, whether slavery narratives or fiction.

We've already looked at twenty-nine writers. Here are another seventy-two.

The list is a hodge-podge; but then, a list of writers working with white themes and characters is a hodge-podge. The list starts with Phillis Wheatley, born two decades before the American Revolution, who rose out of slavery to actually make some money at writing. It took many of her black contemporaries another 100 years before they could expect to even learn to read and write. So whites were quick to fill the gap. John Pendleton Kennedy in the 1830s wrote sketches of Virginia plantation life. A contemporary, George Washington Dixon, wrote about outrageous Zip Coon. Lydia Maria Child wrote about the tragic mulatta in *The Quadroons* (1842). Frederick Douglass recalled his sojourn to freedom. Colonel Prentiss Ingraham created Darkie Dan, the Colored Detective, for the 1880s dime novels. Helen Bannerman created Little Black Sambo for a juvenile audience.

This is meant to be an illustrative list, giving a glimpse of the emergence of black writers from a sea of white writers who clung as long as they could to stereotype. Names from the main section of this book are cross-referenced to create an informal timeline.

This section includes black as well as white writers, as they mingled in their respective eras. Though contemporaries, white and black writers had little in common and certainly did not follow each others' trends.

This listing is not exhaustive and it is not meant to be. Most of these writers are here because they wrote for a wide market; some are novelists or columnists. Poets and song composers and cartoonists and joke writers are included for historical perspective. Why are writers placed here, rather than in the book's main section? Because they were from a different time period, or they didn't have *continuing (usually humorous) characters in short story series appearing in wide-circulation periodicals or newspapers.*

Writers of a literary bent exceed this book's scope and are only minimally included. Check Henry Louis Gates, Jr. and Nellie Y. McKay's *The Norton Anthology of African American Literature* (1997) for an examination in this direction. Too, this book does not examine radio (with one exception, because Correll and Gosden also appeared in print), film or television (except peripherally). A good source in this vein is *Toms, Coons, Mulattoes, Mammies, & Bucks* by Donald Bogle (2004).

Phillis Wheatley
(1753–1784)
Poems (1773)

The first person of African descent to have a book published in North America, and to earn a modicum of income from writing, Phillis Wheatley was born in West Africa and sold into slavery as a girl. She learned to read while in the service of merchant John Wheatley and his wife, Susanna, in Boston. Her *Poems on Various Subjects, Religious and Moral by Phillis Wheatley, Negro Servant to Mr. John Wheatley, of Boston, In New England,* came out from Archibald Bell, Bookseller, in London and Cox & Berry, Boston, in 1773 and earned her a degree of fame in this country and England. George Washington praised her craft. After she obtained her freedom in 1778, she married John Peters, a free black who owned a grocery. She was a strong advocate for the American Revolution.

Robert Roberts
(1780–1860)
The House Servant's Directory (1827)

Robert Roberts, a free man, was the first African American to write a book for commercial publication: *The House Servant's Directory: A Monitor for Private Families* (Monroe and Francis, 1827). There's no little irony that in the North few blacks could read, and in the South they were forbidden to learn to read. Roberts, butler for merchant Nathan Appleton of Boston and later for Massachusetts Governor and Senator Christopher Gore, advised his readers, "This station of life comprises comforts, privileges, and pleasures, which are to be found in but few other stations in which you may enter; and on the other hand many difficulties, trials of temper, &c., more, perhaps than in any other station in which you might enter, in a different state of life." The South Carolina native became a prominent abolitionist.

Thomas D. Rice
(1808–1860)
Jim Crow (1828)

A popular minstrel entertainer, Thomas Dartmouth "Daddy" Rice incorporated black dialect in his song and dance routines. Born in Manhattan, Rice trained as a wood carver but aspired to the stage. He was a traveling actor before the age of twenty, appearing on both New York City and hinterland stages. He adopted the guise of a lazy, meek "Jim Crow" after a "Jump Jim Crow" routine was well received in Louisville in 1828. He is said to have taken on the blackface persona after meeting an old Negro stableman with a bad leg. When he sang his "Jim Crow Song," Rice emphasized each stanza with a quirky jump. Another version has it Rice developed his stereotype through longtime observation of African American performers in Manhattan and in the South. Rice published a songbook, *Jim Crow's Vagaries; or, Black Flights of Fancy* (1840). Some of his plays, such as *Oh, Hush!* (1833) and *Virginia Mummy* (1835), featured variations on Jim Crow. Rice performed for white and black audiences. Jim Crow was at times a scamp of sharp wit and observation, turning the tables on white authority figures. Rice played the title character in *Uncle Tom's Cabin* on Broadway. He traveled to Europe and experienced career highs before suffering progressive speech paralysis and became an alcoholic. He eventually took his own life.

John Pendleton Kennedy
(1795–1870)
Swallow Barn (1832)

John Pendleton Kennedy, U.S. Secretary of the Navy from 1852 to 1853 and later a congressman from Maryland, was born in Baltimore. A graduate of Baltimore College, he fought in the War of 1812. He became a lawyer. His first interest was literature, however. His best-known book, *Swallow Barn; or, A Sojourn in the Dominion*, published in 1832, contained glowing sketches (some of them humorous) of life on a Virginia plantation as seen through the eyes of a northern visitor. While the plantation's owner, Frank Merriwether, believes the institution of slavery is wrong, he believed his slaves "could never become a happier people" in other circumstances.

George Washington Dixon
(1801–1861)
Zip Coon (1834)

George Washington Dixon performed "Coal Black Rose," "Long Tail Blue" and other race songs on New York City and other burlesque stages. Born in Virginia, probably of mixed parentage, he caught the acting bug in his teens and was an early blackface performer in the play *Love in a Cloud* in 1829. He collected his routines in the book *Dixon's Oddities* (1830). In 1833 he started a short-lived newspaper—the first of a succession of newspapers in which he took strong Whig stands. On one occasion, he was convicted of libel for material that appeared in his *Polyanthos* newspaper and served a prison sentence. He played for working-class audiences, for whom he devised his lively, urban, extravagantly dressed "Zip Coon" character. Zip (Scipio) Coon put on airs. L. Hewitt & Co. published *Zip Coon: A Favorite Comic Song* in 1834. The lyrics (to the tune of "Turkey in the Straw") begin: "O ole Zip Coon he is a larned skoler/Ole Zip Coon he is a larned skoler/Ole Zip Coon he is a larned skoler/Sings possum up a gum tree an coony in a holler/possum up a gum tree, coony on a stump/possum up a gum tree, coony on a stump/possum up a gum tree, coony on a stump/Den over dubble trubble Zip Coon will jump."

Augustus Baldwin Longstreet
(1790–1870)
Georgia Scenes (1835)

Georgia Scenes, Characters, Incidents, Etc. in the First Half Century of the Republic (1835), one of Georgia's first important works of literature, was written by an Augusta native, Augustus Baldwin Longstreet. Longstreet attended Yale and studied law at Tapping Reeve's school in Litchfield, Connecticut. He entered the Georgia bar in 1814, married Frances Eliza Parke, served in the Georgia General Assembly and became a Superior Court judge. In grief at the death of his son, Longstreet underwent a Christian conversion and became a traveling Methodist minister. *Georgia Scenes* collected his humorous short writings that had appeared in the *Midgeville Southern Recorder* and elsewhere. Billy Porter, a black musician, is mentioned in one story, "The Dance." Longstreet created the frontier character Ransy Sniffle in his best-known story, "The Fight." The author's later works included *A Voice from the South* (1847), a defense of slavery. It sold few copies.

Caroline Gilman
(1794–1888)
Recollections of a Southern Matron (1838)

Boston-born Caroline Howard married Samuel Gilman in 1819 and moved to Charleston, South Carolina, where he became a Unitarian minister. Her poem "Jephthah's Rash Vow" was published, without her permission, when she was sixteen. She continued to write as she raised a family, and in 1832 founded and edited *The Rose Bud*, a juvenile weekly that attracted such writers as Harriet Martineau and Nathaniel Hawthorne. Her first novel was *Recollections of a Housekeeper* (1835). Her second, *Recollections of a Southern Matron* (1838), includes Negro dialect, for which the author apologizes in an introductory note: "It has only been done when essential to the development of individual character." She wrote about black superstitions and black faithfulness to white masters.

Lydia Maria Child
(1802–1880)
The Quadroons (1842)

Lydia Maria Child pretty much invented the literary type "the tragic mulatta" in her short stories "The Quadroons" and "Slavery's Pleasant Homes," which appeared in *The Liberty*

Bell issues of 1842 and 1843. The heroine is light-skinned, biracial and generally thinks of herself as free and white—until a parent dies and she is thrown into slavery. A running theme is the failure of white fathers to care for their offspring with black women. Child was born in Massachusetts. She was an abolitionist. She often took on issues of male dominance and white supremacy in her stories. She started a private school in 1824 and two years later initiated *Juvenile Miscellany*, a monthly periodical for children. She married Boston lawyer David Lee Child. Her first novel, *Hobomok: A Tale of Early Time* (1824), issued under the pseudonym "An American," was about the marriage between a white woman and an Indian man.

Frederick Douglass
(1818–1895)
Narrative of the Life of Frederick Douglass (1845)

Frederick Bailey was born in Maryland, the son of an enslaved black woman and an unknown white man. Reared by grandparents, exposed to the most brutal of slave conditions, he learned a trade from a ship's carpenter in Baltimore. He learned to read and write. He learned of the abolitionist movement. Obliged to go to work as a field hand, he experienced brutal treatment at the hands of a slave breaker. Escaping to the north in 1838, he settled in New Bedford, Massachusetts, married, and took the name Frederick Douglass. Douglass attended abolitionist meetings. He met social justice leader William Lloyd Garrison, though his beliefs would not become as radical as Garrison's. He gave speeches and published his autobiography, *Narrative of the Life of Frederick Douglass, an American Slave, Written by Himself,* in 1845. Fearing reprisals for revealing his past, he fled to England, Scotland and Ireland. British supporters purchased his freedom and he returned to North America. He met President Abraham Lincoln during the Civil War and helped recruit black soldiers. He held a variety of jobs including with the District of Columbia Registrar of Deeds and the Dominican Republic embassy. He worked tirelessly to improve race relations and change white perceptions of blacks.

William Wells Brown
(1814–1884)
Narrative of William W. Brown (1847)
Clotel; or, The President's Daughter (1853)
The Escape (1858)

Born in Lexington, Kentucky, William Wells Brown was the son of an enslaved woman and a white plantation owner. Hired out to a publican in St. Louis as a teenager, he escaped to freedom only to be captured and punished. He was hired out to a newspaper publisher and learned aspects of the printing trade. He escaped again in 1834 and for two years helped other fugitives run to Canada. He married. He attended abolitionist meetings including the

1843 National Convention of Colored Citizens. He became a public speaker and an agent for the Massachusetts Anti-Slavery Society. In 1847, he published the story of his experiences, *Narrative of William W. Brown, a Fugitive Slave, Written by Himself* (1847). He visited Europe, and, with passage of the Fugitive Slave Law, feared to return to North America. He put his time to good use, writing the first novel by an African American, *Clotel; or, The President's Daughter: A Narrative of Slave Life in the United States*. It was published in England in 1853. It was about Thomas Jefferson and his black mistress Sally Hemings. He eventually returned to the United States and lived in Boston. His next book was the nonfiction *The American Fugitive in Europe: Sketches of Places and People Abroad* (1855). Brown's *The Escape* (1858) is, according to Eric Gardner in *Major Voices: The Drama of Slavery* (2005), "the earliest extant play published in the U.S. by a Black American."

E.D.E.N. Southworth
(1819–1899)
Retribution (1849)

Emma Dorothy Eliza Nevitte shortened her name for her sixty books, several of which became bestsellers. She graduated from her stepfather's academy in Washington, D.C., in 1835 and taught school before she married Frederick Southworth and moved to Wisconsin. She returned to Washington when her husband abandoned the family. She sold a few short stories and the *National Era* serialized her first novel, *Retribution*. One character in the book is the quadroon Henny, who is cruelly treated by her young mistress. Otherwise the slaves shown in the book are happy and content. The author is said to have earned $10,000 a year from her writing.

Harriet Beecher Stowe (1811–1896) *Uncle Tom's Cabin* (1851) see Section I

Mary Henderson Eastman
(1818–1887)
Aunt Phillis's Cabin (1852)

Mary Henderson Eastman and her husband, Seth Eastman, researched and wrote about Native American culture and life. Born in Virginia to a family of planters, she moved to West Point, New York, when her father became a surgeon at the military academy. While they lived in Washington, D.C., she was spurred to write *Aunt Phillis's Cabin; or, Southern Life as It Is* (1852). It sold upwards of 30,000 copies and became the best known of the anti–Tom novels. Among points she makes to refute the Harriet Beecher Stowe work is the suggestion that plantation owners abused their slaves. Rather, as she described them, the owners treated their slaves with compassion. The slaves, she insisted, were happy. The main character is fifty years old and lives on a cotton plantation in Virginia. She disdains drink, though her husband Uncle Bacchus is an alcoholic.

Maria J. McIntosh
(1803–1878)
The Lofty and the Lowly (1853)

Maria J. McIntosh's *The Lofty and the Lowly; or, Good in All and One All Good*, an anti–Tom novel, came out in 1853 and surpassed Mary Eastman's *Aunt Phillis's Cabin* in book sales. The story takes place in Georgia and details efforts of a plantation owner to stay out of bankruptcy. Which he does, with the help of his loyal slave, Daddy Cato. Descended from Scottish Highlanders, McIntosh was born in Georgia, on her parents' plantation. After their deaths, she moved to New York and wrote *Aunt Kitty's Tales* and other books.

Caroline Lee Hentz
(1800–1856)
The Planter's Northern Bride (1854)

Born in Massachusetts, the daughter of a Revolutionary War soldier, Caroline Lee Whiting opposed the abolitionist movement. She became a teacher. She married Nicholas Hentz in 1824 and they lived variously in North Carolina, Ohio and five other states. She found success in writing, though she and her husband also ran a succession of private schools. Her first work in print was "The Sacrifice" for *Godey's Lady's Book* in 1832. *The Planter's Northern Bride* (1854) was a response to Stowe's *Uncle Tom's Cabin*. Hentz made a strong defense of the institution of slavery and lauded caring relationships between masters and slaves. In her book, the villains include a meddling abolitionist who tries to free slaves against their will. She argues through her story that only inexpensive Southern labor (slaves) enabled the industrial revolution to take place in the North.

Mary J. Holmes
(1825–1907)
Lena Rivers (1856)

Mary Jane Hawes was born in Brookfield, Mass., and became a teacher. She married Daniel Holmes in 1849 and they moved to Kentucky, then to New York, where Daniel studied law. Her experiences in the rural South inspired the author to write antebellum fiction. Mary's first novel was *Tempest and Sunshine* (1854), about two girls as they grew to maturity. Proceeds from book sales enabled the author to travel to Europe. She wrote seventeen more books, including *Lena Rivers* (1856), which has a spunky, orphaned heroine who leaves Massachusetts to live with a cranky uncle, a planter in Kentucky, and encounters his dialect-speaking, ignorant, enslaved blacks.

Thomas Chandler Haliburton
(1796–1865)

The Americans at Home (1856)

Crime novelist Robert B. Parker, when he was an English professor at Northeastern University in Boston in the early 1970s, taught a course in "The Novel of Violence." The wilderness in James Fenimore Cooper's Leatherstocking tales, Parker said, is symbolic of innocence, while civilization represents corruption and evil. Cooper's frontier scout turns his back on civilization in order to maintain his integrity. This iconic figure is a good man who is a loner. He often has a male companion of another race; in Herman Meville's *Moby Dick*, it's Ishmael; in *Last of the Mohicans* (1826), it's Chingachgook. In Thomas Chandler Haliburton's *The Americans at Home* (1854), one might add, it's Sam. Haliburton was a businessman and judge from pre–Confederation Nova Scotia. He shaped as a fictional hero Dick Kelsey, an early settler of upper Missouri country. Tall, raw-boned, "his only companion being a negro slave [Sam] who was at once his master's attendant and friend." Haliburton's best-known fictional character was Sam Slick, in the novel *The Attaché; or, Sam Slick in England* (1843). In a tight squeeze, Slick at one point utters a Negro phrase, "Chah!—chah!" and launches into a dialect song: "Oh hab you nebber heerd ob de battle ob Orleens, Where de dandy Yankee lads gave de Britishers de beans." Haliburton often introduced ignorant black characters as comic relief.

Johnson Jones Hooper
(1815–1862)

Simon Suggs (1858)

Making his literary debut with "Taking the Census in Alabama," published in *The Spirit of the Times* in 1843, Johnson Jones Hooper was a newspaper editor and lawyer as well as humorist. He served a term as Alabama's state prosecutor. *Adventures of Captain Simon Suggs, Late of the Tallapoosa Volunteers* (1845) collected his short stories about the rascal gambler that first saw print in the *East Alabamian*. The book went through eleven editions in eleven years. A sequel was *Simon Suggs' Adventures* (1858). Hooper built on the pioneering work of Longstreet. His Suggs is an amoral character, out for his own gain. In one story, "Simon Plays the Snatch Game," a youth manipulates his father into believing a black boy named Bill is responsible for Simon's own misadventure. Some of the stories adapt the African trickster tales known to Southern blacks. Hooper was secretary of the Provisional Confederate Congress in 1861, but died the next year of tuberculosis.

Martin Delany
(1812–1885)

Blake: Or the Huts of America (1859)

Born a free man in West Virginia, Martin Delany was the son of a free black woman and an enslaved black man. He learned to read and write as a boy. He became a barber in

Pittsburgh, and started a black newspaper there in 1843. He married. He took classes at Jefferson College. He apprenticed to a physician. He attended the first National Convention of Men of Color in 1835. He developed ideas of black nationalism. He believed blacks could only find freedom in a predominantly black society. He began to write for, among others, William Lloyd Garrison's *The Liberator*. With Garrison and Frederick Douglass, he established the *North Star* in Rochester, New York, and traveled to promote the publication and sell subscriptions. He was accepted to Harvard Medical School, one of the first three blacks to attend the Massachusetts school, though pressure from white students soon led to their dismissal. He wrote nonfiction books and published a novel, *Blake: Or the Huts of America*, first serialized in *Anglo-African Magazine* in 1859, in response to what he saw as too much passivity in Harriet Beecher Stowe's *Uncle Tom's Cabin*. Delany lived in Chatham, Ontario, Canada, from 1856 to 1859. He traveled to Liberia to investigate the possibilities of establishing a new black nation. During the Civil War, he helped recruit black soldiers in New England and Ohio. He was commissioned a major in the U.S. Army, the first black field officer. After the war he worked for the Freedman's Bureau and advocated strongly for the rights of blacks to own land.

Harriet E. Wilson
(1825–1900)
Our Nig (1859)

Born in New Hampshire of mixed lineage, Harriet E. "Hattie" Wilson is believed to be the first woman of African descent to publish a novel in the United States. It was the autobiographical *Our Nig; or, Sketches from the Life of a Free Black*, a work critical of indentured servitude. Wilson made a living as purveyor of "Mrs. H.E. Wilson's Hair Dressing," a color restorative. She established a Sunday school for Boston children and taught in a white school in the Massachusetts city. She became an active spiritualist, though was often out of step with the general Spiritualist movement. She was an active lyceum speaker. She advocated for women's rights and for improved education.

Harriet Ann Jacobs
(1813–1897)
Incidents in the Life of a Slave Girl (1861)

"I was born a slave; but I never knew till six years of happy childhood had passed away," Harriet Ann Jacobs wrote. She grew up in North Carolina. Her parents were enslaved to owners of neighboring plantations. Her father's abilities as a carpenter allowed Harriet and her brother to live together with their parents. After Harriet's mother died, she became a house servant to a plantation mistress, and learned to read and write. In 1842 she was able to escape to the North. She lived in fear of recapture until a later employer, who was strongly antislavery, purchased and freed her in 1852. The next year she began sending letters to the

New York Tribune and, with the help of Lydia Maria Child, compiled *Incidents in the Life of a Slave Girl*. She had it privately printed in 1861. It forthrightly deals with issues of sexual abuse of enslaved women.

Petroleum V. Nasby
(1833–1888)
The Nasby Letters (1861–1887)

A New York native, journeyman printer, reporter and editor, David Ross Locke was one of a vibrant, pre–Twain triad of 19th-century humorists that included Artemus Ward and Josh Billings. Ward was really Charles Farrar Browne (1834–1867), a Maine native who satirized blacks in "Sixty Minutes in Africa." Billings, king of crackerbox aphorisms with funky spellings, was born Henry Wheeler Shaw (1818–1885) in Massachusetts. He once waxed about "The Negro and the Trout." The most political, Locke in 1861 began a series of letters in his newspaper the *Jeffersonian* in Ohio, bearing the pen name Petroleum Vesuvius Nasby. Nasby was purportedly a pastor of the New Dispensation and a sympathetic Copperhead. He preached to Negro-detesting Southern Democrats in support of the old Confederacy—with enormous irony. He was really a staunch Union supporter and enemy of slavery. The letters were poorly spelled and nearly illiterate. For example, the second newspaper column, "On Negro Emigration," begins: "There is now 15 niggers, men, wimin and children, or ruther, mail, femail and yung, in Wingert's Corners, and yesterday another arrove. I am bekimin alarmed, fer if they inkreese at this rate, in suthin over sixty yeres they'll have a majority in the town, and may, ef they git mene enuff, tyrannize over us, even ez we air tyrannizing over them." When Locke became editor of the *Toledo Blade*, Nasby wrote from "Confedrit X. Roads" in Kentucky, where the hardest workers were Republicans. He continued the Nasby missives until 1887. They were collected in *The Nasby Papers* (1866) and *The Nasby Letters: Being The Original Nasby Letters, as Written During His Lifetime* (1893).

Samuel W. Small
(1851–1931)
Old Si (1876–1885)

Born on a plantation near Knoxville, Tennessee, Samuel White Small enlisted in the Confederate Army reserves in the waning months of the Civil War. After graduating from Emory & Henry College, he became a newspaperman. He was secretary to Senator Andrew Johnson. His newspaper columns for the Atlanta *Constitution* (also carried in the *San Francisco Evening Bulletin* and *Macon Weekly Telegraph*) were collected in *Old Si's Sayings* and *Humorous Sketches of "Old Si"* (both 1886). As an example, in "Old Si Gives His Estimate of Kinfolks (17 January 1878), the sage hears a complaint from his friend Amos, who is beleaguered by in-laws: "I'se boddered 'kase ob de huan kontrariness ob mankin'!" to which Si after a fashion tells, "I'd rudder hab er good fren' date z head cook at er hotel dan er string of kin fokes ez long ez sherman's army!" Alcoholism ended the run of Small's Old Si daily column, and for a time his newspaper career. The *Constitution*'s editor Evan Howell sought out Joel Chandler Harris to write black dialect stories in Small's stead. Small established the *Oklahoman* in Oklahoma City in 1889, the *Norfolk Pilot* in Virginia 1894. Hearing the preaching of the Rev. Sam P. Jones, Small gave up drink and became an evangelist. During the Spanish-American War he was chaplain to the Third U.S. Volunteer Engineers. Small traveled as a lecturer for the Anti-Saloon League.

Mark Twain (1835–1910) Nigger Jim (1876–1884) *see* Section I

Irwin Russell
(1853–1879)
Christmas Night in the Quarters (1878/1917)

A native of Mississippi, Irwin Russell was born to a physician and a teacher at Port Gibson Female College. He read John Milton at a young age and Robert Burns was a favorite poet. He graduated from the University of St. Louis and returned to his hometown to read law. He abandoned that endeavor to take up writing. He sold several dialect poems to *Scribner's*. Nelson Page is said to have been familiar with his works. He wrote stage plays and poetry, the best known of which is his operetta "Christmas Night in the Quarters" (1878). Editor Richard Watson Gilder remarked on his work and Russell went to New York where he wrote black dialect verse featuring people based on ones he'd met in Texas and Louisiana for the "Bric-a-Brac" section in *Scribner's Monthly*. He also wrote about Irish characters. He learned to play the banjo and adapted black spirituals and hoedowns. He went to New Orleans to work for the *Times*, and died not long after. A year later, a small collection of his writings including "Blind Ned," "Mahsr John" and "A Sermon for the Sisters" was published as *Poems by Irwin Russell*, with an introduction by Joel Chandler Harris. The volume was expanded in 1917 and published as *Christmas Night in the Quarters*.

Thomas Worth
(1834–1917)
Darktown Art Prints (1879–1890)

Thomas Worth let his pictures do the talking, though his publishers Nathaniel Currier and James Merrit Ives of the firm Currier & Ives added captions. The Greenwich Village–born artist sold his first art to the famed New York City lithographers before he was twenty. The images were redrawn on stone and color prints were sold to an avid market. He contributed many of the seventy-five Darktown print series issued 1879 through 1890—one of which is said to have sold a remarkable 73,000 copies. The image titled "Great Oyster Eating Match Between the Darktown Cormorant and the Blackville Buster" depicted bloated, buffoonish blacks stuffing their mouths in a competition subtitled "The finish—'You is a tie—De one dat gags fust am a gone Coon.'" Darktown themes ranged from spoofs of lawn tennis to literary debates at the Darktown club to ice cream socials to a raucous baseball game.

Joel Chandler Harris (1848–1908) Uncle Remus (1879) *see* Section I

George Washington Cable (1844–1925) *Old Creole Days* (1879) *see* Section I

Colonel Prentiss Ingraham
(1843–1904)
Darkie Dan, the Colored Detective (1881)

Black characters in the pulp-paper dime novels were rare. African Americans were included in "Mrs. Metta Victor's Maum Guinea and Her Plantation 'Children': or, Holiday-Week on a Louisiana Estate. A Slave Romance," *Dime Novels*, 1861. Black characters were generally companions, such as Pomp the cook in the Ted Strong stories in *Rough Rider Weekly* or Scipio in the Bones series or Samson in the Handsome Harry tales. *Black Tom, the Negro Detective; or, Solving Thompson Street Mystery* (1893) by "Old Cap Collier" (Jameson Torr Altemus) is a faux character; in the last chapter he reveals himself to be a white detective wearing blackface. Another Black Tom, in "Plucky Black Tom; or, The Greatest Curiosity on Earth, *Old Sleuth Library*, in 1887, and "Black Tom in Search of a Father; or, The Further Adventures of a Mischievous Darky," *Old Sleuth Library*, 1888, feature a disguised character created by the Old Sleuth. The only real black hero is Dan, who appears in Colonel Prentiss Ingraham's *Darkie Dan, the Colored Detective; or, The Mississippi Mystery*. The 1881 Beadle & Adams story reprinted in *The Dime Library* No. 1063 in 1902. Ingraham, born in Mississippi, in the waning days of the Civil War became acting commander of Ross's brigade in the Texas Calvary. He went on to fight in the Mexican Revolution and Austro-Prussian War and other overseas conflicts. In London in 1869 he began writing adventure tales, turning out an estimated 600 dime novels and 400 novelettes under his own name and a baker's dozen pen names. Darkie Dan saves his mistress from roving wolves and is given his freedom. He remains at the old plantation and continues to help the planter family there as the King of Diamonds seeks to do them harm.

Louise Clarke Pyrnelle
(1850–1907)
Diddle, Dumps, and Tot (1882)

Teacher, public speaker and children's book author Elizabeth Louise Clarke was born on a cotton plantation in Alabama. Some of her writings dwelt on her happy, romantic years growing up in the antebellum countryside. Her father, captain of the Canebrake Rifle Guards during the Civil War, was wounded in action. After the war, the family was forced to sell the plantation and the author's father established a medical practice. Louise attended school and became a teacher and governess. She studied at Anne Randall Diehl's College of Education and the Delsarte Academy in New York City and toured with elocutionist Mary Scott Siddons. Louise read southern dialect stories. She settled in Natchez, Mississippi, for a time.

She married John Parnell in 1880 and moved to Columbus, Georgia, where she began to write fiction. The Lost Cause novel *Diddle, Dumps, and Tot; or, Plantation Child-Life* came out in 1882 and was praised by some for its use of dialect, blasted by others for its stereotypes. The book is about three white girls and the blacks who care for them. A second dialect novel, *Miss Li'l' Tweetty,* came out in 1917, after the author's death.

Katherine Sherwood Bonner McDowell
(1849–1883)
Dialect Tales (1884)

Katherine Sherwood Bonner McDowell also wrote under the pen name Sherwood Bonner. She was born in Mississippi to a well-to-do family whose fortunes were sapped during the Civil War. Obliged to better her fortune, she married Edward McDowell and moved to Texas and bore a child—and abandoned both in pursuit of a career as a writer. She fled to Boston and, with the help of a friend, Nahrun Capen, and with support from Henry Wadsworth Longfellow, persevered in her craft. Her short fiction appeared in northern periodicals for nearly a decade. She wrote local color stories with an emphasis on Negro vernacular. Her books included *Dialect Tales* (1884) and *Suwanee River Tales* (1884).

Thomas Nelson Page (1853–1922) *In Ole Virginia* (1887) see Section I

Ruth McEnery Stuart
(1849–1917)
Dialect Stories (1888)

Ruth McEnery Stuart was born in central Louisiana of Irish and Scots immigrant parents. Her father became cotton commissioner in the New Orleans Customs House. The family was impoverished after the Civil War. Ruth became a teacher. She married an Arkansas planter, Alfred Oden Stuart, but he died four years into the marriage. *Harper's Monthly* editor Charles Dudley Warner nurtured her early writing in 1888. Her first two stories were tales of "faithful darkies," "Uncle Mingo's 'Speculations'" in *The New Princeton Review* and "The Lamentations of Jeremiah Johnson" in *Harper's*. She relocated to New York and as a southern author developed her own social circle. Her first short story collection was *A Golden Wedding* in 1893. It was made up of stories of plantation life. Blacks are also featured in stories on various southern themes in *The Woman's Exchange of Simkinsville* (1893).

Frances Ellen Watkins Harper
(1825–1911)
Iola Leroy (1892)

An abolitionist, feminist, prohibitionist and suffragist, Frances Ellen Watkins Harper wrote poetry and prose. She was born to free black parents in Baltimore, Maryland. She was orphaned at age three and reared by family members. She attended her uncle, the Rev.

William Watkins', Academy for Negro Youth. She worked as a seamstress. When she was twenty, her book of verse *Forest Leaves* was published. A second volume followed. Three of her novels were serialized in a Christian magazine in the period 1868–1888. In Ohio, Watkins taught at Union Seminary. She became a traveling public speaker for the American Anti-Slavery Society in 1953. She married Fenton Harper in 1860. *Iola Leroy; or, Shadows Uplifted* (1892) was published as a book when she was sixty-seven years old. It was among the earliest published novels by a black writer.

Polk Miller
(1844–1913)
Old Virginia Plantation Negro (1892–1911)

James A. "Polk" Miller, a stage comedian and entertainer, grew up on his father's Virginia plantation. He learned to play banjo by listening to slaves. He served in the Confederate Army. A pharmacist in Richmond, he told humorous tales (not minstrel gags) in auditoriums and presented Negro spirituals and plantation songs. "His recital was a source of pleasurable enjoyment, the audience pulsating with him as he related the ludicrous side of the negro life and as he dropped into the pathetic and pictured the happy scenes on the plantations before the war and the changes which that event had wrought," according to the Columbia (S.C) *State* for 13 May 1894. Mark Twain introduced Miller at Madison Square Concert Hall: "Mr. Miller is thoroughly competent to entertain you with his sketches of the old-time negro, and I not only commend him to your intelligent notice, but personally endorse him. The stories I have heard him tell are the best I ever heard." The Lexington, Kentucky, *Morning Herald* ran the column "Polk Miller's Negro Stories" in 1897. By 1906, Miller had revised his program for younger people. At the same time, he assembled a quartet of black musicians, the Plantation Darkies, to perform with him. *Polk Miller's Stories, Sketches, Songs* came out in 1904. The Old South Quartette joined him to record seven songs on Edison cylinders in 1909. Songs included "Oysters and Wine at 2 a.m." and "Pussy Cat Rag." Travels through the South of what was one of the first integrated bands in the country, often to play for Confederate reunions, prompted some interesting moments under Jim Crow.

John Trotwood Moore
(1858–1929)
Old Wash (1893)

He had a law degree but never practiced. John Trotwood Moore was instead a novelist, historian, journalist and editor who made his mark writing local color and humor. Born in Alabama, he departed that state for Tennessee in the 1880s. He graduated from Howard College. He signed his name "Betsy Trotwood" when he wrote for the *Marion Commonwealth*, later just "Trotwood." He established Moore Academy in 1883 and was a teacher as well as principal. He farmed and owned a pacer racehorse. He wrote for *Clark's Horse Review*, where he introduced his Old Wash black character, a retake on Uncle Remus, but for adults, in 1893. Old Wash was crafty. Often he was out to better his own pockets. The stories were populated with liquor, tobacco, mules, preachers, widows, goats and the Ku Klux Klan. "Old Mistis," a story of a loyal slave named Jake, appeared in the magazine's Christmas 1894 issue. Old Wash stories were collected in *Songs and Stories from Tennessee* (1897). *Uncle Wash: His Stories* came out in 1910. Moore was appointed Tennessee state librarian and archivist in 1919.

Kate Chopin
(1851–1904)
Bayou Folk (1894)

Katherine O'Flaherty was born in St. Louis, her father Irish, her mother French. She married cotton broker Oscar Chopin in 1870 and they settled in New Orleans. When Chopin's business failed, he took his growing family to a series of plantations, which he managed. He died in 1882. For income, Kate Chopin wrote a hundred or so short stories in the 1890s and two novels, most set in the Louisiana bayou country. "Désirée's Baby," which appeared in *Vogue's* 14 January 1893 number, is about Louisiana creoles and confronted issues of mixed race and racism. It was one of twenty-one stories in *Bayou Folk* (1894). She was ahead of her time with her novel *The Awakening* (1899), about a woman who felt confined by an oppressive society.

Opie Pope Read
(1852–1939)
My Young Master (1896)

Gangly Nashville-born Opie Pope Read grew up on his slave-owning family's plantation, though as his newspaper career advanced he became an enlightened paternalist. He founded the humorous *The Arkansas Traveler* with Philo D. Benham in 1882 and worked for traditional newspapers including the *Arkansas Democrat*, *The Evening Ledger* and *The Arkansas Gazette*. He covered the national yellow fever outbreak for *The New York Herald* in 1878. His short stories and novels were set in Arkansas, Tennessee or Kentucky. He gave a slave, Dan, the role of narrator in his 1896 novel *My Young Master*, which begins (blessedly without deep dialect) this way: "I was born in the State of Kentucky, on the bluegrass farm owned by Guilford Gradley. Many changes may have taken place, but in my day the northern boundary line of the farm and the southern corporate limit of the town of Litchford here came together; and I think that one of my earliest recollections is of a Sunday morning, when my young master and I got on the ground and parted the long grass to search for the line. I know it must have been on a Sunday, for the church bells were ringing, and Old Master and Old Miss (as we always called his wife) passed us on their way to town. Old Master was one of the most prominent men in the State (had been a general in the militia), and this influence was felt even by the humblest negro on the place, for to belong to a great man was of itself a social prominence not enjoyed by the bondman of the ordinary individual. Why, I remember seeing a little negro boy weep bitterly because a playmate had taunted him with the humiliating fact that his master lived in a log house. Ah, those old days, by turns a sad and a happy freak in the history of man!"

Bob Cole
(1868–1911)
A Trip to Coontown (1897)

William A. Brown's *The Drama of King Shotaway* (1822), about the struggle for freedom in the Caribbean, is probably the earliest play written by a black and performed by a black cast in New York, according to Eric Gardner in *Major Voices: The Drama of Slavery* (2005). Decades later, playwright and songwriter Robert Allen "Bob" Cole Jr. wrote *A Trip to Coontown* in 1897 (with Billy Johnson), a reworking of an earlier skit called *At Jolly Cooney Island* that Cole had turned out for Black Patti's Troubadours. *A Trip to Coontown* is said to be the first full-length Broadway musical stage production written by a black writer and performed by a black cast. Cole initially only managed to stage the show in "third-rate American and Canadian theaters," according to Krystyn R. Moon in *African American Review* (spring-summer 2011). One of the songs, "The Wedding of the Chinee and the Coon," perpetuated twin stereotypes. After brief runs in New York City in 1898 and 1899 (thanks to support from stage entrepreneurs Klaw and Erlanger), the musical enjoyed a longer stay in 1891 and toured until 1901. In one production it was retitled *The Kings of Koon-dom*. Coon songs had been popular at least since J.P. Skelley's "The Dandy Coon's Parade" (1980). Georgia-born Cole had already published tunes in the subgenre (*Genuine Negro Songs by a Genuine Negro Minstrel*, 1896). Though a modest success, *Coontown* was it for Cole. He could see that the popular, if derogatory, dialect and coon songs were losing their appeal. He took aim at more affluent audiences. As historians David A. Jasen and Gene Jones put it in *Black Bottom Blues* (1988), Coontown was the worst back yard in Tin Pan Alley, and black composers couldn't wait to move out. He collaborated with J. Rosamond Johnson (1873–1954) and (sometimes) James Weldon Johnson (1871–1938)—the brothers who wrote the Negro National Anthem, "Lift Ev'ry Voice and Sing," in 1900—to produce more than 200 songs for stage. Among their works was *The Shoe-Fly Regiment* (1907).

Miss Howard Weeden
(1846–1905)
Shadows on the Wall (1898)

Maria Howard Weeden of Huntsville, Ala., "was a successful painter of Southern subjects and made a specialty of negroes. She was also the author, under the name Miss Howard Weeden, of several volumes of Southern poetry," according to a death notice in the *New*

York Times in April 1905. She was born to a family of slave owners and cotton planters. Her father, however, had died three months before her birth. She sold paintings, after the Civil War, to boost the family's then-meager income. She wrote dialect poems for publication with black-and-white editions of her portraits. She and her sister, Kate, never married and lived in "noble poverty" at the Weeden House, which was occupied by Union troops during the war and is now a house museum. Her poems were published in *Shadows on the Wall* (1898), *Bandanna Ballads* (1899), *Songs of the Old South* (1901) and *Old Voices* (1904).

Martha Sawyer Gielow
(1860–1933)
Mammy's Reminiscences and Other Sketches (1898)

Martha Sawyer, born in Alabama, married Henry J. Gielow but, after having two children, separated from her husband. She lived for a time in Washington, D.C. As director of the Southern Industrial Education Association, Gielow advocated industrial arts education for impoverished Appalachian mountain people. She was known for collecting slave narratives and writing poems and songs, children's stories and novels. She wrote newspaper articles and lectured. Her best known works are lectures collected as *Mammy's Reminiscences and Other Sketches* (1898) and *Old Plantation Days* (1902). "Ef de Lawd takes keer uv eben de li'l teeny, weeny sparrers, honey, den we-all what is created in His 'zac' likenes shouldn' 'spute de jestice uv His laws. De Lawd he wucks in myster'ous ways," Mammy Joe—a female variation on Uncle Remus—says in the opening pages of the first title mentioned.

Charles W. Chesnutt (1858–1932) Uncle Julius McAdoo (1898–1899) *see* Section I

Paul Laurence Dunbar (1872–1906) *Folks from Dixie* (1898) *see* Section I

Helen Bannerman
(1862–1946)
Little Black Sambo (1899)

Brodie Cowan Watson, later to be known as "Helen Bannerman," was born in Edinburgh, Scotland. She passed examinations at the University of St. Andrews to earn an LLA, Lady Literate in Arts, designation. She lived most of her life in India with her husband, William Bannerman, who served in the Indian Medical Service. She wrote and illustrated children's books about India, among them a series of Dumpy Books for Children including *Story of Little Black Sambo* (1899), *Story of Little Black Mingo* (1901), *Story of Little Black Quibba* (1902) and *Little Black Quasha* (1908). Sambo is a South Indian or Tamil boy, though he is often mistaken for a southern black. Sambo was long a derogatory term for a black male. The Bannerman stories echo British colonial prejudice. The parents are named Mumbo and Jumbo. The original illustrations are caricatures.

Alice Dunbar-Nelson
(1875–1935)
The Goodness of St. Rocque and Other Stories (1899)

The daughter of a seamstress and former slave and of a black merchant marine, Alice Ruth Moore grew up in middle-class neighborhoods in New Orleans. She graduated from Straight University in 1892 and became a teacher. Her first collection of short stories and poems, *Violets and Other Tales*, came out in 1895 to modest acclaim. She married Paul Laurence Dunbar in 1898 in New York, where she was then teaching at the White Rose Mission in Brooklyn, New York. The Dunbars moved to Washington, D.C., and she continued to write. *The Goodness of St. Rocque and Other Stories* was published in 1899 and marketed as a companion to her husband's *Poems of Cabin and Field*. The author left her husband in 1902 and moved to Delaware to teach. She now published under the name Alice Dunbar. Publishers favored her use of Creole dialect in her fiction, but backed away when she began to explore themes of race and prejudice. She married two more times, to Dr. Henry A. Callis and then to Robert J. Nelson. She edited the *A.M.E. Review* in 1913 and 1914. She became an activist for African American and women's rights.

Richard F. Outcault (1863–1928) Gallus Coon (1900) and Pore Lil Mose (1900–1902) *see* Section II

Will N. Harben
(1858–1919)
Northern Georgia Sketches (1900)

William Nathaniel Harben came from a well-to-do family. He became a merchant of little success in Georgia and Tennessee. At age thirty, he began to write. The mountain folk of Northern Georgia were a favorite topic. His first novel, the melodramatic *White Marie: A Story of Georgian Plantation Life* (1889), told the story of a white girl raised as a slave. Ten short stories of a generally abolitionist bent, from *Century* and *Lippincott's* magazines, *Ladies Home Journal* and *Black Cat,* made up *Northern Georgia Sketches* (1900). Sketches included "A Humble Abolitionist," "The Whipping of Uncle Henry" and "The Sale of Uncle Rustus." Harben's rustic hillbilly Abner Daniel, a cracker-barrel wit, became a running character.

Booker T. Washington
(1856–1915)
Up from Slavery (1901)

The founder of the Tuskegee Institute, Booker Taliaferro Washington was a nationally known black educator, an outspoken advocate for vocational training for blacks and a spokesman for civil rights. He was born in slavery in Virginia, the son of a black mother and white father. With emancipation, he became a free laborer in West Virginia coal mines and salt furnaces. He attended Hampton Normal and Agricultural Institute and became a teacher. In his Atlanta Compromise address in 1895 at the Cotton States Exposition, he suggested blacks could accept segregation and the lack of voting rights if there were greater economic and educational opportunities. Counter to this, W.E.B. Du Bois urged full equality in all endeavors. Washington wrote an autobiography, *Up from Slavery*, in 1901.

Martha Strudwick Young
(1862–1941)
Plantation Songs (1901)

Martha Strudwick Young was born on the family plantation in Alabama. She attended Greensboro Female Academy, where one of her teachers was Louise Clarke Pyrnelle. She graduated from Livingston Female Academy (now University of West Alabama) and returned to her family's then home in Greensboro to care for her ailing father and siblings. She began to write black dialect stories and songs she had heard as a girl, to preserve them. Her "A Nurse's Tale" appeared in the New Orleans *Times-Democrat* in December 1884, under the byline "Eli Shepperd," and soon others of her works found homes in print in such publications as *Woman's Home Companion*, *Metropolitan Magazine*, *Southern Churchman* and *Cosmopolitan*. *Plantation Songs for My Lady's Banjo* (1901) and *Plantation Bird Legends* (1902) were collected for books, issued under her real name, followed by a children's book, *Bessie Bell* (1903).

John Charles McNeill
(1874–1907)
Four Negro Songs (1902)

John Charles McNeill wrote "Four Negro Songs" for *The Century Magazine*: "The Possum and the Coon," "Profession vs. Practice," "The Stolen Melon" and "The Catfish Song," all illustrated by E.W. Kemble and appearing in the February 1902 issue. Born in North Carolina, McNeill grew up on a farm and attended Wake Forest College. He taught for a year then began a law practice. He went to work for the Charlotte *Daily Observer*, where most of his poetry appeared. He won his state's Patterson Cup in 1905 for the best literary work that year. His book *Songs, Merry and Sad* came out in 1906. "The Coon from the College Town," "Mr. Nigger" and "Nigger Demus" are among verses in *Lyrics from Cotton Land* (1907), illustrated by Kemble and A.B. Frost.

Frederick H. Seymour
(1850–1913)
Uncle Eph (1902)

Frederick O'Hoolihan, known as Lord Gilhooly, came from his ancestral seat at Balryghatally Castle, Ireland, to visit his American cousins at Gilhooly Manor in Virginia, in the 1902 book *Son; or, The Wisdom of Uncle Eph, the Modern*. The book, purportedly written by Gilhooly, was printed on tobacco paper and bound in blue denim by F.A. Stokes. "Among the former slaves of the Virginia Gilhoolys is 'Uncle Eph,' whose sayings in negro dialect are recorded in this book," according to a *School Journal* (27 September 1902) review. One modern-day bookseller catalogued it as "unpaginated dialect drivel—or humor." "Why it was necessary for the author to put his excellent ideas into the dialect of the negro is beyond understanding," a reviewer said in *The Delineator* (December 1902). As an example of Uncle Eph's wisdom: "Son! All de loud prayin' an psalm singin' yo' kin do ain't gwine to help yo' credit at de co'ner grocery." The author's real name was Frederick A. Seymour. Born in Connecticut, he was an artist and inventor of the Acme monkey wrench. He worked for Detroit newspapers including the *Journal* and *Tribune*. His first humorous book, in 1897, was *The God Yutzo of 763 B.C.* (also titled *Ye Wisdom of Confusius*), in which Lord Gilhooly's little ivory idol, purchased in Paris, becomes animated and provides witty wisdom on life. The novel *Dennis Fogarty* (1903) is written in Irish dialect. *Gillhooleyisms* (1904) collects aphorisms from all three books. Seymour also wrote nonfiction, including *Roosevelt in Africa* (1909).

James D. Corrothers
(1869–1917)
The Black Cat Club (1902)

James D. Corrothers was raised in Michigan by his grandfather. He attended public school. He worked as a lumberjack, waiter and barber. He went to work for the *Chicago Tribune* in 1887. A white reporter rewrote one of his stories about a black social event, using dialect. Corrothers quit. He attended Northwestern University and Bennett College but returned to journalism without completing degree requirements. He wrote poetry, and based on Paul Laurence Dunbar's success, wrote stories and verses in dialect, such as "Way in de Woods, an' Nobody Dar," for *Century* in 1899. He wrote a verse about racial protest, *The Snapping of the Bow*, in 1901. He collected his short pieces with urban setting in *The Black Cat Club* (1902). Many were about a lower-class "literary society" guided by a dialect poet named Sandy "Doc" Jenkins. Corrothers' is a rare example of the use of humor by a black writer in this period. Corrothers used dialect only as it served the purposes of his message, and his need to appeal to white editors and readers. One story from the book is about a public debate at the Black Cat Club on the topic "Courage and Common Sense; or, Resolved, 'at a good run's bettah'n a bad stan." The gathering is wildly attended by blacks and whites, begins in good mood, deteriorates minstrel-like into accusations and absurdity until Jenkins restores order by reciting one of his own poems. Corrothers became a minister variously with African Methodist Episcopal, Baptist and Presbyterian churches.

W.E.B. Du Bois
(1868–1963)
The Souls of Black Folk (1903)

Born in Great Barrington, Massachusetts, William Edward Burghardt Du Bois had a comfortable, all–American New England childhood. He attended Fisk University, studied at the University of Berlin and became the first black to earn a doctorate at Harvard. He founded the Niagara Movement, which lead to creation of the National Association for the Advancement of Colored People. His landmark sociological study, *The Philadelphia Negro*, came out in 1899. But his 1903 *The Souls of Black Folk*, in which sorrow songs frame fourteen essays, brought him into blazing prominence as a new spokesman for his race. He took exception to Booker T. Washington's Atlanta Compromise, and fought for more than the teaching of farming and mechanical skills to blacks. He aspired to develop the "talented tenth," a black elite, with rich liberal arts educations. He advocated greater opportunities for blacks, and also for women. He taught at Atlanta University. He edited *The Crisis*, the NAACP journal, from 1910 to 1933. He traveled widely in support of Pan-Africanism. He died in Accra, Ghana, where he had gone to edit the ambitious *Encyclopedia Africana*.

Ella Middleton Tybout
(1871–1952)
Poketown People (1904)

"I recall with affection certain dark-skinned friends of my childhood, whose patience and unfailing kindness endeared them to me then and deserve recognition from me now," Ella Middletown Tybout wrote in the introduction to *Poketown People; or Parables in Black* (1904), published by J. B. Lippincott. "These sketches are simply intended to depict the negro as I have known him or her with their eccentricities, superstitions, strange code of morality, and curious practical application of religion to every-day life. The higher education of the negro is past obliterating the types I have described..." *The New York Times* for 24 December 1904 found the book's characters were "not the Northern 'negro,' but the Southern 'nigger'—shiftless and idle, but infinitely picturesque and even lovable." Tybout, born in Delaware but long a Washington, D.C., resident, began writing at age sixteen. She contributed dialect and other stories to *Lippincott's* and *Frank Leslie's Monthly, New England Magazine* and *Short Stories*. The author also wrote *The Smuggler, Wife of the Secretary of State* and other books.

Silas Xavier Floyd
(1869–1923)
Floyd's Flowers (1905)

Silas Xavier Floyd was born in Georgia, the son of blacks freed after Emancipation. He attended public schools and entered Atlanta University, earning a master of arts degree. He became a teacher, briefly in Boston, mostly in the South. He became an ordained Baptist minister. He received a doctor of divinity degree from Morris Brown College in 1902. He was very active in Sunday school work. He wrote several books, including a biography of Dr. C.T. Walker and *Floyd's Flowers: or, Duty and Beauty for Colored Children, Being One Hundred Short Stories Gleaned from the Storehouse of Human Knowledge and Experience*

(1905). Illustrated with photographs, the stories were morally instructive and uplifting and aimed at black children. It sold 20,000 copies in its initial printing. He wrote for newspapers. In 1915, he became secretary to the National Association of Teachers in Colored Schools and edited its magazine, the *National Note-Book*. He and his wife lived in Augusta.

William Marriner
(1873–1914)
Sambo Johnsin (1905)

Kentucky-born artist William F. Marriner excelled in drawing children. He sold his first cartoons to the humor magazine *Puck*, and from 1900 to 1906 worked for the *Philadelphia Enquirer* and *New York World*. He worked briefly with the McClure Syndicate in 1901, then again from 1905 until his death in 1914. One of his comic strip creations was *Sambo and His Funny Noises* (also called *Sambo* and *Misto Sambo*), about a black boy, Sambo Johnsin, who interacted with, and sometimes rendered come-uppances to, two white boys. It was syndicated from 1905 to 1913. Animator Pat Sullivan (1885–1833), an Australian who worked as Marriner's assistant on the comic strip, secured rights to the character and adapted Sambo to the screen in 1915 and 1916. Because Helen Bannerman's Little Black Sambo predated his efforts, Sullivan changed the character's name to Sammie Johnsin for the ten-cartoon series. An example is *Sammie Johnsin Strong Man*. Sullivan later made Felix the Cat shorts, of which Otto Messmer was the lead animator. "The first black character to appear in an American animated cartoon was the smiling face of Coon in 1907. In 1915 Sullivan developed Sammy Johnsin, a Sambo stereotype and the first black character to star in his own silent animated cartoon series," according to Todd Boyd in *African Americans and Popular Culture* (2008). Of Marriner's several strips, *Wags, the Dog That Adopted a Man* was perhaps the most popular. It ran from 1905 to 1908. He also drew the adventures of Willie White, Benny Brown and Bobby Black as part of the *Captain Kidd* strip for the *Enquirer*, featuring a rich kid and a poor kid, both white, and a black kid. It ran from May to September 1900. Marriner was an alcoholic. He lived and worked in Manhattan.

John F. Dixon Jr.
(1864–1946)
The Clansman (1905)

John F. Dixon Jr. did for racists what Harriet Beecher Stowe did for humanitarians. He polarized the institution of southern slavery. Dixon attended college and was a Southern Baptist minister, playwright, orator, legislator and author in North Carolina. Reconstruction-era confiscation of farmlands and bureaucratic corruption embittered Dixon, whose father had held slaves—disdaining slavery yet refusing to sell them, stating he feared they would be abused. The younger Dixon learned of an incident in which a black man, accused of raping a white woman, was beaten and lynched by the Ku Klux Klan and was of the opinion members of the KKK were the only ones looking out for southern whites. His father and uncle belonged to the Klan for a time. Frustrated in his pursuit of a stage career, he studied law. He ran for the North Carolina General Assembly and was known for advocating for the rights of Confederate veterans. He pastored at First Baptist Church in Goldsboro, North Carolina, and Dudley Street Church in Boston. He wrote a Trilogy of Reconstruction that included *The Leopard's Spot* (1902), *The Clansman: An Historical Romance of the Ku Klux Klan* (1905) and *The Traitor* (1907). The middle novel "opened wider a vein of racial hatred which was to poison further an age already in social and political upheaval," according to historian Thomas D. Clark. "Dixon had in fact given voice in his novel to one of the most powerful latent forces in the social and political mind of the South." *The Clansman* became the basis for D.W. Griffith's artistically innovative but politically provocative film *The Birth of a Nation* (1915). The film triggered a rebirth of the KKK. Dixon did not advocate slavery, but he believed blacks were inferior to whites. A Negrophobe, he believed blacks were uneducable and aggressive toward whites. He favored racial segregation. Dixon eventually lost his fortune and in his last years worked as a court clerk.

Sara Cone Bryant
(1873–?)
Epaminondas and His Auntie (1907)

Sara Cone Bryant (Mrs. Theodore F. Borst) wrote *Best Stories to Tell Children* (1912) and other books for youngsters. Ten of her stories were made into spoken-word Victor recordings, including *Epaminondas* in 1917. Bryant did her own recitation for that cylinder. Artist Inez Hogan illustrated *Epaminondas and His Auntie* with caricatures. The featured black boy character followed directions too literally. Each day he visited his aunt, and each day she sent him home with something for his Mammy. Transporting butter, for example, he stores it in his hat. A puppy ... well, the puppy doesn't make it home alive. Epaminondas falls into the category of noodlehead or numbskull stories, which had origins in folk tales such as "Lazy Hans" and "Lazy Jack."

Henry Edwards Cowen ("Red Buck") Bryant (1873–1967)
Tar Heel Tales (1908–1909) *see* Section II

Bridges Smith (1848–1930) Yamacraw Stories (1909–1918) *see* Section II

Frances Boyd Calhoun
(1867–1909)
Emma Speed Sampson
(1868–1947)
Miss Minerva Stories (1909–1919)

Virginia native Frances Boyd became a teacher in Covington, Tennessee, and wrote for her father's newspaper. Her husband, George Barret Calhoun, died in 1904, a year after their marriage. Illness forced her retirement. The author's juvenile novel *Miss Minerva and William Green Hill* came out in 1909, shortly after her death. The book is about a southern woman who becomes guardian of an unruly nephew. It includes African American characters, stereotypes and dialect. Emma Speed, who was born in Kentucky, studied art in Paris and New York. She married Henry Aylett Sampson and settled in Richmond, Virginia. She wrote juvenile books, some of them as Nell Sampson. She continued L. Frank Baum's Oz series and turned Calhoun's novel into a series with *Miss Minerva on the Old Plantation* (1923) and nine other books featuring Miss Minerva. Her *Mammy's White Folks* (1919) was a stand-alone book of thirty-three dialect stories. She in later years was a member of the Virginia state Board of Motion Picture Censors and was a columnist for the Richmond *Times Dispatch*.

Harris Dickson (1889–1943) Ole Reliable (1910–1923) *see* Section II

Irvin S. Cobb (1876–1944) Jeff Poindexter, Colored (1911–1936) *see* Section II

Joseph S. Cotter, Jr.
(1861–1949)
Negro Tales (1912)

Joseph Seamon Cotter, Jr. was born in Kentucky, the son of a freeborn black mother and a prominent white Louisville father, parties of a common-law marriage. He worked as a laborer and studied at night to become a teacher. He was a school principal for nearly five decades. The *Courier-Journal* published his early poetry. *A Rhyming* (1895) was his first book, followed by *A White Song and a Black One* (1909) and others. He wrote plays. His prose collection *Negro Tales* (1912) was written mostly in Standard English ("The Boy and the Ideal") but some dialect ("Kotchin' de Nines"). It includes folk tales ("The Jackal and the Lion"). He was one of the first black poets of ability, and the first to write protest poetry.

James Weldon Johnson
(1871–1938)
The Autobiography of an Ex-Colored Man (1912)

James Weldon Johnson was internationally known as a novelist, poet, songwriter, journalist, playwright, diplomat and champion of human rights. He was the first black to pass the Florida bar exam. With his brother Rosamond (1873–1954) he composed numerous show tunes during the Harlem Renaissance, the best known the Negro National Anthem, "Lift Ev'ry Voice and Sing" (1899). Johnson wrote two songs for Theodore Roosevelt's 1904 presidential campaign, and became Roosevelt's U.S. consul to Venezuela and Nicaragua (1906–1913). Published anonymously, Johnson's 1912 *The Autobiography of an Ex-Colored*

Man was one of the first works of fiction written by a black author in the first person. Johnson was the NAACP's field secretary beginning in 1915 and with W.E.B. Du Bois led some 12,000 marchers in New York City in a protest of lynching. After a period as NAACP secretary, Johnson taught at Fisk University. All the while, he wrote and published poetry and short fiction.

E.K. (Eldred Kurtz) Means (1878–1957)
Skeeter Butts (1913–1929) *see* Section II

Booth Tarkington (1869–1946) Herman and Verman (1913–1929)
see Section II

Marion F. Harmon
(1861–1940)
Negro Wit and Humor (1914)

Pink Laffin wrote *Coontown: A Negro Joke Book* in 1850. It was typical of dialect books published by whites and distributed throughout the South to entertain other whites. Marion Franklin Harmon continued the humor tradition with his self-published *Negro Wit and Humor: Also containing folk lore, folk songs, race peculiarities, race history,* under the imprint of his Louisville, Kentucky, based Harmon Publishing Co. in 1914. The author claimed to be seriously charting the progress of the race with his anecdotes and said friends "vouch for their accuracy and originality." The book includes a lexicon: "I am" is "I'ze" in Negro speak; "except" is "excusin," "before" is "befo," tuberculosis is "two-bugs-in-a-locus." During this period, books of Negro jokes abound. Historian William Schechter in *The History of Negro Humor in America* (1970) was aghast at the irony: "In 1926, while these joke books were enjoying large sales, thirty blacks were lynched in the United States, events little-noticed during a nation's search for laughs at inveterate 'chicken-stealer,' bootleg liquor and stock market tips." Harmon was born in Mississippi but lived in Kentucky when he operated the Messenger Publishing House and produced the *Messenger*, a Christian weekly. He was later pastor of First Christian Church in Jackson, Mississippi. Harmon's only other book was *The History of Christian Churches (Disciples of Christ) in Mississippi* (1929).

James P. Alley (1885–1934) **Calvin Alley** (1915–1970)
Hambone's Meditations (1916–1968) *see* Section II

Ambrose Gonzales (1857–1926) *Black Border* (1918–1924) *see* Section II

Robert McBlair (1888–1976) Mister Fish Kelly (1918–1927) *see* Section II

Octavus Roy Cohen (1891–1959) Florian Slappey (1918–1952) *see* Section II

Harry Stillwell Edwards (1855–1938) Eneas Africanus (1919–1921)
see Section II

Arthur LeRoy Kaser (1890–1956) Mush and Poke (1920–1934) *see* Section II

Hugh Wiley (1884–1968) "Wildcat" Marsden (1920–1934) *see* Section II

B.B. Valentine
(1862–1919)
Ole Marster (1921)

Emerging from the plantation generation of the South following the Civil War, Benjamin Batchelder Valentine was a staunch defender of the old way in *Ole Marster and Other Verses* (1921). Ellen Glasgow, in praise printed on the dustcover of a Valentine Museum edition of the book, said, "This little book contains some of the very best, the richest, and the most expressive interpretation of the Southern Negro that I have ever read in verse." Valentine, a wealthy businessman (his father marketed "Valentine's Meat Juice," a health tonic) who lived in Richmond, Virginia, was a philanthropist and collector of Native American relics from the Appalachian mountains. He was married to suffragist Lila Meade (1865–1921).

Julia Mead Peterkin
(1880–1961)
Green Thursday (1924)

Julia Mead grew up in South Carolina. Her mother died soon after her birth. Her father was a doctor. She graduated from Converse College and became a teacher. She married a planter, William George Peterkin, in 1903. He owned the 2,000-acre Lang Syne cotton plantation, which became inspiration for his wife's fiction. Her plantation story "Maum Lou" (from *The Reviewer*) received the O. Henry Award for Best Short Story in 1925. "The Diamond Ring" won the same prize in 1930. Her first book was *Green Thursday* (1924), a collection of sketches set around a black plantation family. Although she attempted a sincere and accurate depiction of blacks, including the Gullah dialect, her writings generated some controversy. Her novel *Scarlet Sister Mary* (1928) won a Pulitzer Prize and was made into a Broadway play. Nevertheless, some charged it was obscene. Other works include *Roll, Jordan, Roll* (1933) and *A Plantation Christmas* (1934).

Robert Emmet Kennedy
(1877–1941)
East Green Stories (1924)

Robert Emmet Kennedy was born in Louisiana. He was a painter and pianist and collected black songs and folklore. He reviewed books for *The New York Times*. His *Black*

Cameos came out in 1924, followed by *Gritny People* (1927). Edward Larocque Tinker illustrated *Black Cameos*, which included such stories as "East Green Alligator Charmer" and "Aunt Kizzie's Troubles." The stories took place in an imagined black settlement, East Green, in Gretna, a small town across the Mississippi River from New Orleans. The stories replicate a Negro dialect, as does the novel *Red Bean Row* (1929). Kennedy's songbooks and musician biographies included *Mellows: A Chronicle of Unknown Singers* (1925) and *More Mellows* (1931) and *Negro Spirituals* (1931). In the last two decades of his life, he managed an antiques store in New York.

Jane Baldwin Cotton
(d. 1932)
Wall-Eyed Caesar's Ghost (1925)

Jane Baldwin Cotton is known for two literary efforts: *The Compilation of The Maryland Calendar of Wills Volumes I–VIII*, a research tool, and *Wall-Eyed Caesar's Ghost* (1925), an assembly of four stories illustrated by Frederick J. Cotton, the author's husband, an orthopedic surgeon. The Cottons lived in Boston for many years, maintaining a summer place in Maryland. The title story includes the character of a girl, Posey, who talks this way: "Jes' listen ter de frogs, Pappy. Dey sounds luk birds singin' out dar in de swamp. I wondahs why 'tis dat dey stahts out wid voices luk dat in de spring an' artah a while dey can't do nuttin' but croak." "I donan know," answered Moses reflectively, not being an authority on frogs, "but I reckons dey jes' gits ha'se er else dey grows up an' der voice changes."

Arthur K. Akers (1886–1980) Bugwine Breck (1925–1934) *see* Section II

Charles Correll (1890–1972) and **Freeman F. Gosden** (1899–1982) Sam & Henry (1926–1927) and Amos & Andy (1928–1955) *see* Section II

Roark Bradford (1896–1948) Bugaboo Jones (1927–1940) and Little Bee Bend Plantation (1932–1948) *see* Section II

Nella Larsen
(1891–1964)
Quicksand (1928)

Nellallitea "Nella" Walker was born in Chicago. When her West Indian father left the household, her mother married Peter Larsen, and Nella took her stepfather's last name. She lived briefly in Denmark with her mother's family. She attended Fisk University and studied nursing in New York City. She became head nurse at Tuskegee Institute in Alabama and met Booker T. Washington. She worked in New York City as a public health nurse during the influenza epidemic of 1918. She married Elmer Imes, a physicist, and began to write short fiction. They lived in Harlem, where she knew W.E.B. Du Bois and James Weldon Johnson. Without a college degree, she felt rebuffed for her middle-class lifestyle. She attended the New York Public Library School and became a librarian, eventually at the Harlem branch. As the Harlem Renaissance grew, she turned to writing and published *Quicksand* (1928), an autobiographical novel, followed by *Passing* (1929), which dealt with issues of mixed race and skin color, female perspective and search for identity. She was accused of plagiarism for a story, "Sanctuary," said to, in parts, strongly resemble "Mrs. Adis" by Sheila Kaye-Smith. Larsen's biographer H. Pearce said Larsen's story has similar themes but is longer and better written. She divorced her husband in 1933. She received a Guggenheim fellowship and traveled to Europe.

Charles E. Mack
(1887–1934)
Two Black Crows in the AEF (1928)

Charles E. Mack (real name Charles Sellers) teamed in 1917 with John Swor (1877–1965) as Swor and Mack in a blackface vaudeville act. A year later Mack took a new partner, George Searcy (1881–1949), to perform as the Two Black Crows. Searcy used the stage name George Moran. The pair exaggerated their rustic Buford, Tennessee, characters on the weekly radio show *Majestic Hour* in 1928 on NBC Blue. Mack was the naïve Amos, Moran the lazy jokester Willie. "Why bring *that* up?" Mack would ask in a phrase that caught on with audiences. (*Why Bring That Up?* became the title of one of their films.) They appeared on Broadway with the Ziegfeld Follies. They made audio recordings in 1927. After Moran left in a salary dispute, Bert Swor (1871–1943) became Mack's partner (and took the stage name George Moran) until the real Moran came back. "The early bird catches the worm," Moran would say. "Who wants a worm, anyhow?" Mack would reply. One skit segment from 1928 has the two men in stripes and wielding sledge hammers: Moran: What ah wants to know is what we're supposed to do with these rocks? Mack. Ah believs the idea is to crack 'em. Moran. Crack 'em in halves or in quarters? Mack. Boy, we'll be here long enough to make sand out of 'em. Mack wrote a book, *Two Black Crows in the AEF* (Bobbs-Merrill, 1928, called *Anybody's War* for a motion picture edition, 1930), about Amos and Willie overseas during the First World War. Speaking in character, Mack told interviewer W. Ward Marsh in the *Cleveland Plain Dealer* for 18 November 1930": When we wuz makin' 'Anybody's War,' we needed Dachund puppies fo' de las' scene. Den we foun' out dat o such aniumules could be got, 'n we had to wait seven weeks 'til dem puppies was born, 'n even den we didn't know fo' sho' dat dey'd be Dachunds. BUT WHO CARES 'BOUT DAT?"

Annie Vaughan Weaver
(1905–1982)
Frawg (1930)

Born near Selma, Alabama, Annie Vaughan Weaver grew up on the family's plantation called Emerald Place. She entered Smith College in Massachusetts to study theology, intending to become a missionary. After a time, she went to New York to study art. She wrote and illustrated three children's books to raise money for her studies. Her books, based on plantation stories, were *Frawg* (1930), *Boochy's Wings* (1931) and *Pappy King* (1932). While many suggest *Frawg* perpetuates negative black stereotypes (in one story, Frawg overeats on watermelon), others believe its characters are well-rounded and positive. Frawg is a boy growing up impoverished in the post–Civil War south. She continued her studies, won two Carnegie Foundation Travel fellowships, and became a teacher in Florida, where she married a gallery owner named Nelson. She later took up sculpture.

Inez Hogan
(1895–1973)
Nicodemus (1932)

Inez Hogan wrote and illustrated some sixty-three children's books, many of them animal stories, and illustrated another nineteen. Born in Washington, D.C., she studied at Wilson Teacher College and Cape Cod School of Art. She lived in Provincetown, Massachusetts, and New York City. She taught. But from 1930 on, she supported herself by her books. Her best known were twelve volumes about Nicodemus, an American boy of African descent. Critics say Nicodemus was a pickaninny, a clumsy, lazy, slow-witted character in tattered clothing and bare feet. The first book was *Nicodemus and His Little Sister* (1932). A *Kirkus Review* reviewer discussing *Nicodemus and the Gang* in 1939 found Hogan "has a freshness of approach, a child quality, humor and a sense of the value of repetition that gives the special quality to the little stories and pictures of the small darky and his little sister."

E.V. White
(1879–1955)
Chocolate Drops (1932)

Chocolate Drops from the South: A Book of Negro Humor and Philosophy (1932) includes stories of Rastus and Sambo—the expected degrading dialect stories. The writer was Edmund Valentine White, who self-published three Negro joke books. Eleanor Roosevelt for some reason recommended his writing in one of her newspaper columns. White was a graduate of the University of Texas and Baylor University. He served in the military in the Spanish-American War. He was dean of Texas State College for Women from 1915 to 1948. He also wrote texts on algebra and mathematics. (White's grandson, Edmund White III, is a well-known gay novelist.)

Zora Neale Hurston
(1891–1960)
Moses, Man of the Mountain (1939)

Zora Neale Hurston was born in Alabama, her mother a teacher, her father a tenant farmer, carpenter and Baptist preacher. When she was a child, the family moved to an all-black town in Florida, Eatonville, where her father became mayor. She traveled with a theatrical company before she enrolled at Morgan Academy, part of Morgan College in Baltimore, Maryland. She cofounded the student newspaper when she attended Howard University. She was the only black student when she went to Barnard College. In New York, she was invigorated by the Harlem Renaissance. She wrote short stories and poetry. She, Langston Hughes and Wallace Thurman, calling themselves the Niggerati, started *Fire!!*, a literary magazine. In 1927 she married Herbert Sheen, a jazz musician who became a doctor. She collaborated with Hughes on *Mule Bone*, a play. She favored the self-help philosophy of Booker T. Washington rather than socialist or New Deal policies. She later taught at North Carolina College for Negroes. Hurston was a folklorist and anthropologist and traveled to the Caribbean throughout the American south. A result was *Mules and Men* (1925), a folklore classic and basis for her later novels such as *Jonah's Gourd Vine* (1934). *Their Eyes Were Watching God* came out in 1937, *Moses, Man of the Mountain* two years later. Some, such as Richard Wright, objected to Hurston's use of the vernacular in her novels. But her dialect expressions came from her research. Her works received new attention following an appreciation by Alice Walker, "In Search of Zora Neale Hurston," in the March 1975 issue of *Ms.*

Paul Ernst (1899–1985) Joshua and Rosabel Newton (1939–1944) *see* Section II

Will Eisner (1917–2005) Ebony White (1940–1952) *see* Section II

Richard Wright
(1908–1960)
Native Son (1941)

African American authors made serious literary strides. Richard Wright in particular grappled with issues of race in his novels, short stories and poems. Wright grew up in Mississippi in a broken and poor household. He sold his first story to the newspaper *Southern Register* when he was fifteen. In Chicago in 1927, working as a mail clerk or laboratory orderly, he attended meetings of the Marxist-leaning John Reed Club. He wrote and found a few markets. He moved to New York City in 1937 and the next year *Uncle Tom's Children* was published and brought him a Guggenheim Fellowship. His naturalistic novel about Bigger Thomas, *Native Son: The Biography of a Young American*, came out in 1941. It was acclaimed one of the best books written on America's racial divide. His autobiographical *Black Boy*, about growing up in the repressive Jim Crow South, became a bestseller in 1945. He became an American expatriate in Paris in 1946 and traveled extensively.

Ellen Tarry
(1906–2008)
Hezekiah Horton (1942)

Hezekiah Horton, in Ellen Tarry's 1942 novel of the same title, is a ten-year-old Harlem boy who spends most of his waking moments dreaming about automobiles. The author was born in Birmingham, Alabama. She became a teacher. She wrote a newspaper column. She moved to New York City in 1929 to join the Harlem Renaissance authors and artists. A convert to Catholicism, she was a founder of Friendship House's Chicago branch. She was the first African American writer of children's picture books, starting with *Janie Belle* in 1940. Oliver Harrington illustrated *Hezekiah Horton* and its sequel in 1950, *The Runaway Elephant*. She also wrote biographies. She participated in the 1963 March on Washington.

Langston Hughes (1902–1967) Jesse B. Semple (1942–1965) *see* Section II

Enid Blyton
(1897–1968)
Golliwogs (1944)

The British children's book author known for the Famous Five, Secret Seven and other juvenile series also wrote about the Golliwogs. Born in London, the author was educated at St. Christopher's School. Family dysfunctions accounted for her emotional immaturity, according to biographers. She was a pianist of some ability, but abandoned music as a career in favor of becoming a teacher. She married Hugh Alexander Pollock in 1924. He was an editor with the firm George Newnes, which published her early books. *The Three Golliwogs* came out in 1944 and there were three sequels. Many of her books, even Famous Five books, are riddled with "black as a nigger with soot" and other language in an era when "Negro" was in wide and acceptable usage. There were also sexist elements to the narratives. Golliwogs were odd ragdoll characters (Blyton didn't create them, they already existed in folklore) wearing red pants and blue jackets. Dark skinned, the characters had near Afro hair. Florence Kate Upton of New York—her parents were British—also wrote stories about Golliwogs.

Jackie Ormes
(1911–1985)
Patty-Jo 'n' Ginger (1945–1956)

Jackie Ormes was the first nationally syndicated female African American newspaper cartoonist. Her *Torchy Brown Dixie to Harlem* (1937–1938) in the *Pittsburgh Courier* was about a starry-eyed country girl from Mississippi who travels to New York City to seek her fortune at the Cotton Club in Harlem. The cartoonist was born Zelda Mavin Jackson in Pennsylvania. She became a political activist as well as journalist. She wrote and drew *Candy*, about a snarky housemaid, for the *Chicago Defender*, in the mid–1940s. Her one-panel *Patty-Jo 'n' Ginger* strip about two middle-class black sisters, the younger one given to wisecracks (sometimes about race or social justice), the older one more of a pinup, was printed in the *Courier* from 1945 to 1956. The younger girl inspired the Patti-Jo doll from the Terri Lee doll company in 1947. The artist revived Torchy Brown for the *Courier*, which ran *Torchy in Heartbeats* from 1950 to 1954.

Ralph Ellison
(1914–1994)
Invisible Man (1952)

Ralph Ellison wrote one novel, the National Book Award–winning *Invisible Man* (1952). It took him seven years to complete, and it remains one of the most mature and significant works of black fiction of its day. Born in Oklahoma, he studied music at Tuskegee Institute and sculpture at a New York City studio. He served in the Merchant Marine. He became a protégé of Richard Wright. Ellison wrote essays and review and short stories. Though it is far more than a protest novel, *Invisible Man* expresses the author's disillusion with the Communist Party for failing to offer a path to the end of class and race oppression. Later in his career Ellison taught at New York University. He received the Presidential Medal of Freedom in 1969.

James Baldwin
(1924–1987)
Go Tell It on the Mountain (1953)

James Baldwin wrote frequently about racial and social issues. His *Notes of a Native Son* (1965) and *The Fire Next Time* (1963) speak loudly for and about the civil rights movement and social and sexual justice. Born in Harlem, the writer and playwright took several jobs to support his single mother and other siblings. Settling in Greenwich Village, he eventually found markets for his stories and essays. He was gay. He disdained organized religion. Modern Library called his novel *Go Tell It on the Mountain* one of 100 Best English Language Novels of the 20th Century. In the semiautobiographical work, the author looks at the relationship of African Americans and the Christian Church. Disgusted with prejudices he encountered in the United States, he left for Paris in 1948. There he strove to establish an identity, not as a black, but as a novelist.

Lorraine Hansberry
(1930–1965)
A Raisin in the Sun (1959)

Lorraine Hansberry had a bright, if brief, career as a dramatist. Her play *A Raisin in the Sun* (1959) was the first drama by an African American to be produced on Broadway, and she became the youngest and first black recipient of the New York Drama Critic's Circle Award for Best Play. It ran for 530 performances. The playwright grew up in Chicago and encountered prejudice when her family moved to a restricted white neighborhood. After attending university, and living in New York, she wrote short stories and poetry. She wrote another play, *The Sign in Sidney Brustein's Window* (1964), but died on closing night, after 101 shows. She wrote a teleplay for NBC, *The Drinking Gourd* (1960), which was unproduced.

Index

Adventures of Captain Simon Suggs 251
Adventures of Huckleberry Finn 23–25
Aiken, George L. 22
Akers, Arthur K. 179–183
Alabama 122–159, 181, 251, 255, 257, 260, 261, 262, 271, 272, 273
All-Story Cavalier Weekly 94
All-Story Weekly 88, 94–95
Alley, Calvin 106–113
Alley, James P. 106–113
Alley, James P., Jr. 110
Alley, Nona Lane 110–111
Altemus, Jameson Torr 255
American Magazine 86
Americans at Home 251
Amos 'n' Andy stories 129, 199–215
Anstead, W.H. 38
anti-Tom novels 23, 249, 250
Argosy All-Story Weekly 89, 95
Arnold, Everett M. "Busy" 219
Atlanta Constitution 25–28, 254
Atlantic Monthly 33
Augusta Chronicle 108
Aunt Phillis's Cabin 249
Autobiography of an Ex-Colored Man 267
Avenger stories 216–218

Baldwin, James 275
Bannerman, Helen 260, 265
Baum, L. Frank 267
Bayou Folk 258
Bigger and Blacker 155
Billings, Josh 253
Birmingham stories 122–159
Birth of a Nation 266
Black and Blue 155
Black Border stories 113–118
Black Boy 273
Black Cameos 270
Black Cat Club 263
Black to Nature 155

Blake: Or the Huts of America 251–252
blowhard character 16
Blue Book 88, 179, 182–183
Blue Steel stories 197
Bly, Nellie 39
Blyton, Enid 274
Bonner, Sherwood 256
Bradford, Roark 183–199
Brooks, Walter 8
Brown, William A. 259
Brown, William Wells 248–249
Browne, Charles Farrar 253
Bryant, H.E.C. *see* Henry Edwards Cowen Bryant
Bryant, Henry Edwards Cowen ("Red Buck") 45–49
Bryant, Sara Cone 266
Bubber stories 197
buck character 16, 183–199
Bugaboo Jones stories 183–199
Bugwine Breck stories 170–183
Bunn, Martin 8
Burns, Robert 14, 254
Butler, Ellis Parker 8

Cable, George Washington 19, 29–30
Caldwell, J.P. 45, 47
Calhoun, Frances Boyd 266
Captain Kidd cartoon 265
cartoonists *see* Alley, Calvin; Alley, James P.; Eisner, Will; Marriner, William; Ormes, Jackie; Outcault, R.F.; Worth, James
Cavalier 89, 94
Century 25, 31, 262
Charlotte Daily Observer 45–49
Chesnutt, Charles W. 19, 32–35
Chicago Daily News 205
Chicago Defender 228–243, 274
Chicago Tribune 201–205, 211–212
Child, Lydia Maria 247–248
Ching Chow 109

Chocolate Drops 272
Chopin, Kate 258
Christmas Night in the Quarters 254
Chute, M.G. 7
Clansman 265
Clotel 248
Cobb, Irvin S. 8, 77–88
Cohen, Octavus Roy 5, 8, 122–159, 175
Cole, Bob 259
Collier, Old Cap 255
Collier's 2, 118, 183–199
colloquial language *see* creative language; dialect
columnists *see* Bryant, Henry Edwards Cowen; Cohen, Octavus Roy; Correll, Charles; Dickson, Harris; Gosden, Freeman; Hughes, Langston; Smith, Bridges
Come Seven 135–136, 154, 155
comic strips *see* Alley, Calvin; Alley, James P.; Cohen, Octavus Roy; Correll, Charles; Eisner, Will; Gosden, Freeman; Outcault, R.F.
Commercial Appeal 106–113
The Conjure Woman and Other Conjure Tales 32–34
Contract with God 223
coon character 16
Coontown: A Negro Joke Book 268
Correll, Charles 13, 199–215
Corrothers, James D. 263
Cosmopolitan 86, 97, 103–104
Cotter, Joseph S., Jr. 267
Cotton, Jane Baldwin 270
creative language 19, 47, 131, 141, 176, 192, 205, 271
Currier & Ives 254

Dark Days and Black Knights 155
Darkie Dan, the Colored Detective 255
Darktown art prints 254

Darktown stories 122–159
Dean, Dud 8
Delany, Martin 251–252
Dent, Lester 216
Detective Fiction Weekly 118
dialect 10, 12–14, 53, 115, 245, 246, 247, 351, 256, 263, 273
Dialect Tales 256
Dickson, Harrison 71–77
Diddle, Dumps, and Tot 255
Dixon, George Washington 246–247
Dixon, John F., Jr. 265–266
Douglass, Frederick 248
Drama of King Shotaway 259
Drinking Gourd 275
Du Bois, W.E.B. 10, 14, 81, 139, 203, 263–264
Dunbar, Paul Laurence 13, 19, 35–36, 261, 263
Dunbar-Nelson, Alice 261

East Green stories 269
Eastman, Mary Henderson 249
Ebony White stories 218–227
Edwards, Harry Stillwell 159–164
Eisner, Will 15, 218–227
Eisner-Iger Studio 219
Ellery Queen's Mystery Magazine 86, 154
Ellison, Ralph 275
Elonka, Steve 8
Eneas Africanus stories 159–164
Epaminondas and His Auntie 266
Epic Peters stories 122–159
Ernst, Paul F. 215–218
Everybody's Magazine 97, 103

Felix the Cat 265
films *see* motion pictures
Fire Next Time 275
Fitzgerald, F. Scott 8
Florian Slappey Goes Abroad 155
Florian Slappey stories 122–159
Floyd, Silas Xavier 264–265
Floyd's Flowers 264
Fo' Meals a Day 176, 179
Folks from Dixie 35–36
Four Negro Songs" 262
Frawg 271–272
Frost, A.B. 26

Gallus Coon cartoons 39
Gardner, Erle Stanley 8
Georgia 25–29, 49–71, 113–118, 159–164, 260, 256, 259, 261, 264
Georgia Scenes 247
Gibson, Walter 216
Gielow, Martha Sawyer 260
Gilman, Caroline 247
Gilpatrick, Guy 7
Go Tell It on the Mountain 275

Golden Wedding 256
Golliwog stories 274
Gonzales, Ambrose E. 113–118
Gonzales, Narciso Gener 113
Gonzales, William E. 114
Goodness of St. Rocque and Other Stories 261
Gosden, Freeman 13, 199–215
Green Thursday 269
Griffith, D.W. 266
Gullah stories 113–118

Haliburton, Thomas Chandler 251
Hambone's Meditations 106–113
Hansberry, Lorraine 275
Harben, Will N. 261
Harmon, Marion F. 268
Harper, Frances Ellen Watkins 256–257
Harper's 35, 160, 186, 256
Harris, Joel Chandler 12, 25–29
Hays, Ethel 109
Hearst, William Randolph 79
Hentz, Caroline Lee 250
Herman and Verman stories 98–102
Hezekiah Horton 273
Hibbs, Ben 134
high yellow character 16
Highly Colored 155
Hogan, Inez 272
Hogan's Alley 39
Holmes, Mary J. 250
Hooper, Johnson Jones 251
House Servant's Directory 245
Howells, William Dean 13
Hughes, Langston 2, 13, 228–243
Hurston, Zora Neale 13, 272–273

Iger, Jerry 219
In Ole Virginia 30–32
Incidents in the Life of a Slave Girl 252
Indiana 96–106, 165
Ingraham, Colonel Prentiss 255
Invisible Man 275
Iola Leroy 256

J. Poindexter, Colored 79
Jacobs, Harriet Ann 252–253
Jeff Poindexter stories 79–87
Jesse B. Semple stories 228–243
Jim Crow era 3, 5, 13–15, 38, 39, 229
Jim Crow Guide 15
Jim Crow's Vagaries 246
Jim Hanvey, Detective 134
John Henry 186–187, 192
Johnson, James Weldon 267–268
Johnson, Rosamund 267
Jordan, Louis 131

Joshua and Rosabel Newton stories 215–218
Judge Priest stories 79–87

Kansas City Journal 110
Kaser, Arthur Leroy 164–170
Kelland, Clarence Budington 7
Kennedy, John Pendleton 246
Kennedy, Robert Emmet 269
Kentucky 77–88, 88–96, 179–183, 228, 249, 250, 258, 265–267, 268
Kingfish character 18, 176, 206–207

Lady Luck 178
Laffin, Pink 268
Larsen, Nella 270
Lawyer Chew stories 122–159
Lena Rivers 250
Liberty 212
Little Bee Bend Plantation stories 183–199
Little Black Sambo stories 260
Locke, David Ross 253
Lofty and the Lowly 250
Longstreet, Augustus Baldwin 247
Lord Gilhooly 262
Lorimer, George Horace 79, 133, 139, 143, 174
Lost Cause novel 14, 19, 54, 79, 159, 256
Louisiana 29, 88–96, 174, 183–199, 256, 258, 271

Mack, Charles E. 271
Macon Evening News 163
Macon Telegraph 50–71, 253
mammy character 16, 37–45, 140, 260, 266
Mammy's Reminiscences and Other Sketches 260
Marriner, William 265
McBlair, Robert 118–121
McClure's Magazine 179
McDowell, Katherine Sherwood Bonner 256
McIntosh, Maria J. 250
McNeill, John Charles 262
Means, E.K. 9, 88–96
Metropolitan Magazine 103
Midnight Film stories 122–159
Miller, James A. "Polk" 257
minstrelsy 164–170, 245–246
Miss Minerva stories 266–267
Mississippi 23, 71–77, 89, 181, 183–199, 254, 256, 268, 274
Mister Fish Kelly stories 118–121
Mr. Wong stories 177
Mooney, C.P.J. 106
Mooney, Hugh J. 108
Moses, Man of the Mountain 272–273

motion pictures *see* Bradford, Roark; Cobb, Irvin S.; Cohen, Octavus Roy; Correll, Charles; Dixon, John F., Jr.; Eisner, Will; Gosden, Freeman; Harris, Joel Chandler; Mack, Charles E.; Tarkington, Booth; Twain, Mark; Wiley, Hugh
Munsey's 89, 94–96
Mush and Poke skits 164–170
music *see* Correll, Charles; Dixon, George Washington; Gosden, Freeman; Miller, Polk; Outcault, R.F.; Rice, Thomas D.; Russell, Irwin
My Young Master 258

Nanovic, John 216
Narrative of the Life of Frederick Douglass 248
Nasby, Petroleum V. 253
Nasby Letters 253
National Era 20
Native Son 273
navigator character 16
NBC Blue Network 206
Negro Tales 267
Negro Wit and Humor 268
New York City 37–45, 78, 135, 184, 187, 207, 210, 245–246, 254, 255–256, 270–271, 272–273
New York Herald 40, 44
New York Journal American 39
New York Post 233
New York World 39
News and Courier 113
Nicodemus and His Little Sister 272
North Carolina 32–35, 45–49, 265
North Star 252
Northern Georgia Sketches 261

Ol' Man Adam an' His Chillun 186, 188
Old Si's Sayings 253
Old Sleuth 255
Old Wash stories 258
Ole Creole Days 29–30
Ole Marster and Other Verses 269
Ole Reliable stories 71–76
Oregonian 103
Ormes, Jackie 274
Our Nig 252
Outcault, R.F. 37–45
Outcault, Richard *see* R.F. Outcault

Paducah News 78
Page, Thomas Nelson 12, 30–32
Penrod stories 96–106
"Perfect Song" 208

Peterkin, Julia Mead 269
Photoplay 130, 152
pickaninny character 16
Pittsburgh Courier 274
Plantation Songs 262
Planter's Northern Bride 250
plays *see* Brown, William Wells; Cobb, Irvin S.; Cohen, Octavus Roy; Cole, Bob; Correll, Charles; Cotter, Joseph Jr.; Dickson, Harris; Gosden, Freeman; Hansberry, Lorraine; Hughes, Langston; Rice, Thomas D.; Stowe, Harriet Beecher; Tarkington, Booth
poets *see* Corrothers, James D.; Cotter, Joseph S. Jr.; Dunbar, Paul Laurence; Edwards, Harry Stillwell; Gilman, Caroline; Hansberry, Lorraine; Harper, Frances Ellen Watkins; Hughes, Langston; Hurston, Zora Neale; Johnson, James Weldon; McBlair, Robert; McNeill, John Charles; Weeden, Miss Howard; Wheatley, Phillis
Poketown People 264
Polished Ebony 154
Polk Miller's Stories, Sketches, Songs 257
Popular Magazine 88, 121
Pore Lil Mose cartoons 38–43
"Preaching in Yamacraw" 53–71
PS Magazine 223
pulp magazines *see* Cohen, Octavus Roy; Ernst, Paul F.; Ingraham, Colonel Prentiss; McBlair, Robert; Means, E.K.
Pyrnelle, Louise Clarke 255–256

Quadroons 247
Quicksand 270

radio *see* Bradford, Roark; Cobb, Irvin S.; Correll, Charles; Ernst, Paul; Gosden, Freeman; Kaser, Arthur LeRoy; Tarkington, Booth
Raine, Norman Reilly 7
Raisin in the Sun 275
Rastus 11, 12, 36, 46–47, 217, 272
Read, Opie Pope 258
Recollections of a Southern Matron 247
Red Book 88, 179, 182
Red Buck" *see* Bryant, Henry Edwards Cowen
Retribution 249
Rice, Thomas D. 245
Richard Benson stories 215–218
Rinehart, Mary Roberts 7
Roberson, Y. Andrew 9
Roberts, Robert 245

Robeson, Kenneth 215–218
Roll, Jordan, Roll 269
Ruark, Robert 141
Russell, Irwin 254
Ryatts 111

Saint Detective Magazine 86
Sam 'n' Henry stories 199–215
Sambo and His Funny Noises 265
Sambo character 4, 6, 11, 16, 244, 260, 265, 272
Sammie Johnson cartoons 265
Sampson, Emma Speed 266–267
Saturday Evening Post 2, 72–88, 97, 103, 122–159, 160, 170–179
schemer character 16, 207
Seymour, Frederick H. 262
Shadows on the Wall 259
Shaw, Henry Wheeler 253
shrill wife character 16
sidekick character 16
Silhouettes columns 117
Simms, William Gilmore 115
Simple stories 228–243
Skeeter Butts stories 88–96
slave narrative 244, 248, 249, 260
Small, Samuel W. 253–254
Smith, Bridges 49–71
Smith, Frank Leon 8
Smith, Sidney 109
Son; or, The Wisdom of Uncle Eph, the Modern 263
Souls of Black Folk 263
South Carolina 113–118, 122–159, 245, 269
Southworth, E.D.E.N. 249
Spirit stories 218–227
Startling Detective Adventure 206
State 113–114
"Stories in Black" 52–63
"Stories in Black and White" 56, 63–70
Stout, Wesley Winans 134
Stowe, Harriet Beecher 19, 20–22
Strange Detective Mysteries 206
Stuart, Ruth McEnery 256
Sullivan, Pat 265
Sunclouds 155
Swallow Barn 246
Swor, John 271

"Tales of the Town and the Times" 46–49
Tar Heel Tales 45–49
Tarkington, Booth 8, 10, 96–106
Tarry, Ellen 273–274
television *see* Cobb, Irvin S.; Cohen, Octavus Roy; Correll, Charles; Gosden, Freeman
Tennessee 106–113, 184, 253, 257, 258, 261, 267
Their Eyes Were Watching God 273

Index

This Week 130, 154
Three Golliwogs 274
Tickfall stories 88–96
Times-Picayune 76
Torchy Brown Dixie to Harlem 274
tragic mulatta 90, 247
Train, Arthur 7
trickster 25–29, 91, 115, 189, 251
Trip to Coontown 259
Trotwood, Betsy 257
Twain, Mark 10, 23–25
Two Black Crows 271
Two Black Crows in the AEF 271
Tybout, Ella Middleton 13, 264

Uncle Julius McAdoo stories 32–34
Uncle Rastus stories 46–47
Uncle Remus: His Songs and Sayings 25–28
Uncle Tom character 16
Uncle Tom's Cabin 20–22
Uncle Tom's Children 273
United Features Syndicate 149–151
Up from Slavery 261
Upson, William Hazlett 7
Upton, Florence 274

Valentine, B.B. 269
vernacular *see* dialect
Virginia 30–32, 118, 181, 200, 244–245, 249–250, 251–252, 254, 257, 262–263, 266–267, 269,

Wall-Eyed Caesar's Ghost 270
Ward, Artemus 253
Washington, Booker T. 261–262
Weaver, Annie Vaughan 271–272
Weeden, Miss Howard 259–260
Weird Tales 215
WGN 201
Wheatley, Phillis 245
White, E.V. 272
Widow Duck stories 183–199
Wildcat Marsden stories 170–179
Wiley, Hugh 8, 170–179
Williams, Dudley 183
Wilson, Harriet E. 252
WMAQ 205–206
Wodehouse, P.G. 7
Worth, Thomas 254
Wright, Farnsworth 215
Wright, Richard 273

Yamacraw stories 49–71
Young, Martha Strudwick 262

Zip Coon: A Favorite Comic Song 246

www.ingramcontent.com/pod-product-compliance
Lightning Source LLC
Chambersburg PA
CBHW081543300426
44116CB00015B/2737